Historical War Crimes Trials in Asia

LIU Daqun and ZHANG Binxin (editors)

2016
Torkel Opsahl Academic EPublisher
Brussels

EDITORS' PREFACE

In recent years, there has been a growing recognition among practitioners and scholars that the common narratives of the development of international criminal law have omitted or ignored a large part of the picture. The generally referred to "history" of international criminal law starts with a recounting of the Nuremberg and Tokyo trials (or at times goes back to the post-First World War trials and attempted trials), then to the United Nations *ad hoc* tribunals and the permanent International Criminal Court. It is not difficult to discern a Western-centric perspective to this storyline, in which even the Tokyo trial does not receive the attention and thorough study as its counterpart in Nuremberg has.

To mention this is not really to criticise. It is merely recognition of a reality that needs to be changed. In fact, this is an unfortunate reality not only in the West, but in other parts of the world as well. The Tokyo trial and post-Second World War national trials in China, for example, remain an underexamined area of study even in the Chinese literature. One of the reasons for this is the lack of first-hand materials, many of which have only become available recently, while many others are still inaccessible. For Western researchers there is also the obvious barrier of language. Despite these difficulties, studies on these largely unexplored trials and events are vitally important. Their importance lies not only with the understanding of history itself but also the mapping of the whole picture of the evolution of international criminal law, the understanding of China and Asia's current attitudes towards international criminal law, and also the removal of our often misplaced bias.

Fortunately, in recent years we have been witnessing a growing interest in the studies of these "forgotten" trials and events. In China, the transcripts and court documents of the Tokyo trial were published for the first time. New research centres in related areas of study have been established, and more discussions on related topics are appearing in the literature. This anthology was made possible also thanks to this new development and the growing interest in these topics.

In an attempt to cover different historical events and discussions and their various aspects, this anthology consists of papers on the Tokyo trial, as well as national trials conducted by different authorities including the Chinese Nationalist government's trials, the People's Republic of China's trials and the British trials in Hong Kong. Both thematic topics and reflections on the general impact of the trials are included. There are discussions that challenge or re-evaluate previously held opinions, by looking at the trials from a different perspective or exploring previously overlooked materials. The anthology also contains papers on methodological aspects of studying historical trials and on the compilation of relevant historical materials. These historical trials are not only judicial events relevant to legal study. They are also, or perhaps even more importantly, historical events that would leave historical records. Perhaps this could also be said in respect to today's criminal tribunals, which are creating a historical record for the future. With such understanding, the anthology also includes a chapter on new developments in evidence collection and presentation in today's international criminal courts.

This project has received enthusiastic support from many talented and committed individuals. We would like to thank the authors for their excellent contributions. Our editorial assistants, Ms. YU Wei and Ms. Elisabeth Pirotta, provided valuable assistance in the early stage of the editing process. We owe sincere gratitude to each member of the editorial team of the Torkel Opsahl Academic EPublisher, in particular, Mr. Gareth Richards, whose professionalism and outstanding contribution guaranteed the quality of the copy-editing, as well as Ms. FAN Yuwen and Dr. SONG Yan. This project started with a conference held in Fudan University, co-organised by Fudan University Law School and the Centre for International Law Research and Policy. This anthology would not have been possible without the generous support of these two institutions.

LIU Daqun, ZHANG Binxin

FOREWORD BY JUDGE LIU DAQUN

The seventieth anniversary of the end of the Second World War is a bittersweet and poignant occasion. It is a moment for the world to pause and reflect upon what has become known as the deadliest conflict in history, and to commemorate the millions of lives lost in the cataclysm. I cannot commemorate the memory of the Second World War without also paying tribute to the "forgotten" holocaust, an event which has been largely overlooked for the greater part of the twentieth century and which has only garnered renewed interest in recent years. I am speaking of the Nanjing (Nanking) Massacre or Rape of Nanjing,[1] six weeks of carnage that would, in retrospect, become one of the greatest atrocities committed during the Second World War era.

After the fall of Nanjing, then China's capital, on 13 December 1937, the Imperial Japanese Army proceeded to murder, rape, loot and torture in a wanton fashion. The first concern of the Japanese was to eliminate any threat from the 90,000 Chinese soldiers who surrendered. Some of the Chinese prisoners of war were simply mowed down by machine-gun fire while others were tied up, soaked with petrol and burned alive. After the destruction of the prisoners of war, the soldiers turned their attention to the women of Nanjing and an outright animalistic hunt ensued. Old women over the age of 70, as well as girls under the age of eight, were dragged off to be sexually abused. More than 20,000 females were gang-raped by Japanese soldiers, then stabbed to death with bayonets or shot so they could never bear witness. Throughout the city of Nanjing, random acts of murder occurred as soldiers frequently fired their rifles into panicked crowds of civilians, killing indiscriminately. According to the findings of Nanjing War Crimes Tribunal, over 300,000 civilians and prisoners of war were brutally murdered during the Nanjing Massacre.

Immediately following the conclusion of the Second World War, the Allies in Asia began to try Japanese war criminals. According to the Special Proclamation by the Supreme Commander for the Allied Powers of 19 January 1946, the International Military Tribunal for the Far East

---

1   The modern pinyin romanisation, Nanjing, is used here rather than the previous spelling, Nanking.

('IMTFE') was established to prosecute Japanese war criminals. At the same time, in 10 different Chinese cities the government also established military tribunals to prosecute Japanese war criminals. The Nanjing War Crimes Tribunal was established on 15 February 1946 under the Ministry of Defence to deal with crimes committed mainly in Nanjing at the end of 1937 and the beginning of 1938. The Nanjing War Crimes Tribunal concluded its proceedings on 26 January 1949 and acquitted General Okamura Yasuji, the commander-in-chief of the China Expeditionary Army in late 1944. Twenty-four suspects were tried; eight were sentenced to death, 14 were sentenced to imprisonment, one was acquitted and one died in custody.

Yet despite the egregious nature of the crimes committed by the Japanese and the subsequent international trial proceedings, the horrors of the Nanjing Massacre and the findings of Nanjing trials remain virtually unknown to people outside Asia. Their legacy is transient and fading into the recesses of history. This was unfortunately due to a complex myriad of political and military circumstances after the Second World War and the subsequent Cold War that prevented the Nanjing trials fulfilling their long-term aims and hence their historical neglect.

It is true that the Nanjing trials had many shortcomings and problems. First, political implications and negotiations between Japan and the United States led to the granting of immunity to Japan's Emperor Hirohito. Immunity was not only granted to the emperor but also to his relatives. For example, Prince Asaka Yasuhiko, an imperial kinsman and commander of the entire Japanese army that attacked Nanjing, was indicted as the principal perpetrator of the Nanjing Massacre due to his alleged order to "kill all captives". The extradition request that the Chinese government filed against him was refused by General Douglas MacArthur, the Supreme Commander for the Allied Powers, because the prince was a relative of the Japanese emperor.

Second, the Nanjing trials were conducted in great haste due to the domestic situation in China after 1945. The trials also did not delve into all the atrocities committed throughout the rest of China, especially those occurring in the northern and north-eastern regions. For symbolic purposes, the tribunal only chose to try a few events, such as the Nanjing Massacre. Numerous crimes committed during the war were not investigated and prosecuted, such as the use of chemical weapons, bacteriological warfare, the use of poison gas against soldiers and civilians, biological experiments on prisoners of war and civilians, the forced prostitution of so-called comfort women, and the subjugation of Chinese as forced labourers in Japanese domestic industries.

Finally, the convicted Japanese war criminals, who should have served their sentences in special prisons set up in China, were sent back to Japan. This was because the Chinese Nationalist government lost territory north of the Yangtze River in late 1948, and so it decided to send convicted individuals back to Japan. Predictably, upon arrival in Japan they were all released and some convicted persons even became important officials in the Japanese government after the war, thereby perpetuating the impunity of their criminal acts.

It was the sum of these factors that contributed to the gradual erosion of the Nanjing Massacre from people's consciousness following the conclusion of the Second World War through to the early twenty-first century. However, in the past decade, I have witnessed a resurgence of interest in the Nanjing Massacre and the totality of crimes committed during the anti-Japanese war. In 1985 the Nanjing Massacre Memorial Hall was built by the Nanjing municipal government in memory of the victims who lost their lives. In February 2014 China's top legislature decided to set 13 December as the National Memorial Day to mourn Nanjing Massacre victims and all those killed by the Japanese invaders, and to reveal war crimes committed by the Japanese. The Chinese President XI Jinping attended the state ceremony for the first National Memorial Day on 13 December 2014. He pointed out in his speech that after the victory of the Second World War, the IMTFE and China's military tribunals for the trial of war criminals investigated the Nanjing Massacre and made their verdict and conclusion. It was the first time that a supreme leader of China had made a positive appraisal on the Nanjing War Crimes Tribunal and its findings.

It is here that I want to take a moment to reflect upon the legacies of the Nanjing trials. In particular, I want to give consideration to how this criminal tribunal, along with the Nuremberg and Tokyo tribunals, set the foundation stone for what has now emerged as a flourishing realm of international criminal law.

While the Nanjing trials could not end the impunity of international crimes, its contribution is no less important to international justice. It was the first time that China, as a victorious nation, conducted public criminal trials instead of summarily executing war criminals, as historically war criminals were executed upon capture. Instead, in this case, a court was set up to address the question of responsibility after the conclusion of the war. This was a monumental moment in China's thousands of years of history. The Nanjing trials, conducted fairly, fulfilled the requirements of justice and contributed to international and regional peace and stability. In addition, the trials greatly raised the moral and legal consciousness in the Chinese people and became a central milestone for the rule of law. While the tribunal's procedures were not perfect, the precedents set by the judgments undoubtedly constituted a landmark in international law.

Furthermore, despite the many problems faced by the Nanjing War Crimes Tribunal, the trials also commanded great significance in China's history. The tribunal was able to produce and preserve historic records through all the indictments, judgments, testimonies of witnesses, and victims and records of the court proceedings. This labyrinth of records, tested through examinations at trial, document the dark history of Japan's invasion of China. Accordingly, they render the commission of the atrocities very difficult to deny and serve as a reminder for the nation of China.

Since the achievement of an international order is based on reason and justice, we have a historical responsibility to provide definite and exhaustive answers about the value and place of the Nanjing trials in China's history, and their impact on the development of the contemporary rule of law in China and in Asia. President XI also pointed out that "[f]orgetting history is a betrayal, and denying a crime is to repeat a crime". Not forgetting history does not mean that we should hate a people just because a small minority of militarists set off an invasion and war. It means that we will never let the atrocity happen again. Understanding the past is crucial in addressing the challenges of today.

Reflecting on what happened in Nanjing nearly 80 years ago, we must recognise that the Nanjing Massacre was not just a Chinese tragedy; it was a tragedy for humankind as a whole. The same is true in that the Holocaust was not just a Jewish tragedy and Rwanda's genocide was not just a catastrophe for the Tutsi ethnic group. Those atrocities were in violation of the basic values of human beings. We are all the victims wherever they happen. If we do not fight against those crimes that trample basic human rights we will be the next victims. So it is the responsibility of everyone on this planet to prevent and condemn those atrocities, no matter where they occur and whoever directly suffers.

Reverend Martin Niemöller said in a speech on 6 January 1946 to the representatives of the Confessing Church in Frankfurt:

> When the Nazis came for the communists, I remained silent; I was not a communist. When they locked up the social democrats, I remained silent; I was not a social democrat. When they came for the trade unionists, I did not speak out; I

was not a trade unionist. When they came for the Jews, I remained silent; I wasn't a Jew. When they came for me, there was no one left to speak out.[2]

In his speech, President XI also expressed thanks to the foreigners who protected Nanjing residents and recorded the atrocities of the Japanese invaders, despite the risks. The German businessman John Rabe, Bernhard Arp Sindberg from Denmark and the American priest John Magee were among the foreign friends. President XI added: "The Chinese people will never forget their humanitarian spirit and brave and righteous acts".

The most important thing is to educate our next generation. We criticised the Japanese ultranationalists who altered the facts of the invasion of China, the Nanjing Massacre and the comfort women in secondary school textbooks. This is absolutely right. But did the Nanjing Massacre or Nanjing trials ever appear in Chinese textbooks?

Unfortunately, those who risked their own lives to save thousands of Chinese during the Nanjing Massacre never appeared in the textbooks of Chinese schools. How many Chinese know about Dr. HO Feng-Shan, the Chinese consul-general in Vienna during the Second World War? In spite of orders from his superior to the contrary, he issued Chinese visas to Jews in Vienna so that thousands of lives were saved. He was the only Chinese who was given the title of Righteous Among the Nations for his humanitarian courage by the Yad Vashem organisation of Israel. A survivor of Auschwitz tells us:

> Our schools and our religious institutions and the state itself all have an obligation to instill into future generations the will and ability to resist aligning themselves with political movements and ideologies that advocate hatred. Tolerance and respect for other human beings regardless of their race, religion, national or ethnic origin, or sexual preference must be taught in our schools, in our military academies and religious institutions.[3]

---

[2] There are many versions of the poem by Reverend Martin Niemöller. As claimed by Richard John Neuhaus, when "asked in 1971 about the correct version of the quote, Niemöller said he was not quite sure when he had said the famous words but, if people insist upon citing them, he preferred a version that listed 'the Communists', 'the trade unionists', 'the Jews', and 'me'". Richard John Neuhaus, "September 11 – Before and After", in *First Things*, November 2001, p. 4.

[3] Thomas Buergenthal, "Reflecting on Auschwitz, Six Decades Later", a speech on the occasion of the annual "Auschwitz Never Again" organised by the Netherlands Auschwitz Committee, Centre for Holocaust and Genocide Studies and Pension and Benefit Board, 27 January 2009, cited in Thomas Buergenthal, *A Lucky Child: A Memoir of Surviving Auschwitz as a Young Boy*, Little, Brown, New York, 2010, p. 8.

After nearly 70 years things are beginning to change. Research institutions on the Tokyo and Nanjing trials are in the process of being established around the world. In the spring of 2014 Fudan University Law School held a seminar on war crimes trials in Asia and the Centre for International Law Research and Policy launched a broadly based research project on the historical origins of international criminal law. Hopefully, these initiatives will serve as the start of an increased awareness and better understanding of the Second World War mass atrocity trials in China, which are not only of significance to the development of international criminal law but also manifest important implications for our understanding of history and reality.

Against this background, this anthology forms part of this renewed wave of interest, and I am truly honoured to be able to contribute to it. The purpose of this volume is to reintroduce the world to the Tokyo and Nanjing trials, both of which, despite its many flaws, attempted to prosecute those responsible for committing egregious crimes, at a time when the notions of war crimes and crimes against humanity were still in their infancy. It was impossible to try all those responsible for their nefarious crimes committed in the Second World War. But what we can do is to remember and to commemorate, and to undertake a process of continuous learning about those events of history, such as the Nanjing Massacre, that have been swept into the cobwebbed alcoves of humanity's memory. It may be too late for the prosecution of those crimes against humanity, but to allow history to selectively fade would truly be the greatest crime against humanity. In conclusion, I would like to quote what Thomas Buergenthal has said:

> Let us not forget the children who are killed or die of starvation in never-ending armed conflicts, those who were murdered in Rwanda, in the Balkans, in Cambodia, who will keep dying in other parts of the world unless and until we can create a world in which "Never Again" really means "Never Again" and not "Never Again until the next time".[4]

---

[4] *Ibid.*

FOREWORD BY PROFESSOR SUN XIAOXIA

This anthology is based on papers presented at a conference held in Fudan University, Shanghai, on "Old Evidence Collection and War Crime Trials in Asia", which also marks the inauguration of the Fudan International Criminal Law Center. As the Dean of Fudan University Law School, I am very pleased and honoured to see the results of these events, namely the publication of this important anthology.

You might remember the Chinese judge at the International Military Tribunal for the Far East, Judge MEI Ju-ao. Judge MEI was a professor of Fudan Law School. Before he set off for Tokyo at 19:00 on 9 January 1946, the Politics Society of Fudan University held a farewell party in its auditorium. On 31 January Judge MEI requested to resign in writing to the then president of Fudan University, ZHANG Yi, who replied: "I regard this as a request for leave and you could still come back to Fudan when you return". Judge MEI's departure and his service as a judge hit the headlines in many of the main newspapers in Shanghai, including *Ta Kung Pao* and *Shun Pao*. On 19 March the US military jet that Judge MEI took to Tokyo flew from Jiangwan military airport near Fudan. This airport has now been turned into the beautiful Jiangwan campus of Fudan University, where the Law School is located. These might be just a chance occurrence in the progress of the society and the development of the university, but from these traces we can follow the footsteps of the precursors of the legal profession, and understand the noble responsibility that their generation shouldered.

Fudan Law School has always been dedicated to the internationalisation of its education and research, and international law has long been one of its strong disciplines. We concentrate not only on research in international law but also on the education of new generations of international lawyers. Now, in the era of globalisation, many social and legal matters are transnational. Traditional international law has been expanded to include international intellectual property law, international financial law, international environment law, international criminal law and so on. Therefore, we use the concept of transnational law to replace the traditional international law. Transnational law has a wider coverage of similar legal matters, and within this context we are able to consolidate our faculty members specialising in different fields of law to pursue joint research. The Fudan Law School Criminal Law Department has also been focusing on and dedicated to research in transnational criminal law. We have already forged a team concentrating on the research of international criminal law, international criminal trials and international human rights.

In March 2014 Fudan Law School, Fudan Human Rights Research Center and Fudan International Criminal Law Center and the Centre for International Law Research and Policy co-organised the conference on "Old Evidence Collection and War Crime Trials in Asia". Of note is the fact that Fudan Human Rights Research Center is the earliest institution for human rights education and research among Chinese universities. Since the early 1990s Fudan Human Rights Research Center has started interdisciplinary human rights research, in fields such as law, politics, sociology and so on. The Center has also conducted international research with jurists and sociologists from Europe and North America and experts from the International Committee of the Red Cross. Fudan International Criminal Law Center is a newly established institution, and its work starts with this important conference and now this anthology. I hope that the papers presented at the conference, and included in this anthology, will help to raise interest in and awareness of the forgotten or ignored trials in Asia, and from hereon we can see more research on these important events.

FOREWORD BY JUDGE HANS-PETER KAUL[*]

The Rome Statute ('ICC Statute') – the founding treaty of the International Criminal Court – is nowadays regarded by many as the most important treaty since the adoption of the Charter of the United Nations ('UN') in San Francisco in October 1945.[1] The ICC Statute, which established the first permanent international criminal court in the history of mankind, entered into force on 1 July 2002 with 66 ratifications. Today the ICC Statute has 124 states parties.[2] It contains a comprehensive codification of genocide,[3] crimes against humanity,[4] war crimes[5] and the crime of aggression.[6] This comprehensive codification is based – and this is significant if not revolutionary – on the free and voluntary consent of the international community. The ICC will prosecute these crimes if and when national criminal systems fail. We are a court of last resort. The principle of complementarity, as provided for in particular in Article 17 of the ICC Statute, is the decisive basis of the entire ICC system. It is the principle of complementarity which safeguards and protects the sovereign and primary right of states to exercise criminal jurisdiction, if they are able and willing to do so. You could say that Article 17 is, maybe together with Article 12 on jurisdiction, the most important provision of the entire ICC Statute. The ICC is the first permanent, general, future-orientated court that is based on the general principle of law – "equality before the law, equal law

---

[*] This foreword is based on a speech delivered by the late Judge Hans-Peter Kaul on 5 March 2014 at the occasion of the inauguration of the Fudan International Criminal Law Center ('ICLC Fudan') and the symposium on Old Evidence Collection and War Crime Trials in Asia, hosted by Fudan University Law School, Shanghai, China. It has been updated by Eleni Chaitidou and Gareth Richards in light of developments at the ICC up to March 2016, and has been reviewed by Elisabeth Kaul.

[1] Rome Statute of the International Criminal Court, adopted 17 July 1998, entry into force 1 July 2002 ('ICC Statute') (http://www.legal-tools.org/doc/7b9af9/).

[2] Since this speech was delivered, Palestine became the 123rd state party to the ICC Statute on 1 April 2015 and El Salvador became the 124th state party on 3 March 2016.

[3] ICC Statute, Art. 6, see *supra* note 1.

[4] *Ibid.*, Art. 7.

[5] *Ibid.*, Art. 8.

[6] *Ibid.*, Art. 8*bis*.

for all" – and is not imposed upon by powerful states or by the UN Security Council as, for example, the statutes of the *ad hoc* tribunals were.[7]

I will deal with two sets of issues. First, what is the current situation of the Court? This will be in particular a rather brief recapitulation of the situations before the ICC and an overview of the cases which are currently entertained by its chambers. Second, what are some of the most important challenges and difficulties confronting the Court now and in the future? I will conclude with some personal thoughts on China and the ICC, which will also reflect my personal hope that China, in the foreseeable future, may become a state party to the ICC Statute.

Current Situation

What is the Court's current situation and what progress has been made since its establishment in 2003? Admittedly, the ICC's first 11 years have not been easy. When the first judges of the ICC arrived in The Hague in 2003 – I was the first judge to be called to serve full-time – we were quite concerned about the future of the Court. We seriously wondered whether it would survive the hostility it was then facing from many sides, in particular from the United States during the Bush administration.[8] In the last 11 years, however, we managed to turn the ICC from a court on paper into a fully functioning world criminal court, a leading actor in the field of international criminal justice.

The complete administrative infrastructure of the chambers, the Office of the Prosecutor and the Registry had to be developed from scratch. Five field offices[9] and a UN liaison office in New York were opened. In

---

[7]   United Nations, Updated Statute of the International Criminal Tribunal for the Former Yugoslavia, adopted 25 May 1993 by resolution 827 (1993), last amended 7 July 2009 by resolution 1877 (2009) (http://www.legal-tools.org/doc/b4f63b/); United Nations, Statute of the International Criminal Tribunal for Rwanda, adopted on 8 November 1994 by resolution 955 (1994), last amended 16 December 2009 by resolution 1901 (2009)) (http://www.legal-tools.org/doc/8732d6/).

[8]   See, for example, John R. Bolton, "The Risks and Weaknesses of the International Criminal Court from America's Perspective", in *Law and Contemporary Problems*, 2001, vol. 64, no. 1, p. 167; William A. Schabas, "United States Hostility to the International Criminal Court: It's All About the Security Council", in *European Journal of International Law*, 2004, vol. 15, no. 4, p. 701; Anne K. Heindel, "The Counterproductive Bush Administration Policy Toward the International Criminal Court", in *Seattle Journal for Social Justice*, 2004, vol. 2, no. 2, p. 345.

[9]   The ICC entertains field offices in Kampala (Uganda), Kinshasa and Bunia (Democratic Republic of the Congo), Nairobi (Kenya) and Abidjan (Côte d'Ivoire). Due to security concerns, the field office in Bangui (Central African Republic) was closed in November 2013.

the past few years the focus of activity has steadily shifted from establishing the Court to concrete action concerning prosecution and judicial proceedings. Employee numbers have grown from five to 1,100. Only five individuals formed the advance team, which I founded in 2002/2003, to start the build-up of the Court. The Office of the Prosecutor, Pre-trial, Trial and Appeals Chambers are nowadays all fully functional and cope with a heavy workload.

The ICC is currently dealing with international crimes allegedly committed in eight countries – Democratic Republic of the Congo, Uganda, Central African Republic,[10] Sudan, Kenya, Libya, Côte d'Ivoire and Mali. In addition, the prosecutor has yet to take a decision whether to open an investigation in relation to the events on the registered vessels of the Union of the Comoros, Greece and Cambodia.[11] Six situations have been referred to the prosecutor by states parties.[12] Two situations, Dar-

---

[10] It is noted that two different situations have been referred to the prosecutor in relation to the Central African Republic, see *infra* note 11.

[11] On 6 November 2014 the prosecutor took the decision not to open an investigation into the situation. Subsequently, the Comoros requested on 29 January 2015 that the competent pre-trial chamber review the prosecutor's decision. See ICC, Application for Review Pursuant to Article 53(3)(a) of the Prosecutor's Decision of 6 November 2014 Not to Initiate an Investigation in the Situation, 29 January 2015, ICC-01/13-3-Red (http://www.legal-tools.org/doc/b60981/). At the time of writing, the pre-trial chamber has not yet rendered its decision on the matter.

[12] In December 2003 the Government of Uganda referred the situation to the prosecutor; see ICC, Presidency, Decision Assigning the Situation in Uganda to Pre-Trial Chamber II, 5 July 2004, ICC-02/04-1 (http://www.legal-tools.org/doc/b904bb/). In March 2004 the Government of the Democratic Republic of the Congo referred the situation to the prosecutor; see ICC, Presidency, Decision Assigning the Situation in the Democratic Republic of Congo to Pre-Trial Chamber I, 5 July 2004, ICC-01/04-1 (http://www.legal-tools.org/doc/218294/). On 21 December 2004 the Government of the Central African Republic referred the situation to the prosecutor; see ICC, Presidency, Decision Assigning the Situation in the Central African Republic to Pre-Trial Chamber III, 19 January 2005, ICC-01/05-1 (http://www.legal-tools.org/doc/5532e5/). On 18 July 2012 the Government of the Republic of Mali referred the situation to the prosecutor; see ICC, Presidency, Decision Assigning the Situation in the Republic of Mali to Pre-Trial Chamber II, 19 July 2012, ICC-01/12-1 (http://www.legal-tools.org/doc/793de5/). On 14 May 2013 the Government of the Union of the Comoros referred the situation to the prosecutor; see ICC, Presidency, Decision Assigning the Situation on Registered Vessels of the Union of the Comoros, the Hellenic Republic and the Kingdom of Cambodia to Pre-Trial Chamber I, ICC-01/13-1, 5 July 2013 (https://www.legal-tools.org/doc/8e4e80/). On 30 May 2014 the Government of the Central African Republic referred a second situation to the prosecutor (for events taking place in the Central African Republic since 1 August 2012); see ICC, Presidency, Decision Assigning the Situation in the Central African Republic II to Pre-Trial Chamber II, 18 June 2014, ICC-01/14-1 (http://www.legal-tools.org/doc/9304eb/).

fur/Sudan and Libya, have been referred by the UN Security Council.[13] Most noteworthy, the Libya situation was referred on 17 March 2011 by a unanimous Security Council decision. With regard to two further situations,[14] the prosecutor requested authorisation to commence with an investigation *proprio motu*.[15] The first *proprio motu* investigation in Kenya was authorised by Pre-trial Chamber II to commence by the prosecutor, the latter being triggered by a request of, in particular, Kofi Annan who mediated an end to the post-election violence in early 2008. The second *proprio motu* investigation was authorised by Pre-trial Chamber III for Côte d'Ivoire, a non-state party at the time,[16] but which had accepted the jurisdiction of the Court.[17]

Three cases are currently at the pre-trial stage,[18] including proceedings against Saif Al-Islam Gaddafi, the son of Muammar Gaddafi, and Dominic Ongwen.[19] The latest confirmation of charges decisions were issued by the Court's pre-trial chambers in June and November/December 2014. On 9 June 2014 Pre-Trial Chamber II confirmed the charges of

---

[13] On 31 March 2005 the UN Security Council referred the situation in Darfur/Sudan to the Prosecutor; see United Nations Security Council, Resolution 1593 (2005), 31 March 2005, UN doc. S/RES/1593 (2005) (http://www.legal-tools.org/doc/4b208f/); on 17 March 2011, the UN Security Council referred the situation in Libya to the Prosecutor, see Security Council Resolution 1973 (2011) dated 17 March 2011, UN doc. S/RES/1973 (2011).

[14] Situation in the Republic of Kenya, see ICC, Presidency, Assigning the Situation in the Republic of Kenya to Pre-Trial Chamber II, 6 November 2009, ICC-01/09-1 (https://www.legal-tools.org/doc/0ae588/); Situation in Côte d'Ivoire, see ICC, Presidency, Decision Assigning the Situation in the Republic of Côte d'Ivoire to Pre-Trial Chamber II, 20 May 2011, ICC-02/11-1 (https://www.legal-tools.org/doc/aa6613/).

[15] ICC Statute, Arts. 13(c) and 15(1), see *supra* note 1.

[16] Côte d'Ivoire became the 122nd state party to the ICC Statute, which entered into force for Côte d'Ivoire on 1 May 2013.

[17] On 18 April 2003, 14 December 2010 and 3 May 2011, Côte d'Ivoire lodged a declaration with the registrar accepting as a non-state party the exercise of jurisdiction by the ICC, pursuant to ICC Statute, Art. 12(3).

[18] Pre-Trial Chamber I currently entertains the case of *Prosecutor v. Saif Al-Islam Gaddafi* (ICC-01/11-01/11); and *Prosecutor v. Simone Gbagbo* (ICC-02/11-01/12). Pre-Trial Chamber II currently entertains the case of *Prosecutor v. Dominic Ongwen* (ICC-02/04-01/15). Since the delivery of this speech, the case against Abdullah Al-Senussi has been declared inadmissible before the ICC and proceedings have been terminated accordingly.

[19] Dominic Ongwen was sought by a warrant of arrest issued on 8 July 2005 (unsealed on 13 October 2005). On 16 January 2015 Dominic Ongwen consented to appear voluntarily before the ICC and, on the same day, was transferred to the custody of the Court. On 21 January 2015 he arrived at the detention centre of the Court and made his first appearance before Pre-Trial Chamber II on 26 January 2015. The case has been committed to trial. See Pre-Trial Chamber II, Decision Postponing the Date of the Confirmation of Charges Hearing, 6 March 2015, ICC-02/04-01/15-206 (http://www.legal-tools.org/doc/5a0ab1/).

crimes against humanity and war crimes against Bosco Ntaganda,[20] a Congolese warlord known in Africa as "the Terminator". He had walked into the US embassy in Rwanda on 22 March 2013 and voluntarily appeared before the Court on 26 March 2013.[21] The crimes against humanity charges against Laurent Gbagbo, the former President of Côte d'Ivoire, were confirmed by Pre-Trial Chamber I on 12 June 2014,[22] after the chamber had adjourned the confirmation hearing and requested the prosecutor to consider conducting further investigation with respect to the contextual elements of crimes against humanity.[23] On 11 November 2014 charges were confirmed against five suspects for offences against the administration of justice;[24] and on 11 December 2014 charges of crimes against humanity were confirmed against Charles Blé Goudé, the former minister for youth, professional training and employment in the government of Laurent Gbagbo in Côte d'Ivoire.[25]

Six other cases are currently at the trial stage.[26] In total, seven accused/suspects are currently detained by the Court in the ICC detention

---

20 ICC, Pre-Trial Chamber II, *Prosecutor v. Bosco Ntaganda*, Decision Pursuant to Article 61(7)(a) and (b) of the Rome Statute on the Charges of the Prosecutor against Bosco Ntaganda, 9 June 2014, ICC-01/04-02/06-309 (http://www.legal-tools.org/doc/a9897d/).

21 ICC, Pre-Trial Chamber II, *Prosecutor v. Bosco Ntaganda*, Transcript of Hearing, 26 March 2013, ICC-01/04-02/06-T-2-ENG (http://www.legal-tools.org/doc/a525ff/).

22 ICC, Pre-Trial Chamber I, *Prosecutor v. Laurent Gbagbo*, Decision on the confirmation of charges against Laurent Gbagbo, 12 June 2014, ICC-02/11-01/11-656-Red (http://www.legal-tools.org/doc/5b41bc/).

23 ICC, Pre-Trial Chamber I, *Prosecutor v. Laurent Gbagbo*, Decision adjourning the hearing on the confirmation of charges pursuant to article 61(7)(c)(i) of the Rome Statute, 3 June 2013, ICC-02/11-01/11-432 (http://www.legal-tools.org/doc/2682d8/).

24 ICC, Pre-Trial Chamber II, *Prosecutor v. Jean-Pierre Bemba Gombo et al.*, Decision pursuant to Article 61(7)(a) and (b) of the Rome Statute, 11 November 2014, ICC-01/05-01/13-749 (http://www.legal-tools.org/doc/a44d44).

25 ICC Pre-Trial Chamber I, *Prosecutor v. Charles Blé Goudé*, Decision on the confirmation of charges against Charles Blé Goudé, 11 December 2014, ICC-02/11-02/11-186 (http://www.legal-tools.org/doc/0536d5/), with a partly dissenting opinion of Judge Christine van den Wyngaert annexed thereto (http://www.legal-tools.org/doc/7485d0/).

26 Trial Chamber I entertains the case of *Prosecutor v. Laurent Gbagbo and Charles Blé Goudé* (ICC-02/11-01/15); Trial Chamber III entertains the case of *Prosecutor v. Jean-Pierre Bemba Gombo* (ICC-01/05 -01/08); Trial Chamber IV entertains the case of *Prosecutor v. Abdallah Banda Abakaer Nourain* (ICC-02/05-03/09); Trial Chamber V(a) entertains the case of *Prosecutor v. William Samoei Ruto and Joshua Arap Sang* (ICC-01/09-01/11); Trial Chamber VI entertains the case of *Prosecutor v. Bosco Ntaganda* (ICC-01/04-02/06); and Trial Chamber VII entertains the case of *Prosecutor v. Jean-Pierre Bemba Gombo, Aimé Kilolo Musamba, Jean-Jacques Mangenda Kabongo, Fidèle Babala Wandu and Narcisse Arido* (ICC-01/05-01/13). Trial Chamber II conducts reparation proceedings in the case of *Prosecutor v. Thomas Lubanga Dyilo* (ICC-01/04-01/06) and *Prosecutor v. Germain Katanga* (ICC-01/04-01/07).

centre. Furthermore, an additional nine situations are currently being monitored by the Office of the Prosecutor, that is to say they are in a preliminary stage before a possible commencement of investigations. This concerns the situations in Columbia, Afghanistan, Georgia, Guinea, Nigeria, Honduras, Palestine, Iraq and Ukraine.

In March 2012 there was a particularly significant development: we had the first judgment in the case of Thomas Lubanga Dyilo.[27] For the first time in the history of international criminal law, a person was convicted for the war crime of recruiting children below the age of 15 years and of using them in armed hostilities. A second judgment was rendered against Mathieu Ngudjolo Chui acquitting him on 18 December 2012 because of lack of sufficient evidence.[28] The third judgment was delivered against Germain Katanga who was convicted for crimes against humanity and war crimes to 12 years' imprisonment.[29] These first instance judgments were upheld in appeal.

In total, the ICC judges have issued 31 warrants of arrest[30] and nine summonses to appear.[31]

---

[27] ICC, Trial Chamber I, *Prosecutor v. Thomas Lubanga Dyilo*, Judgment pursuant to Article 74 of the Statute, 14 March 2012, ICC-01/04-01/06-2842 (http://www.legal-tools.org/doc/677866/).

[28] ICC, Trial Chamber II, *Prosecutor v. Mathieu Ngudjolo Chui*, Judgment pursuant to article 74 of the Statute, 18 December 2012, ICC-01/04-02/12-3-tENG (https://www.legal-tools.org/doc/e5aa90/).

[29] ICC, Trial Chamber II, *Prosecutor v. Germain Katanga and Mathieu Ngudjolo Chui*, Jugement rendu en application de l'article 74 du Statut, 7 March 2014, ICC-01/04-01/07-3436 (http://www.legal-tools.org/doc/9813bb/).

[30] The Court issued a warrant of arrest against Thomas Lubanga Dyilo (10 February 2006); Germain Katanga (2 July 2007); Mathieu Ngudjolo Chui (6 July 2007); two warrants against Bosco Ntaganda (22 August 2006 and 13 July 2012); Callixte Mbarushimana (28 September 2010); Sylvestre Mudacumura (13 July 2012); two warrants against Jean-Pierre Bemba Gombo (the first warrant on 23 May 2008, which was replaced by a warrant of arrest dated 10 June 2008; and the second warrant on 20 November 2013); Aimé Kilolo Musamba (20 November 2013); Jean-Jacques Mangenda Kabongo (20 November 2013); Fidèle Babala Wandu (20 November 2013); Narcisse Arido (20 November 2013); Joseph Kony (8 July 2005); Vincent Otti (8 July 2005); Okot Odhiambo (8 July 2005); Dominic Ongwen (8 July 2005); Raska Lukwiya (8 July 2005, rendered without effect 1 July 2007 following his death); Ahmad Muhammad Harun (27 April 2007); Ali Muhammad Ali Abd-Al-Rahman (27 February 2007); two warrants against Omar Hassan Ahmad Al Bashir (4 March 2009 and 12 July 2010); Abdel Raheem Muhammad Hussein (1 March 2012); Walter Osapiri Barasa (2 August 2013); Muammar Mohammed Abu Minyar Gaddafi (27 June 2011, rendered without effect following his death); Saif Al-Islam Gaddafi (27 June 2011); Abdullah Al-Senussi (27 June 2011); Laurent Gbagbo (23 November 2011); Charles Blé Goudé (21 December 2011); and Simone Gbagbo (29 February 2012).

Challenges for the Future Work of the Court

Twelve years after the ICC Statute entered into force it is obvious that the Court continues to face difficult, ongoing tasks and challenges, which, to make matters worse, all need to be dealt with simultaneously. Let me mention some of these challenges, which relate either to the work of the Court itself or are difficulties inherent in the ICC system.

First, there are many areas where the Court must improve and make its own work more efficient. This includes areas of an administrative nature, such as the budgeting system, but also judicial work. The judges are currently engaged in a lessons learned exercise, which aims at identifying ways and means to improve the efficiency of the judicial process.

Second, the Office of the Prosecutor, above all, must continue to develop into a more effective body for prosecuting international crimes. High expectations rest on the shoulders of Fatou Bensouda, from Gambia, the second prosecutor since June 2012. In my view, she should be given enough time to review, redirect and strengthen her office according to her own ideas and objectives.

Third, the Court needs greater international recognition and more members than the current 124 states parties. It is, however, encouraging that Tunisia and the Maldives joined the ICC in 2011,[32] and that other Arab and Asian states are considering accession.

Fourth, a particularly serious problem in the judicial work is the necessary provision of protection to witnesses and victims. Far more so than in central Europe, witnesses and victims from African "situation states", such as Kenya, Democratic Republic of the Congo, Uganda or Darfur/Sudan, who are prepared to testify, are often at great risk and face concrete threats. And this is where the problems start: procedural rules explicitly permit witnesses and victims to be made anonymous through

---

A warrant of arrest was also issued against Abdallah Banda Abakaer Nourain, replacing a previous summons to appear (11 September 2014).

[31] The Court issued summonses to appear against Bahar Idriss Abu Garda (7 May 2009); Abdallah Banda Abakaer Nourain (27 August 2009) which was later replaced by a warrant of arrest; Saleh Mohammed Jerbo Jamus (27 August 2009, proceedings terminated following his death); William Samoei Ruto (8 March 2011); Henry Kiprono Kosgey (8 March 2011); Joshua Arap Sang (8 March 2011); Uhuru Muigai Kenyatta (8 March 2011); Francis Kirimi Muthaura (8 March 2011); and Mohammed Hussein Ali (8 March 2011).

[32] Tunisia and the Maldives deposited their instruments of accession of the ICC Statute on 24 June 2011 and 21 September 2011, respectively.

"redactions" – that is, the blacking out of details, especially their names[33] – and to make them unrecognisable in submissions and witness statements. However, this also fundamentally threatens the rights of the accused to a fair trial.

Fifth, there is still dispute between the Court's chambers about the role that victims of crimes (and their organisations) can play in the various stages of the proceedings. The dilemma is clear: yes, we want victim participation as envisaged by the ICC Statute[34] – but how to achieve this without affecting the proceedings, in particular without delays? To illustrate this issue, the Court has received, up to the present, more than 11,000 victims' applications of which roughly 45 per cent were authorised by the respective chambers to participate in the proceedings. In general, it is my impression that the chambers have gradually found, especially in recent years, better ways for victims' participation.[35]

Beyond these challenges, let me now recall some of the inherent limitations and continuing difficulties that the Court has simply to live with and that we cannot change however much we would like to.

First, it has become more apparent in the last years that the ICC is absolutely, 100 per cent, dependent on effective co-operation with states parties in preparing criminal cases, in particular when it comes to the key issue of arrest and surrender of the suspect. This lack of any form of executive power is another weakness of the Court, its Achilles' heel, so to speak. The matter is simple: no arrests, no trials.

Second, another limiting factor is the unprecedented, indeed gigantic difficulty that the Court must, in order to obtain the evidence required, conduct the necessary, complex investigations in regions thousands of kilometres away from The Hague; in regions where travel is difficult, security volatile and where evidence is difficult to collect.

---

[33] See ICC, Rules of Procedure and Evidence, adopted 3 –10 September 2002, rule 81(4) (http://www.legal-tools.org/doc/8bcf6f/).

[34] See ICC Statute, Art. 68(3), *supra* note 1.

[35] See, for example, ICC, Pre-Trial Chamber I, *Prosecutor v. Laurent Gbagbo*, Decision on issues related to the victims' application process, 6 February 2012, ICC-02/11-01/11-33 (http://www.legal-tools.org/doc/da3e22/), in which collective victims' applications were encouraged. See also ICC, Pre-Trial Chamber II, *Prosecutor v. Bosco Ntaganda*, Decision Establishing Principles on the Victims' Application Process, 28 May 2013, ICC-01/04-02/06-67 (http://www.legal-tools.org/doc/f6fa38/), establishing a simplified application form and instructing the Victims Participation and Reparation Section to assist in processing the applications.

Third, genocide, crimes against humanity and war crimes are usually committed during armed conflict as a result of orders "from the top" issued by all kinds of rulers, who at the same time make every effort to cover up their responsibility for the crimes. This means that, first of all, the prosecution is faced with the difficult task to lay open the so-called chain of command – in other words, that powerful leaders at the top were responsible for the crimes. At the same time, these powerful leaders have quite often political allies or supporters who then – and this comes as no surprise – heavily criticise the intervention by the Court or seek to fight against it.

In pursuing its task, therefore, the Court will almost inevitably be caught between the poles of brutal power politics, on the one hand, and law and human rights, on the other. Consequently, the work of the Court will often continue to be hampered by adverse political winds or indeed political reproach of every colour. This is the reality – despite all our efforts to demonstrate, time and again, that we are, that we remain a purely judicial, non-political, neutral, fair and objective institution. Likewise, all must be done against further attempts, by whomever, to politicise the work of the Court.

Future Perspectives

In the preceding part you have been made aware again of the many limitations, many ongoing tasks and many challenges the Court has to cope with, also in the future. This is necessary for a reality check so that we all have a realistic idea of the conditions under which the ICC will have to work, now and in the future. But we have come a long way. When I first joined the ICC negotiations at the UN in New York in 1996, there was a myriad of unresolved issues; the whole idea of a future world court for international crimes seemed to be some kind of utopia, a dream. It is worthwhile to recall what has been achieved since the Rome diplomatic conference of 1998.

First, it is a huge success. This means real progress in that we managed to establish the first permanent international criminal court in the history of humankind in the past 12 years; this against the forces of *Realpolitik*, against so many odds. What illustrates this achievement in a very concrete way is that on 14 December 2015 the ICC moved into its new permanent premises – built for the next 50 to 100 years.

Second, today the Court is a functioning reality, an internationally accepted and respected guardian or watchtower against core crimes when justice cannot be delivered at the national level. In my presentations, I sometimes compare the Court with a lighthouse which constantly sends out a double message of fundamental importance, a very serious warning indeed. 1) To engage in genocide, crimes against humanity, war crimes or the crime of aggression is no longer tolerated by the international community. There can be no impunity for these crimes. And 2) if you are a political or military leader, obsessed by power, and you play with the idea of using brutal force against your opponents, or your own population, you face the risk of ending up in court, be it in a national court or before the ICC. This is because more and more men and women in this world are united by the conviction that nobody is above the law, regardless of the nationality and the rank of the perpetrators.

Some Personal Observations

Let me now conclude with some personal observations and also hopes for the future. This anthology is based on papers presented at a conference held in Fudan University, Shanghai, marking the inauguration of the Fudan International Criminal Law Center ('ICLC'). This conference and the establishment of the ICLC are, in my view, further concrete proof of the commitment of China to international peace and justice, and to the rule of law in this somehow disorderly world, which therefore urgently needs this rule of law and more international justice.

I was born in 1943, during the Second World War. So my childhood was heavily marked by the suffering, misery and destruction that the crimes committed by Adolf Hitler and his followers have brought over Europe and also the German people. I still remember that, as children, our favourite playground was the ruins of bombed-out houses in our neighbourhood. Soon after, as a young man, I also became aware that China, this great country in the distance, was badly destroyed and had suffered terribly during the Second World War and in the years afterwards. Ever since then, I have followed, with growing admiration, from a distance, the rise of China and of the Chinese people, from the ashes of war to their current position, as a leading country in Asia and the world, as a permanent member of the Security Council, and as a country whose commitment to international justice and to peaceful co-existence in this world are a hope for many.

It is my hope that, with efforts like the Fudan conference, we all may have a better common understanding of why the International Criminal Court is no threat to the sovereignty and constitutional order of states, and no threat to the principle of non-intervention in the domestic jurisdiction of states. Otherwise, why would 124 states from all regions of the world already be signatories to the ICC Statute?

It is also my hope that, with such efforts, we all may have a better common understanding of the principle of complementarity, which maintains, even strengthens, the primacy and priority of functioning criminal justice systems. The principle of complementarity and its implication must be explained time and again, in the most careful manner so that unjustified fears and concerns regarding the ICC disappear.

Finally, it is my hope that over time it will be better understood, also through the work of the new ICLC Fudan, that the ICC indeed merits and deserves to be fully supported also by China. The 18 judges of the Court would welcome a judge colleague from China on the bench, just as with Judge LIU Daqun in the International Criminal Tribunal for the former Yugoslavia and Judge XUE Hanqin at the International Court of Justice. It is also very clear to me that all the 124 states parties, including Germany and the German government, would like to see China as their partner in the ICC. Full support by China for the ICC would also be a great encouragement for many small developing and other states, mainly from the Third World, who look up to China, and who await a positive signal from this great nation to support the International Criminal Court. Chinese accession to the ICC Statute would also weaken all those who are against the rule of law, and would strengthen international peace and justice.

FOREWORD BY JUDGE THEODOR MERON

Although international criminal law as we know it today is still a new and growing area of the law, I submit to you that over the course of just two decades it has become clear that an understanding of international criminal law and of the rulings of international criminal courts is essential, not just for law professors focused on public international law but also for lawyers working on issues related to the rule of law in post-conflict countries, for diplomats who must consider how best to address crimes that take place during armed conflicts on the other side of the world, for government officials who must advise their governments on the scope of obligations under international humanitarian law, for those responsible for providing humanitarian aid in war zones, and for military officers who must train and lead their troops in accordance with governing law. In short, a nuanced understanding of international criminal law and justice has become vital to a great many areas of undertaking. So it is only fitting that we are having this important anthology, consisting of papers presented at a seminar held in March 2014 at Fudan University, given the university's illustrious connection to one of the very first judges of an international criminal tribunal, MEI Ju-ao, who served his nation with distinction as a member of the International Military Tribunal for the Far East. I followed a very similar path to the bench as Judge MEI, having long served as a law professor – as he did – and as legal counsellor to my country's State Department before becoming a judge, so it is a very special honour for me to provide this foreword.

In my remarks I would like to provide you with an overview of the legacy of the first international criminal tribunal of the modern age, the International Criminal Tribunal for the former Yugoslavia ('ICTY'), and to give you an introduction to the world's newest international criminal tribunal: the United Nations Mechanism for International Criminal Tribunals. Before we can understand the remarkable changes that have taken place over the past 20 years with the rise of international criminal law, however, we must look first to the past.

Throughout most of human history, the conduct of war and concepts of individual *criminal* liability were not seen to overlap. In many cases, mistreatment of civilians was expected or even embraced as a useful tool of war. Even where armies chose to enforce particular disciplinary standards as an internal matter, any punishment meted out for the mistreatment of civilians or opponents generally focused on low-ranking individuals. Insofar as liability for actions against civilians and mistreatment of combatants during wars was addressed, it was generally in the context of state-paid reparations by the losing side of the conflict. There was no notion of individual liability, much less of individual *criminal* responsibility.

I do not mean to paint an entirely grim picture. A number of civic and religious leaders have, over the centuries, decried particular practices during warfare, or appealed for limits on civilian suffering. However, in the past, such appeals rested on broad moral principles, or codes of chivalry, rather than on any legal framework.

Starting in the nineteenth century, however, some of these moral principles found their way into military manuals and, eventually, into international treaties. The signing of the first Geneva Convention and subsequent agreements among nations gave rise to the idea that particular laws of war restricted the behaviour of forces during conflicts. Importantly, however, these restrictions were framed as obligations undertaken by state parties, and any failure to abide by the restrictions was to be addressed solely on the state-to-state plane.

In the early part of the twentieth century, the scope and content of conventions and treaties governing conduct in times of war and armed conflict expanded significantly, and the contours of the law of war became increasingly well defined. At the same time, and in response to the horrors of the First World War, notions of individual obligation – and, at times, individual liability – slowly came to the fore. For example, the Versailles Treaty signed in 1919 provided at Article 227 that: "The Allied and Associated Powers publicly arraign William II of Hohenzollern, formerly German Emperor, for a supreme offence against international morality and the sanctity of treaties", and specified that "[a] special tribunal will be constituted to try the accused". This marked the first time that a treaty addressed the individual responsibility of a head of state for initiating and conducting what we now call a crime of aggression or crime against peace. As a practical matter, however, Article 227 was a dead letter. As one commentator has suggested, this Article set forth a *moral* rather than a *legal* offence. Although the Versailles Treaty contained two other provisions related to the prosecution of individuals for war crimes, these clauses did not call for an international criminal court; instead, they merely contemplated the use of military tribunals and were limited in scope, with even more limited impact when they were eventually implemented.

In the aftermath of the Second World War, there were important advances and changes in the law of war, both in terms of the protections offered and in terms of notions of international crimes and individual responsibility. The Geneva Conventions of 1949, for instance, included grave breaches clauses explicitly requiring state parties to prosecute, or to turn over for prosecution in another state, individuals who committed serious violations of the Conventions during international conflicts. In practice, however, little was done to prosecute those alleged to be responsible under the grave breaches clauses within national jurisdictions. And while the commentaries to the Geneva Conventions noted the possibility of an international court judging those who committed grave breaches, no action was taken in this regard.

To be sure, the well-known criminal trials that took place at Nuremberg and Tokyo after the Second World War involved the trial of individuals for crimes under international law. But these post-war tribunals were, undeniably, courts of the victorious states which had militarily defeated Germany and Japan. They were, in other words, victors' courts rather than being truly international, and despite some efforts to provide due process and fair procedures, doubts as to their fundamental fairness persisted as a result. While some trials of individuals accused of committing crimes in the context of the Second World War took place on a national level, including the trials of assorted Nazi officials in the Federal Republic of Germany, these proceedings were restricted in both scope and ambition.

National prosecutions for war crimes and other similar acts in the nearly half century that followed the Second World War were virtually non-existent. And it is fair to say that during the Cold War the idea that the nations of the world would support the operation of an independent, international court that would be mandated to adjudicate individuals' criminal liability – without regard to which side of a conflict those individuals belonged – appeared fanciful at best.

In sum, for many years the notion of prosecuting those believed to be responsible for grave breaches of the Geneva Conventions, much less for other serious breaches of the law of war (or "international humanitarian law" as it came to be known following the humanising innovations adopted following the Second World War), was almost entirely theoretical. And as a result, the expectation was that if such crimes were committed, they could be committed with impunity.

All of this changed a little over 20 years ago when, on 25 May 1993, the United Nations Security Council adopted Resolution 827, establishing the International Criminal Tribunal for the former Yugoslavia. Resolution 827 was, in many ways, the result of a fortuitous set of circumstances – the end of the Cold War, the unprecedented level of media attention paid to the Yugoslavia conflict, the resulting enhanced ability of non-governmental organisations and others to mobilise public opinion, and the increased focus of members of civil society and others on notions of accountability, including and perhaps particularly by those who are or were government or military leaders.

At the time of the ICTY's founding, of course, the significance of the Security Council's step was not fully understood. Many observers, and even some members of the Security Council itself, had doubts as to what this new institution – this new *court* – could achieve. They had doubts that there would be arrests, doubts that there would, in fact, be trials, doubts as to the legitimacy any verdicts might have – doubts, in sum, as to whether the court that they had created on paper would become a viable institution. No one, in short, could have known in 1993 how the ideal of holding individuals to account for serious violations of international humanitarian law – the ideal embodied in the resolution that created the ICTY – would translate into practice.

To be sure, over the years, the ICTY faced a great many challenges. Although the international military tribunals at Nuremberg and Tokyo were important predecessors for the ICTY, in a very real way the judges and staff who arrived in The Hague in the early 1990s had to construct a new court from the ground up. General legal principles had to be made concrete, judicial and practical precedents drawn from a host of differing national legal traditions had to be appropriately melded, and jurisdictional boundaries adhered to. In the early years, co-operation from states was often not readily forthcoming, and the ICTY struggled at times to demonstrate that it could and would accomplish all that had been mandated to do.

But today I am proud to report that the ICTY has put to rest the early doubts and achieved far more than many would have expected two decades ago. Not only has the tribunal successfully carried out the mandate that was established for it by the Security Council but, in the process, it has set a vitally important precedent for a number of other international criminal courts and tribunals that were established in the years since 1993, as well as for a growing array of national jurisdictions increasingly intent on prosecuting international crimes within their domestic systems. Indeed, many of the advances made since 1993 in the world of international criminal justice were made possible thanks to the pioneering example set by the ICTY, and when the tribunal eventually closes its doors – as it will soon – it will leave behind an important legacy.

In some respects, the ICTY's legacy is quite tangible. As a result of its trials and thanks to the efforts of both the prosecution and the defence, the tribunal has become the guardian of an extraordinary quantum of evidence and information concerning events that took place during the conflicts in the former Yugoslavia. This unparalleled compilation of material will serve students and researchers for generations to come.

Over the past two decades the tribunal has also crafted practical processes and policies to address a wide range of responsibilities, including the enforcement of sentences, the transfer of accused persons across state borders, and the protection of vulnerable victims and witnesses. Key rules of evidence and procedure were formulated, adopted – and revised – over time as necessary. As the first international criminal court of the modern era, the ICTY's advances in relation to these and other key court management matters have served as valuable models for other international courts, and for judiciaries and practitioners in national jurisdictions as well.

More fundamentally, the ICTY has demonstrated that it is possible to try even the most complex of cases, involving allegations of some of the worst crimes imaginable and brought against senior military and political leaders – and to do so not once or twice but time and again. It is not simply the fact that the ICTY has held so many trials that I wish to emphasise but also the non-discriminating nature of its approach to individual responsibility more generally. The ICTY's prosecutor has indicted, and the ICTY has tried, not just individuals who were alleged to be physically involved in committing crimes, but military and political leaders who are accused of masterminding crimes or failing to prevent subordinates from committing crimes or failing to punish the subordinates thereafter. And the ICTY has indicted and put on trial political and military leaders from all over the former Yugoslavia – in the process helping to dismantle the age-old assumption that military commanders and other leaders may avoid responsibility through political manoeuvring or deploying scapegoats.

And of course, over the past two decades the tribunal has issued hundreds if not thousands of rulings, creating a vast corpus of substantive and procedural decisions and other rulings: a body of functioning law built onto the bare, statutory skeleton that the judges of the tribunal faced in 1993. The ICTY's procedural rulings have addressed everything from the different ways in which evidence can be collected, translated and heard, to the scope of defendants' rights, including the right to self-representation, to the best practices for addressing almost unprecedented volumes of evidence concerning alleged crimes. This focus on procedural fairness reflects the tribunal's deep commitment to respect for human rights – and, in particular, to fair trial rights, which are enshrined in the ICTY Statute. The centrality of due process and fair trial principles to the work of the tribunal is, undeniably, an important advance as compared with the approach of earlier courts trying those accused of war crimes and other violations in the wake of the Second World War.

Although these procedural rulings have been critically important to the ICTY's achievements and the perceptions of the legitimacy of its work, it is the ICTY's rulings on matters of substantive law that have, in many ways, been at the core of its success. Starting with its first court proceedings and continuing to this day, the tribunal's judges have delineated, in much more concrete fashion than had ever been done before, the parameters of the core crimes in the ICTY Statute – genocide, crimes against humanity, grave breaches of the Geneva Conventions of 1949, and violations of the laws and customs of war – and the scope of basic modes of liability governing individual criminal responsibility. In doing so, the tribunal's judges have looked not simply to the text of the ICTY Statute, to treaty-based law like the Genocide Convention, and to judicial precedents from the Tokyo and Nuremberg tribunals, but also to the body of law known as customary international law. This reliance on customary international law has been crucial to the tribunal's ability to abide by the key legal principle of *nullum crimen sine lege* – but it has also been at the core of some of the tribunal's truly groundbreaking rulings, including the 1995 ruling in the *Tadić* case, in which the late, great Judge Antonio Cassese and his colleagues made plain that many of the rules and principles governing *international* armed conflicts apply to *internal* armed conflicts as well.

By accomplishing all that I have just discussed, the ICTY has played an important role in paving the way for the establishment of other international and hybrid criminal tribunals, including the Special Court for Sierra Leone, the ICTY's sister tribunal, the International Criminal Tribunal for Rwanda ('ICTR'), and the world's first permanent international criminal court. More generally, however, the ICTY – together with the other international and hybrid criminal courts – has helped to introduce a new era in our thinking about crimes that take place during war and other armed conflict. Today the debate in diplomatic and legal circles is not so much whether an individual should be held criminally responsible for his or her actions but the means and modalities according to which the individual will be tried – whether a person should be tried at an international court in The Hague, for instance, or whether he or she should be tried in his or her home jurisdiction, and whether holding a trial locally can be done fairly and appropriately. We are, in many ways, at the beginning of a new era in international law and international relations: one based on notions of individual accountability, and one that owes a great deal to what the ICTY has accomplished over the past 20 years.

As I mentioned earlier, the ICTY – which has now accounted for each of the 161 individuals it has indicted and is in the process of completing its last few remaining trials and appeals – is soon expected to close its doors. The impending completion of ongoing trials and appeals at the ICTY does not, however, signal the end of the tribunal's responsibilities. To the contrary, even after these trials and appeals are concluded much work will remain, including: the continued protection of witnesses; the determination of applications for review of judgments, for variation of protective measures granted to witnesses, and for access to evidence; and the supervision of the enforcement of sentences and determination of applications for early release and clemency. It was in light of this remaining work, the remaining work of the ICTY's sister tribunal, the ICTR, and the UN Security Council's goal to encourage the completion of both tribunals' judicial work without further delay that the Security Council decided to establish the United Nations Mechanism for International Criminal Tribunals ('Mechanism') on 22 December 2010 in Security Council Resolution 1966.

As this resolution and the accompanying statute make plain, the Mechanism is designed to assume responsibility for core functions of both the ICTY and the ICTR, and to begin to assume such responsibility even as the two original tribunals are in the process of completing their remaining judicial work. The creation of the Mechanism reflects the international community's strong conviction that the closure of the ICTY and the ICTR should not open the door to impunity for those who have yet to be brought to justice – and that certain key functions of the tribunals must be maintained even after the ICTY and ICTR cease to hear cases.

The core functions of the Mechanism include some of those I have already described – such as the enforcement of sentences and the provision of continued protection to victims and witnesses – as well as others, such as ensuring continued co-operation with requests from national jurisdictions. The Mechanism is also – and importantly – entrusted with responsibility for the archives of both the ICTY and the ICTR, and will be responsible for the conduct of proceedings involving any of the remaining fugitives indicted by the ICTR, if and, I would like to say, when they are taken into custody. And following the completion of the ICTY's remaining trials, any appeals from the judgments in those cases will be heard by the Mechanism, rather than by the ICTY.

In many ways, the Mechanism will look and behave much as its predecessor tribunals, the ICTY and the ICTR, did; indeed, the Mechanism was designed with a goal of ensuring normative continuity with the ICTY and the ICTR. In other ways, however, the Mechanism presents a host of new challenges. It is designed to be a lean, efficient institution, with a small staff, yet – with offices in Tanzania, Rwanda and the Netherlands – it is also the world's first international criminal tribunal spanning two continents, and it must develop internal policies and procedures to address this special status and the different traditions and practices it has inherited from both of its predecessors.

The Mechanism is also the only international tribunal with judges who do not – with the exception of the president – work full time. This circumstance may well give rise to novel managerial challenges. When Judge MEI was called upon to be a member of the International Military Tribunal for the Far East in Tokyo 70 years ago, he was willing and ready to fly to Tokyo to serve. But only time will tell if the judges on the Mechanism's roster will be prepared to answer the call to come to hear a case in The Hague or in Arusha if they are otherwise engaged in full-time work on the other side of the globe.

Notwithstanding these challenges, if the Mechanism proves to be a success – as I hope it will – it may well offer a new and more efficient model for other courts and tribunals around the world.

TABLE OF CONTENTS

1

Crimes against Peace in the Tokyo Trial

XUE Ru[*]

The International Military Tribunal for the Far East ('IMTFE'), also known as the *Tokyo Tribunal*, was established on 26 July 1945. The Tokyo Tribunal was the Pacific counterpart of the Nuremberg Tribunal. However, one of the differences between the two tribunals is that crimes against peace played a more important role before the IMTFE.[1] Consequently, 36 of the 55 counts submitted by the prosecutors related to crimes against peace, and all but one of the accused were convicted of crimes against peace.[2] Some 85 per cent of the entire judgment was devoted to crimes against peace and all five separate and dissenting opinions expressed different views on the basis or application of crimes against peace.[3] Most importantly, the IMTFE's jurisdiction on crimes against

---

[*] **XUE Ru** is a Lecturer at the Military Law Department, Xi'an Academy of Political Science of the Chinese People's Liberation Army ('PLA'). She holds a Ph.D. from China University of Politics and Law, an LL.M. from Xi'an Academy of Political Science of the PLA. She is temporarily doing research work in the Military Court and was awarded a doctoral scholarship by the Hague Academy of International Law in 2013. Her article, "On the Effect of Security Council on the Crimes of Aggression in the Jurisdiction of the International Criminal Court", was published in *Chinese Yearbook of International Law 2014*.

[1] International Military Tribunal for the Far East ('IMTFE'), Charter, Tokyo, enacted 19 January 1946 and amended 25 April 1946 ('IMTFE Charter') (http://www.legal-tools.org/doc/a3c41c/). Article 5 states: "The Tribunal shall have the power to try and punish Far Eastern war criminals who as individuals or as members of organizations are charged with offences which include Crimes against Peace". The interpretation suggested the Tokyo Tribunal's jurisdiction was limited to those persons charged with offences which included crimes against peace. This explains why the 28 defendants consisted only of those who could be charged with the commission of crimes against peace.

[2] IMTFE, Indictment ('IMTFE Indictment') (https://www.legal-tools.org/doc/59771d/).

[3] See IMTFE, *United States of America et al. v. Araki Sadao et al.*, Judgment, 1 November 1948 the majority opinion of the Tribunal ('IMTFE Judgment') (http://www.legal-tools.org/doc/3a2b6b/). For the dissenting and separate opinions: IMTFE, *United States of America et al. v. Araki Sadao et al.*, Opinion of Mr. Justice Roling Member for the Netherlands, 12 November 1948 (http://www.legal-tools.org/doc/fb16ff/); IMTFE, *United States*

peace aroused considerably more debate both within and outside the courtroom than the other two crimes within its jurisdiction. In other words, crimes against peace were the primary focus of the IMTFE. This fact compels a thorough review of international law in this regard before the Second World War and the application of crimes against peace before the tribunal.

1.1. The Prohibition on Aggressive War before the Second World War

The prohibition on aggressive war in international law evolved over a rather long period of time. From a historical perspective, wars were originally deemed a normal feature of international relations and a part of the sovereign rights of states. International law aimed to regulate war as an institution rather than to sanction the act of war.[4] As a result, the law of war (*jus in bello*) and the lawfulness of the use of force (*jus ad bellum*) emerged. The lawfulness or otherwise of the active use of force by a state was estimated by various standards in different periods of history.

At the time of the conclusion of the Peace of Westphalia in 1648 no effective restraints had been imposed on nation states and their leaders in making wars abroad. As Cicero long ago noted: "*Inter arma silent leges*" (In time of war, the law is silent).[5] While the theory of state sovereignty was deeply entrenched, state elites held that waging war should not be regulated under international law since it fell under the power of state sovereignty. In developing the doctrine of *bellum justum* in detail, Hugo Grotius argued that the state's right to initiate war was recognised. Until the early twentieth century "the predominant conviction was that every

---

of America et al. v. Araki Sadao et al., Separate Opinion of the President, 1 November 1948 (http://www.legal-tools.org/doc/1db870/); IMTFE, *United States of America et al. v. Araki Sadao et al.*, Judgment of the Hon'ble Mr. Justice Pal Member from India, 1 November 1948 ('Pal Dissenting Judgment') (http://www.legal-tools.org/doc/712ef9/); IMTFE, *United States of America et al. v. Araki Sadao et al.*, Dissenting Judgment of the Member from France, 12 November 1948 (http://www.legal-tools.org/doc/d1ac54/); and, IMTFE, *United States of America et al. v. Araki Sadao et al.*, Concurring Opinion By the Honorable Mr. Justice Delfin Jaranilla Member from the Republic of the Philippines, 1 November 1948 (http://www.legal-tools.org/doc/67f7b0/).

4   Jackson Nyamuya Maogoto, *War Crimes and Realpolitik: International Justice From World War I to the 21st Century*, Lynne Rienner, Boulder, CO, 2004, p. 2.

5   Cited in Quincy Wright, *A Study of War*, University of Chicago Press, Chicago, 1965, p. 863.

State had a right – namely, an interest protected by international law – to embark upon war whenever it pleased".[6]

At the end of the nineteenth century, because of the development of science and technology, rising nationalism and other relevant factors, the mode of warfare gradually transformed into a much more devastating form of total war that inflicted horrifying casualties on both armed forces and civilians. The severe consequence of warfare objectively spurred more states to legislate against the unlimited use of force and aggressive war. The first steps, designed to somewhat curtail the freedom to wage war in general international law, were taken at the two Hague Peace Conferences of 1899 and 1907.[7]

The League of Nations, founded in 1920, created a considerable advance by inscribing the prevention of aggressive war into its Covenant and promoting the conclusion of a series of resolutions and protocols for world peace. All the state parties were required to mutually respect and preserve the territorial integrity and political independence of one another against "external aggression",[8] and the state parties agreed "in no case to resort to war until three months after the award by the arbitrators or the judicial decision, or the report by the Council".[9]

In addition to the restriction on the power to resort to war, the disastrous outcome of the First World War focused minds on the moral and legal responsibilities for the outbreak of the war. Article 227 of the Versailles Treaty stipulated that the last German emperor, Kaiser Wilhelm II, should be punished for waging the war. Although this article was eventually not carried out because of the diplomatic asylum provided for the Kaiser by the Netherlands (which was neutral and not a party to the peace negotiations), the significance of the post-war process of sanctions was to put into place individual criminal responsibility of military and civilian officials for their violation of the "sanctity of treaties".[10]

---

[6]   Yoram Dinstein, *War, Aggression and Self-Defence*, 3rd ed., Cambridge University Press, Cambridge, 2004, p. 71.

[7]   *Ibid.*, p. 74.

[8]   Covenant of the League of Nations, December 1924, Art. 10 (http://www.legal-tools.org/doc/106a5f/).

[9]   *Ibid.*, Art. 12.

[10] Versailles Treaty, 28 June 1919, Art. 227, Part VII, Penalties (http://www.legal-tools.org/doc/a64206/).

The purpose of the Kellogg-Briand Pact, the so-called Pact of Paris of 1928, was to outlaw wars as an instrument of national policy. Eventually the Pact was signed by most states in the world at that time, including Germany, Italy and Japan. The conclusion of the Kellogg-Briand Pact can be regarded as a milestone towards the prohibition of threatening or the use of armed force. From then on, a state party having initiated a war might be held responsible for violating its treaty obligations.

The eruption of the Second World War greatly inspired the idea not only of outlawing but also of criminalising aggressive war, which culminated in the formulation of the United Nations Charter ('UN Charter') in 1945. The most remarkable achievements of the UN Charter were the prohibition of the threat or use of force in international relations and the implementation of the doctrine of collective security into reality by empowering the Security Council to prevent aggression and restore peace by coercive measures whenever international security was at risk.

In practice, the strong will to punish war criminals was shown by the establishment of two historic tribunals, namely, the International Military Tribunal ('IMT') at Nuremberg and the IMTFE at Tokyo. The IMT and IMTFE Charters "criminalized the aggressive warfare under the heading of crimes against peace instead of crime of aggression because of political consideration, and there were no elements of the crime besides a compact definition because the drafters intended to leave the task of determining what constituted a war of aggression to the judges".[11]

1.2. Jurisdiction over Crimes against Peace in the Tokyo Tribunal

The jurisdiction of the IMTFE refers to the scope with regard to who could be prosecuted, for which crimes and under what circumstances. Although the subject-matter jurisdiction on crimes against peace is the focus of this chapter, the territorial, temporal and personal jurisdiction related to crimes against peace also affects the jurisdiction on this crime, all of which, taken together, highlight the very essence of the IMTFE. The three types of jurisdiction are discussed briefly and then the subject-matter jurisdiction of crimes against peace is highlighted.

---

[11] Nicolaos Strapatsas, "Aggression", in William A. Schabas and Nadia Bernaz (eds.), *Routledge Handbook of International Criminal Law*, Routledge, London, 2011, pp. 156–57.

1.2.1. Territorial, Temporal and Personal Jurisdiction Relating to Crimes against Peace

The IMTFE Charter did not define the territorial jurisdiction of the tribunal beyond the Far Eastern region where the aggressive wars initiated by Japan prevailed[12] and the territory of the states with which Japan had been at war.[13] This territorial confinement was further clarified by the IMTFE judgment.

> So far as the wishes of the conspirators crystallized into a concrete common plan we are of the opinion that the territory they had resolved that Japan should dominate was confined to East Asia, the Western and South Western Pacific Ocean and the Indian Ocean, and certain of the islands in these oceans. We shall accordingly treat Count 1 as if the charge had been limited to the above object.[14]

Then the jurisdiction over crimes against peace had territorial scope within East Asia, the western and south-western Pacific Ocean and the Indian Ocean.

There was no explicit expression of the temporal jurisdiction of the IMTFE in its Charter, but a discussion about the time period during which the crimes should be dealt with did take place among the prosecutors. In the end, the prosecutors decided to charge the offences that happened between 1 January 1928 and 2 September 1945.[15] The reason choosing 1928 as the starting point was because in that year Marshal ZHANG Zuolin[16]

---

12 IMTFE Charter, Art. 1: "the International Tribunal for the Far East is hereby established for the just and prompt trial and punishment of the major war criminals in the Far East", see *supra* note 1.

13 *Ibid.*, Art. 8.

14 IMTFE Judgment, p. 1137, see *supra* note 3.

15 IMTFE Indictment, count 1, para. 1: "[A]ll the defendants together with divers other persons, between the 1st January, 1928 and the 2nd September, 1945, participated as [...]", see *supra* note 2.

16 See also the old phonetic spelling as Marshal Chang Tso-lin, who was the commander-in-chief of the Chinese armies in Manchuria and the head of last cabinet of the so-called northern warlord government. In April 1927, when Tanaka Giichi took office as the Japanese prime minister, the expansionists gained their first victory. The new cabinet was committed to a policy of peaceful penetration into Manchuria in north-eastern China. But, whereas Tanaka proposed to establish Japanese hegemony over Manchuria through negotiation with its separatist leaders, elements within the Kwantung Army were impatient with this policy. In June 1928 members of the Kwantung Army murdered ZHANG, with whom Tanaka was negotiating.

was murdered by members of the Japanese Kwantung Army,[17] an act that was regarded as the very genesis of aggression by Japan towards China. This point of view was confirmed by the IMTFE in its judgment.[18] The closing date of the temporal jurisdiction was obviously the date on which Japan signed the Instrument of Surrender. The IMTFE believed that dealing with the history of these attacks and the exploitation by Japan of the resources of the territories it occupied could help in assessing the responsibility of individuals for these attacks.

Personal jurisdiction was laid out in Article 5 of IMTFE Charter.[19] It seems that those who were charged individually or as members of organisations with crimes against peace would fall into the personal jurisdiction. The boundaries of personal jurisdiction could be further clarified if the provisions of the Potsdam Proclamation – which defined the terms for the Japanese surrender – could be read in conjunction with the Charter.[20] Since crimes against peace were the major crime to be tried at the IMTFE, and the accused alleged to have committed this crime were called class A criminals, the tribunal exercised personal jurisdiction on those who had sufficient political or military authority and influence so as to lead Japan into a war of conquest. Such a narrowly delimited personal jurisdiction could be implied not only by the legal documents but also by the characteristic of crimes against peace as "leadership crimes".[21]

---

[17] The Kwantung Army was the Japanese unit maintained in Manchuria under the Treaty of Portsmouth, which ended the 1904–5 Russo-Japanese War, for the protection of Japanese interests, including the South Manchuria railway.

[18] IMTFE Judgment, p. 83, see *supra* note 3: "In dealing with the period of Japanese history with which this Indictment is mainly concerned it is necessary to consider in the first place the domestic history of Japan during the same period. In the years from 1928 onwards Japanese armed forces invaded in succession the territories of many of Japan's neighbors".

[19] IMTFE Charter, Art. 5, see *supra* note 1: "The Tribunal shall have the power to try and punish Far Eastern war criminals who as individuals or as members of organizations are charged with offences which include Crimes against Peace".

[20] Proclamation Defining Terms for Japanese Surrender, Potsdam, 26 July 1945, para. 6 ('Potsdam Declaration'): "There must be eliminated for all time the authority and influence of those who have deceived and misled the people of Japan into embarking on world conquest, for we insist that a new order of peace, security and justice will be impossible until irresponsible militarism is driven from the world" (http://www.legal-tools.org/doc/f8cae3/).

[21] See also American Military Tribunal, *United States of America, v. Wilhelm von Leeb et al.,* Judgment, 27 October 1948, p. 25: "The criminality which attaches to the waging of an aggressive war should be confined to those who participate in it at the policy level" ('High Command case') (http://www.legal-tools.org/doc/c340d7/).

First, only decision makers could be held accountable. This crime was committed only by perpetrators who assumed leadership in either the military or the civilian government of a state. "Crimes against peace were not a crime that could be committed by people acting in a private capacity, or by low-level political or military officials of a State".[22] The International Law Commission ('ILC') in 1950 arrived at a similar conclusion that only "high-ranking military personnel and high State officials" can be guilty of waging war of aggression.[23] In its 1996 draft Code of Offences against the Peace and Security of Mankind, the ILC strictly defined the crime of aggression as limited to leaders or organisers.[24] Actually, both high-ranking state and military leaders could play key roles in the waging of aggressive war. If a person was a commander-in-chief of the navy or head of a state department or foreign office, then that person might very well have played a role in the commission of the crime of aggression so that the conviction would be easier than was otherwise the case.[25]

Second, the ability and competence implied by a high position to shape and influence state policy towards aggressive war was the key factor in relating individual responsibility to a state act. The High Command case judgment stated:

> It is not a person's rank or status, but his power to shape or influence the policy of his state, which was the relevant issue for determining his criminality under the charge of crimes against peace.
>
> International law condemns those who, due to their actual power to shape and influence the policy of their nation, prepare for, or lead their country into or in an aggressive war.[26]

---

22 Mauro Politi, "The Debate within the Preparatory Commission for the International Criminal Court", in Mauro Politi and Giuseppe Nesi (eds.), *The International Criminal Court and the Crime of Aggression*, Ashgate, Aldershot, 2004, p. 47.

23 United Nations, Report of the International Law Commission to the General Assembly on the Work of its Second Session, *Yearbook of the International Law Commission*, vol. II, para. 117, 29 July 1950, UN doc. A/CN.4/24 (http://www.legal-tools.org/doc/be570a/).

24 United Nations, Report of the International Law Commission to the General Assembly on the Work of its Forty-eighth Session, *Yearbook of the International Law Commission*, vol. II, part 2, 1996, UN doc. A/CN.4/SER.A/1996/Add.1(Part 2) (http://www.legal-tools.org/doc/e5f28b/).

25 Larry May, *Aggression and Crimes against Peace*, Cambridge University Press, Cambridge, 2008, p. 178.

26 High Command case, Judgment, p. 489, see *supra* note 21.

Before the IMTFE, among those sentenced to death were Doihara Kenji, a lieutenant general on the General Staff of the Imperial Japanese Army who played a prominent part in the political intrigue to initiate the war of aggression in Manchuria;[27] Hirota Kōki, the Japanese foreign minister and prime minister from 1933 to 1938 when the national policy of expansion and aggressive war was formulated and adopted;[28] Itagaki Seishirō, a divisional commander who took part in fighting at Marco Polo Bridge in 1937 and a war minister in 1938 who participated in intensifying and extending attacks on China;[29] Kimura Heitarō, the chief of staff for the Kwantung Army and later a deputy minister of war well aware of all governmental decisions to initiate hostilities in China and the Pacific War, and who actually played a prominent role in conducting those wars;[30] Tōjō Hideki, chief of staff of the Kwantung Army and later a minister of war and prime minister who consistently supported the policy of conquering China.[31]

1.2.2. Subject-matter Jurisdiction over Crimes against Peace

Before both the Tokyo and Nuremberg Tribunals the defendants challenged the jurisdiction over crimes against peace for the violation of the principle of *nullum crimen sine lege*, which was accepted as a maxim by all the civilised nations.[32] This most intensely debated issue focused on two elements: first, the lawfulness of the tribunal and the jurisdiction on crimes against peace; and second, individual criminal liability for crimes of aggression.[33]

As the Tokyo Tribunal's counterpart and forerunner, the IMT confronted similar challenges from the defendants and delivered its judgment prior to that of the IMTFE. The majority judgment of the Tokyo Tribunal followed the IMT's opinion in practically all aspects of the law, expressly

---

27 IMTFE Judgment, pp. 1148–1150, see *supra* note 3.

28 *Ibid.*, pp. 1158–1161.

29 *Ibid.*, pp. 1164–1165.

30 *Ibid.*, pp. 1174–1177.

31 *Ibid.*, pp. 1206–1207.

32 *Ibid.*, p. 24. See also International Military Tribunal ('IMT'), *Nuremberg Tribunal v. Goering et al.*, Judgment, 1 October, 1946 ('IMT Judgment') (https://www.legal-tools.org/doc/45f18e/).

33 MEI Ju-Ao, 远东国际军事法庭 [International Military Tribunal for the Far East], Law Press, Beijing, 1988, p. 17; IMT Judgment, pp. 445–447, see *supra* note 32.

adopting its reasoning in relation to key issues such as the binding nature of the Charter and the criminality of aggressive war.[34] Accordingly, the point of view that derived from the IMT quoted below can be regarded as part of the perspective of the IMTFE as well.

1.2.2.1. The Charge of Crimes against Peace

The first issue was whether it was lawful for the tribunals to charge the defendants with crimes against peace. The defence argued that they should be tried by a court martial rather than an international tribunal and that aggressive war was not illegal *per se*.[35] More specifically, they suggested that there was no authority for the IMTFE to include crimes against peace within its jurisdiction because aggressive war had not been made an international crime at the time the alleged criminal acts were committed and no penalty had been fixed for its commission. Therefore, the defence claimed that the charge violated *nullum crimen sine lege* and caused *ex post facto* punishment that was abhorrent to the law of all civilised nations.[36]

Both the Nuremberg and Tokyo Tribunals made definite answers to these challenges in two respects. First, it was lawful for the tribunals to exercise jurisdiction over the defendants. According to the IMT judgment, the jurisdiction of the Nuremberg Tribunal was defined in the London Agreement and its Charter. The making of the Charter was an exercise of sovereign legislative power by the countries to which Germany unconditionally surrendered and the undoubted right of these countries to legislate for the occupied territories had been recognised by the civilised world.[37] The creation of the IMT and its jurisdiction was merely the collective exercise of the right of each signatory power to set up special courts to administer law and to define the law it was to administer.

The establishment of the IMTFE was more complicated than that of the Nuremberg Tribunal. The IMTFE was established by virtue of four international legal instruments: the Cairo Declaration released on 1 December 1943, the Potsdam Declaration of 26 July 1945, the Instrument of Surrender of 2 September 1945 and the Moscow Conference Agreement

---

[34] IMTFE Judgment, pp. 25–27, see *supra* note 3.

[35] *Ibid.*, p. 24.

[36] IMT Judgment, p. 445, see *supra* note 32.

[37] *Ibid.*, p. 444.

of 26 December 1945. According to the Cairo Declaration, the three major Allies were "fighting the war to restrain and punish the aggression of Japan".[38] With respect to the prosecution of crimes committed by Japanese nationals, the Potsdam Declaration read: "the terms of the Cairo Declaration shall be carried out. [...] We do not intend that the Japanese shall be enslaved as a race nor destroyed as a nation, but stern justice shall be meted out to all war criminals, including those who have visited cruelties upon our prisoners".[39] It was from this provision, which was also accepted in the Instrument of Surrender, that the Supreme Commander for the Allied Powers, Douglas MacArthur, explicitly derived his powers by the special proclamation to establish the Tokyo Tribunal. Japan assumed obligations directly derived from the Instrument of Surrender. By this instrument, the Japanese authorities undertook to carry out the provisions of the Potsdam Declaration in good faith, and to issue whatever orders and to take whatever action for the purpose of giving effect to the declaration.[40] What is more, by the Moscow Conference Agreement, the Supreme Commander was entitled to issue all orders for the implementation of the terms of surrender.[41]

All these provisions, taken together, created a solid legal basis for the prosecution of Japanese defendants. The Supreme Commander of the Allied Powers was entitled to apply not only the Instrument of Surrender but also other legal instruments agreed between Japan and the Allied powers. The Hague Regulations, which were recognised to be in effective force in Japan and most of the Allied powers, acknowledged the authority of the legitimate power in the hands of the occupier to take all measures necessary to restore and ensure public order and safety. Without doubt

---

[38] Cairo Declaration on Japan, jointly released by the United States, the Republic of China and Great Britain, 1 December 1943, para. 8 ('Cairo Declaration').

[39] Potsdam Declaration, paras. 8, 10, see *supra* note 20.

[40] Instrument of Surrender by Japan, 2 September 1945, para. 6 ('Instrument of Surrender'): "We hereby undertake for the Emperor, the Japanese Government and their successors to carry out the provisions of the Potsdam Declaration in good faith, and to issue whatever orders and take whatever actions may be required by the Supreme Commander for the Allied Powers or by any other designated representative of the Allied Powers for the purpose of giving effect to that Declaration" (https://www.legal-tools.org/doc/4059de/).

[41] Moscow Conference Agreement: Soviet-Anglo-American Communiqué, Interim Meeting of Foreign Ministers of the United States, the United Kingdom and the Union of Soviet Socialist Republics, Moscow, 27 December 1945, p. 4 ('Moscow Agreement') (https://www.legal-tools.org/doc/653d48/).

establishing a special tribunal to pursue the justice required by the Potsdam Declaration fell into the category of the possible measures. What is more, the IMTFE recognised that belligerent powers might act only within the limits of international law, and therefore the right of the Allied powers to authorise a special tribunal for the trial and punishment of war criminals did not conflict with recognised international rules and principles.[42]

Second, both the IMT and IMTFE confirmed the criminality of aggressive war in the international law of that time. The Nuremberg Tribunal dismissed the defendants' claim by ruling that ever since the 1928 Kellogg-Briand Pact aggressive war had been a crime under international law because the solemn renunciation of war as an instrument of national policy necessarily involved the proposition that such a war was illegal. Therefore those who planned and waged such a war, with its inevitable and terrible consequences, were committing a crime in so doing.[43] Apropos of the argument that the pact did not expressly enact that such a war was a crime, the IMT made reference to the relevant enforcement of the international conventions in the field of international humanitarian law. The actions prohibited by the Hague Conventions of 1907 had long been deemed indisputably as crimes and been brought into force at the domestic level, although no provisions relating to the criminalisation of the relevant conduct were contained in the Conventions. What is more, punishment was the inherent power of a tribunal, so long as the tribunal was lawfully established, the act had been criminalised and the conviction was proved beyond reasonable doubt.

The IMT and IMTFE depended heavily, but not solely, in their reasoning on the Kellogg-Briand Pact. A long list of the treaties violated by Japan and Germany was clearly enumerated. These included the Hague Conventions of 1907, the Versailles Treaty of 1919, the treaty of mutual assistance sponsored by the League of Nations of 1923, the League of Nations Protocol for the Pacific Settlement of International Disputes of 1924, the declaration concerning wars of aggression adopted at the meeting of the Assembly of the League of Nations of 1927, the resolution at the Pan-American Conference of 1928, which were solemnly made to condemn the war of aggression not merely as illegal but criminal. As for Japan, the

---

[42] IMTFE Judgment, p. 23, see *supra* note 3.
[43] *Ibid.*, p. 446.

IMTFE provided an even longer list of treaties to which Japan had assumed obligations.[44]

The purpose of the tribunals invoking the provisions of these treaties was to illustrate that over the previous 20 years a general trend of states accepting war of aggression as a crime had emerged as a new development of international law. Thus, far from creating new international law, outlawing wars of aggression in the Kellogg-Briand Pact did no more than to express and define for more accurate reference the principles of law already in existence, which was the true interpretation of the treaty. As concluded by the IMT judgment, the Charter was not an arbitrary exercise of power on the part of the victorious nations, but the expression of international law existing at the time of its creation, and to that extent was itself a contribution to international law.[45] According to the IMTFE, aggressive war was a crime in international law long before the date of the Potsdam Declaration.[46]

1.2.2.2. Individual Responsibility for Crimes against Peace

As to the second question – whether the accused should be personally accountable for waging war – the defence argued that war was an act of state for which there was no individual responsibility under international law and there was no provision of sanction against individuals in international law. As such the tribunals violated the principles of *nullum crimen sine lege* and *nulla poena sine lege* and their charges amounted to *ex post facto* legislation.[47]

The IMT affirmed that international law had long recognised both state obligation and individual liability. The tribunal made reference to both domestic trials such as the *Ex parte Quirin* case before the United States Supreme Court and international instruments such as Article 227 of the Versailles Treaty which had inculpated individuals for the crime under international law.[48]

---

[44] *Ibid.*, Annex B.
[45] IMT Judgment, p. 445, see *supra* note 32.
[46] IMTFE Judgment, p. 27, see *supra* note 3.
[47] *Ibid.*, pp. 23–24; IMT Judgment, p. 447, see *supra* note 32.
[48] IMT Judgment, p. 448, see *supra* note 32.

In fact, individuals could be punished under international law and the argument of the non-existence of individual liability in international law ran up against long-standing practice and theory of international law. Over 300 years earlier, Hugo Grotius had expressed the idea that the offender who had violated international law could be sentenced to death by an adjudicator.[49] The IMT's point of view was supported by the established practice of the enforcement of international humanitarian law. Most countries had legislated the provisions in international treaties to which they assumed obligation to their domestic legal instruments and then punished individuals under their domestic judicial systems. In this way, individuals assumed liability for crimes of an international nature. Long before the IMT and IMTFE came into being, military tribunals or domestic courts in various countries had applied to individuals the laws and customs of war found in the relevant treaties. Those suspected of committing war crimes had been brought to trial and been convicted. Further, individuals had taken responsibility for acts of state. A well-known example is Napoleon, who was denounced and outlawed by European nations as an enemy and disturber of the peace and was sentenced to banishment to St Helena in 1815. At the end of the First World War the idea of trying war criminals not only came into being but was already reflected in Articles 228 and 229 of the Versailles Treaty.

1.2.2.3. Reflections on the Debate

The debates before the IMT and IMTFE reflect the tensions between the principle of justice and the principle of legality. A proper understanding of the principle of legality would be conducive to resolving this tension. *Nullum crimen, nulla poena sine lege* – the prohibition of retroactive application of criminal prohibitions and penalties without the principle of legality – provides a fundamental safeguard of the rights of the accused. This maxim had two purposes. For one thing, the function of criminal law to guide the behaviour of individuals can be achieved since anyone could reasonably foresee the legal response to his action under pre-existing law. For another, the principle aimed to protect the accused as far as possible from abuses of power by the authorities and excessive judicial discretion through arbitrary interpretation or creation of the terms of law. The two

---

[49] Hugo Grotius, *De Jure Belli ac Pacis*, 1625, book III, ch. XI, sec. 10., cited in MEI, 1988, p. 23, see *supra* note 33.

purposes are examined below to analyse whether or not they were satisfied in the present case.

In the first place, the issue could be safely transformed into a question of whether the defendant convicted by the tribunals understood that his conduct would violate international law as a crime at the time these offences were committed. It is evident that as leaders having the power to control the state, the defendants should have known the obligations they assumed under international law. According to the IMT judgment, the defendants must have known of the treaties signed by Germany outlawing recourse to war for the settlement of international disputes and they must have known that they were acting in defiance of all international law.[50] It is simply too naive to deem the Japanese leaders as being ignorant and innocent as they claimed themselves to be in virtue of the scope and gravity of the atrocities which had been supported by solid evidence. So long as the accused waged war with bold ignorance of their international obligation, the prosecution was not arbitrary or unjust.

In the second place, it is questionable whether the principle of legality could justifiably apply to the Tokyo Tribunal. As a principle of human rights, the principle of legality intended to protect ordinary citizens from the enormous power of the state. To this effect, it is doubtful whether the defendants who were themselves in the seats of state power could assert this principle in an international tribunal.[51] Even in domestic legal systems, *nullum crimen sine lege* is not an overriding principle. This maxim is adopted in common law countries in a qualified way. Common law offences may lack those requirements of rigidity, foreseeability and certainty proper to written legislation.[52] Further, the interpretation of the principle of legality should not impair the value judgment under the principle of justice. In the rhetoric of justice, "the legal order must primarily aim at prohibiting and punishing any conduct that was socially harmful or caused danger to society, whether or not that conduct had already been legally criminalized at the moment it was taken".[53] Where conduct was *malum in se* (evil in itself) by brutally intruding on the rights and legiti-

---

[50]   IMT Judgment, p. 446, see *supra* note 32.

[51]   Chihiro Hosoya, Nisuki Ando, Yasuaki Onuma and Roy Minear (eds.), *The Tokyo War Crimes Trial: An International Symposium*, Kodansha, Tokyo, 1986, p. 53.

[52]   Antonio Cassese, *International Criminal Law*, Oxford University Press, Oxford, 2003, p. 142.

[53]   *Ibid.*, p. 139.

mate interests of others, perpetrators could not be excused from blame when international legal rules were underdeveloped. In any case, the interpretation of the principle of legality should not compromise justice that is the fundamental value underpinning international formulations of all the other principles. Those who took a narrow perspective on the issue of legality, and hence criticised the Tokyo Tribunal as victor's justice, merely ignored the human right and justice value on the part of the victims. As the Nuremberg Tribunal stated, so far from being unjust to punish the war criminals, it would be unjust if their wrongs were allowed to go unpunished.[54]

It is true that with the perfection of the codification of legal norms in international criminal law and the rise of international human rights law, it is accepted that certain fundamental principles such as *nullum crimen sine lege* have now become more entrenched in international criminal law than ever before. During the negotiations for the Rome Statute of the International Criminal Court ('ICC Statute'), for example, the participating states made a move to define the crimes within its jurisdiction with the clarity and precision needed for criminal law, which resulted in the definitions of crimes and drafting of the elements of crimes later on. The ICC Statute itself contains a strong restatement of the *nullum crimen* principle in Article 22. However, the many criticisms of the violation of legality principle in the IMT and IMTFE are due to a misplaced application and interpretation of the maxim nowadays to the situations that occurred well over half a century ago. At least at that time, before the modern law of human rights and when the codification of international legal norms was rather rudimentary, the IMTFE was correct about the law on the point that substantive justice prevailed over the procedural limitation.

1.3. Elements of Crimes against Peace

On 1 November 1948 the IMTFE delivered its judgment on the major Japanese war criminals. Of the 25 defendants being sentenced, 24 were found guilty of crimes against peace and of participating in a common plan or conspiracy to commit this crime.[55] The IMTFE devoted a large portion of its judgment to the contextual elements of crimes against peace,

---

[54] IMT Judgment, p. 445, see *supra* note 32.
[55] The convictions for each defendant were identified in the appendix.

that is, the act of aggression by Japan,[56] and discussed both the material elements and mental elements of the accused in its verdicts.

1.3.1. Contextual Elements

The contextual elements are the broader circumstances in which the material elements of international crimes must be placed and in which the evidence should be introduced. The contextual elements are usually the *sine qua non* for the establishment of the individual criminal liability for an international crime although its *actus reus* may be the same as a corresponding domestic offence. "Individual liability for aggression presupposes state responsibility, and persons can be convicted for aggression only if a state act of aggression has taken place".[57]

According to Article 5 of the IMTFE Charter, in order to fall within the definition of crimes against peace the crimes should be committed in the context of "a declared or undeclared war of aggression, or a war in violation of international law, treaties, agreements or assurances". Thus isolated military operations or border clashes do not meet the criteria; otherwise the seriousness of this crime might be diluted. Crimes against peace can only be committed by individuals who have decision-making power on behalf of a state and as part of a state plan or policy. The contextual elements are therefore crucial to establishing a link between state responsibility and individual criminal liability.[58] An act of aggression by a state is the contextual element of crimes against peace, which could be verified from the substance of the IMTFE judgment.

This special reference to a "declared or undeclared" war of aggression implied that it made no difference whether the war was declared while judging whether the war was aggressive or not. As the United Nations War Crimes Commission made clear, heralding the initiation of war by a formal declaration, as required by the Hague Conventions, did not deprive such a war of its criminal nature if it was "aggressive".[59] Whether

---

[56] The preparation and waging of war by Japan were thoroughly discussed in the IMTFE Judgment, Chapters IV, V, VI and VII, see *supra* note 14.

[57] Beatrice I. Bonafè, *The Relationship between State and Individual Responsibility for International Crimes*, Martinus Nijhoff, Leiden, 2009, p. 109.

[58] *Ibid.*, p. 15.

[59] United Nations War Crimes Commission, *History of the United Nations War Crimes Commission and the Development of the Laws of War*, His Majesty's Stationery Office, London, 1948, p. 258.

or when a declaration of war was issued made no difference to the nature of the war itself.

By virtue of the intricacy of the wars started by Japan, the IMTFE judgment expounded on the waging of aggressive wars in line with the target of the wars. After a lengthy and detailed statement of the relevant facts and circumstances relating to each of the alleged wars of aggression, the tribunal ultimately concluded that Japan had waged wars of aggression against all of the countries named in the indictment except the Philippines and Thailand – the Philippines because it was not a completely sovereign state but part of the United States,[60] while Thailand acted as an ally of Japan, as the evidence demonstrated.[61] The actions of Japan thus amounted to an act of aggression even under the criteria adopted later in the UN General Assembly.[62] Japan's armed forces invaded, attacked and then occupied the territory of China; bombarded the airfield at Hangzhou;[63] needlessly bombed Shanghai[64] and Nanjing;[65] and blockaded the coast of China.[66] Japan initiated the bombardment of the German Club in Manila,[67] and established the military occupation over the Far Eastern territories of the Soviet Union.[68] The famous attack on the US fleet at Pearl Harbor amounted to an "attack by the armed forces of a State on the land, sea or air forces, or marine and air fleets of another State".[69]

Furthermore, the IMTFE stressed the offensiveness of the war. With regard to a military operation in Lake Khassan, it concluded that Japan deliberately planned and launched the first attack, and that there was no evidence of Soviet troops initiating the fighting which would have

---

[60] IMTFE Judgment, p. 1000, see *supra* note 3.

[61] *Ibid.*, p. 998.

[62] The General Assembly of the UN adopted resolution 3314 on 14 December 1974 to provide for a definition of aggression; United Nations General Assembly, Resolution 3314, Definition of Aggression, 14 December 1974, UN doc. GA.Res.3314 ('UN Resolution 3314') (http://www.legal-tools.org/doc/90261a/).

[63] IMTFE Judgment, p. 598, see *supra* note 3.

[64] *Ibid.*, p. 599.

[65] *Ibid.*, p. 698.

[66] *Ibid.*, p. 205.

[67] *Ibid.*, p. 1039.

[68] *Ibid.*, p. 776.

[69] UN Resolution 3314, Art. 3(d), see *supra* note 62.

justified the attack by Japan.[70] The facts of waging aggressive wars were discussed in a long narration, which concluded that to win or lose a war made no difference to judging the nature of the war itself. What is more, a lack of offensiveness was exactly the reason why the IMTFE found the charge against Japan for waging an aggressive war against Thailand could not been proved.[71]

1.3.2. Material Elements

Material elements, or *actus reus*, can be summarised as meaning "an act indicated in the definition of the offence charged together with any surrounding circumstances and any consequences of that act which are indicated by that definition".[72] They are the specific elements of the offence which could give rise to individual liability. The IMTFE was empowered to try and punish Japanese war criminals who had, *inter alia*, committed crimes against peace, including "planning, preparing, initiating or waging a declared or undeclared war of aggression or a war in violation of international law, treaties, agreements or assurances, or participating in a common plan or conspiracy to accomplish any of the above".[73] In other words, under the heading of crimes against peace, the IMTFE Charter provided the sub-categories of this crime, which were planning, preparation, initiation and waging aggressive war and conspiracy for the accomplishment of any of the foregoing. It is submitted that waging aggressive war was the commission of this crime, while there was no hint in the IMTFE Charter and judgment as to whether the rest of the sub-categories were inchoate crimes or forms of liability for the crimes against peace, since the aggressive war planned, prepared, initiated or conspired did eventually take place. It remained unclear what kind of verdict could have

---

[70] IMTFE Judgment, pp. 828–33, see *supra* note 3.

[71] *Ibid.*, pp. 996–98: "There is no evidence that the position of complicity and confidence between Japan and Thailand, which was then achieved, was altered before December 1941. [...] The Japanese troops marched through the territory of Thailand unopposed on 7 December 1941. [...] No witness on behalf of Thailand has complained of Japan's actions as being acts of aggression. In these circumstances we are left without reasonable certainty that the Japanese advance into Thailand was contrary to the wishes of the Government of Thailand and the charges that the defendants initiated and waged a war of aggression against the kingdom of Thailand remain unproved".

[72] Richard Card, *Card, Cross and Jones Criminal Law*, 12th ed., Butterworths, London, 1992, p. 50.

[73] IMTFE Charter, Art. 5, see *supra* note 1.

been rendered if the planning, preparation or conspiracy of an aggressive war had been carried out without actually giving rise to the aggressive war itself. When the verdict for each of the accused is scrutinised, it is clear that Shiratori Toshio was convicted of preparation and conspiracy but acquitted of waging aggressive war, while Ōshima Hiroshi was convicted of conspiracy only. What is more, the IMTFE Charter defined conspiracy as to "accomplish any of the above", which meant that it amounted to a conspiracy to reach a common agreement not only on waging aggressive war itself but also planning or preparing aggressive war. It seems that the planning, preparation, initiation and conspiracy of aggressive war had an inherently independent feature. Thus, the planning, preparation, initiation and conspiracy of aggressive war were assessed as inchoate crimes rather than forms of liabilities before the IMTFE.

The indictment submitted to the IMTFE on 29 April 1946 contained three groups of charges consisting of 55 counts against 28 accused, with 52 of the counts relating to crimes against peace. Group one contained counts 1 to 36 concerning crimes against peace, while group two contained counts 37 and 38 concerning acts of murder as crimes against peace.[74] But the tribunal reduced the number of charges that it would consider because some of the charges were cumulative or alternative charges.[75] The IMTFE did a lot to rationalise the relationship among the charges alleged by the prosecutors and decided not to consider the charges relating to planning with respect to any accused convicted of conspiracy, since there was a close relationship between planning an aggressive war and participating in a common plan or conspiracy to do so. Similarly, the IMTFE decided not to consider the charges contained in counts 18 to 26 because of the close relationship between initiating and waging an aggressive war. Although "a war in violation of international law, treaties, agreements or assurances" was included in IMTFE Charter, the tribunal itself did not find it necessary to consider this type of war as specified in the particulars annexed to count one because conspiracy to wage wars of aggression was already criminal in the highest degree.[76] What is more, the

---

[74]   IMTFE, Transcript of Proceedings, 3 May 1946, pp. 33–73 (http://www.legal-tools.org/doc/6faa21/).

[75]   IMTFE Judgment, p. 34–35, see *supra* note 3.

[76]   *Ibid.*, p. 1142.

IMTFE decided not to consider any of the charges relating to murder as crimes against peace.[77]

After the efforts to clarify the charges, the IMTFE actually reviewed the accusations and made the conviction of crimes against peace in terms of waging aggressive war and two inchoate crimes, namely, preparing aggressive war and conspiracy for aggressive war. Their material elements were reflected in the IMTFE judgment and their mental elements are examined below.

1.3.2.1. Preparing Aggressive War

Generally, preparation for an offence consists of devising or arranging means or measures necessary for its commission. "Preparation is spawned by the various steps taken to implement the plan before the actual outbreak of hostilities".[78] Sometimes it consists of the formulation of a design or scheme for a specific war of aggression as planning. The specific act of preparation and its substantial consequences are both necessary. The IMTFE judgment elaborated the development and formulation of the Japanese military's aggressive plans and policies. The tribunal traced the gradual rise of the military to such predominance in the government that no other organ could impose an effective check on its aggressive ambitions. It also traced the preparation of virtually every segment of Japanese society for war, including the military, the civilian population, the educational system, the media, the economy and the essential industries.[79] Further, the IMTFE attributed particular importance to the conclusion of the Tripartite Pact between Germany, Italy and Japan on 27 September 1940 as a necessary step in preparing for Japan's aggressive actions and as a clear indication of the aggressive aims of those countries.

The period for Japan to prepare for a war of expansion to meet its established goals lasted from 1928 to 1940, during which time the conquest of China would be a minor affair, according to Tōjō.[80] Following this logic, out of 25 accused being convicted, only Doihara, Oka Takazu-

---

77 *Ibid.*, p. 34–37.

78 Dinstein, 2004, p. 120, see *supra* note 6.

79 *Ibid.*, pp. 83–520.

80 IMTFE Judgment, p. 188, see *supra* note 3.

mi, Ōshima, Shigemitsu Mamoru, Shimada Shigetarō and Tōgō Shigenori did not participate in preparing the war of aggression.[81]

1.3.2.2. Waging Aggressive War

Waging a war of aggression is a continuous offence. Periodic reviews of the changing situation are inevitable in the course of every prolonged war. Those who decide to persist in the illegal use of force may be charged with waging aggressive war.[82] The IMTFE stressed the planning, conduct and effect of waging aggressive war. First, the planning of waging aggressive war was articulated in order to distinguish the war of aggression from minor boundary friction. In the Japanese war against the Soviet Union, for example, the IMTFE found evidence for Japan's detailed plans for control of occupied Soviet territories[83] and noted that Japan undertook extensive preparations for war against the Soviet Union.[84] The IMTFE concluded that a war of aggression against the Soviet Union was contemplated and planned throughout the period under consideration, and that it was one of the principal elements of Japan's national policy.[85]

Second, the conduct and facts of waging aggressive war were fully elaborated as a requisite element. In the war against China, the IMTFE not only described the broad outlines of the war but also continued with a lengthy and detailed statement of the facts, including the objectives of territorial expansion, colonisation and the exploitation of the resources of China and various armed incidents used as pretexts for military action.[86]

Finally, the effect and consequences of waging aggressive wars were also mentioned. Occupation was usually a consequence of waging aggressive war, as in the war against France. The IMTFE stressed in a long statement that the occupation by Japanese troops of portions of French Indochina, which Japan had forced France to accept, did not remain peaceful.[87] After assessing counts 27 to 36 relating to waging aggressive wars, the IMTFE convicted all but three of the accused of this

---

[81] See Appendix A below.
[82] Dinstein, 2004 p. 123, see *supra* note 6.
[83] IMTFE Judgment, p. 812, see *supra* note 3.
[84] *Ibid.*, p. 782.
[85] *Ibid.*, p. 308.
[86] *Ibid.*, pp. 521–775.
[87] *Ibid.*, p. 994.

charge. For example, as a high-ranking officer in the Japanese army hierarchy and high-level cabinet position in the government, Araki Sadao approved, supported and played a prominent part in developing and carrying out the military and political policies pursued in Manchuria and Jehol, and the successive military steps taken for the occupation of that portion of the territories of China.[88] The three accused acquitted of waging wars of aggression were Matsui Iwane, Ōshima and Shiratori.[89]

1.3.2.3. Conspiracy to Commit Crimes against Peace

The notion of conspiracy in the IMT and IMTFE Charters was borrowed from the corresponding concept in common law, in which conspiracy was defined as "an agreement of two or more individuals to commit a criminal or unlawful act or a lawful act by unlawful means".[90] To qualify as a conspirator, a person must be shown to have participated in a concrete and criminal common plan. The material elements of the conspiracy to commit crimes against peace were supported by the IMTFE in the following manner.

First, there existed a group of persons. There should be a group of persons contributing to a common goal by virtue of the complexity of crimes against peace. As the IMTFE judgment notes:

> These far-reaching plans for waging wars of aggression, and the prolonged and intricate preparation for and waging of these wars of aggression were not the work of one man. They were the work of many leaders acting in pursuance of a common plan for the achievement of a common object. [...] The conspiracy existed for and its execution occupied a period of many years. Not all of the conspirators were parties to it at the beginning and some of those who were parties to it had ceased to be active in its execution before the end. All of those who at any time were parties to the criminal conspiracy or who at any time with guilty knowledge played a part in its execution are guilty of the charge contained in count one.[91]

---

[88] *Ibid.*, pp. 1146–47.

[89] See Appendix A below.

[90] Richard G. Singer and John Q. La Fond, *Criminal Law*, 6th ed., Wolters Kluwer, New York, 2013, p. 342.

[91] IMTFE Judgment, pp. 1141–43, see *supra* note 3.

Second, there existed a common purpose or aim among such a group of persons. The IMTFE discussed personal responsibility by addressing in great detail the changes in the high-level government officials and the consequential changes in government policies. It concluded that the fundamental aggressive aim of Japan remained constant throughout the years of planning and preparation for a sequence of aggressive acts.[92] The tribunal then addressed the criminal nature of the common plan or conspiracy.[93]

Third, participation and execution of the conspiracy is a necessary element. The IMTFE showed that the defendants were parties to the plan or conspiracy, or, knowing of the plan, furthered its purpose and objectives by participating in the preparation for aggressive war. All but two accused were convicted of conspiracy by the IMTFE; these were Matsui and Shigemitsu, because there was no evidence to prove beyond reasonable doubt that they participated in the execution of the conspiracy. By contrast, Araki both approved and actively supported the policies undertaken by the Japanese army in Manchuria and Jehol to separate that territory politically from China, to create a Japanese-controlled government, and to place its economy under the domination of Japan. The IMTFE found him to have been one of the leaders of the conspiracy set out in count one and thus guilty under that count.[94] Hashimoto Kingorō was an army officer and joined the conspiracy early on. After the initial years, he figured mainly as a propagandist in the execution of the conspiracy.[95] Hiranuma Kiichirō became a member of the conspiracy, if not at the beginning then shortly afterwards. He was a member of the group of conspirators, and from 1936 president of the Privy Council until 1939, when he became prime minister; he later served in succession as a minister without portfolio and home minister in the second and third Konoye cabinets.[96] As a war minister and commander-in-chief of expeditionary forces

---

92   *Ibid.*, p. 468.

93   *Ibid.*, p. 1141: "The common object, that they should secure Japan's domination by preparing and waging wars of aggression, was a criminal object. Indeed no more grave crimes can be conceived of than a conspiracy to wage a war of aggression, for the conspiracy threatens the security of the peoples of the world, and the waging disrupts it. The probable result of such a conspiracy, and the inevitable result of its execution is that death and suffering will be inflicted on countless human beings".

94   *Ibid.*, p. 1146.

95   *Ibid.*, p. 1151.

96   *Ibid.*, p. 1156.

in China, Hata Shunroku contributed substantially to formulating and executing the aggressive plan and exerted considerable influence on Japanese government policy;[97] he also favoured Japanese domination of East Asia and the areas to the south and took concrete measures to achieve that objective. The acts of most of the accused met the material element requirements for both conspiracy and the commission of aggression. They could then be convicted separately of the two crimes since conspiracy and waging aggressive war were two different crimes with different criminal aims and purposes.

In the sense of agreeing to commit a crime or to reach a criminal objective, conspiracy could be regarded as the embryo of and compared with the theory of joint criminal enterprise ('JCE') that evolved at the International Criminal Tribunal for the former Yugoslavia in the 1990s and 2000s. Joint criminal enterprise is a theory of common purpose liability which permits the imposition of individual criminal liability on an accused for his knowing and voluntary participation in a group acting with a common criminal purpose or plan. As Gideon Boas, James L. Bischoff and Natalie L. Reid note:

> The advantage of JCE lies in its utility in describing and attributing responsibility to those who engage in criminal behavior through oppressive criminal structures or organizations, in which different perpetrators participate in different ways at different times to accomplish criminal conduct on a massive scale.[98]

The Japanese militarist government that initiated the aggressive war was similar to this kind of criminal structure or organisation, in which the accused worked in co-ordination. That is why Ōshima was convicted of conspiracy of crimes against peace but acquitted of waging aggressive war. He was the first military attaché of the Japanese embassy in Berlin and later promoted to the post of ambassador. Holding no diplomatic post for about one year from 1939, he returned to Berlin as ambassador to Germany, where he remained until the surrender of Japan in 1945. He showed his consistent support for and promotion of the aims of the main conspiracy by his efforts to involve Japan in a full military alliance with

---

[97] *Ibid.*, pp. 1152–1153.

[98] Gideon Boas, James L. Bischoff and Natalie L. Reid, *Forms of Responsibility in International Criminal Law*, vol. 1, Cambridge University Press, Cambridge, 2007, p. 9.

Germany. However, he took no part in the direction of the war in China or the Pacific War.[99] The conviction of Ōshima and Tōgō, who was foreign minister, for playing a similar role to Ōshima was used to criticise the broad interpretation of conspiracy.[100] But in the author's view, since Ōshima's criminal material elements had been satisfied, as well as his state of mind, that is, intent to further and contribute to the aggression was proved, it was justified to convict him of conspiracy.

1.3.3. Mental Elements

The mental element, namely *mens rea*, refers to the state of mind expressly or by implication required by the definition of the offence charged.[101] Usually the mental element for crimes against peace is the intent to commit aggression or simply the knowledge that certain conduct contributes to the perpetration of aggression.[102] In fact, the IMTFE assessed the psychological state of the accused according to the standard of the intent to commit aggressive war rather than simply the knowledge of such.

With regard to the mental element for preparing aggressive war, it was proved that perpetrators' actions intentionally led to the eruption of aggressive wars. For example, Umezu Yoshijirō knew and approved of the plans of the conspirators to carry on the war when the fighting in China broke out anew in July 1937 at Marco Polo Bridge.[103] Tōjō helped to organise Manchuria as a base for that attack. At no time thereafter did he abandon the intention to launch such an attack if a favourable chance should occur.[104]

As mental elements for waging aggressive war, clear intention or purpose to reach the goal of aggressive wars were mentioned very fre-

---

[99] IMTFE Judgment, pp. 1188–89, see *supra* note 3.

[100] Robert Cryer, Håkan Friman, Darryl Robinson and Elizabeth Wilmshurst, *An Introduction to International Criminal Law and Procedure*, 2nd ed., Cambridge University Press, Cambridge, 2010, p. 116; Neil Boister, "The Application of Collective and Comprehensive Criminal Responsibility for Aggression at the Tokyo International Military Tribunal", in *Journal of International Criminal Justice*, 2010, vol. 8, no. 2, p. 429.

[101] Card, 1992, p. 57, see *supra* note 72.

[102] See International Criminal Court, Assembly of State Parties, Resolution RC/Res.6, The Crime of Aggression, Annex II: Amendments to the Elements of Crimes, Elements 4 and 6 11 June 2010 (http://www.legal-tools.org/doc/0d027b/).

[103] IMTFE Judgment, p. 1210, see *supra* note 3.

[104] *Ibid.*, p. 1206.

quently. For example, after the outbreak of the Pacific War, Tōgō collaborated with other members of the Japanese cabinet in its conduct as well as in waging the war in China.[105] As a member of the Military Affairs Bureau of the War Ministry, Suzuki Teiichi insisted that the Soviet Union was the absolute enemy of Japan and assisted in preparing to wage aggressive war against it.[106] Oka participated in forming and executing the policy to wage aggressive war against China and the Western powers.[107] Doihara was intimately involved in the initiation and development of the war of aggression waged against China in Manchuria and in the subsequent establishment of the Japanese-dominated state of Manchukuo.[108]

As mental elements of the conspiracy, the defendants intended to contribute for the common purpose or participated in the conspiracy with a clear knowledge of the purpose. After the acts of substantial participation by certain defendants were established by overwhelming proof, the IMTFE further examined that the acts were accompanied by the intentional state of mind requisite in law to establish individual guilt. For example, the IMTFE discussed the knowledge of the criminal nature of the policies as one of important criteria while assessing the conviction of Satō Kenryō.[109] Koiso Kuniaki joined the conspiracy in 1931 by participating as one of the leaders of the so-called March Incident, an abortive *coup d'état* attempt in Japan, and later contributed for the purpose of the conspiracy.[110]

---

[105] *Ibid.*, p. 1204

[106] *Ibid.*, p. 1202.

[107] *Ibid.*, p. 1187.

[108] *Ibid.*, p. 1148.

[109] *Ibid.*, p. 1191: "The matter is put beyond reasonable doubt by a speech which Sato delivered in August 1938. He states the Army point of view on the war in China. He shows complete familiarity with the detailed terms, never revealed to China, upon which Japan was prepared to settle the war against China. [...] This speech shows that Sato did not believe that Japan's actions in China had been dictated by the wish to secure protection for Japan's legitimate interests in China as the defence would have us believe. On the contrary, he knew that the motive for her attacks on China was to seize the wealth of her neighbor. We are of opinion that Sato, having that guilty knowledge, was clearly a member of the conspiracy from 1941 onwards".

[110] *Ibid.*, pp. 1177–78. Koiso joined the conspiracy in 1931 by participating as one of the leaders of the March Incident, the purpose of which was to overthrow the Hamaguchi government and put in office a government favourable to the occupation of Manchuria. Later, as overseas minister in the Hiranuma and Yonai cabinets, Koiso supported and took part in the direction of the war in China, the beginning of the occupation of French Indochina, and

Besides the intent or knowledge of crimes against peace, it is submitted that specific intent for this crime is justifiable. The specific intent requirement presupposes that only those attacks that cross borders with the specific goals of achieving territorial gains, obtaining economic advantages or interfering in the internal affairs of the victim state, and therefore causing a severe infringement of the victim state's sovereignty, will necessitate condemnation as crimes against peace. In other words, minor boundary friction would not suffice to give rise to criminal liability. It should be noted that this specific intent requirement applies only to aggression as a crime, that is, as an offence involving individual criminal liability, not state delinquency. The specific intent as a requisite *mens rea* exclusively connects with individuals who conduct this offence. The merit of the requirement of specific intent would enable courts to "distinguish, for the purpose of establishing guilt or at least for sentencing purposes, between leaders planning or ordering aggression and those persons who merely carry out their plans or aid and abet aggression",[111] because the former have both the specific and general intent while the latter possess only general intent, that is, the intent to occupy a small part of a foreign territory or intent to attack strategic facility on part of the adversary, and so on.

1.4.   Significance of Crimes against Peace at the IMTFE

From the perspective of international criminal law with regard to the development of the crime of aggression, the IMTFE held the significance of its contribution as a judicial precedent to the punishment of aggression as the severest international crime. The IMTFE's efforts to establish individual criminal liability for aggression helped to crystallise the conviction that aggressive war was culpable. Even heads of state could no longer shield behind the privilege of immunity vested with them in traditional international law, which helped to stop impunity and promoted the theory of international law. The fruits of both the IMT and the IMTFE were confirmed and inherited in General Assembly resolutions 95(I) of 1946 and 3314 of 1974, the draft Code of Crimes against the Peace and Security of Mankind by the ILC of 1996 and even the ICC Statute of 1998. There is

---

the negotiations intended to obtain concessions from and eventual economic domination of the Netherlands East Indies.

[111]   Cassese, 2003, p.116, see *supra* note 52.

no doubt that the criminality of aggressive war has been firmly established in international law.

Furthermore, the IMTFE recorded proof in the huge amount of documents, testimonies and other varieties of evidence of the Japanese aggressive war against victim states, especially China, which were thoroughly tested during the court proceedings. "The process of subjecting evidence to forensic scrutiny will set down a permanent record of the crimes that will stand the test of time".[112] In other words, the most important legal value of the IMTFE was the work of collecting and making public the verified evidence and the rich juridical records left for study – all of which are difficult to contradict.

Japanese right-wing forces have attached great importance to the dissenting opinion of Justice Radhabinod Pal of India who held an opinion similar to that of the Japanese defendants: that the use of force by Japan during the Second World War aimed at either self-defence or the liberation of Asian colonies from the Western powers rather than aggression.[113] From the perspective of criminal law, the reason or aim of the Japanese government initiating the invasion of China and the Pacific War fell into the category of the motive. "A person's motive is his reason for acting as he did".[114] This motive for committing a crime was "not intent and not even *mens rea*";[115] therefore it did not matter while establishing that crime. Whether the defendant's motives might be benign or bad is irrelevant to his guilt and criminal liability. So long as the elements of the crime are satisfied, the crime can be definitively established. Even assessed under the narrowest and most uncontroversial definition of aggression agreed upon by the entire international community, as enshrined in General Assembly resolution 3314, the acts of Japan during the Second World War would meet the requirement of aggression. With such authenticity and such detailed and established evidence before the IMTFE, there could be no arbitrary denial of these crimes in the future. The denial of the Holocaust itself is now a crime in Germany. As a matter of fact, Japan's

---

[112] Antonio Cassese, "Reflections on International Criminal Justice", in *Modern Law Review*, 1998, vol. 61, no. 1, pp. 6–7.

[113] Justice Pal express his approval of the defendants' opinion in many parts of his dissenting opinion, such as part II, "What Is Aggressive War" and part IV about conspiracy. See Pal Dissenting Judgment, *supra* note 3.

[114] Card, 1992, p. 83, see *supra* note 72.

[115] Singer and Fond, 2013, p. 59, see *supra* note 90.

military invasion over seven decades ago was a competition for colonies, and not at all a quest for national liberation. Judge Pal showed great sympathy for colonised people in East and Southeast Asia but wrongly ignored the agony the Japanese inflicted on them. In any case, it is fallacious to assert that Japanese colonisation, as a substitute for the Western colonies, would turn out to be benevolent. Thanks to the court records made in the courtroom of the IMTFE, and the heated arguments outside the courtroom, younger generations have an opportunity to make their own judgments about that crucial historic period as well as their own choices for a more peaceful future.

Appendix A: Verdicts on the Accused at the International Criminal Tribunal for the Far East

No.	Name	Highest position	Preparation of aggressive war (1928–1940)	Waging aggressive war	Conspiracy
1	Araki	Minister of war	Yes	Yes	Yes
2	Doihara	Commander in 7th Area Army	No	Yes	Yes
3	Hashimoto	Military commander in the field	Yes	Yes	Yes
4	Hata	Commander-in-chief of expeditionary forces in China	Yes	Yes	Yes
5	Hiranuma	Prime minister	Yes	Yes	Yes
6	Hirota	Prime minister	Yes	Yes	Yes
7	Hoshino	Chief cabinet secretary	Yes	Yes	Yes
8	Itagaki	War minister	Yes	Yes	Yes
9	Kaya	Finance minister	Yes	Yes	Yes
10	Kido	Education minister	Yes	Yes	Yes

11	Kimura	Commander-in-chief of Burma Area Army	Yes	Yes	Yes
12	Koiso	Prime minister	Yes	Yes	Yes
13	Matsui	Commander-in-chief of Central China Area Army	No	No	No
14	Minami	Governor general of Korea	Yes	Yes	Yes
15	Mutō	Chief of Military Affairs Bureau, Ministry of War	Yes	Yes	Yes
16	Oka	Chief of Naval Affairs Bureau	No	Yes	Yes
17	Ōshima	Ambassador	No	No	Yes
18	Satō	Chief of Military Affairs Bureau	Yes	Yes	Yes
19	Shigemitsu	Minister and ambassador	No	Yes	No
20	Shimada	Chief of Navy General Staff	No	Yes	Yes
21	Shiratori	Ambassador to Sweden	Yes	No	Yes
22	Suzuki	President of Cabinet Planning Board and minister without portfolio	Yes	Yes	Yes
23	Tōgō	Foreign minister	No	Yes	Yes
24	Tōjō	Prime minister	Yes	Yes	Yes
25	Umezu	Commander of Kwantung Army	Yes	Yes	Yes

2

From Tokyo to Rome: A Chinese Perspective

ZHU Dan[*]

2.1. Introduction

The Tokyo trial was China's very first experience of direct engagement with an international criminal tribunal. Being a key member of the global anti-fascist alliance and the biggest victim of Japanese atrocities during the Second World War, China had a considerable stake in the Tokyo trial. The Nationalist government played a constructive role in both the establishment and the operation of the International Military Tribunal for the Far East ('IMTFE'). Although the trial convicted 28 high-ranking Japanese political and military leaders for class A crimes, many of the Japanese atrocities committed in China were left untouched, including, among others, the accountability of Emperor Hirohito, the biological weapons experiments conducted by Unit 731, the so-called "comfort women" issue, and the use of atomic weapons and poisonous gas.

The failure to establish accountability on these issues does not nullify the historical significance of the Tokyo trial, but it inevitably affects the extent to which justice was delivered to China by the IMTFE. Some justice was actually achieved through a series of national military trials conducted between 1945 and 1947 in 10 Chinese cities, which tried Japanese for class B and C war crimes. The pursuit of justice by the Chinese people for the heinous crimes committed in occupied China did not stop at the conclusion of the Tokyo trial. In 1956 two special military tribu-

[*] **ZHU Dan** is an Assistant Professor in Public International Law at Fudan University Law School and member of the Chinese Bar. She holds a Ph.D. from the University of Edinburgh, an LL.M. from Xiamen University, and an LL.B. from Jilin University. Before joining Fudan, she worked at the Registry Legal Advisory Service Section and the Appeals Chamber of the International Criminal Court. She is currently a member of the International Law Association Study Group on Individual Responsibility in International Law. Her academic interests include international criminal law, human rights law and international dispute settlement. She also does research on issues related to China's engagement with international law-making and international adjudication.

nals, one in Shenyang and the other in Taiyuan, were set up in order to conduct additional trials of Japanese war crimes suspects. The ongoing demands for compensation in recent years by the Chinese victims in relation to the "forgotten crimes" demonstrate that a notion of injustice still lingers. While the International Military Tribunal ('IMT') at Nuremberg and the crimes for which Nazi leaders were punished have been widely acknowledged and accepted in Germany, the Japanese attitude towards the Tokyo trial is often characterised by passivity and apathy.[1] These facts more or less cast doubt on the significance of the Tokyo trial for China. However, taking into consideration China's political, economic, military and judicial influence in the world, and its domestic situation after the Second World War, the Tokyo judgment was perhaps the best result China could have expected at that time. The recent seventieth anniversary of the end of the war serves as an important opportunity for China to review the significance and deficiencies of the Tokyo trial. While fully acknowledging its historical and legal legacies,[2] this chapter seeks to offer reflections, from a Chinese perspective, on the factors that have affected the adequacy of the Tokyo trial in delivering justice to China.

The Tokyo trial is not necessarily an isolated incident that happened in the remote past. As much of what occurred in Tokyo continues to resonate with more recent international criminal justice practice, a close study of the trial may offer invaluable insights into the general workings of the international criminal justice system today. Reflections on the past provide a window through which a better appreciation of the possibilities and limitations of what present-day international criminal tribunals can achieve. This chapter thus attempts to draw some contemporary relevance from the establishment and operation of the Tokyo trial that may still be relevant today, with a view to understanding how the Chinese perception of it influences China's current approach towards the permanent International Criminal Court ('ICC').

---

[1] Madoka Futamura, "Japanese Societal Attitude towards the Tokyo Trial: From a Contemporary Perspective", in Yuki Tanaka, Tim McCormack and Gerry Simpson (eds.), *Beyond Victor's Justice? The Tokyo War Crimes Trial Revisited*, Martinus Nijhoff, Leiden, 2011, p. 52.

[2] JIA Bing Bing, "The Legacy of the Tokyo Trial in China", in Yuki Tanaka, Tim McCormack and Gerry Simpson, (eds.), *Beyond Victor's Justice? The Tokyo War Crimes Trial Revisited*, Martinus Nijhoff, Leiden, 2011, pp. 207–27.

2.2. China's Involvements in the Tokyo Trial

It was China, the major victim of wartime Japan, that first raised a clear voice in support of the international prosecution of Japanese war crimes suspects. One of the first statements on the punishment of offences in the Pacific sphere came on 13 January 1942 when Chinese delegates to the signing of the St James's Declaration, which called for the punishment of German war leaders, stated that it was China's "intention to apply the same principles to the Japanese occupying authorities in China when the time comes".[3]

On 1 December 1943 the leaders of the United States, China and Britain adopted the Cairo Declaration, in which they made it clear that they were "fighting this war to restrain and punish the aggression of Japan".[4] The United Nations War Crimes Commission ('UNWCC'), which was established in October 1943 to prepare for the prosecution of Axis war crimes, at first dealt exclusively with the European theatre. The Chinese ambassador, V.K. Wellington KOO (GU Weijun), actively participated in the constituent meeting of the UNWCC, and some of his suggestions were taken on board and adopted by the meeting.[5] In 1944 a Far Eastern and Pacific Sub-Commission of the UNWCC was established in Chongqing (Chungking). The legal basis for punishing Japanese aggression took on a more tangible form when the leaders of the United States, China and Britain adopted the Potsdam Declaration on 26 July 1945.[6]

The Chinese legal experts, whose participation was actively supported by the Nationalist government, played an important role in the operation of the IMTFE. The Chinese prosecution team was headed by HSIANG Che-chun (XIANG Zhejun), then chief prosecutor in Shanghai. There were significant differences among the International Prosecution Section of the Supreme Commander for the Allied Powers ('SCAP') as to

---

3   Louise W. Holborn, *War and Peace Aims of the United Nations, September 1, 1939– December 31, 1942*, vol. 1, World Peace Foundation, Boston, 1943, pp. 387–88.

4   Cairo Declaration on Japan, jointly released by the United States, the Republic of China and Great Britain, 1 December 1943.

5   Society for Research on the Diplomacy of the Republic of China, (ed), 中日外交史料丛编 [A Series of Documents Illustrating the Diplomatic Relations between China and Japan], 1966, vol. 7, pp. 432–40.

6   Proclamation Defining Terms for Japanese Surrender, Potsdam, 26 July 1945 ('Potsdam Declaration') (http://www.legal-tools.org/doc/f8cae3/).

the starting date of the Japanese war crimes. At HSIANG's insistence, 1 January 1928, when the Japanese bombed ZHANG Zuolin, was finally adopted as the starting date in terms of the prosecution strategy.[7] This was three years earlier than the Mukden or 918 Incident in 1931, nine years earlier than Marco Polo Bridge Incident in 1937, and 13 years earlier than the bombing of Pearl Harbor in 1941 – each of which was proposed by prosecutors from other states as dates for the start of Japanese aggression. Among the 11 judges on the bench was the jurist MEI Ju-ao, who insisted that the judgment on Japan's crimes committed in China should be drafted by the Chinese. After fierce debates, other judges agreed to set the Chinese part as a separate chapter, and MEI was responsible for drafting it. Judge MEI also convinced the IMTFE to apply death penalties to the accused, which was an issue initially opposed by some judges from the common law system.[8]

The Chinese prosecution team's efforts in gathering evidence received considerable support from the Nationalist government.[9] The official government newspaper also extensively covered the progress of the Tokyo trial in a timely manner.[10] At the same time, a War Damage Investigation Committee was set up by the Nationalist government to gather evidence for war crimes trials in China as well as for the IMTFE, and held its own trials before 13 military tribunals against the background of a civil war.[11]

---

[7] XIANG Longwan, 东京审判–中国检察官向哲浚 [Tokyo Trial – The Chinese Prosecutor XIANG Zhejun], Preface III, Shanghai Jiaotong University Press, Shanghai, 2010, p. 9.

[8] MEI Ju-ao, 远东国际军事法庭 [International Military Tribunal for the Far East], Law Press, Beijing, 2005, pp. 7–8.

[9] XIANG Longwan and SUN Yi, "东京审判中的中国代表团" [The Chinese Delegation in the Tokyo Trial], in *Republican Archives*, 2014, p. 65.

[10] For example, "严惩日本战争罪犯：联合国战争委员会声明已备名单送各国批准" [Inflict Severe Punishments on Japanese War Criminals: The United Nations War Crimes Commission Has Declared Readiness of the List of Names for Ratification by States], in 中央日报 [*Central Daily News*], 10 September 1945, p. 3; see also "东京国际法庭即将审判战犯：天皇受审与否尚未决" [The Tokyo Tribunal Is About to Try War Criminals: Whether the Emperor Will Stand Trial Is Still Pending], 中央日报 [*Central Daily News*], 2 December 1945, p. 3.

[11] Mark Eykhold, "Aggression, Victimization, and Chinese Historiography of the Nanjing Massacre", in Joshua A. Fogel (ed.), *The Nanjing Massacre in History and Historiography*, University of California Press, Berkeley, 2000, pp. 11–69.

2.3. Restricting Factors on the Adequacy of the Tokyo Trial

2.3.1. The Political Dimensions of the Tokyo Trial

The IMTFE was established by the Allied powers as the Pacific counterpart of the Nuremberg trial in the immediate aftermath of the Second World War. However, the political context in which the Tokyo trial was conducted differed from that of Nuremberg. In fact the IMTFE was far more susceptible to the politics of the Cold War than Nuremberg, which closed in October 1946. While the United States played an important role in planning and establishing the Tokyo tribunal, its policy towards postwar Japan dominated many aspects of the trial. This American dominance hindered the IMTFE to a certain extent from delivering greater justice to the most victimised state – China. As Judge B.V.A. Röling noted: "In fact the Americans were in control of most aspects of the trial".[12]

The issuing of the IMTFE Charter took the form of an executive decree of General Douglas MacArthur in his capacity as the Supreme Commander for the Allied Powers. It was the International Prosecution Section, which was initially composed only of US prosecutors, that drafted the Charter.[13] After arriving in Japan, the associate prosecutors (including the Chinese prosecutor) were only given an opportunity to suggest revisions to the Charter. The structure of the tribunal also reflected the central role of the United States. Unlike the IMT, where there were four chief prosecutors, one each from the major Allied powers, in Tokyo the prosecution consisted of one chief prosecutor from the United States (Joseph B. Keenan) and 10 associate prosecutors from other countries, including China. Rather than being on an equal footing, these associate prosecutors were actually subordinate to the chief prosecutor.[14] According to the IMTFE Charter, MacArthur had the authority to appoint judges as well as the president of the tribunal,[15] and to review their judgments.[16]

---

[12]   B.V.A. Röling and Antonio Cassese, *The Tokyo Trial and Beyond: Reflections of a Peacemonger*, Polity Press, Cambridge, 1993, p. 31.

[13]   Solis Horowitz, "The Tokyo Trial", in *International Conciliation*, 1950, no. 465, p. 483.

[14]   MEI, 2005, p. 86, see *supra* note 8.

[15]   International Military Tribunal for the Far East ('IMTFE'), Charter, Tokyo, enacted 19 January 1946 and amended 25 April 1946, Arts. 2 and 3 ('IMTFE Charter') (http://www.legal-tools.org/doc/a3c41c/).

In addition, as a result of political calculation and pragmatic choices by the United Statues, several important issues and people were exempted from the trial's prosecution. The decision to grant immunity to the Japanese Emperor Hirohito was clearly a political decision. Given Japanese public support for the emperor, the US policy was to "save" Hirohito in order to maintain public order within newly occupied Japan.[17] Also due to the intervention of the United States, the fate of Unit 731 – the notorious military unit that experimented with bacteriological weapons on live humans – was omitted from the indictment.[18] The conduct of Unit 731, together with Japan's alleged use of biological weapons in the war in China, was given immunity in exchange for the results of their research work.[19] As noted by Judge Röling, "apparently the American military were eager to profit from the crimes committed by the Japanese, to enhance their knowledge of biological warfare".[20] The IMTFE did not include the charge of indiscriminate bombing or bombing of civilian areas in China, which was arguably an issue the United States deliberately tried to avoid in order to evade prosecution for the atomic bombings they undertook on Hiroshima and Nagasaki.

Due to the rapid changes in international relations and the increasing prominence of Chinese communists, the United States gradually shifted its punitive policy against Japan to a conciliatory policy of transforming Japan into a stronghold against communism in Asia. Following the execution of some accused in December 1948, 19 class A war crimes suspects waiting for the second round of the Tokyo trial were released. The policy of "no more trials on major war criminals in Japan" was officially announced by MacArthur in February 1949.[21] As M. Cherif Bassiouni points out, the trial was an exercise in realpolitik rather than accountabil-

---

[16] *Ibid.*, Art. 17 allowed MacArthur "at any time [to] reduce or otherwise alter the sentence except to increase its severity".

[17] Herbert P. Bix, *Hirohito and the Making of Modern Japan*, HarperCollins, New York, 2000.

[18] Sheldon Harris, *Factories of Death: Japanese Biological Warfare, 1932–1945, and the American Cover-up*, Routledge, New York, 1995.

[19] Yves Beigbeder, *Judging War Criminals: The Politics of International Justice*, Palgrave Macmillan, London, 1999, p.73.

[20] Röling and Cassese, 1993, p. 31, see *supra* note 12.

[21] Madoka Futamura, *War Crimes Tribunals and Transitional Justice: The Tokyo Trial and the Nuremberg Legacy*, Routledge, London, 2008, p. 62.

ity, because MacArthur "structured [it] to function as a strategy for achieving control over the occupied territories".[22] All the accused before the IMTFE, apart from having Japanese defence lawyers, were also supported by American lawyers, which was another way for the United States to exert its influence on the Tokyo trial and shield Japanese war criminals.[23] As MEI Ju-ao notes, trials in Japan for class B and C war criminals were similarly controlled by the Americans.[24] One possible way to avoid US manipulation was to extradite these criminals to the victimised states' territory for trials.[25] In fact, influenced by the American Cold War strategy, all the prisoners under sentence, including class B and C war criminals held by the Allies – except the Soviet Union and China – were released by the end of 1958.[26]

2.3.2. Difficulties in Collecting Evidence

The work of the IMTFE was actually dominated by the rules of the common law system, in which evidence plays a vital role. As MEI notes, "the IMTFE is an international tribunal, but common law has absolute advantage in terms of language and trial proceedings. There was also an overwhelming number of judges from the common law system".[27] The differences between the common law system and the civil law system on trial procedures and rules of evidence are significant. The Chinese legal tradition, based primarily on the civil law model, overemphasised the role of judges but neglected the collection of evidence.

The Nationalist government, which underestimated the complexity of the Tokyo trial, merely assumed that the trial of the Japanese war criminals was a formality.[28] As NI Zhengyu, who was part of China's prosecution team in Tokyo, observes: "The Nationalist government did not expect

---

22 M. Cherif Bassiouni, "Justice and Peace: The Importance of Choosing Accountability over Realpolitik", in *Case Western Reserve Journal of International Law*, 2003, vol. 35, pp. 196–97.

23 MEI, 2005, p. 12, see *supra* note 8.

24 *Ibid.*, p. 83.

25 *Ibid.*

26 Richard H. Minear, *Victors' Justice: Tokyo War Crimes Trial*, Princeton University Press, Princeton, NJ, 2001, p. 173.

27 MEI, 2005, p. 73, see *supra* note 8.

28 NI Zhengyu, "Memories of the Tokyo Trial", in 东京审判文集 [Collected Works of the Tokyo Trial], Shanghai Jiaotong University Press, Shanghai, 2011, p. 8.

the application of the rules of evidence would be so rigid. They simply took for granted that it was a punishment of the vanquished".[29] When the Chinese legal team first arrived in Tokyo, as MEI recalls, "the evidence that China was able to submit was very limited".[30] He argues that "more evidence should have been produced, as there had been around 15 years of Japanese aggressive war in China".[31] On the other hand, the Chinese prosecution team in Tokyo was seriously understaffed compared to other states.[32] For example, the Soviet Union, which had only declared war with Japan for a week, sent around 100 people to Tokyo for prosecutorial work. This was in sharp contrast to China, which had fewer than 10 people on its prosecution team.[33]

In spite of time and resource constraints, the Chinese prosecution team made tremendous efforts and contributions to the collection of evidence on Japanese atrocities committed in China. Shortly after his arrival in Tokyo, the prosecutor XIANG Zhejun sent several telegrams to the Nationalist government, requesting further collection of evidence.[34] The Ministry of Foreign Affairs and several other sections were actively involved in the process of locating evidence.[35] The Nanking Massacre Investigation Committee was subsequently established in China.[36] A local newspaper also issued an appeal for witnesses to the Nanking massacre.[37] The collection of evidence was in part constrained by the internal convulsions going on at that time. Although the Chinese prosecution team planned a trip to the north-east region of China to gather evidence, it was cancelled due to changes in the domestic political atmosphere and the difficulties in travelling.[38]

---

[29] *Ibid.*

[30] MEI Xiaoao and MEI Xiaokan, (eds.), 梅汝璈东京审判文稿 [The Tokyo Trial Manuscripts of MEI Ru'ao], Shanghai Jiaotong University Press, 2013, p. 65.

[31] *Ibid.*

[32] NI, 2011, p. 8, see *supra* note 28.

[33] *Ibid.*

[34] XIANG and SUN, 2014, p. 65, see *supra* note 9.

[35] *Ibid.*

[36] Taiwan Historica, International Military Tribunal for the Far East Trial Materials, 172-1-0899(2) Epson 0101, pp. 14–15.

[37] XIANG, 2010, pp. 184–85, see *supra* note 7.

[38] NI, 2011, p. 11, see *supra* note 28.

Compared to the heinous atrocities committed by Japanese soldiers on the ground, the evidence on the formation of Japan's aggressive policy and the initiation of its aggressive war was even more difficult to obtain. As noted by QIN Dechun, then mayor of Beijing, none of the Chinese military commanders would think of persevering evidence for the purpose of accusing Japanese war criminals at a later stage, at least while fighting.[39] The Chinese prosecution team faced tremendous challenges in securing evidence of criminal orders because of the massive destruction of documents orchestrated by the Japanese government prior to its surrender.[40] With co-ordination and help from the Chinese military delegation in Japan, the Chinese prosecution team was able to get access to the sealed archives of the former Imperial Japanese Army to search for evidence.[41] Despite the language barrier, many useful documents were found.[42] This evidence, which was presented in XIANG's submissions in court, played an important role in the trial proceedings.[43] The efforts and the achievements of the Chinese prosecution team were somehow undermined by the inaccurate reports by several foreign newspapers, according to which, among the 3,700 pieces of admitted evidence on atrocities committed by class A war criminals, only 17 pieces were provided by the Chinese prosecution team.[44] This kind of report inevitably undercut the significance of China's involvement at the IMTFE.[45] In fact, according to XIANG, no less than 700 pieces of evidence were submitted by China after several months' intensive search.[46]

Although the Chinese prosecution team did provide a number of key witnesses to testify before the tribunal, the pursuit of witnesses did not go smoothly, which was partly caused by the ongoing domestic tur-

---

[39] *Ibid.*

[40] Yuma Totani, "The Case against the Accused", in Yuki Tanaka, Tim McCormack and Gerry Simpson (eds.), *Beyond Victor's Justice? The Tokyo War Crimes Trial Revisited*, Martinus Nijhoff, Leiden, 2011, p. 154.

[41] NI, 2011, p. 13, see *supra* note 28.

[42] *Ibid.*, p. 14.

[43] XIANG, 2010, pp. 56–110, see *supra* note 7.

[44] Taiwan Historica, International Military Tribunal for the Far East Trial Materials, 172-1-0916 Epson 0088, p. 22.

[45] XIANG and SUN, 2014, see *supra* note 9, p. 70.

[46] Taiwan Historica, International Military Tribunal for the Far East Trial Materials, 172-1-0916 Epson 0088, pp. 37–40.

moil. Many people were reluctant to give evidence due to the fear of being mistreated by the Japanese again.[47] One witness, who had a legal background, changed his mind on giving written testimony after hearing the rumour that Japan would win an imminent third world war.[48] The Chinese witnesses also lacked familiarity with Anglo-American court proceedings and techniques. One witness testifying before the tribunal repeatedly stated that the Japanese "kill people everywhere, set everywhere on fire, and do all manner of evil against the Chinese".[49] However, without any substantive supporting evidence, his testimony was fiercely challenged by the accused and dismissed by the tribunal.[50]

2.3.3. The Prosecutorial Strategy

The primary goal of the IMTFE was to address the individual criminal responsibility of the major war criminals in East and Southeast Asia. The Allied governments, in particular the United States, pursued this prosecutorial policy as a concrete step towards instituting an international legal system for deterring future aggressors and preventing the kind of devastation that Axis aggression had caused.

The focus on crimes against peace was considerable. The IMTFE Charter required that the principal charges against the defendants be crimes against peace, while deeming charges on war crimes and crimes against humanity as optional. Article 5 of the IMTFE Charter restricted war criminals tried and punished by the tribunal to those who "are charged with offences which include crimes against peace".[51] In other words, no defendant was prosecuted without a charge of committing crimes against peace. The IMTFE's focus on crimes against peace made the collection of evidence more difficult, since it concentrated more on the reasons Japan had conducted the war rather than on how Japan had committed atrocities.

---

[47] 我国控诉日战犯：物证多于人证 [China Accused Japanese War Criminals: Evidence Outnumbered Witnesses], 申报 [Shen Bao], 4 April 1946, p. 3.

[48] NI, 2011, p. 11, see *supra* note 28.

[49] *Ibid.*, p. 8.

[50] *Ibid.*

[51] IMTFE Charter, Art. 5, see *supra* note 15.

The fact that crimes against peace were the central charge of the trial also made the IMTFE more controversial. Crimes against peace, or aggressive war, were a much more disputed concept than conventional war crimes. This is because crimes against peace deal directly with the nature and cause of war, which are recognised in different ways during various periods of history. The defendants at the IMTFE contended that "whatever the nature of the war or character of the war, the planning, the preparing, the initiating and the waging of war cannot be considered as 'crimes against peace' in accordance with the conception of war held by the civilized nations of the world up to July, 1945".[52] It was also submitted that waging war had not been explicitly criminalised prior to the outbreak of the Second World War.[53] A similar challenge was made at the IMT by the defendants, who argued that crimes against peace, or wars of aggression, were not clearly codified at the time the alleged acts were committed.[54]

In response, the IMT judgment referred to the Kellogg-Briand Pact, which was binding on Germany at the outbreak of war in 1939. The contracting parties in Article 1 of the pact declared that they "condemn recourse to war for the solution of international controversies and renounce it as an instrument of national policy in their relations to one another". In the opinion of the IMT, "the solemn renunciation of war as an instrument of national policy necessarily involves the proposition that such a war is illegal in international law; and that those who plan and wage such a war, with its inevitable and terrible consequences, are committing a crime in so doing".[55] The defendants, however, submitted that "the Pact does not expressly enact that such wars are crimes, or set up courts to try those who make such wars".[56] In order to rationalise its leap from state responsibility to individual criminal responsibility, the IMT made an analogy with the Hague Convention. The tribunal pointed out that the Hague Convention IV prohibiting certain means and methods of warfare did not declare an

---

[52] IMTFE, Transcript of Proceedings, 13 May 1946, p. 122 (https://www.legal-tools.org/doc/397ff7/).

[53] *Ibid.*

[54] International Military Tribunal, *Trial of the Major War Criminals Before the International Military Tribunal: Proceedings, 25 June–8 July 1946*, vol. 17, Secretariat of the Tribunal, Nuremberg, 1947, p. 478.

[55] International Military Tribunal (Nuremberg), "Judgment and Sentences", in *American Journal of International Law*, 1947, vol. 41, no. 1, p. 218.

[56] *Ibid.*

act to be criminal, but tribunals had exercised criminal jurisdiction over those breaching such prohibitions, which had been enforced long before the date of the Convention.[57] In the view of the IMT, those who waged aggressive war were doing somthing that was equally illegal, and of much greater moment than a breach of one of the rules of the Hague Convention. In interpreting the Kellogg-Briand Pact, the IMT further pointed out:

> The law of war is to be found not only in treaties, but in the customs and practices of states which gradually obtained universal recognition, and from the general principles of justice applied by jurists and practised by military courts. This law is not static, but by continual adaption follows the needs of a changing word.[58]

In addition, the Nuremberg Tribunal referred to a series of drafts and other efforts leading up to the Kellogg-Briand Pact that used the term "international crime".[59]

The IMTFE adopted the rationale of the Nuremberg Tribunal and dismissed the defendants' argument by referring to the IMT judgment, although Judge Radhabinod Pal of India maintained in a dissenting opinion that the rule concerning crimes against peace constituted *ex post facto* legislation.[60] Nevertheless, it has been observed that: "had the Tokyo defendants been tried on conventional war crimes charges only – as lesser Japanese suspects were – most likely no substantial controversy or criticism of the Tokyo Trial would have arisen".[61]

2.3.4. The Limitations of International Criminal Trials

The IMTFE attempted to convey a notion of justice served by punishing individual guilty defendants. It rejected the notion of collective guilt and the idea of placing responsibility on the Japanese nation as a whole. The

---

[57] *Ibid.*, pp. 218–19.

[58] *Ibid.*

[59] *Ibid.*, pp. 219–20.

[60] IMTFE, *United States of America et al. v. Araki Sadao et al.*, Judgment of the Hon'ble Mr. Justice Pal Member from India, 1 November 1948, pp. 151–153 (http://www.legal-tools.org/doc/712ef9/). Judge Pal noted: "no category of war became a crime in international life up to the date of commencement of the world war under our consideration. Any distinction between just and unjust war was only remained in the theory of international legal philosophers".

[61] Futamura, 2008, p. 66, see *supra* note 21.

Allies' policy on targeting individuals was initially laid down in paragraph 10 of the Potsdam Declaration:

> We do not intend that the Japanese shall be enslaved as a race or destroyed as a nation, but stern justice shall be meted out to all war criminals, including those who have visited cruelties upon our prisoners.[62]

Although the IMTFE sentenced several top Japanese officers, it was impossible to try everyone – from the commanding general to the foot soldier – within a short amount of time. In fact, due to the political influence of the United States, certain individuals were absent from the Tokyo trial in spite of their active role in the war. The dubious selection criteria with regard to the defendants made it unclear to the Chinese whom and what the IMTFE was targeting and thus diluted the impact of individual criminal punishment. Rather than the Tokyo trial, in which only major war criminals were judged and punished, it was the national trials conducted in China that brought to justice a significant number of Japanese class B and C war criminals.

The IMTFE judgment, while demonstrating the guilt of individual criminals, did not satisfy the Chinese population who continued to demand compensation and an official apology from the Japanese government. The Tokyo trial, in the same manner as the Nuremberg trial, did not provide redress to war victims for criminal acts. The Sino-Japanese Joint Statement of September 1972 renounced the state claim by the Chinese government against Japan. However, a settlement at the government level does not necessarily eradicate the dissatisfaction of the Chinese people on the issue. Since the 1990s there have been various private claims brought by Chinese citizens in Japanese courts regarding atrocities committed by Japanese troops in China during the war, including the Nanjing massacre,[63] Unit 731 atrocities,[64] "comfort women",[65] the massacre of civilians in Liaoning province,[66] and injuries suffered as a result of the toxic chem-

---

[62] Potsdam Declaration, para. 10, see *supra* note 6.

[63] "Japan Court Refuses to Compensate Victims", in *China Daily*, 19 April 2005.

[64] "Chinese Victims of Japanese Germ Warfare Demand Apology", in *China Daily*, 26 December 2001.

[65] "Japan: No Compensation for Chinese 'Comfort Women'", in *China Daily*, 18 March 2005.

[66] "Japanese Court Rejects Compensation to Chinese", in *China Daily*, 13 May 2005.

ical weapons left in China by Japanese troops in Heilongjiang province.[67] In 2012 15 victims who suffered in the mass bombings in Chongqing between 1938 and 1944 filed a lawsuit against the Japanese government for the first time in a Chinese court. These victims demanded a worldwide apology to the Chinese people and compensation for economic losses.[68]

It is obvious that there have been some shifts in Chinese demands for justice: from those of criminal indictment, to ones of monetary compensation and an official apology, where Japan itself (rather than individual Japanese) is required to bear responsibility for crimes committed. However, the IMTFE, which was only concerned with individual criminal responsibility, was an inadequate forum to address some kinds of state responsibilities. While setting up the Tokyo trial to pursue the individual responsibility of wartime leaders the international community failed to question the responsibility of Japan as a state for its acts of aggression in other judicial forums. This approach gave the impression, to a certain extent, that issues that were not dealt with by the IMTFE were guilt-free, and there was no state responsibility on the part of Japan for its aggressive war.

2.4. The Tokyo Trial's Contemporary Relevance

The factors discussed above, which affected the adequacy and effectiveness of the Tokyo trial, are not entirely foreign to more recent international criminal justice systems. Unlike in domestic courts, where it is expected that all crimes should be investigated and prosecuted, a degree of selectivity is a functional necessity for international criminal tribunals that do not have the capacity to entertain all the cases due to time and resource constraints. The key issue is the criteria for which defendants and which crimes to prosecute. The IMTFE's core selectivity problem was that the tribunal lacked sufficiently clear standards to justify its decision to immunise, among others, Emperor Hirohito, Unit 731 and the Americans from being prosecuted. Despite past and present war and conflict in other regions, all the cases that the ICC is currently investigating and prosecuting have to do with crimes allegedly committed in African countries,

---

[67] "Chinese to Seek Justice in Tokyo Court", in *China Daily*, 14 October 2003.

[68] "Japanese Government Sued over Chongqing Bombing", in *China Daily*, 11 September 2012.

---

which have similarly prompted critiques of selectivity and illegitimacy.[69] While the problem of selectivity at the ICC is primarily one of prosecutorial discretion,[70] the Court's relationship with the Security Council may further add to the perception of selective justice.[71] The Security Council has referred some cases – Libya and the Sudanese region of Darfur – but not others, such as Israel and Syria. The Security Council's decision with regard to which situation it deems deserves the attention of the ICC is essentially a political one, which by no means offers clear selection standards. This kind of political selectivity is institutionally inherent in the ICC Statute in order to extend the jurisdiction of the ICC to cover even non-state parties.

While the IMTFE dispensed justice to the extent that it conformed to political expediency for the United States, the ICC is not totally immune from the political influence of powerful states. However, the political dimensions of international criminal tribunals should be properly separated from the issue of politicisation.[72] In other words, not all political aspects of international criminal trials are subject to the charge of politicisation. This is manifest from Article 16 of the ICC Statue, which provides that the Security Council can defer an investigation or prosecution before the ICC for a renewable period of 12 months by adopting Chapter VII of the UN Charter.[73] Article 16 actually allows for a limited intervention in the Court's jurisdiction by the Security Council where the demands of peace so require.

There are considerable similarities between the challenges that the Allied powers confronted historically and those that we are facing today. The Security Council has been split on issues with regard to whether to

---

69 Margaret M. deGuzman, "Choosing to Prosecute: Expressive Selection at the International Criminal Court", in *Michigan Journal of International* Law, 2012, vol. 33, no. 2, p. 265.

70 William A. Schabas, "Prosecutorial Discretion v. Judicial Activism at the International Criminal Court", in *Journal of International Criminal Justice*, 2008, vol. 6, no. 4, p. 731.

71 Robert Cryer, *Prosecuting International Crimes: Selectivity and the International Criminal Law Regime*, Cambridge University Press, Cambridge, 2005, p.222.

72 ZHU Dan, "Who Politicizes the International Criminal Court?", in *FICHL Policy Brief Series*, 2014, no. 28, Torkel Opsahl Academic EPublisher.

73 Chapter VII of the UN Charter provides the framework within which the Security Council may take enforcement action. It allows the Security Council to "determine the existence of any threat to the peace, breach of the peace, or act of aggression" and to make recommendations or to resort to non-military and military action to "maintain or restore international peace and security".

defer the ICC's proceedings against the Sudanese president as well as the Kenyan president and his deputy. The discussion over possible deferral of the situation in Darfur came when the Office of the Prosecutor, on 14 July 2008, submitted an application for an arrest warrant against the Sudanese President Omar Al-Bashir.[74] In response to this application the African Union called upon the Security Council to apply Article 16 and "defer the process initiated by the ICC".[75] The views of the permanent members of the Security Council were deeply divided. The United States essentially held an ambiguous view in this regard.[76] While France and the United Kingdom issued statements against a deferral,[77] China and Russia contended that an arrest warrant would be detrimental to the Darfur peace process and harm the fragile security situation.[78] In the Kenya situation, the Security Council was once again asked to consider a deferral resolution, which would have postponed the ICC proceedings against the Kenyan President Uhuru Kenyatta and Vice President William Ruto, who face charges related to post-election violence in 2008.[79]

The same kind of debate took place among the leaders of the Allied governments some 70 years ago, when they were poised to decide their policy regarding the trial or non-trial of the Japanese emperor. The Allies' ultimate decision, which was manipulated by the United States, was to use Hirohito's unique power and authority in order to achieve international peace and security rather than taking legal action against him. However, at the time of the IMTFE there was no legal basis for subordinating justice

---

[74] International Criminal Court ('ICC'), Situation in Darfur, Sudan, Public Redacted Version of the Prosecutor's Application under Article 58 filed on 14 July 2008, ICC-02/05-157-AnxA, 13 September 2008 (http://www.legal-tools.org/doc/1ecabc/).

[75] African Union, Communique of the 142nd Meeting of the Peace and Security Council, PSC/MIN/Comm(CXLII), 21 July 2008, paras. 3, 5, 9, 11(i).

[76] United Nations Security Council ('UNSC'), Statement by Mr. Wolff (USA), 5947th Meeting, UN doc. S/PV.5947, 31 July 2008, p. 8; UNSC, Statement by Ms. Dicarlo (USA), 6028th Meeting, UN doc. S/PV.6028, 3 December 2008, p. 15.

[77] UNSC, Statement by Mr. De Rivi.re (France), 5947th Meeting, UN doc. S/PV.5947, 31 July 2008, p. 9; UNSC, Statement by Ms. Pierce (UK), 6028th Meeting, UN doc. S/PV.6028, 3 December 2008, p. 18.

[78] UNSC, Statement by Mr. Wang Guangya (China), 5947th Meeting, SCOR, UN Doc. S/PV.5947, 31 July 2008.

[79] UNSC, Azerbaijan, Burundi, Ethiopia, Gabon, Ghana, Kenya, Mauritania, Mauritius, Morocco, Namibia, Rwanda, Senegal, Togo and Uganda: Draft Resolution, UN doc. S/2013/660, 15 November 2013.

to peace. In contrast, when negotiating the ICC Statute, the political dimensions of international criminal trials were explicitly acknowledged by the delegates and Article 16 was designed to provide a legal basis for the Security Council to exert its political influence for the sake of peace. The application of Article 16, however, has not been collectively endorsed by the present-day superpowers in both the Darfur and Kenya situations, where the Security Council refused to act on the requests for a deferral of ICC proceedings against the incumbent political leaders.

While the ICC Statute is not oblivious to the political realities surrounding international criminal trials, compromise should not be confused with unjustified political interference in the judicial processes of international tribunals. Due to the intense political pressure exerted by the African Union at the twelfth session of the Assembly of States Parties to the ICC Statute on 28 November 2013, the Assembly decided to amend, by consensus, rule 134 of the ICC Rules of Procedure and Evidence ('RPE'), which opened the possibility for high-ranking government officials to be excused from being present in the courtroom during their trials at the ICC. New rules of procedure – RPE 134*bis*, *ter* and *quarter* – were designed for excusals from physical presence at trial "due to extraordinary public duties".[80] The amendments allow persons in authority to participate in the trial through the use of video technology or representation by counsel. The two tiers of accused created by rule 134*quater* are arguably incompatible with Article 27 of the ICC Statute, which provides that all alleged perpetrators of international crimes should be held accountable for their crimes, regardless of their official capacity. This amendment not only introduces the very element of selectivity that the ICC was in part designed to reject but also sends an unfortunate message that the operation of the ICC is still subject to the political calculations of certain states.

Like the IMTFE, the ICC has also encountered some difficulties in the collection of evidence. In 2013 the ICC prosecutor had to request an adjournment of the trial date of the Kenyatta case following the withdrawal of two key witnesses.[81] It is still unclear whether sufficient evi-

---

[80] ICC, Assembly of State Parties, 12th session, Resolution 7, 27 November 2013, ICC-ASP/12/Res.7 (http://www.legal-tools.org/doc/c50839/).

[81] ICC, Kenyatta Case: Statement of the Prosecutor of the International Criminal Court, Fatou Bensouda, Following an Application Seeking an Adjournment of the Provisional Trial Date, 19 December 2013 (https://www.icc-cpi.int/iccdocs/PIDS/wu/ED194_ENG.pdf).

dence can be collected, given "the widespread perception that the witnesses have been intimidated and bribed" by the Kenyan government.[82] Under the ICC Statute, the prosecutor enjoys a significant degree of autonomy to select where, and against whom, the ICC directs its efforts. Though it cannot be compared with the IMTFE chief prosecutor's broad prosecutorial power, the exercise of the ICC prosecutor's discretion is not without controversy. There have been criticisms that the Court has unfairly targeted Africans.

While certain deficiencies, which the IMTFE also suffered from, may continue to haunt the operation of the ICC, there are some positive developments in the ICC Statute. While the Tokyo trial was subject to the accusation that it deliberately did not question the past conduct of the Allied powers, the ICC has looked into crimes committed by both sides in its practice. It can be recalled that Uganda first attempted to refer the situation of the Lord's Resistance Army ('LRA') to the ICC under Article 13(a) of the ICC Statute. The prosecutor, nonetheless, opened an investigation into northern Uganda more generally, covering both parties (the government of Uganda and the LRA) to the conflict.[83] Though the ICC is not isolated from the influence of political powers, the international community has made an effort to transfer the unilateral privilege to a broader common will. An example can be drawn from the negotiations on Article 16 of the ICC Statute, which replaced the "negative" veto – given to the five permanent members of the Security Council by the International Law Commission text to shield their own nationals – with a "positive" consensus in stopping the ICC from acting.[84] Some safeguards and oversight mechanisms were also introduced in the ICC Statute to control or filter the broad discretionary power of the ICC prosecutor.[85]

---

[82]   "Uhuru Kenyatta's trial: A case study in what's wrong with the ICC", in *Global Post*, 6 February 2014.

[83]   Payam Akhavan, "The Lord's Resistance Army Case: Uganda's Submission of the First State Referral to the International Criminal Court", in *American Journal of International Law*, 2005, no. 99, p. 411.

[84]   Lionel Yee, "The International Criminal Court and the Security Council: Articles 13(b) and 16", in Roy S. Lee (ed.), *The International Criminal Court: The Making of the Rome Statute: Issues, Negotiations, Results*, Kluwer Law International, The Hague, 1999, p.151.

[85]   For example, the Rome Statute of the International Criminal Court ('ICC Statute'), Art. 15(3) obliges the prosecutor to seek authorisation from the Pre-Trial Chamber before proceeding with an investigation on his or her initiative (http://www.legal-tools.org/doc/7b9af9/).

With the establishment of the ICC, some "forgotten" crimes, including the comfort women, biological experiments, and the use of chemical and biological weapons, will no longer be ignored by the international community. The ICC Statute is the first international treaty that criminalises and defines – beyond the act of rape – sexual and gender-based violence as crimes against humanity,[86] war crimes[87] and (to some extent) genocide.[88] Furthermore, the ICC Statute explicitly provides that the conduct of biological experiments is a kind of war crime.[89] It also criminalises the use of poison or poisoned weapons,[90] which arguably includes chemical and biological weapons. In contrast to the IMTFE, the ICC pays significant attention to victims. The ICC Statute created the Trust Fund for Victims, which is responsible for implementing the reparations mandated by the ICC.[91] In 2012 the ICC issued its first-ever decision on reparations for victims in the case against Thomas Lubanga.[92] Rather than being dominated by common law, some provisions of the ICC Statute combine features of both common law and civil law systems.[93] While Asian judges were under-represented in the Tokyo trial, one relevant consideration in the election of ICC judges is the need for "equitable geographical representation".[94]

2.5. The Implications of the Tokyo Trial on China's Approach to International Criminal Tribunals

From Tokyo to Rome, China has long supported the establishment of international criminal courts. It engaged in a consistent manner with the establishment of international criminal tribunals as a permanent member of

---

86 *Ibid.*, Art. 7(g).

87 *Ibid.*, Art. 8(2)(B)(xxii).

88 *Ibid.*, Art. 6(d).

89 *Ibid.*, Art. 8(2)(a)(ii).

90 *Ibid.*, Art. 8(2)(b)(xvii).

91 *Ibid.*, Art. 79.

92 ICC, Situation in the Democratic Republic of the Congo, *Prosecutor* v. *Thomas Lubanga Dyilo*, Trial Chamber, Decision Establishing the Principles and Procedures to be applied to Reparations, ICC-01/04-01/06, 7 August 2012 (http://www.legal-tools.org/doc/a05830/).

93 Adrian Hoel, "The Sentencing Provisions of the International Criminal Court: Common Law, Civil Law, or Both?", in *Monash University Law Review*, 2007, vol. 33, no. 2, pp. 264–89.

94 ICC Statute, Art. 36(8)(a)(ii), see *supra* note 85.

the UN Security Council. This can be traced to the establishment of International Criminal Tribunal for the former Yugoslavia[95] and International Criminal Tribunal for Rwanda.[96] Even though China had reservations about the way in which the *ad hoc* tribunals were created, it did not seek to use its veto power within the Security Council to block the adoption of the resolutions establishing these tribunals. China actively participated in every stage of the negotiating process leading up to the creation of the ICC.[97] The inadequacy of the IMTFE in addressing its demands for justice nonetheless planted seeds of distrust in China's impression of the international criminal justice system, which can be seen from its current concerns regarding the ICC. At the end of the Rome diplomatic conference in 1998, China cast a negative vote against the ICC Statute and articulated several reasons for doing so.[98] One of them was about the *proprio muto*

---

[95] UNSC, Statement by Mr. CHEN Jian (China), Provisional Verbatim Record of the 3175th Meeting, UN doc. S/PV.3175, 22 February 1993, p. 7, para. 5; UNSC, Statement by Mr. LI Zhaoxing (China), Provisional Verbatim Record of the 3217th Meeting, UN doc. S/PV.3217, 25 May 1993, p. 33, para. 1.

[96] UNSC, Statement by Mr. LI Zhaoxing (China), Provisional Verbatim Record of the 3453rd Meeting, UN doc. S/PV.3453, 8 November 1994, p. 11, para. 7.

[97] JIA Bing Bing, "China and the International Criminal Court: Current Situation", in *Singapore Year Book of International Law*, 2006, vol. 10, p. 88.

[98] Statement by WANG Guangya (China) on the Statute of the International Criminal Court, in *Legal Daily*, 29 July 1998:

> (1) The jurisdiction of the ICC is not based on the principle of voluntary acceptance; the Rome Statute imposes obligations on non-States Parties without their consent, which violates the principle of state sovereignty and the Vienna Convention on the Law of Treaties. Furthermore, the complementary jurisdiction principle gives the ICC the power to judge whether a state is able or willing to conduct proper trials of its own nationals. As a result, the Court becomes a supra-national organ. (2) War crimes committed in internal armed conflicts fall under the jurisdiction of the ICC. Further, the definition of "war crimes" goes beyond that accepted under customary international law and Additional Protocol 2 to the Geneva Conventions. (3) Contrary to the existing norms of customary international law, the definition of "crimes against humanity" does not require that the state in which they are committed be "at war". Furthermore, many actions listed under that heading belong to the area of human rights law rather than international criminal law; this deviates from the real aim of establishing the ICC. (4) The inclusion of the crime of aggression within the jurisdiction of the ICC weakens the power of the UN Security Council. (5) The *proprio motu* power of the Prosecutor under Article 15 of the Rome Statute may make it difficult for the ICC to concentrate on dealing with the most

power of the ICC prosecutor, which, in the view of China, would be abused for politically motivated prosecutions.[99] This concern clearly echoes China's past experience of biased prosecutions in the Tokyo trial. While acknowledging that the creation of the ICC was a positive addition to the international legal architecture, China insisted that international crimes should be dealt with by national courts, which, it believed, "have apparent advantages over the ICC in prosecuting these types of crimes".[100] This Chinese position can be linked to its successful prosecutions of thousands of Japanese war criminals at the domestic level, which was in sharp contrast with Tokyo's limited convictions.

China, as a permanent member of the Security Council, carries special responsibility for the maintenance of world peace and security. When facing the choice between peace and justice, as the Allied powers were confronted with in history, China seems to advance an approach that acknowledges the limitations of international criminal justice and allows more flexibility in dealing with complex situations. In the view of China, "the work of the International Criminal Court should be pursued in a way that does not impede or jeopardize the relevant peace process".[101] China believes that "the pursuit of international judicial justice should be carried out with the ultimate aim of putting an end of conflict and in the wider

---

serious crimes, and may make the Court open to political influence so that it cannot act in a manner that is independent and fair.

[99] *Ibid.*

[100] *Ibid.*

[101] UN General Assembly, Position Papers of the People's Republic of China at the 63rd (2008), 65th (2010), 66th (2011), 67th (2012) Sessions of the UN General Assembly. See also UNSC, Statement by Mr. Li Baodong (China), 6849th Meeting, SCOR, UN doc. S/PV.6849, 17 October. 2012. According to Li:

China believes that justice cannot be pursued at the expenses of peaceful process, nor should it impede the process of national reconciliation. [...] The ICC, as an integral part of the international system of the rule of law, must abide by the purposes and principles of the Charter and play a positive role in maintaining international peace and security. [...] Since the Charter entrusts the Security Council with the primary responsibility for the maintenance of international peace and security, we hope that the ICC will exercise caution in carrying out its functions and avoid impeding the work of the Security Council by seeking political settlements to international and regional conflicts.

context of restoring peace".[102] To this end, China actively sought for deferrals with regard to both Sudan[103] and Kenya.[104]

When it comes to the crime of aggression China seems to have drawn lessons from the IMTFE's politically manipulated prosecutions. When voting against the ICC Statute China clarified its position in the following terms:

> Crime of aggression is a state act, and there is no legal definition of the crime of aggression. To avoid political abuse of litigation, it is necessary to have the UN Security Council first determine the existence of aggression before pursuing individual criminal responsibility, as is stipulated in Article 39 of the UN Charter.[105]

The IMTFE's inability to deal with Japan's state responsibility for aggressive war against China also finds echoes in its current approach towards the crime of aggression. China argues:

> Since the precondition for an individual to bear the criminal responsibility is that the state commits an act of aggression, in the absence of a determination by the Security Council on the situation of aggression, the court lacks the basis to prosecute the individual for his criminal liability. Besides, allowing the court to exercise jurisdiction before the Security Council makes the determination was practically bestowing on the court the right of determination on the state act of aggression. This runs counter to the provision of the Charter.[106]

---

[102] Statement by China on the Eighth Report of the Prosecutor of the ICC Pursuant to Resolution 1593 (2005), 3 December 2008.

[103] UNSC, Statement by Mr. WANG Guangya (China), 5947th Meeting, SCOR, UN doc. S/PV.5947, 31 July 2008. According to WANG, "seeking to resolve the issue of impunity through the indictment of the Sudanese leader by the ICC will only derail the process of resolving the Darfur issue".

[104] UNSC, Statement by LIU Jieyi (China), UNSC, 7060th Meeting, 15 November 2013, UN doc. S/PV.7060, p. 12. LIU noted that "deferring the ICC proceedings against the leaders of Kenya is not only a matter of concern to Kenya, but also a matter of concern for the entire African continent".

[105] WANG, 1998, see *supra* note 98.

[106] Permanent Mission of the People's Republic of China to the United Nations Office at Geneva, Statement by Chinese delegate at the Sixth Session of the Preparatory Commission (2000) (http://www.china-un.ch/eng/qqwt/hflygz/t85684.htm).

What China has been suggesting is that individual criminal responsibility for aggression should not be allowed to go ahead before international criminal tribunals in the absence of a determination of state responsibility for acts of aggression by an appropriate body.[107] Should the international community have followed this approach in the aftermath of the Second World War, rather than leaving aside Japan's responsibility for aggression towards China, justice could have been delivered to China more sufficiently. By selecting a handful of symbolic figures for criminal punishment, the international community gave the impression that what was examined at the IMTFE was all that mattered and allowed Japan to move forward without bearing its state responsibility towards the victimised states, in particular China.

Although it was difficult to set up other means to deal with Japan's state responsibility at the end of the Second World War, due to various limitations, the international community today is in a better position to re-evaluate its approach to punishing aggression. On the one hand, the determination of the Security Council, which is a political organ with wide discretionary powers, as to whether an act of aggression has taken place, is not automatic but a result of political considerations. On the other, in the absence of a Security Council determination on an act of aggression, the ICC may have to engage with highly political questions, which are likely to lie outside the scope of its judicial function. The Kampala amendment to the ICC Statute on the crime of aggression, however, moved the question of resort to armed force from the exclusive purview of the Security Council, and granted the ICC prosecutor the ability to proceed with an investigation of an alleged crime of aggression without a Security Council filter, albeit only with the approval of the ICC pre-trial division. In this sense, the ICC Statute's current provision on the crime of aggression has not fully addressed China's concerns, part of which derived from its past experience with the IMFTE.

In view of the dubious use of broad prosecutorial powers by the chief prosecutor at Tokyo, China has been very cautious in granting the ICC prosecutor the ability to initiate his/her own investigations. According to China, "the *proprio motu* power of the Prosecutor under Article 15

---

[107] For further discussion, see ZHU Dan, "China, the Crime of Aggression, and the International Criminal Court", in *Asian Journal of International Law*, 2015, vol. 5, no. 1, pp. 94–122.

of the Rome Statute may make it difficult for the ICC to concentrate on dealing with the most serious crimes, and may make the Court open to political influence so that it cannot act in a manner that is independent and fair".[108] At the Rome diplomatic conference, unlike the majority of states, China did not consider the authorisation by the pre-trial chamber to constitute a sufficient system of checks and balances on the powers conferred to the prosecutor.[109] In Kampala, a special regime was adopted to the exercise of *proprio motu* power with respect to the crime of aggression. If prosecution for the crime of aggression results from the prosecutor exercising *proprio motu* authority, it is the pre-trial division that authorises the commencement of an investigation.[110] Though this is similar to the mechanism that applies to *proprio motu* prosecution for the other three crimes pursuant to Article 15 of the ICC Statute, the threshold of checks has been increased; the task belongs not to the pre-trial chamber, which is composed of three judges, but to the pre-trial division, which has a minimum of six judges. Whether China's concern about politically motivated investigations, which has historical resonance with the IMTFE, will materialise largely depends on the ICC's post-Statute practice.

One of the discomforts that China had at the IMTFE was the application of rules of common law by the Western judges. To some extent this has contributed to China's distrust of Western-dominated international law and the international adjudicative process of international judicial bodies.[111] Though China does not view the ICC Statute as subject to the same criticism as the IMTFE Charter, it is still sceptical about certain rules, in particular the definitions of crimes against humanity and war crimes. While the IMTFE did not win China's trust in the adjudicative process of international criminal tribunals, with more and more international law experts being elected as judges on the benches of the *ad hoc*

---

[108] WANG, 1998, see *supra* note 98.

[109] United Nations Diplomatic Conference of Plenipotentiaries on the Establishment of an International Criminal Court, Statement by Mr. LIU Daqun (China), 9th Plenary Meeting, 17 July 1998, UN doc. A/CONF.183/SR.9, para. 39.

[110] ICC, Assembly of State Parties, Amendments to the Rome Statute of the International Criminal Court on the Crime of Aggression, Resolution RC/Res.6, 11 June 2010, Annex I, Art. 15*bis*(8) (http://www.legal-tools.org/doc/0d027b/).

[111] ZHU Dan, "China, the International Criminal Court, and International Adjudication", in *Netherlands International Law Review*, 2014, vol. 61, no. 1, p. 55.

tribunals for the former Yugoslavia and Rwanda,[112] China's attitude has been gradually changing. But its distrust has not entirely disappeared. The lack of expertise in collecting and presenting evidence was another obstacle that stood in the way of China's pursuit of justice at the Tokyo trial. Through direct engagement with the *ad hoc* tribunals, where there were several Chinese experts on board, China has accumulated some experience and expertise. However, this is currently missing in the context of the permanent International Criminal Court. From the Office of the Prosecutor to the chambers of the ICC there has been very limited Chinese involvement at a professional level.

2.6. Concluding Remarks

With the benefit of historical hindsight, some lessons can be learned from China's initial pursuit of international criminal justice in Tokyo, which was hindered by a range of issues. The IMTFE, a special organ established at the end of the Second World War, had some structural deficiencies. As discussed above, some of these deficiencies, to a greater or less extent, have been overcome in the evolution of the international criminal courts. The ICC, in particular, has been designed in a way that would trigger fewer Chinese anxieties than its past experience with the Tokyo trial, though not all of the issues have been addressed to its satisfaction.

There were, however, more fundamental problems caused by some inherent limitations of international criminal trials, which still have significant contemporary relevance. As demonstrated by the IMTFE, there are three major limitations. First, international criminal courts are seldom immune from the influence of politics. International crimes, due to their nature, are frequently and almost exclusively committed in circumstances which directly or indirectly challenge international peace and security in a manner that triggers the international community's collective response. Situations may exist where the pursuit of justice by international criminal tribunals contribute to the achievement by the Security Council of its peace and security mandate. The establishment of the *ad hoc* tribunals by

---

[112] From 1993 to 1997 Professor LI Haopei served as a judge at the Appeals Chamber of the International Criminal Tribunal for the former Yugoslavia ('ICTY'); he also served as a judge at the International Criminal Tribunal for Rwanda from 1995 to 1997. Professor WANG Tieya was elected in 1997 as a judge at the ICTY. Since 2000 Professor LIU Daqun has been a permanent judge at the ICTY.

the Security Council was inspired by the conviction that the prosecution of major international crimes constitutes a means to maintain international peace and security. However, this is not always the case. A political decision to maintain peace and security may sometimes require a different approach from that being pursued by international criminal courts, as with the case of the immunity of the Japanese emperor.

Second, an international criminal trial that only addresses individual criminal responsibility is not a catch-all solution to meet justice demands, especially when states' involvement is explicit in the commission of international crimes. The Chinese people's call for compensation and an official apology would be better dealt with in the context of state responsibility, which is beyond the purview of a criminal trial. A sense of injustice may arise where individuals were convicted of serious international crimes, but the government who orchestrated these atrocities then denied the nature of its state act. It would create a sentiment within the victimised nation that justice has not been done. This problem overshadowed the IMTFE, and might well continue to exist with the adoption of the Kampala amendment on the crime of aggression. There may be cases where the Security Council does not consider that aggression has materialised, while the ICC takes a contrary position and consequently finds individuals criminally responsible for aggression.

Third, due to the personnel and financial limitations on international legal processes, it would be impossible to try everyone involved in committing atrocities. Some low-ranking suspects may be left unpunished if not tried by domestic courts. By providing that the ICC should be complementary to national criminal jurisdiction, the ICC Statute assigns primary responsibility for prosecution of the core crimes to national criminal jurisdiction.[113] The ICC prosecutor also gradually developed a prosecutorial strategy of "positive complementarity", which encourages and facilities states to conduct national proceedings against the crimes within the ICC's jurisdiction.

Drawing on its past experience with the IMTFE, China seems to have understood these limitations of international criminal trials, and has gradually developed its own approach in dealing with these issues. In the view of China, peace should take priority over the pursuit of justice and

---

[113] ICC Statute, Art. 17, see *supra* note 85.

accountability; national courts are better equipped to deal with international crimes; and the prosecution of the crime of aggression should not be allowed to proceed without a prior explicit determination of the existence of a state act of aggression by the Security Council.

Apart from the structural flaws of the IMTFE and the inherent limitations of an international criminal trial, the lack of expertise was another factor restricting the adequacy of the Tokyo trial. Though China still regards the ICC with a degree of suspicion due to identifiable concerns, gaining greater expertise would provide China with more flexibility when it considers new developments in the Court's practice, and, from time to time, re-evaluates its approaches to the international criminal justice system. On the other hand, building national capacity to prosecute international criminals would allow China to continue its legacy of prosecuting war criminals domestically.

3

Japanese Receptions of Separate Opinions
at the Tokyo Trial

Yuma Totani[*]

On the early afternoon of 12 November 1948 Justice Sir William F. Webb, member for Australia and president of the International Military Tribunal for the Far East ('IMTFE') at Tokyo, Japan, finished reading the judgment and verdicts. Before announcing the sentences to individual accused, he let it be known to all present in the courtroom that the judgment and verdicts thus delivered did not reflect the unanimous decision of the 11-member tribunal. "The Member for India dissents from the majority Judgment and has filed a statement of his reasons for such dissent", he announced, and "the members for France and the Netherlands dissent as to part only from the majority Judgment and have filed statements of their reasons for such dissents". The member for the Philippines, too, submitted a separate opinion, although his was concurring with the majority. Webb himself filed another. "Generally, I share the view of the majority as to facts", he stated, but he produced a separate opinion to express his own reasoning "for upholding the Charter [of the Tribunal] and the jurisdiction of the Tribunal and of some general considerations that influenced me in deciding on the sentences".[1] In short, the decision of the tribunal was split between the majority opinion of eight justices and five concurring and dissenting opinions. Webb informed that the defence counsel's prior request for the reading of separate opinions in the open court was denied.

---

[*] **Yuma Totani** earned her Ph.D. in history from the University of California, Berkeley, in 2005, and is presently an Associate Professor of history at the University of Hawaii. She authored *The Tokyo War Crimes Trial: The Pursuit of Justice in the Wake of World War II*, Harvard University Asia Center, Honolulu, 2008, and *Justice in Asia and the Pacific Region, 1945–1952: Allied War Crimes Prosecutions*, Cambridge University Press, Cambridge, 2015, and rendered their Japanese-language translations, *Tōkyō saiban: dai-niji taisen go no hō to seigi no tsuikyū*, Misuzu shobō, Tokyo, 2008, and *Futashikana seigi: BC-kyū senpan saiban no kiseki*, Iwanami shoten, Tokyo, 2015.

[1] Neil Boister and Robert Cryer (eds.), *Documents on the Tokyo International Military Tribunal: Charter, Indictment and Judgments*, Oxford University Press, Oxford, 2008, p. 626.

However, he assured that all the separate opinions would be included in the official record of the trial and that they would become "available to the Supreme Commander [for the Allied Powers], to Defense Counsel and to others who may be concerned".[2]

Duly distributed in the days immediately following the conclusion of the international proceedings at Tokyo ('Tokyo Trial'), separate opinions caused much stir among those who had direct access to them, including the 25 defendants themselves. The dissenting opinion by the Indian member, Judge Radhabinod Pal (in which all the defendants were found "not guilty" of any of the charges), especially received enthusiastic responses. General Matsui Iwane, who was convicted and sentenced to death by hanging in connection with the Rape of Nanjing, confided to Hanayama Shinshō, a prison chaplain at the war criminals' compounds at Sugamo, Tokyo, that Pal's dissent "articulated our position in full and, as might be expected of an Indian, he looks at things from the philosophical standpoint". General Itagaki Seishirō, who was a former staff officer of the Kwantung Army that instigated the invasion of Manchuria in 1931 and who was convicted of multiple counts of crimes against peace and war crimes, spent three days reading Pal's dissent and was "extremely impressed", so much so that he composed two poems in its appreciation.[3] Shigemitsu Mamoru, who served as foreign minister in the second half of the Pacific War, and who was similarly convicted of crimes against peace and war crimes (but received an unusually light sentence of seven years in prison), also read Pal's dissent. He reached the conclusion that this text was "a must read" (*hitsudoku no sho*) for all. In Shigemitsu's opinion, this dissenting opinion was an articulation of the judge's fearless commitment to the principle of justice, on the one hand, and his dogged adherence to the principle of neutrality, on the other, the latter quality ostensibly representing the national trait of modern-day India, the then emerging leader of the Third World.[4]

Similar views were expressed elsewhere. In their retrospective account of the Tokyo Trial, a group of court reporters for *Asahi Shinbun* – a

---

[2]   *Ibid.*

[3]   Ushimura Kei, "'Paru hanketsu' to sengo Nihon" [The Pal Judgment and Post-war Japan], in Ushimura Kei, *"Sengo sekinin" ron no shinjitsu: sengo Nihon no chiteki taiman o danzu* [The Truth about the "Post-war Responsibility" Debates: Criticism of Intellectual Idleness in Post-war Japan], PHP Kenkyūjo, Tokyo, 2006, pp. 151–52.

[4]   *Ibid.*, pp. 158–59.

leading centre-left national daily newspaper – recalled that "the majority judgment on first reading gave an impression of falling within the bounds of the prosecution's opening statement". By contrast,

> the dissenting opinion by the Indian member Justice Pal outstripped the majority judgment in terms of its volume, its retention of a high level of discernment as regards its quality, and its taking on of certain characteristics as a critique of civilization; all in all, one cannot help but feeling that this is the very thing to be regarded as the rightful historical document [*korekoso tadashiku rekishiteki bunken*].

That said, the *Asahi* reporters did not forget to note the importance of other separate opinions, especially the ones submitted by the French justice Henri Bernard, the Dutch justice B.V.A. Röling, and the president of the tribunal Webb. Their opinions, too, "carried considerably interesting materials", the *Asahi* reporters maintained, and "it is by no means a small matter to contemplate the ramifications of these minority opinions having not been read [in the courtroom]".[5]

What were the "considerably interesting materials" in the separate opinions that the Japanese newspaper reporters were referring to? How did the Japanese public receive the opinions by these justices? How about Pal's dissenting opinion? Why did the *Asahi* reporters maintain that this particular piece set itself apart from the rest of the judicial opinions arising from the Tokyo Trial? The purpose of this chapter is to address these questions by exploring the Japanese-language publications on the five separate opinions in the post-trial period.

3.1. Assessing the Separate Opinions

It was known to the Japanese public contemporaneously that the Tokyo Trial ended in split decisions, but it took more than a decade for the translation of the separate opinions to gain broad circulation. A comprehensive Japanese-language sourcebook of the separate opinions was published by the *Asahi* newspaper in 1962 under the title *Tōkyō saiban, gekan* (The Tokyo Trial, volume 2). This publication consisted of a summary of the majority judgment (including some excerpts); full texts of separate opinions by Bernard, Pal and Webb; excerpts from separate opinions by Jara-

---

5   Asahi shinbun hōtei kishadan [The Asahi Newspaper Court Reporters] (ed.), *Tōkyō saiban* [The Tokyo Trial], vol. 2, Tōkyō saiban kankōkai, Tokyo, 1962, p. 47.

nilla and Röling; and a short introductory statement for each separate opinion. *Tōkyō saiban* was part of the expanded, two-volume edition of the reportage that the *Asahi* court reporters had originally published at the time of the Tokyo Trial. The eighth and the last instalment of the original reporting, published in 1949 as *Hanketsu-hen* (The Volume on the Judgment), contained no more than brief summaries and excerpts from the decisions, due to limited pages allowed for the series.[6] The 1962 edition was a considerable improvement in this regard. It was the first of its kind that carried in Japanese translation a near-complete set of all five separate opinions, and hence constituted an important milestone in the existing literature on the Tokyo Trial.

It should be noted that, in the intervening years, a full translation of the majority judgment came in print (in 1949).[7] However, no effort to publish the separate opinions in either English or Japanese materialised in the ensuing decade except Pal's dissenting opinion.[8] A group of individuals who had been closely associated with the accused Matsui launched publicity campaigns to establish Pal's credentials as the only justice qualified to adjudge the case against the Japanese defendants. They mass-circulated versions of Pal's dissenting opinion for that purpose, touting it as the "truthful judgment" (*shinri no sho*) that advanced the "Japan is not guilty thesis" (*Nihon muzai-ron*). They also invited over to Japan the Indian justice himself to have him play a proactive role in building his image as a staunch advocate of world peace, justice and the rule of law. The publicity campaigns proved to be a tremendous success. During his visits to Japan in 1952, 1953 and 1966, Pal pleased his hosts by willingly taking part in an array of media events whereby he reportedly befriended convicted war criminals and bereaved families; condemned the self-righteousness of the West; expressed rage over the seeming meekness of

---

[6] Asahi shinbun hōtei kishadan [Asahi Newspaper Court Reporters], (ed.), *Tōkyō saiban* [The Tokyo Trial], 8 vols., Nūsusha, Tokyo, 1946–1949.

[7] Mainichi shinbunsha [Mainichi Newspaper] (ed.), *Kyokutō kokusai gunji saibansho hanketsu* [The Judgment of the International Military Tribunal for the Far East], Mainichi shinbunsha, Tokyo, 1949.

[8] For a discussion of Justice Pal's post-trial tours in Japan and their impacts on the Japanese understanding of the Tokyo Trial, see Yuma Totani, *The Tokyo War Crimes Trial: The Pursuit of Justice in the Wake of World War II*, Harvard University Asia Center, Cambridge, MA, 2008, ch. 8; and Nakazato Nariaki, *Paru hanji: Indo nashonarizumu to Tōkyō saiban* [Justice Pal: Indian Nationalism and the Tokyo Trial], Iwanami shoten, Tokyo, 2011.

the people of Hiroshima in criticising the victors' use of atomic bombs; and advocated the "Eastern" ideals of solidarity, law, justice and world peace. Pal's public persona as a jurist-pacifist of Asian origin grew in sufficient importance that he was chosen in 1966 to be the recipient of the First Order of the Sacred Treasure (*kun ittō zuihōshō*) from the government of Japan, which Emperor Hirohito personally presented, in recognition presumably of the Indian justice's unique contribution to promoting law and world peace.[9] Memorial sites that celebrated Pal's words and deeds came to dot the Japanese archipelago after his death in January 1967, the latest of which being a new memorial stone built in 2005 at the precinct of the controversial Yasukuni Shrine in central Tokyo. Pal's dissenting opinion, in this manner, gained popularity and came to define the Japanese perception of the Tokyo Trial.

When seen against this backdrop, the publication of the *Asahi* reporters' *Tōkyō saiban* can be understood as addressing the existing imbalances in the Japanese knowledge about the Tokyo Trial. It went beyond the narrow focus on Pal's dissenting opinion and promoted instead comparative assessments of all the five separate opinions in relation to the majority judgment. This publication suffered certain editorial shortcomings, however. For one thing, it carried only a fraction of the majority judgment for the stated reason that its main points were already well known to the Japanese public.[10] *Tōkyō saiban* also omitted some sections from the separate opinions by Jaranilla and Röling. No satisfactory explanation was given for these omissions. Jaranilla's separate opinion was short enough to have caused no editorial problems had it been printed in full. Röling's separate opinion was possibly considered as being too lengthy to be printed in its entirety, but this scenario is unlikely. The editor of the volume was prepared to adopt special typesetting to reproduce Pal's dissenting opinion in full, that is, by using double-column formatting and narrower line spacing. This course of action was taken despite the fact that Pal's dissenting opinion had already enjoyed broad circulation in various versions in the preceding decade. One can only surmise that Pal's dissent was believed to be too important to be included in any other form but its entirety. It is still unclear, however, as to why the other less-known – but by

---

[9]   Nakazato, 2011, p. 227, see *supra* note 8.

[10]   Asahi shinbun hōtei kishadan, 1962, vol. 2, p. 54, see *supra* note 5.

no means less important – separate opinions could not have been accommodated in the same way as Pal's dissenting opinion.

Tōkyō saiban provides a short introductory statement for each separate opinion to familiarise the readers with its unique features. The highlighted points can be summarised as follows. With regard to Webb's separate opinion, the *Asahi* reporters introduced it as an "interesting piece" that offered a useful window through which one could appreciate "the main concerns of the Tribunal", and, more specifically, various legal controversies that arose in connection with the charges of crimes against peace. The discussion of the emperor's culpability also stood out to the *Asahi* reporters as a distinct feature in Webb's separate opinion. While acknowledging that Webb touched on "the issues of the emperor" (*tennō-ron*) for the limited purpose of determining the adequacy of the sentences against the defendants, the *Asahi* reporters found his comments "highly suggestive" (*ganchiku ni tomu*). [11] Having stated so, however, they stopped short of elaborating in what regard, exactly, Webb's comments were highly suggestive and merited the readers' attention.

The separate opinion by Jaranilla, too, appealed to the *Asahi* reporters as being "of considerable interest" for the unique stances the Philippine justice took on certain points of law and fact. Especially noteworthy were the following: 1) that he gave full and unqualified endorsement to the legal principles arising from the Nuremberg trial, that is, the principles subsequently applied at the Tokyo Trial; 2) that he deemed the Allied use of atomic bombs justifiable from the military standpoint, or as he put it, "a means is justified by an end"[12]; 3) that he criticised Justice Pal's defiance of the IMTFE Charter, referring to this action as his "exceeding of authority" (*ekken*); and 4) that Jaranilla disapproved of the sentences rendered by the majority justices, which he found too lenient.[13] The *Asahi* reporters took no position for or against any of these issues that the Philippine jus-

---

[11]   *Ibid.*, p. 164.

[12]   The following passage can be found in Jaranilla's concurring opinion: "If a means is justi-fied by an end, the use of the atomic bomb was justified, for it brought Japan to her knees and ended the horrible war. If the war had gone on longer, without the use of the atomic bomb, how many more thousands and thousands of helpless men, women and children would have needlessly died and suffered, and how much more destruction and devastation, hardly irreparable, would have been wrought?" Boister and Cryer, 2008, p. 655, see *supra* note 1.

[13]   Asahi shinbun hōtei kishadan, 1962, vol. 2, pp. 176–77, see *supra* note 5.

tice raised as if to maintain the attitude of a neutral observer. However, they took exception with Jaranilla's opinion on atomic bombs. Voicing dissent, the *Asahi* reporters held that the use of unconventional weapons, including atomic bombs, had already been outlawed under international law, and that Jaranilla was mistaken in finding its use as being militarily justifiable.[14]

The *Asahi* reporters expressed less enthusiasm when introducing Bernard's separate opinion, which they heard to have been "written in a rush" and which was not guided by any careful writing plan "unlike the Pal Judgment".[15] But they still gave some credit to Bernard's dissent with regard to the following points: 1) that it concluded the charges of crimes against peace as valid based on natural law, but *not* the Pact of Paris of 1928 (thus disputing the legal position taken by the majority justices); 2) that it advanced an important critique of the theories of liability the majority adopted relative to war crimes; 3) that it criticised procedural shortcomings of the Tokyo Trial; 4) that it denounced the exemption of Emperor Hirohito from prosecution; and 5) that it "boldly disclosed that the method by which the Tribunal had carried out its oral deliberations greatly lacked transparency". On the last point, Bernard did not explain in any great detail the alleged opacity of the tribunal's deliberation processes. Even so, the *Asahi* reporters found Bernard's criticism weighty enough that it "warrants special attention".[16]

With respect to Röling's dissenting opinion, it is introduced as a relatively lengthy piece whose scope of dissent, however, was quite limited. Its main goal was to record the Dutch justice's points of dissent in light of the possible remission of sentences of the defendants. Another feature that stood out to the *Asahi* reporters in Röling's dissent was an in-depth analysis of factual issues relative to crimes against peace, in which the Dutch justice appeared to give sympathetic treatment to some of the defendants' contentions, such as those concerning the Japanese invasion of China. The *Asahi* reporters took pains not to portray Röling as a Japan apologist, however, as they were quick to point out that the Dutch justice minced no words in denouncing the Japanese advocacy of the Greater East Asia Co-Prosperity Sphere, the vision of empire with which the war-

---

[14]   *Ibid.*, p. 177.

[15]   *Ibid.*, p. 193.

[16]   *Ibid.*, p. 194.

time government of Japan justified its war effort. Röling wrote – and the *Asahi* reporters quoted from his dissenting opinion – that "during the years of occupation, Japan not only failed to fulfil the pledges based on the principle of amity and assistance, but did not even live up to the rules of conduct as formulated in the Hague Convention based on the principles of decent belligerency".[17]

Having highlighted these stern words in the dissenting opinion, however, the *Asahi* reporters still speculated that Röling might have had some pro-Japanese sentiments or, at least, been sympathetic to Hirota Kōki, a former diplomat and the only civilian defendant who was convicted and sentenced to death.[18] Röling *did* discuss the case of Hirota at length – along with the cases of some other defendants – because he did not agree with the majority justices about the basis of Hirota's conviction. "It is not entirely unwarranted to conjecture that Justice Röling wrote this dissenting opinion to save Hirota from the death penalty", the *Asahi* reporters commented, and added that "while it is perhaps unrelated to the present issue" (*honron towa mukankei de arōga*), Hirota had once served as ambassador to the Netherlands and that "rumor has it that a flower named 'Hirota Tulip' [*Hirota chūrippu*] still exists in the said country".[19] By this passing remark, the *Asahi* reporters implied that Röling was favourably disposed to leniency for Hirota, in part because of friendship Hirota had purportedly cultivated with the people of the Netherlands.

When it came to Pal's dissenting opinion, the *Asahi* reporters introduced it in a manner quite unlike any other separate opinions. Instead of maintaining the stance of a neutral observer, they praised the dissenting opinion for its bold and thoroughgoing criticism of the majority opinion. They particularly noted: 1) that the Indian member refused to be bound by the IMTFE Charter and criticised the victor nations for the "exceeding of authority" (*ekken*) by its issuance; 2) that he analysed various existing literature on international law "with thoroughness" (*amasutokoro naku*) before reaching his definitive conclusion on points of law; 3) that when assessing the charges of conspiracy, he delved into the modern history of

---

[17] Boister and Cryer, 2008, p. 742, see *supra* note 1; Asahi shinbun hōtei kishadan, 1962, vol. 2, p. 219, see *supra* note 5.

[18] For Hirota's brief biographical information and verdict, see Boister and Cryer, 2008, pp. 64–65, 603–4, see *supra* note 1.

[19] Asahi shinbun hōtei kishadan, 1962, vol. 2, p. 219, see *supra* note 5.

Japan since the time of *kaikoku* – the opening of Japan to the Western world in the mid-nineteenth century – through the Pacific War with "clarity and discernment" (*kaimei, dōsatsu*); 4) that he "criticised scathingly" (*koppidoku hihyō*) the tribunal's unfair application of the rules of evidence; and 5) that, as regards war crimes, he investigated the facts in "minute detail" (*kokumei ni*) and "set forth his argument concretely" (*gutaiteki ni tenkai*), before reaching the reasoned verdicts of not guilty.[20] Above all, the *Asahi* reporters praised Pal for his ability to think *beyond* the Tokyo Trial when contemplating the future of world peace, justice and the rule of law. The *Asahi* reporters quoted from the last segment of Pal's dissenting opinion in this connection, which partly read as follows:

> The name of justice should not be allowed to be invoked only for the prolongation of the pursuit of vindictive retaliation. The world is really in need of generous magnanimity and understanding charity. The real question arising in a genuinely anxious mind is, "can mankind grow up quickly enough to win the race between civilization and disaster".[21]

The *Asahi* reporters attached importance to the quote above, commenting that this particular passage urged one to turn one's attention to "the real big issues of international society".[22] By so stating, the *Asahi* reporters appeared to trivialise the historical significance of the Tokyo Trial and the majority judgment.

Assessments of the five separate opinions similar to those expressed by the *Asahi* reporters were repeated in other contemporaneous publications. *Kyōdō kenkyū: Pāru hanketsusho* (Collaborative Research: The Pal Judgment, 2 volumes), is one representative example. Published in 1966 by Tokyo Saiban Kenkyūkai ('Tokyo Trial Research Group'), *Kyōdō kenkyū* consisted of a complete translation of Pal's dissenting opinion and six analytical articles on its historical context and significance.[23] The pur-

---

20 *Ibid.*, pp. 346–47.

21 Boister and Cryer, 2008, p. 1425, see *supra* note 1; Asahi shinbun hōtei kishadan, 1962, vol. 2, p. 347, see *supra* note 5.

22 *Ibid.*

23 Tōkyō saiban kenkyūkai [The Tokyo Trial Research Group] (ed.), *Kyōdō kenkyū: Paru hanketsusho* [Collaborative Research: The Pal Judgment], 2 vols., Kōdansha, Tokyo, 1984. This was originally published in 1966. The research group was appointed by the Ministry of Legal Affairs in June 1964 to analyse and assess the records of war crimes trials that the ministry had collected in preceding years. The research group continued its activities until

pose of this publication appears to have been to improve public access to Pal's dissenting opinion and also to provide a forum for its scholarly discussion. However, the research group's handling of Pal's dissenting opinion is neither dispassionate nor impartial. The preface to *Kyōdō kenkyū*, for instance, introduced Pal's dissent as "the 'truthful text' that will endure in history in perpetuity" (*eien ni rekishi ni nokoru 'shinri no sho'*), on account of its offering a bold opinion on world peace, justice and the rule of law from the standpoint of "Eastern philosophy" (*Tōyō-teki tetsuri*). The research group particularly praised Pal for his open denunciation of the American use of atomic bombs "without regard to the potential threat to personal safety" (*mi ni furikakaru yamo shirenu kiken o kaerimizu*). The courage the Indian justice purportedly demonstrated impressed the members of the research group so much that they concluded Pal as being "comparable" to the towering seventeenth-century jurist of international law, Hugo Grotius.[24]

As regards other separate opinions, the research group of *Kyōdō kenkyū* did not have much to comment on. One of the articles for the volume by Ichimata Masao, a scholar of international law and a member of the research group, contained a mere 11-page summary of the remaining four separate opinions.[25] The general indifference to other separate opinions is best manifested in an off-hand remark by Ichimata that Webb's separate opinion, for one, was "nothing special" (*taishita mono dewa nai*), but perhaps "interesting when read as the opinion of the president [of the tribunal]".[26] The only thing Ichimata considered worth mentioning relative to this separate opinion was that Webb recognised "the emperor's

---

March 1969. For more information regarding this group, see Nakazato, 2011, pp. 215–25, see *supra* note 8.

[24] Tōkyō saiban kenkyūkai, 1984, vol. 1, p. 3, see *supra* note 23. Concerning the atomic bombs, Pal wrote in his dissenting opinion as follows: "As I have already pointed out, there were in evidence at the Nurnberg trial many orders, circulars and directives emanating from the major war criminals indicating that it was their policy to make war in such a reckless, ruthless way. We know that during the first World War, also, the German Emperor was charged with issuing directives like that. [...] In the Pacific war under our consideration, if there is anything approaching what is indicated in the above letter of the German emperor [authorising indiscriminate wholesale massacre of the civilian population], it is the decision coming from the allied powers to use the atom bomb". Boister and Cryer, 2008, pp. 1354–55, see *supra* note 1.

[25] Ichimata Masao, "Paru hanketsusho no naiyō" [The Substance of the Pal Judgment], in Tōkyō saiban kenkyūkai, 1984, vol. 1, pp. 119–30, see *supra* note 23.

[26] *Ibid.*, p. 120.

love of peace and the role he played in the termination of the war".[27] This remark is somewhat misplaced, however, as the relevant part in the actual separate opinion read: "In fairness to him [Emperor Hirohito] it should be stated that the evidence indicates that he was always in favour of peace, *but as he elected to play the part of a constitutional Monarch he accepted ministerial and other advice for war*, most probably against his better judgment".[28] In other words, Webb found the emperor responsible for the planning and waging of the war as well as ending it. But Webb did not mean to advocate the trial of the emperor; he simply recommended that the emperor's exemption from trial be taken into account when determining the sentences of his wartime subordinates. He was personally of the opinion that they should be spared of the death sentence.[29]

The Tokyo Trial Research Group, in this manner, celebrated Pal's dissenting opinion while relegating the rest of the judicial opinions arising from the Tokyo Trial to the realm of unimportance. That said, its members had certain misgivings about the quality of Pal's dissenting opinion. Nakazato Nariaki's path-breaking study of Pal's biography, *Paru hanji: Indo nashonarizumu to Tōkyō saiban* (Justice Pal: Indian Nationalism and the Tokyo Trial), shows that some actually expressed in private unflattering views on both stylistic and substantive aspects of the dissenting opinion.[30] For instance, Ichimata complained about the poor organisation of Pal's dissenting opinion, such as the repetitiveness and redundancy of arguments, and his frequent use of bulk quotations without much regard to their readability or materiality. Ichimata also expressed personal doubts about the impact of Pal's dissenting opinion in the field of international law. He predicted that, while this dissenting opinion had some merits, the larger legal community was likely to pay no attention to it.[31] A former navy officer and another member of the research group, Toyoda Kumao, commented meanwhile that those who became familiar with Pal's argu-

---

[27] *Ibid.*, p. 121.

[28] Boister and Cryer, 2008, p. 639, see *supra* note 1. Emphasis added.

[29] Webb indicated in his separate opinion that he did not intend to suggest the emperor should have been prosecuted. "That is beyond my province", he wrote. However, "this immunity of the Emperor, as contrasted with the part he played in launching the war in the Pacific, is I think a matter which this Tribunal should take into consideration in imposing sentences". Boister and Cryer, pp. 638–39, see *supra* note 1.

[30] Nakazato, 2011, pp. 220–23, see *supra* note 8.

[31] *Ibid.*, p. 221.

ment found it not only agreeable but also "slightly flattering" (*sukoshi kusuguttai*, literally, slightly tickling) because Pal defended the legality of the Japanese invasion of China and other neighbouring countries far more adamantly than the defence lawyers had done in the courtroom.[32] Another member of the research group, Bandō Junkichi, added that Hayashi Fusao, an author and a Japan apologist who was known for popularising the "affirmation of the Greater East Asia War thesis" (*dai-Tōa sensō kōtei-ron*), had not studied Pal's dissenting opinion well enough to make his case more compelling.[33] These comments did not converge onto any systematic critiquing of Pal's dissenting opinion. However, they show that the members of the research group had some doubts as to whether or not this dissenting opinion was, in fact, the "truthful judgment" of enduring consequences.

A number of books and articles that celebrated Pal's dissenting opinion in a similar manner as the *Asahi* reporters' *Tōkyō saiban* and the Tokyo Trial Research Group's *Kyōdō kenkyū* came in print in ensuing decades, and they remain highly influential in the Japanese debates on the Tokyo Trial. Not entirely satisfied with the established knowledge of Pal and his dissenting opinion, however, some scholars took new lines of inquiry into the life of the Indian justice and his dissenting opinion. Three scholars deserve mention. One of them is Higurashi Yoshinobu, a leading scholar of the Tokyo Trial in Japan today. Higurashi made his debut in the field in the late 1980s when he published several research pieces that explored international politics, law and diplomacy surrounding the Tokyo Trial. One of his early publications, "Paru hanketsu saikō: Tōkyō saiban ni okeru bekko iken no kokusai kankyō" (Rethinking the Pal Judgment: The International Environment of the Separate Opinion at the Tokyo Trial), investigated the circumstances of Pal's appointment to the IMTFE, his relationship with other members of the same tribunal, the substance of Pal's dissent, and its impacts on the British and Indian foreign policies. A main scholarly contribution of this piece was that it elucidated two contradictory intellectual currents that ran through Pal's dissenting opinion. One of them is narrow legalism – or "legal empiricism" (*hō jisshō shugi*) to use Higurashi's words – and the other is a strand of anti-Western imperialism. Higurashi argued: "In Pal's logic, there is an intermingling of the

---

[32]   *Ibid.*, p. 222.

[33]   *Ibid.*

minute legal technicality [on the one hand] and pronounced politicisation [on the other]", and that this commingling of contradictory ideas "confuses the observers". Consequently, the interpretative position one takes could be at variance with another depending on which aspect of "these constitutive elements" one would attach importance.[34] Pal's dissent may thus be regarded as a doggedly legalistic judicial opinion that advanced conservative interpretations of the law *or* a political tract that offered a heavy-handed critique of Western imperialism.

Ushimura Kei, a professor of comparative literature and intellectual history at the International Research Center for Japanese Studies, shed further light on the second of the two intellectual currents that were pointed out in Higurashi's article. In his book, *"Bunmei no sabaki" o koete: Tai-Nichi senpan saiban dokkai no kokoromi* (Beyond the "Trial in the Name of Civilisation": A Reading of the War Crimes Trials Brought against the Japanese),[35] Ushimura drew upon the existing scholarship on Orientalism and argued that the core issue of the dissenting opinion was not so much to advance the "Japan is not guilty thesis" as to question the validity of the Western *paradigm* on civilisation. The prosecution at the Tokyo Trial claimed to be trying and punishing the Japanese war criminals in the name of civilisation. According to Ushimura's interpretation, Pal questioned *that very premise* of the prosecution, and deemed the Tokyo proceedings nothing but "ritualised vengeance" (*gishikika sareta fukushū*).[36]

Nakazato Nariaki, a professor emeritus at the University of Tokyo and a scholar of the modern history of South Asia, explored in the aforementioned *Paru hanji* the Indian justice's intellectual biography in relation to twentieth-century Bengali nationalism. Pal is commonly known in the existing Japanese-language historical literature as a Gandhian pacifist, but Nakazato's study cast doubts on this assumption. In his account of

---

[34] Higurashi Yoshinobu, "Paru hanketsu saikō: Tōkyō saiban ni okeru bekko iken no kokusai kankyō" [Rethinking the Pal Judgment: The International Environment of the Separate Opinion at the Tokyo Trial], in Itō Takashi (ed.), *Nihon kindaishi no saikōchiku* [Reconstruction of the Modern History of Japan], Yamakawa shuppansha, Tokyo, 1993, p. 399.

[35] Ushimura Kei, *"Bunmei no sabaki" o koete: tai-Nichi senpan saiban dokkai no lokoromi* [Beyond the "Trial in the Name of Civilisation": A Reading of War Crimes Trials Brought against the Japanese], Chuokoron shinsha, Tokyo, 2000.

[36] *Ibid.*, p. 187.

Pal's intellectual biography, Nakazato shed light on Pal as a typical Bengali jurist of his time who 1) identified himself with the Bengali colonial elite known as *bhadralok*; 2) aligned closely with the anti-communist, radical Hindu nationalist movement in the region of Bengal; and 3) was generally unsympathetic to the plight of the Chinese people under Japanese military control. On the last point, Nakazato observed that the Bengali elite in those years tended to identify itself with a powerful Asian nation such as Japan while commonly holding China with contempt for its relative weakness. This, in Nakazato's opinion, was "an expression of the colonial elite's warped consciousness".[37] Given the prevailing intellectual current of the Bengali elite, and given the ideological stance of Pal personally, Nakazato found it hardly surprising when Pal defended the Japanese war policy vis-à-vis China and insisted on its legality.

Nakazato's study also questioned the common belief that Pal was a qualified jurist in international law. The biographical records Nakazato scrutinised rather produced no evidence that Pal had any expert knowledge on international law prior to joining the Tokyo Tribunal. Pal did make a career as an international law jurist after the Tokyo Trial, that is, by way of accepting the nomination to serve as a member of the International Law Commission of the United Nations. He served in the commission from 1952 until his death in 1967, as well as accepting the appointment as its chair between 1958 and 1962.[38] Even so, Nakazato's study showed that Pal made no constructive contribution to furthering the development of international law. Pal generally abstained from voting when the commission deliberated new proposals that aimed at consolidating the legal principles arising from Nuremberg and Tokyo in statutory form. If anything, he *opposed* such proposals on grounds that the international community had not developed sufficiently to guarantee fair trial to accused persons at international criminal trials. According to Nakazato, the image of Justice Pal that emerged from the records of proceedings at the International Law Commission was "a jurist who had scant interest in issues of peace or human rights but extremely sensitive on the issues of state rights".[39]

---

[37] Nakazato, 2011, p. 137, see *supra* note 8.

[38] *Ibid.*, p. 173.

[39] *Ibid.*, p. 182.

As the studies of Pal's dissenting opinion gained greater depth over time, fresh research initiatives concerning the rest of judicial opinions gathered some momentum. B.V.A. Röling, formerly the Dutch member of the Tokyo Tribunal, can be counted as one of the contributors in the new initiatives. He was one of the three dissenting justices who expressed deep misgivings about the laws applied at the Tokyo Trial, especially those pertaining to crimes against peace. However, he came to fashion himself in the post-trial period as a jurist-cum-peace activist, advocating the importance of advancing the legal principles arising from the Nuremberg and Tokyo proceedings. The post-trial transformation in Röling's intellectual outlook is evidenced in the special lecture he delivered at an international symposium on the Tokyo Trial, held at the capital of Japan in 1983 to mark the thirty-fifth anniversary of the Tokyo judgment. Röling was the keynote speaker at the event.[40]

He stated during his lecture that "notwithstanding several negative aspects of the verdicts of Nuremberg and Tokyo, they did undeniably contribute to a legal development that mankind urgently needed". He went on to point out that the United Nations adopted the principles set out by the two tribunals thereafter, and that, consequently, "the crime against peace has become an accepted component of international law".[41] When asked by the audience about his opinion regarding Pal who "adopted the dispassionate objectivity that informed his quest for peace", Röling replied that Pal's dissent was "a more or less belated reaction against the [Western] aggressive wars by which the [Western] colonial system was established centuries ago".[42] While expressing respect for Pal's position, Röling characterised Pal's opinion to be backward-looking that failed to appreciate the contribution of the Tokyo Trial in strengthening the international peace mechanism. As he put it, "I think Pal's judgment is understandable if we look at the past, but not when we look at the future".[43] This remark is significant, since Röling was implicitly presenting to the audience an

---

[40] Hosoya Chihiro, Andō Nisuke, Ōnuma Yasuaki, and Richard H. Minear (eds.), *The Tokyo War Crimes Trial: An International Symposium*, Kodansha International, Tokyo, 1986. For the original Japanese, see Hosoya Chihiro, Andō Nisuke and Ōnuma Yasuaki (eds.), *Kokusai shinpojiumu: Tōkyō saiban o tou* [The International Symposium: Questioning the Tokyo Trial], Kōdansha, Tokyo, 1984.

[41] *Ibid.*, p. 132.

[42] *Ibid.*, p. 152.

[43] *Ibid.*, p. 153.

alternative to rallying around Pal in advancing the post-war pacifist agenda. Röling's version of pacifism did not appear to impress the audience, however, as this particular point elicited no follow-up questions. Instead, Röling had to field such queries as to whether or not he could verify various procedural defects and misjudgments that were believed to have occurred at the Tokyo Trial.[44]

Research initiatives in more recent years shed light on other judges whose contributions to the making of the majority opinion and the separate opinions have been overlooked. Higurashi Yoshinobu can be credited once again in this regard. In his *Tōkyō saiban to kokusai kankei: Kokusai seiji ni okeru kenryoku to kihan* (The Tokyo Trial and International Relations: Power and Norm in International Politics), he explored archival materials in Australia, Britain and the United States to bring to light the complex internal workings of the IMTFE and to trace how the majority justices coalesced.[45] Higurashi's work showed 1) that the president of the tribunal, Webb, and the rest of the justices had a rocky relationship from early on, due partly to conflicting legal positions concerning crimes against peace, and due partly to personality differences; 2) that the possibility of split judgment was present from the start, because the Indian member refused to sign an agreement not to publicise the individual members' opinions or votes should there be any differences;[46] and 3) that, after much soul searching, the British member Lord Patrick acted as a mediator to put together the majority and prevent the tribunal from falling into utter disintegration.

---

[44] *Ibid.*, pp. 154–56. For other commentaries that shed light on the Japanese reception of Röling at the time of the international symposium, see also Ōnuma Yasuaki, *Tōkyō saiban kara sengo sekinin no shisō* [From the Tokyo Trial to Thoughts on Post-war Responsibility], Tōshinsha, Tokyo, 1987, pp. 80–84; Hosoya Chihiro, "Tōkyō saiban Oranda daihyō hanji no shōgen" [Testimony of the Justice Representing the Netherlands at the Tokyo Trial], *Chūō kōron*, July 1983, pp. 142–43; and Bernard Röling, "Yuiitsu no bunkan shiikei hikoku, Hirota Kōki o saishin suru" [Reviewing the Case of Hirota Kōki, the Only Civilian Accused Sentenced to Death], *Chūō kōron*, July 1983, pp. 144–62.

[45] Higurashi Yoshinobu, *Tōkyō saiban no kokusai kankei: Kokusai seiji ni okeru kenryoku to kihan* [The Tokyo Trial and International Relations: Power and Norm in International Politics], Bokutakusha, Tokyo, 2002. See also Higurashi Yoshinobu, *Tōkyō saiban* [The Tokyo Trial], Kōdansha, Tokyo, 2008.

[46] Higurashi, 2002, p. 407, see *supra* note 45. See also Higurashi, 1993, p. 389, *supra* note 34; and Nakazato, 2011, pp. 102–3, *supra* note 8.

Nagai Hitoshi, a leading scholar of the Philippine war crimes programme, has also contributed to the study of the Tokyo Trial by bringing back Justice Jaranilla into the picture. Titled "Wasurerareta Tōkyō saiban Firipin hanji: Derufin Haranīrya hanji no shōgai" (The Forgotten Philippine Justice at the Tokyo Trial: The Life of Delfin Jaranilla), Nagai's research piece showed 1) that Jaranilla was a jurist of considerable legal experience in his home country; 2) that he was also a man of high social and political standing in the Philippines; and 3) that, while being a survivor of the Bataan Death March, he maintained a high degree of professionalism and attitude of impartiality throughout the Tokyo proceedings. Moreover, Nagai found Jaranilla's legal positions as expressed in the concurring opinion to be generally sound.[47] But one aspect of the concurring opinion bothered him. It pertained to Jaranilla's approval of the American use of the atomic bombs. With a tone of reproach, Nagai remarked that Jaranilla was sensitive to the sufferings of the victims of Japanese atrocities but failed to make an objective judgment on matters of the atomic bombs, possibly because "he was trapped in the [victim] mentality of the [Philippines'] colonial period".[48]

Ōoka Yūichirō is relatively new to the study of the Tokyo Trial, but he made an important contribution to the field by way of producing a biography of the French justice Bernard, titled *Tōkyō saiban: Furansujin hanji no muzairon* (The Tokyo Trial: The Not Guilty Thesis by the French Justice). Ōoka was well positioned to undertake this particular book project as he had years of experience living and working in France as a journalist, was fluent in the French language, and had an in-depth appreciation of the French people, culture and politics. Based on extensive archival research and fieldwork, Ōoka brought to light Bernard's unique upbringing as a would-be Jesuit priest in his youth and his subsequent career as a prosecutor in French Africa prior to serving as a member of the Tokyo Tribunal. According to Ōoka, certain idiosyncrasies in Bernard's dissenting opinion can be explained partly by Bernard's insistence on representing the voice of France in the international arena, on the one hand, and his personal propensity to position himself as a perpetual outsider vis-à-vis

---

[47] Nagai Hitoshi, "Wasurerareta Tōkyō saiban Firipin hanji: Derufin Haranīrya hanji no shōgai" [The Forgotten Philippine Justice at the Tokyo Trial: The Life of Delfin Jaranilla], in Awaya Kentarō (ed.), *Kingendai Nihon no sensō to heiwa* [War and Peace in Modern Japan], Gendai shiryō shuppan, Tokyo, 2011.

[48] *Ibid.*, p. 344.

the mainstream, on the other. By illustration, Bernard affirmed in his dissenting opinion the validity of the charges of crimes against peace but on a legal ground entirely different from the one recognised by the Anglo-American countries, thus continuing the time-honoured French tradition of being a good "ally but without conforming" (*dōmei suredomo dōchō sezu*.[49] By the same token, Bernard criticised the majority justices for faulty deliberation processes but refrained from specifying the problems, *thereby* straining French relations with its Anglo-American allies but never breaking them. In short, Ōoka found French exceptionalism as the defining characteristic of Bernard's dissenting opinion and its major intellectual contribution to the Tokyo Trial.

3.2. Concluding Remarks

This chapter has explored a representative range of Japanese-language publications on the Tokyo Trial in order to bring to light the Japanese assessments of the five separate concurring and dissenting opinions. It has been shown that the Japanese people gained familiarity with the gist of each separate opinion from early on, but that substantive discussions have been rather limited. As of today, studies of the separate opinions remain underdeveloped despite the passage of nearly seven decades since the conclusion of the Tokyo Trial. It is true that scholars such as Higurashi and Nakazato broke new ground in their cutting-edge research of Pal's intellectual biography. Nagai and Ōoka, too, can be credited for bringing back into the picture Justices Jaranilla and Bernard respectively, and hence broadening the horizon of the Japanese understanding of the separate opinions. It may be a matter of time before new research initiatives will be taken on biographies of Röling and Webb as well. However, it is also true that what has animated the Japanese research of separate opinions is their political and ideological content, and not so much the *judicial* one. The task for the future researchers is to go beyond these conceptual limitations, and produce a more balanced assessment of the separate opinions and their contributions to the making of the Tokyo Trial.

---

[49] Ōoka Yūichirō, *Tōkyō saiban: Furansujin hanji no muzairon* [The Tokyo Trial: The Not Guilty Thesis by the French Justice], Bungei shunjū, Tokyo, 2012, p. 22.

4

Dissent at Tokyo: The Opinion of Justice Henri Bernard at the International Military Tribunal for the Far East

David Cohen[*]

It is one of the striking features of the scholarship on the trial of major Japanese war criminals before the International Military Tribunal for the Far East ('IMTFE') that there has been so little scholarly analysis of the separate opinions published alongside the majority judgment. To be sure reference is often made to the fact that there were five dissenting and concurring opinions promulgated alongside that of the majority of seven judges (out of 11) that produced the final judgment of the tribunal. The most famous (or infamous) of these five opinions is that of the Judge Radhabinod Pal of India who announced before the trial began that he would dissent and, true to his word, produced a thousand-page dissenting opinion that bears more similarity to a political tract than to a judicial document. Pal was elevated to the status of a heroic figure in post-war Japan and second place was accorded to Judge B.V.A. Röling of the Netherlands who was lauded for having argued in his dissenting opinion that five of the accused, and most notably former foreign ministers Hirota Kōki and Shigemitsu Mamoru, should have been acquitted. Critics of the Tokyo Trial who take Röling as one of their champions tend to overlook that, while dissenting on these five defendants, Röling agreed with the majority that all the others should have been convicted and nine of them

[*] **David Cohen** is Director of the WSD HANDA Center in Human Rights and International Justice at Stanford University, USA, where he is also a Distinguished Visiting Fellow at the Hoover Institution. He is Professor of Law at the University of Hawaii School of Law, where he co-directs the Center for ASEAN Law and Integration. He taught at the University of California Berkeley from 1979 to 2012 as the Ancker Distinguished Professor for the Humanities and the founding Director of the War Crimes Studies Center (which moved to Stanford as the WSD HANDA Center in 2013). He now holds the title of Professor in the Graduate School at UC Berkeley. At the East-West Center he is Director of the Asian International Justice Initiative and Senior Fellow in International Law.

sentenced to death. While much is made of these two dissenting opinions their legal content has rarely been seriously analysed. They are viewed more from the standpoint of the result they reached than the legal justifications for those results.

There was, of course, a third dissenting opinion, that of Justice Henri Bernard of France. From a jurisprudential standpoint it is at least as interesting as those of Röling and Pal but has been largely neglected. This is likely due to the fact that it does not provide ammunition for the critics of the tribunal in the way that the opinions of Pal and Röling are felt to. The two other separate opinions, those of the Australian Justice Sir William F. Webb, the president of the tribunal, and of Judge Delfin J. Jaranilla of the Philippines, are also rarely accorded serious attention. Even more neglected is the most interesting of all the separate opinions, which is the massive unpublished opinion of Webb, which he had hoped to be the majority judgment, but which was not accepted as such by enough of his colleagues. Webb decided, for reasons that go beyond the scope of this chapter, to submit a vastly shorter version of his separate opinion and to withdraw the more than 600-page draft he had prepared.

An assessment of the Tokyo Trial, and particularly of how the tribunal reached its final decision, demands that proper attention be paid to the legal content of the majority judgment and of all the separate opinions. Aside from the political polemics that have too often obscured the legal issues at stake in the proceedings, the Tokyo Trial was a judicial process to determine the guilt or innocence of 25 individuals accused of the most serious international crimes. It was the obligation of the tribunal to reach a verdict on each of these individuals and it is on the basis of how they justified those verdicts, as well as the fairness of the trial process as measured by international fair trial standards, that the performance of the judges must be assessed. Under international fair trial standards and due process, as well as under fundamental principles of judicial ethics, it was the duty of the IMTFE to provide a reasoned account of how it reached its decisions on each of the accused individuals based upon a careful analysis and weighing of the evidence presented by the prosecution and the defence, leading to factual findings on all of the elements of all of the charges. It is also the obligation of a reasoned final decision to clearly articulate the applicable legal standards and explain how these standards were applied to the factual findings so as to reach ultimate decisions of guilt or innocence.

As noted above, the majority judgment has seldom been analysed according to such criteria. Likewise, the legal content of the separate opinions has been significantly neglected. This chapter examines the separate opinion of Justice Bernard because of all the separate opinions it has received the least attention. At the same time, the opinion of Bernard sheds light on internal differences among the judges as to some of the most fundamental jurisprudential issues before the court. It also reveals the way in which the legal culture of these 11 judges from such disparate backgrounds shaped the way they viewed such issues. While Bernard's separate opinion may not have had the political impact as those of Pal and Röling, it is striking that it did not. For the thrust of Bernard's objection to the proceedings at the IMTFE is that the Japanese emperor was not also on trial. This uncomfortable fact for many Japanese critics of the trial may explain why Bernard has received so much less attention than Röling and Pal. The grounds of this neglect are also interesting because Bernard's opinion is in some ways similar to those of Pal and Röling in offering an alternative account of the basis of international law and the conceptual and philosophical foundations of the very idea of international justice. For this reason alone it should compel our attention.

At the outset of his opinion Bernard rejects the defence and Pal arguments on the legitimacy of the tribunal. He states that the Allied nations were, by virtue of the criminal nature of the war waged by Japan, "perfectly qualified to create the International Military Tribunal for the Far East". He also finds that the charge of "victors' justice" is without merit because 1) the Allies created a tribunal and turned the accused over to them; 2) there was no alternative mechanism because of the lack of an international authority; and 3) the Allies provided the procedural basis for a fair trial. He concludes his discussion of the issue of the legitimacy of the IMTFE by saying that failure to create such a court "would have deprived the world of a verdict, the necessity of which is universally felt".[1] It is small wonder that critics of the tribunal prefer to focus on Pal and generally ignore the salient points made by Bernard which discredit him. This is also the case because, as will appear, the central thrust of Ber-

---

[1] Henri Bernard, "The Dissenting Opinion of the Member for France", in Robert Cryer and Neil Boister (eds.), *Documents on the Tokyo International Military Tribunal: Charter, Indictment and Judgment*, Oxford University Press, Oxford, 2008, p. 665.

nard's objections to the outcome of the tribunal's proceedings is that Emperor Hirohito was not the principal defendant.

Bernard, like Webb in his unpublished judgment, criticises the position taken by the majority on conspiracy. He finds that the majority erred in dismissing the counts of the indictment on planning and preparation of aggressive war on the grounds that findings of guilt on conspiracy subsume the other modes of liability. On Bernard's view, "planning and preparation are more serious matters than the mere conspiracy; consequently they must be taken into consideration by the Tribunal and should be taken as the basis for conviction if found established".[2] Bernard's view seems to proceed from the position that sole reliance on the vague notion of conspiracy obscures the nature of the accused's individual participation in the crimes of which they have been found guilty. When he states that planning and preparation are "more serious" than "mere" conspiracy he points to the different gravity that may be attached to different modes of liability.

His argument, though not articulated in detail, seems to be that subsuming all accused in a grand conspiracy, and at the same time refraining from making specific findings on counts of the indictment that charge specific modes of conduct by which crimes were perpetrated, makes it difficult to fairly assess the culpability of individual accused. Such culpability should, of course, be based upon factual findings that establish the role of each individual in planning, perpetrating, instigating, waging and so on. The majority's conspiracy theory obscures this. Bernard is indeed correct that taking part in the actual planning and preparation of an aggressive war is more serious than merely being part of a group that has agreed that Japan should wage such a war. Such differential roles should be reflected in sentencing and should be based upon factual findings that support the conclusions about the culpability of each accused. In this regard, as argued above, the majority judgment is sorely deficient.

A major thrust of Bernard's judgment, and one of its most interesting aspects, bears not upon the findings of guilt or innocence, but upon the majority's position on the foundation of the law of the tribunal. According to Bernard, the majority position is that objections made by the defence to the jurisdiction of the tribunal (and echoed by Pal) must be re-

---

2   *Ibid.*, p. 666.

jected because "the law of the Charter is decisive and binding".[3] These objections include that aggressive war is not illegal, that there is no individual responsibility for war, and that the IMTFE Charter is *ex post facto* legislation and thus itself illegal.

The majority judgment addresses objections to the legitimacy and jurisdiction of the tribunal through a lengthy citation of the Nuremberg judgment which bases the binding nature of the Charter on the "sovereign legislative power" of the victorious Allies to whom Germany unconditionally surrendered. Although Bernard, as indicated above, recognises the right of the Allies to convene such a tribunal, he nonetheless believes that there is a foundation for what he calls the "substantive law" of the tribunal that transcends such "legislative" authority.[4] Bernard, in articulating this view, goes beyond the Nuremberg judgment's discussion of the evolution of international law in the first half of the twentieth century as the basis for the criminalisation of aggressive war. Implicitly rejecting this justification rooted in legal positivism he invokes another, and on his view higher, source of law.

The Nuremberg judgment went beyond the statement of the binding nature of the Charter and elaborated at some length upon the justification for establishing aggressive war as a crime. It explained this manner of proceeding by indicating that even though the Charter was legitimate and binding the issues raised by the defence objections were important for international law. The majority judgment does not engage in such an extended jurisprudential discussion, though Webb does so in his unpublished draft judgment. It is the majority's bald reliance on the Charter alone that is the focus of Bernard's objection.[5]

How, then, does Bernard justify his position that aggressive war is indeed an international crime and a crime for which there is individual criminal responsibility? In contradistinction to the approach of the majority and of Webb, he turns to the European tradition of natural law jurisprudence. He rejects the majority's view that in accepting appointment as a judge at the IMTFE they accept the validity of all of the substantive law

---

[3]   *Ibid.*, p. 668.

[4]   *Ibid.*

[5]   Bernard acknowledges that the majority at times indicates its awareness of other grounds but he argues that the positivistic reliance on the IMTFE Charter is the real basis of its position. *Ibid.*, p. 669.

articulated by the Charter. On Bernard's view such legitimacy must be measured against a higher source of law and not, for example, on interpretation of the Pact of Paris and so on. His position is quite clear:

> There is no doubt in my mind that such war is and always has been a crime in the eyes of reason and universal conscience, – expressions of natural law upon which an international tribunal can *and must* base itself to judge the conduct of the accused tendered to it.[6]

Bernard goes even further, however, and maintains that it is natural law, and not the Charter, which also establishes the responsibility of individuals for state organised criminality:

> There is no doubt either that the individual cannot shelter behind the responsibility of the community the responsibility which he incurred by his own acts. Assuming there exists collective responsibility, obviously the latter can only be added to the individual responsibility and cannot eliminate the same. It is because they are inscribed in natural law and not in the constitutive acts of the Tribunal by the writers of the Charter, *whose honor it is, however, to have recalled them*, that those principles impose themselves upon the respect of the Tribunal.[7]

With regard to the substantive issue of the legitimacy of charging aggressive war as an international crime for which there is individual responsibility, Bernard is in complete agreement with the majority and with Webb. It is in regard to how this position is justified that he dissents. He reverts to the natural law tradition in maintaining that the judges of the IMTFE are only "recalling" principles already grounded in an eternal natural order. He does not elaborate upon the philosophical basis of such claims but it is clear that he is both standing in a certain European tradition and also that his position must be seen in the context of jurisprudential debates that raged in the post-war years over the status of the positive law as against higher principles of justice. In attacking the legitimacy of, for example, the laws of the Nazi regime, scholars such as Gustav Radbruch and others turned to the natural law tradition to argue that an unjust and iniquitous law is not a law at all and may be set aside. Bernard stands in this tradition in claiming that the legitimacy of the IMTFE and of the

---

6   *Ibid.*, p. 670. Emphasis added.
7   *Ibid.* Emphasis added.

law it applied can only be found in the "higher" sphere of natural law and universal reason.[8]

One of the most substantial sections of Bernard's opinion concerns conventional war crimes. The first sentence of this section makes clear his differences with Pal and why his judgment is generally not examined by those who take a revisionist view:

> There can be no doubt that *on all steps of its hierarchy* the members of the Japanese Army and Police made themselves guilty of the most abominable crimes in respect to the prisoners of war, internees and civilians of occupied territories.[9]

Bernard then goes on to focus on crimes against prisoners of war and criticises not holding the accused liable for such mistreatment but rather the legal grounds on which the majority relies. He agrees with the majority that the four groups specified in the majority judgment can be held liable for such crimes:

> (1) Members of the Government; (2) Military or Naval officers in command of formations having prisoners in their possession; (3) [...]; (4) officials, *whether civilian, military, or naval*, having direct and immediate control of prisoners.[10]

He disagrees, however, that Article IV of the Hague Convention IV of 1907 provides the correct legal basis for their liability and he further disagrees with the majority's reasoning as to what conditions are required to hold members of the specified groups accountable.[11] Although his interpretation of Article IV is implausible and unconvincing, his critique of the majority's reasoning is far more well founded.[12] As will appear, the real

---

8   See, for example, Gustav Radbruch, *Rechtsphilosophie*, 4th ed., Koehler, Stuttgart, 1950 and in the Anglo-American context the famous Hart-Fuller debate. For an overview of the literature and issues in regard to the legal legacy of the Nazi era, see Christian Joerges and Navraj Singh Ghaleigh (eds.), *Darker Legacies of Law in Europe: The Shadow of National Socialism and Fascism over Europe and its Legal Tradition*, Hart Publishing, Oxford, 2003.

9   Bernard, 2008, p. 671, see *supra* note 1.

10 *Ibid.*, p. 671. Emphasis added.

11 *Ibid.*, pp. 671–73.

12 Bernard, without providing any reasoning to back up his assertion, interprets the provision that prisoners of war "are in the power of the hostile government but not of the individuals or corps who capture them" to mean that those individuals or corps who capture the pris-

reason for rejecting the majority's citation of Article IV appears to be that Bernard prefers to rely on natural law rather than international statutory law as the basis for assessing liability.

Bernard's analysis of the defects of the majority's reasoning follows a similar line as to his objections to the exclusive focus on conspiracy in regard to proving crimes against peace: the lack of individuation with regard to the specific conduct and specific culpability of each accused person before the tribunal. His disagreement with the majority is well founded. He objects to the majority's generalisation of liability based upon institutional position rather than individual conduct and argues that culpability, and hence appropriate sentencing, must differ from individual to individual. One sees here again how much better served the tribunal would have been in adopting the Webb draft judgment as it, to a significant degree, addresses precisely Bernard's concerns.

The essence of Bernard's analysis is that "no-one can be held responsible for other than the necessary consequences of his own acts or omissions". In regard to omissions, for example the crucial category for failure to prevent mistreatment of prisoners of war, Bernard correctly argues that an attribution of responsibility must rely upon "proving that the author of the omission could by an action of some kind prevent the commission and its direct harmful consequences".[13] That an individual cannot be punished for the acts of others of which he had no knowledge or was powerless to prevent is well established not only in the contemporary jurisprudence of the international criminal tribunals but also in fundamental principles of criminal law. The greatest failing of the Yamashita Tomoyuki case was that the prosecution absolutely failed to prove either that Yamashita was aware that crimes were being committed or that it would have been in his power to prevent the crimes that were perpetrated by various Japanese forces scattered across the Philippines. Bernard points to the failure of the majority to provide factual findings on these issues for each of the accused who were convicted of such war crimes charges. Bernard specifically and justifiably rejects the imputation of knowledge to all of these accused on the general grounds that the crimes were widespread. He correctly holds: "No general rule can be made upon

---

oners have absolutely no responsibility for any war crimes which they perpetrate against them. *Ibid.*, p. 671.

[13]   *Ibid.*, p. 673.

this point and proof that omission is the cause of harm done must be furnished in each case by the prosecution".[14] In other words, he rejects the general categorisation of classes of individuals who can be held liable by virtue of their positions and places the burden upon the prosecution of making the case against each of them.

Unlike the majority or Pal, Bernard articulates a clear standard of liability based upon what he takes to be established principles of criminal jurisprudence and natural law, to which he again reverts.[15] He maintains that there are two bases on which guilt may be established for the failure to prevent mistreatment. Although the first basis could be far more clearly formulated, in essence it provides that when a person is accused of a failure to prevent war crimes it must be proved that 1) he or she was able to prevent the commission of the crimes – no legal presumption suffices to establish such proof; 2) the crimes must be the direct result of their omission or negligence. The second basis of liability is more clearly formulated and provides that an individual may be held liable for a failure of duty to protect prisoners of war when their imprudence, negligence or disregard of regulations or orders "created a state of fact suited to the multiplication of violations of the laws of war".[16] In concluding the discussion of this section on conventional war crimes we should note that Bernard focused only on prisoners of war and did not consider crimes against the other two groups he mentioned at the beginning of the section. Given that he there indicated his conviction that Japanese forces were also responsible for the most serious crimes against these groups we are left in the dark as to whether he also had disagreements with the approach of the majority on convictions for such crimes.

The most striking feature of Bernard's standard of liability, however, is that he provides no basis for it either in international practice and custom or in the considerable body of conventional law represented by the Hague and Geneva Conventions. Considering that Japan had declared that it would respect the 1929 Geneva Convention on Prisoners of War one would have thought it appropriate that Bernard would at least refer to its

---

[14] *Ibid.*

[15] He concludes this section on conventional war crimes by criticising the view that the treaties, conventions, and customary law encompass the whole of the legal sphere that applies to the regulation of conflict. He points to the universal and natural law "exists outside and above nations". *Ibid.*, p. 674.

[16] *Ibid.*

provisions. He does not. What he does instead is to refer again to natural law as what he takes to be the proper basis for adjudicating war criminality. Needless to say, he does not cite any authority whatsoever either for the general applicability of natural law or for the specific standards of liability that he articulates. Indeed, his position is baffling in its scope: "Several times in expressing my opinion I preferred the expression of natural or universal law to that of international law".[17]

Bernard here appears to venture into metaphysical terrain with his apparent disdain for the body of international legal doctrine. For his twin proposition that the natural law is higher and "above nations" and that concrete norms to define offences and theories of responsibility can somehow be derived from it, he provides no argument, citation or foundation. He contents himself with the sole remark that although there are differences of opinion as to the nature of natural law, "its existence is not seriously contested *or contestable* and the *declaration* of its existence is sufficient for our purpose".[18]

Bernard's assertion that the mere "declaration" of natural law suffices and cannot be contested indicates that he leans on the natural law tradition that is grounded in faith and belief in a metaphysical higher authority. It is beyond the scope of this analysis to assess the biographical origins of Bernard's approach. More salient for present purposes is Bernard's apparent conviction that he can simply sweep away any discussion of international law jurisprudence with a vague reference to metaphysics. When he states that natural law as the basis for substantive law is not "seriously contested or contestable" he also ignores major traditions of legal philosophy that do precisely that. Indeed, in Bernard's epoch theories of legal positivism, associated with figures like Hans Kelsen but going back much further in the European tradition, were in the ascendancy and it is perhaps for this reason that he wanted to make a stand against it for reasons briefly alluded to above. In any event, it is clear that Bernard stands apart from all of his fellow judges in his belief that the tribunal does have the authority to punish individuals for crimes against peace and for war crimes but that this authority, and the doctrines through which it is implemented, derive not from charters, declarations, conventions or custom, but rather from the metaphysical realm of natural and universal law.

---

[17] *Ibid.*

[18] *Ibid.* Emphasis added.

Thus far, Bernard's dissent has supported the legitimacy of the tribunal and of the charges against the accused. He has provided alternative rationales for the proceedings but has not challenged the results. The final two sections of his dissenting opinion, however, do just that. In the penultimate section, "Opinion relative to the Proceedings of the Tribunal", Bernard articulates three grounds on which the fairness of the trial might be contested. What is perhaps most peculiar about these grounds is that they are not based upon any reference to the "natural and universal law" which he has previously emphasised as the ultimate and authoritative source of applicable norms.

The first objection made by Bernard is striking in its narrowly chauvinistic view of justice and fair trial rights. Bernard argues that principles of justice have been violated because the tribunal did not employ an investigating judge to collect and analyse the evidence for both prosecution and defence. Bernard's apparent belief that only the French civil law procedural provisions can deliver a fair trial is baffling in its insularity and implication that all trials conducted under the common law and other civil law systems which do not follow the French civil law model are inherently and inescapably unfair. It is also striking that Bernard relies here not upon a reference to his "preferred" standard of natural law but rather upon the positivistic national institutional arrangements of particular countries (unless, of course he believes that the French system derives from divine law, but he does not say so). The inherent contradiction is clear.

The second objection made by Bernard has a valid political foundation, but Bernard cites neither legal authority nor natural law as its basis. Bernard argues that the prosecution of the accused was "unequal" because Emperor Hirohito was not among those indicted. While I wholeheartedly agree on the substance of his claim that Hirohito should have been among the accused, Bernard makes no plausible or reasoned argument as to why it was unjust to convict those who were in fact demonstrated to be guilty of what he himself calls "the most abominable crimes".[19] Here he appears to confuse the political and moral objections that might be made to exclusion of Hirohito with legal standards of fair trial rights. Where, one might ask, is there a recognised norm in international or domestic criminal law that if one individual potentially implicated in a crime is not indicted then

---

[19] *Ibid.*, p. 671.

no one else can be brought to trial for the same or related crimes? Further, at the time of the IMTFE judgment there was no bar to subsequent prosecutions against other class A war criminals, including the emperor.[20]

Bernard's third and final ground is also puzzling. The essence of his objection on the grounds of fair trial rights was that "the eleven judges which compose the Tribunal were never called to meet" to orally discuss the judgment.[21] Bernard explains that a committee of seven prepared a draft majority judgment and that the opinions of the other judges were distributed among all the judges for comment. In fact, the archival records of the tribunal provide us with a substantial body of such memoranda that commented upon, proposed revisions for and debated many parts of this draft judgment. Those participating in that exercise included Bernard. Bernard acknowledges this and also notes that the majority in fact modified parts of their judgment in response to such suggestions. He also notes that drafts of two dissenting opinions were also circulated.[22] He provides no legal basis whatsoever for the assertion that the lack of an oral deliberation of all the judges violated fundamental principles of fair trial rights to such a degree to invalidate the proceedings as a whole.

In sum, none of the three procedural grounds which Bernard views as such serious violations of fair trial rights that they invalidate the proceedings has a firm legal basis. One is rooted in a blind belief in the unique superiority of the French system, seemingly unaware of the serious objections that had been raised inside and outside France of its fairness to the rights of the accused. The second is a political critique of the decision to try Japan's political and military leaders without Hirohito and offers no legal basis for claiming this as a violation of fair trial rights and due process. The third has no basis whatsoever either in the IMTFE Charter or in international law. One is left to wonder whether perhaps Bernard simply felt slighted or left out when the majority did not accept his eccentric view of the foundation of the trial in "natural law". He concludes this section of his opinion with the even more puzzling remark that although he in fact signed the judgment of the IMTFE his signature does not indicate an

---

[20] See the discussion of the subsequent Tokyo trials of Toyoda and Tamura in Yuma Totani, *Justice in Asia and the Pacific Region, 1945–1952: Allied War Crimes Prosecutions*, Cambridge University Press, Cambridge, 2015, chs. 2 and 6.

[21] Bernard, 2008, p. 675, see *supra* note 1.

[22] *Ibid.*

"acknowledgement thereof".[23] One again must wonder why a lawyer and judge would sign a judgment which he does not "acknowledge".

The trajectory of Bernard's opinion is a strange one. While the earlier sections make cogent legal arguments about the defects of the majority's approach to liability for war crimes or its sole reliance upon a conspiracy narrative to the exclusion of specific findings on individual accused with regard to their specific conduct in planning, initiating, preparing or waging aggressive war, the opinion increasingly wanders into questionable territory. The culmination of this tendency is perhaps most plainly seen in the two final sections, the second of which turns to the "Verdict and Sentences".

While Bernard has, correctly on my view, criticised the majority judgment for its failure to individualise the culpability of the accused with specific findings on their individual conduct, he appears to be guilty of the same error. His entire critique of the verdicts and sentences occupies less than two pages and does not refer to any of the individual accused but treats them as a group. Bernard articulates three grounds for his objection to the verdicts.

With regard to the charges related to aggressive war he argues that the meaning of the terms "conspiring", "planning", "preparing", "waging" and "initiating" were too vague for the accused to have known what conduct in relation to the war in which they participated was illegal. He states that only "the formal proof" that the accused had "succeeded" in understanding the meaning of these terms could ground their responsibility. This is a strange argument to make considering that Bernard, as seen above, had accepted the illegality of aggressive war as founded in natural and universal law. If this was the natural and universal law which superseded the law of the IMTFE Charter and all relevant international treaties, how could the accused have been unaware of it? It is perhaps for this reason that Bernard tries to rely on his assertion of the "vagueness" of what it means to plan, prepare, initiate or wage war. But it surely stretches the imagination to contend that the Japanese General Staff was unaware of what it meant to "wage war" or to prepare or plan it. What Bernard appears to aim at here is to establish the crime of aggressive war as rooted in immutable natural law, and hence not *ex post facto*, but at the same time

---

[23]   *Ibid.*, p. 676.

to find a way to exculpate the accused. The true reason for this strategy appears in his second and most interesting objection to the verdicts.

The second objection of Bernard addresses the conspiracy charge but quickly turns again to the role of Emperor Hirohito, and it is here that Bernard's difficulty with the tribunal appears to reside. Bernard states that he regards the "declaration of the Pacific war" as "the most serious of acts committed against peace".[24] Why the 14 years of the Japanese war and occupation in China were less "serious" he does not indicate. What he does state, however, is of this "most serious act" there was "a principal author who escaped all prosecution and of whom in any case the present Defendants could only be considered as accomplices".[25] That "principal author", he makes clear in the subsequent paragraph, was Emperor Hirohito.

Bernard's revulsion against the decision by the US and British governments to exclude the emperor from the proceedings so they could continue to use him for their own purposes is understandable. The Australian, Chinese and Soviet judges all objected to this manner of proceeding, often vehemently. It must have indeed been galling for a judge convinced of the ultimate responsibility of the emperor to have sat through a trial that only accused those who regarded him as their superior authority. Whatever his objections, however, Bernard's responsibility as a judge was to make findings against each of the accused on the basis of the evidence against them. He did not need to rely on the evidence adduced by the majority alone, for he had access to the complete record of the trial and could have, as Webb did in his draft judgment, analysed this evidence and arrived at his own conclusions as to guilt and innocence. Indeed, since he criticised the majority for not meeting this standard he was surely bound to do so himself. What he did instead was to imply, though not state explicitly, that none was guilty of aggressive war because the emperor did not join them in the defendants' dock. He rather refuses to take a firm stand and instead of analysing the evidence himself he contents himself with stating that the "defects of the procedure followed by the Prosecution did not permit me to formulate a definite opinion concerning the questions raised by the accusations of crimes against peace".[26]

---

[24] *Ibid.*, p. 677.

[25] *Ibid.*

[26] *Ibid.*

In this regard Bernard fails in his fundamental duty as a judge by refraining from clearly stating his findings on the guilt and innocence of the accused based on the facts brought into evidence. His apparent disgust at the exclusion of Hirohito does not justify either invalidating the whole proceedings without a legal justification for this position or in refusing to make findings against the other accused. If they were "accomplices", as he himself states, that characterisation needs to be documented for each of them, as he required of the majority. And if the evidence in fact supports the attribution of accomplice liability then the guilty verdicts would be justified. The fact that he disapproves of the treatment of Hirohito does not relieve him of his responsibility as a judge, and if he found it morally distasteful to participate in such proceedings he should have resigned and in any event should not have signed the majority judgment.

Bernard's treatment of the verdicts with regard to war crimes and crimes against humanity is even more questionable on the same grounds just advanced with regard to his treatment of crimes against peace. He disposes of these charges in seven obscurely formulated lines, though not by indicating that the accused bear no responsibility for them. This final paragraph speaks for itself in testifying to Bernard's abdication of his judicial responsibilities. He has rejected the majority's approach and articulated his own standards for assessing the liability of the accused for war crimes, yet he fails to apply these standards to indicate where he may differ from the majority on their individual verdicts. He finds, as he has already indicated, that Japanese forces perpetrated the most serious international crimes. He also proposes standards for analysing the individual responsibility of the accused for these crimes, yet he concludes his opinion as follows (quoted in full):

> The most abominable crimes were committed on the largest scale by the members of the Japanese police and navy I esteemed I could say nevertheless, and I will add there is no doubt in my mind that certain Defendants bear a large part of the responsibility for them, that others rendered themselves guilty of serious failings in the duties towards the prisoners of war and towards humanity. I could not venture further in the formulation of verdicts, the exactitude of which would be subject to caution or to sentences, the equity of which would be far too contestable.[27]

---

[27] *Ibid.*

5

The Tokyo Trial and Its Influence on Contemporary International Criminal Justice

GAO Xiudong[*]

5.1. The Establishment of the International Military Tribunal of the Far East and the Tokyo Trial

On 19 January 1946, in order to implement the Cairo Declaration of 1 December 1943, the Potsdam Declaration of 26 July 1945, the Instrument of Surrender of 2 September 1945 and the Moscow Conference Agreement of 26 December 1945,[1] General Douglas MacArthur established by special proclamation of the Supreme Commander for the Allied Power the International Military Tribunal for the Far East ('IMTFE') and its Charter.[2] The IMTFE intended to try Japanese accused of war crimes. The IMTFE was composed of judges from 11 countries: China, the Soviet Union, the

---

[*]   **GAO Xiudong** is Professor of Law at China Foreign Affairs University. Her research area focuses on domestic and international criminal law. She has authored and edited numerous books and articles. She is dedicated to organising and mentoring students to participate in the International Criminal Court Moot Court competition. She holds an LL.B. and an LL.M. from Peking University and a Ph.D. from Beijing Normal University. She was a Visiting Scholar at WSD HANDA Center for Human rights and International Justice, Stanford University, USA in 2014–2015.

[1]   Cairo Declaration on Japan, jointly released by the United States, the Republic of China and Great Britain, 1 December 1943; Proclamation Defining Terms for Japanese Surrender, Potsdam, 26 July 1945 ('Potsdam Declaration') (http://www.legal-tools.org/doc/f8cae3/); Instrument of Surrender by Japan, 2 September 1945 (https://www.legal-tools.org/doc/4059de/); Moscow Conference Agreement: Soviet-Anglo-American Communiqué, Interim Meeting of Foreign Ministers of the United States, the United Kingdom and the Union of Soviet Socialist Republics, Moscow, 27 December 1945 (https://www.legal-tools.org/doc/653d48/). See International Military Tribunal for the Far East ('IMTFE'), *United States of America et al. v. Araki Sadao et al.*, Judgment, 1 November 1948 ('IMTFE Judgment') (http://www.legal-tools.org/doc/3a2b6b/).

[2]   Special Proclamation Establishing an International Military Tribunal for the Far East, 19 January 1946, Washington, DC, US Government Printing Office (https://www.legal-tools.org/doc/242328/); International Military Tribunal for the Far East ('IMTFE'), Charter, Tokyo, enacted 19 January 1946 and amended 25 April 1946 ('IMTFE Charter') (http://www.legal-tools.org/doc/a3c41c/).

United States, Britain, France, the Netherlands, Canada, Australia, New Zealand, India and the Philippines. As designated by MacArthur, Joseph B. Keenan of the United States was appointed the chief counsel in charge of the investigation and prosecution of charges against war criminals within the jurisdiction of the tribunal. Any Allied state that had been at war with Japan was entitled to appoint an associate counsel to assist the chief counsel.[3]

On 28 April 1946 the IMTFE named 28 class A war crimes suspects, including Tōjō Hideki, the chief of staff of the Kwantung Army and later prime minister of Japan. The next day, the International Prosecution Section officially brought charges against the 28 defendants for crimes against peace, war crimes and crimes against humanity. The charges covered 55 counts committed from 1 January 1928 to 2 September 1945.[4] The trial lasted for two years and seven months, from the announcement of indictment on 3 May 1946 to the end of the trial on 29 December 1948. There were 818 sessions, 419 witnesses, 779 written witnesses and 4,336 pieces of admissible evidence. The IMTFE was the only court that tried class A criminals, among more than 50 tribunals worldwide trying Japanese war criminals after the Second World War; it was the only international tribunal. Of the 28 defendants, two died of illness, one was designated *nolle prosequi* for mental disease, while the other 25 were all found guilty.[5] As for the convictions, seven were sentenced to death, including Tōjō Hideki, Doihara Kenji and Itagaki Seishirō; 16 were sentenced to life imprisonment; and two others were sentenced to 20 years and seven years of imprisonment.[6]

Since the establishment of the IMTFE it has been subjected to both persistent queries and blame. Some scholars point out that in the opinion of most international criminal lawyers the Tokyo Trial can be summed up by the name of Richard H. Minear's book, *Victors' Justice*.[7] The notion of

---

[3] IMTFE Charter, Art. 8, see *supra* note 2.

[4] IMTFE Judgment, p. 7, see *supra* note 1. In fact, the Allied military prosecutions in the Far East were only for crimes against peace and war crimes; they did not include crimes against humanity. The IMTFE did not make a decision on crimes against humanity.

[5] IMTFE Judgment, ch. X: Verdict, see *supra* note 1.

[6] IMTFE, *United States of America et al. v. Araki Sadao et al.*, Sentences, 12 November 1948 (https://www.legal-tools.org/doc/75a5f4/).

[7] Richard H. Minear, *Victors' Justice, The Tokyo War Crimes Trial*, Tuttle, Tokyo, 1971. See also Robert Cryer, Håkan Friman, Darryl Robinson and Elizabeth Wilmshurst, *An In-*

"victors' justice" originated from Tōjō's sworn statement in 1948.[8] His standpoint was to some extent supported by the Japanese people. According to the maxim of "might is right", the Japanese saw the findings of the Tokyo Trial as the "necessity of natural law" for a vanquished country.[9] Later, Japan repeatedly applied similar opinions to deny that a sense of justice emerged from the tribunal. According to the newspaper *Mainichi Shimbun*, as recently as 12 March 2013 Japan's prime minister Abe Shinzō expressed this opinion about the Tokyo Trial: "The conclusion of war was not made by us Japanese but by the judgment of the victorious Allied countries".[10]

Although the Tokyo Trial had some notable defects due to historical limitations, its importance in the progress of international criminal justice cannot be denied and its great achievements are beyond doubt. The IMT-FE was not a unilateral trial organised by victorious countries over vanquished countries. By its nature it was a trial of evil fascist forces by international justice. The Tokyo Trial, together with the International Military Tribunal ('IMT') at Nuremberg, realised the human dream that had been present since the First World War of creating an international tribunal to try war criminals. It established a series of basic principles in international criminal law and contributed to the development of that law. Their great and constant influence on the development of international criminal justice lasts to today.

---

troduction to International Criminal Law and Procedure, 2nd ed., Cambridge University Press, Cambridge, 2010, p. 118.

8   Kiyose Ichirō, *Secret Memoir: The Tokyo Trial*, Chuo Koronsha, Tokyo, 1986, p. 195, cited in Fujita Hisakazu, "The Tokyo Trial: Humanity's Justice v Victors' Justice", in Yuki Tanaka, Tim McCormack and Gerry Simpson (eds.), *Beyond Victor's Justice? The Tokyo War Crimes Trial Revisited*, Brill, Leiden, 2011, p. 4.

9   Madoka Futamura, "Japanese Societal Attitude towards the Tokyo Trial: From a Contemporary Perspective", in Tanaka *et al.*, 2011, p. 43, see *supra* note 8.

10   WANG Yang, "Japan's Prime Minister Shinzo Abe's Remarks on Questioning Tokyo Trial May Lead to Criticism from China, Korea and the United States", in *Xinhua*, 13 March 2013 (http://news.xinhuanet.com/world/2013-03/13/c_115015249.htm).

5.2. Main Contributions of the Tokyo Trial to International Criminal Law

5.2.1. Confirmation and Practice of the Nuremberg Principles

On 11 December 1946 the United Nations General Assembly resolution 95 (1) affirmed the Charter of the IMT and its judgment, and directed the International Law Commission ('ILC') on the codification of the principles recognised in the IMT Charter and judgment. The resolution pointed out clearly that similar principles had been adopted in the IMTFE Charter, proclaimed in Tokyo on 19 January 1946.[11] During a UN conference held on 21 November 1947 the ILC was assigned to codify the IMT Charter and the international law principles accepted at the Nuremberg trial.[12] On 12 April 1950 the ILC laid down seven principles: 1) individual criminal responsibility for international crimes; 2) the non-exemption from individual international law responsibility despite immunity under domestic law; 3) the non-exemption from responsibility despite the accused's status of head of state or responsible government official; 4) the non-exemption from responsibility despite government or superior orders; 5) fair trial for a person charged with an international crime; 6) crimes against peace, war crimes and crimes against humanity are punishable as crimes under international law; and 7) complicity in the commission of crimes against peace, war crimes or crimes against humanity is a crime under international law.[13]

These Nuremberg principles are adopted in following international legal documents: the Convention on the Non-Applicability of Statutory Limitations to War Crimes and Crimes against Humanity of 1968;[14] the

---

[11] United Nations General Assembly, Resolution 95 (1), Affirmation of the Principles of International Law Recognized by the Charter of the Nürnberg Tribunal, 11 December 1946, UN doc. A/RES/95(I) (http://www.legal-tools.org/doc/bb7761/).

[12] United Nations General Assembly, Resolution 177 (II), Formulation of the Principles Recognized in the Charter of the Nürnberg Tribunal and in the Judgment of the Tribunal, 21 November 111, UN doc. A/RES/177 (II).

[13] International Law Commission ('ILC'), Principles of International Law Recognized in the Charter of the Nürnberg Tribunal and in the Judgment of the Tribunal, with Commentaires, Adopted by the ILC at its second session, 1950, Yearbook of the International Law Commission, vol. II, 1950, UN doc. A/CN.4/L.2 (http://www.legal-tools.org/doc/038f9a/).

[14] United Nations General Assembly, Resolution 2391 (XXIII), Convention on the Non-Applicability of Statutory Limitations to War Crimes and Crimes against Humanity, 26 November 1968, UN doc. A/RES/2391 (XXIII).

Declaration on Principles of International Law concerning Friendly Relations and Co-operation among States in accordance with the Charter of the United Nations of 1970;[15] the Statute of the International Criminal Tribunal for the former Yugoslavia ('ICTY Statute') of 1993;[16] the Statute of the International Criminal Tribunal for Rwanda ('ICTR Statute') of 1994;[17] and the Rome Statute of the International Criminal Court passed by Rome diplomatic conference of 1998.[18] After the Second World War countries prosecuted war criminals in accordance with national laws, applying principles recognised by the IMT and the IMTFE. The United Nations pointed out clearly, when establishing the ICTY, that the Nuremberg principles provided the basis for its Statute, which demonstrates that these principles had undoubtedly become part of international customary law.[19] No matter how we examine it, the Tokyo Trial established a significant legal precedent, providing important guidance to all subsequent international trials.[20]

5.2.2. Prosecution of the Crime of Aggression

Like Article 6 of the IMT Charter,[21] Article 5 of the IMTFE Charter established crimes against peace as the first crime subject to the tribunal's jurisdiction.[22] Defendants charged with crimes against peace were class A perpetrators. Thirty-six out of 55 charges in the indictment constituted

---

15 United Nations General Assembly, Resolution 2625 (XXV), Declaration on Principles of International Law concerning Friendly Relations and Cooperation among States, 24 October 1970, UN doc. A/RES/25/2625.

16 United Nations, Updated Statute of the International Criminal Tribunal for the Former Yugoslavia, adopted 25 May 1993 by resolution 827 (1993), last amended 7 July 2009 by resolution 1877 (2009) (http://www.legal-tools.org/doc/b4f63b/).

17 United Nations, Statute of the International Criminal Tribunal for Rwanda, adopted on 8 November 1994 by resolution 955 (1994), last amended 16 December 2009 by resolution 1901 (2009)) (http://www.legal-tools.org/doc/8732d6/).

18 Rome Statute of the International Criminal Court, adopted 17 July 1998, entry into force 1 July 2002 ('ICC Statute') (http://www.legal-tools.org/doc/7b9af9/).

19 United Nations Security Council, Report of the Secretary-General pursuant to paragraph 2 of Security Council Resolution 808 (1993), 3 May 1993, para. 44, UN doc. S/25704.

20 JIA Bing Bing, "The Legacy of the Tokyo Trial in China", in Tanaka et al., 2011, p. 279, see supra note 8.

21 International Military Tribunal, Charter, 8 August 1945, Art. 6 (https://www.legal-tools.org/doc/64ffdd/).

22 IMTFE Charter, Art. 5, see supra note 2.

crimes against peace and the main goal of the IMTFE was indeed to prosecute crimes against peace. The object of punishing persons liable for war was to prevent such destructive war to human civilisation from ever happening again.

Several months before the surrender of Japan in 1945 the Allies had created a policy to ensure the post-war international courts in Europe and the Far East should concentrate on the prosecution of individual criminal liabilities for breaking the peace.[23] This policy was seen by the Allies, especially by the United States, as a concrete step towards the formulation of a legal system to impede the launching of aggressive war, and was written into the IMTFE Charter. At Tokyo the main charges against the defendants were crimes against peace, but war crimes and crimes against humanity were regarded as alternatives.[24]

In fact, the international community had been devoted to the peaceful settlement of international disputes and preventing war since the first and second Hague Peace Conferences in 1899 and 1907, and then redoubled its efforts. After the First World War, the Commission on the Responsibilities of the Authors of the War and on Enforcement of Penalties stated expressly: "in the hierarchy of persons in authority, there is no reason why rank, however exalted", in violation of the established laws and customs of war and the elementary laws of humanity, "should in any circumstances protect the holder of it from responsibility when that responsibility has been established before a properly constituted tribunal. This extends even to the case of heads of states".[25] The Commission sorted crimes into two categories: premeditation of the war; and violations of the laws and customs of war and the laws of humanity.[26] But due to serious disagreements over the definition of the crime of aggression, only war crimes were prosecuted.[27]

---

[23] Potsdam Declaration, Art. 10, see *supra* note 1.

[24] See Yuma Totani, "The charges against the accused and convicted", in Tanaka *et al.*, 2014, pp.185–86, see *supra* note 8.

[25] Commission on the Responsibilities of the Authors of the War and on Enforcement of Penalties, "Report Presented to the Preliminary Peace Conference", in *American Journal of International Law,* 1920, vol. 14, nos. 1/2, p. 116.

[26] *Ibid.*, pp. 99–115.

[27] *Ibid.*, p. 123.

Another effort aiming at punishing the crime of aggression was the Inter-Parliamentary Union Conference in 1925. The conference adopted a resolution,[28] by which it decided to set up a permanent sub-committee to study the causes of wars of aggression and to draw up a preliminary draft of an international legal code for the repression of international crimes.[29] In an annex to the resolution, the conference recognised the criminal responsibility of individuals for the act of declaring a war of aggression, as well as all acts of the preparation or the setting in motion of a war of aggression.[30]

The draft Treaty of Mutual Assistance of the League of Nations in 1923 proposed to make a war of aggression illegal.[31] The preface of the Protocol for the Pacific Settlement of International Disputes of 1924 by League of Nations asserted that a war of aggression constitutes an international crime.[32] The preface of Declaration Concerning Wars of Aggression of 1927 passed by the League of Nations pointed out that a war of aggression can never serve as a means of settling international disputes and is, in consequence, an international crime.[33]

Meanwhile, the most remarkable achievement of the international community in preventing aggressive war the Kellogg-Briand Pact (or Pact of Paris) of 1928.[34] As an international agreement signed by most countries in the world at that time, the Kellogg-Briand Pact first renounced war as the instrument to carry out national policy in international relationships, laying the legal foundation of the mutual non-aggression principle

---

[28] See International Law Commission, "Resolution of the Inter-Parliamentary Union on the Criminality of Wars of Aggression and the Organization of International Repressive Measures (1925)", in *Historical Survey of the Question of International Criminal Jurisdiction* (Memorandum submitted by the Secretary-General), UN doc. A/CN.4/7/Rev.1, United Nations, New York, 1949, p. 70.

[29] *Ibid.*, p. 14.

[30] *Ibid.*, p. 71.

[31] League of Nations, Text of the Treaty of Mutual Assistance, Records of the Fourth Assembly, Minutes of the Third Committee, League of Nations Official Journal (Special Supplement no. 16), 1923, pp. 203–6.

[32] League of Nations, Protocol for the Pacific Settlement of International Disputes, 2 October 1924, A.25.1925.IX.

[33] League of Nations, Declaration Concerning Wars of Aggression, League of Nations Official Journal (Special Supplement no. 53), 24 September 1927, p. 22.

[34] Treaty between the United States and other Powers Providing for the Renunciation of War as an Instrument of National Policy, Paris, 27 August 1928 ('Kellogg-Briand Pact').

in international law.[35] When the Second World War broke out in 1939 the pact was binding on 63 countries, including Germany, Italy and Japan. As for the defence argument brought up at the IMTFE that crimes against peace was *ex post facto* law, the Tokyo Trial quoted the IMT judgment, affirmed the legal validity of the Kellogg-Briand Pact and pointed out:

> The Nations who signed the pact or adhered to it uncondi-
> tionally condemned recourse to war for the future as an in-
> strument of policy and expressly renounced it. After the
> signing of the pact any nation resorting to war as an instru-
> ment of national policy breaks the pact. In the opinion of the
> Tribunal, the solemn renunciation of war as an instrument of
> national policy necessarily involves the proposition that such
> a war is illegal in international law; and that those who plan
> and wage such a war, with its inevitable and terrible conse-
> quences, are committing a crime in so doing.[36]

Thus, the Nuremberg and Tokyo Trials drew on illustrations of the existence of the law against the crime of aggression that existed before the Potsdam Declaration. As Keenan announced at the beginning of the IMT-FE, it had been publicly recognised and solemnly declared by all civilised societies that the action of invasion constituted an international war crime. It had by then become an international law principle that invasive wars are illegal.[37] The consensus reached at Tokyo and Nuremberg was that as long as a person participated in wars of aggression, he would certainly bear individual criminal responsibility, regardless of what stage he was involved in. This consensus is regarded as the principle of individual responsibility in terms of a war of aggression.[38]

The Tokyo and Nuremberg Trials probed into many legal issues related to aggression, including the definition of aggression, identification of invasive behaviour, the content of a conspiracy to aggression, the material and mental elements of aggression, and whether the non-retrospective nature of law is violated when aggression is prosecuted and when individ-

---

[35]   LIU Daqun, "On the Crime of Aggression", in *Wuhan University International Law Review*, 2005, vol. 1.

[36]   IMTFE Judgment, p. 25, see *supra* note 1.

[37]   Minear, 1971, p. 50, see *supra* note 7.

[38]   MEI Ju-Ao, 远东国际军事法庭 [International Military Tribunal for the Far East], Law Press, Beijing, 1988, pp. 23–24.

ual responsibility are considered. These judicial practices profoundly enriched the jurisprudence and precedents of the crime of aggression.

5.2.3. The IMTFE as an Inspiration for the International Criminal Court

According to a newspaper report approximately 9,000 Nazi criminals fled to South America after the Second World War,[39] but only 22 of them were prosecuted by the IMT. Similarly, some 5,700 Japanese were confirmed as war criminals after the Second World War.[40] However, the IMTFE only prosecuted 28 accused based on the "main political figures who were responsible for war crimes",[41] while many class B and C criminals were tried in national courts. This pattern has been inherited by the *ad hoc* international criminal tribunals established in the 1990s and beyond. After the genocide in Rwanda, more than 100,000 suspects were kept in domestic custody, while only 93 of them were prosecuted and tried by the ICTR.[42] Meanwhile, only 161 defendants were prosecuted at the ICTY.[43] A large number of criminals were left to be tried by domestic courts.

Article 53 of the Rome Statute of the International Criminal Court ('ICC Statute') sets out the terms for the initiation of an investigation with regard to the role of a defendant in an alleged crime in order to ascertain a "reasonable basis" for determining prosecution. During the 12 years of its existence there have only been 21 cases investigated and tried by the ICC. Article 1 of Statute of the Special Court for Sierra Leone confined the subject of prosecution to "persons who bear the greatest responsibility for serious violations of international humanitarian law and Sierra Leonean

---

[39] ZHU Yingku, "秘密文件披露 9000 名纳粹战犯二战后逃往南美" [Secret Documents Disclosed that 9000 Nazi War Criminals Fled to South America after World War II], Hanqui, 3 March 2012 (http://history.huanqiu.com/world/2012-03/2540521.html).

[40] John W. Dower, *Embracing Defeat: Japan in the Wake of World War II*, W.W. Norton, New York, 1999, p. 447.

[41] Awaya Kentarō, "Selecting the Defendant at the Tokyo Trial", in Tanaka *et al.*, 2011, p. 71, see *supra* note 8.

[42] United Nations Security Council, Report on the Completion Strategy of the International Criminal Tribunal for Rwanda, 22 May 2012, para. 3, UN doc. S/2012/349.

[43] United Nations Security Council, Letter from the President of the International Tribunal for the Prosecution of Persons Responsible for Serious Violations of International Humanitarian Law Committed in the Territory of the Former Yugoslavia since 1991, 16 May 2014, Annex I, p. 3, UN doc. S/2014/351.

law committed in the territory of Sierra Leone since 30 November 1996".[44] Both Article 1 of the agreement between the United Nations and the government of Cambodia concerning the prosecution of crimes committed during the period of Democratic Kampuchea,[45] and Article 1 of the Law on the Establishment of the Extraordinary Chambers in the Courts of Cambodia limited the subject of prosecution to

> senior leaders of Democratic Kampuchea and those who were most responsible for the crimes and serious violations of Cambodian penal law, international humanitarian law and custom, and international conventions recognized by Cambodia, that were committed during the period from 17 April 1975 to 6 January 1979.[46]

The purpose of international society in establishing an international tribunal is not to replace the traditional jurisdiction of states with international jurisdiction.

> In establishing an international tribunal for the prosecution of persons responsible for serious violations [...], it was not the intention of the Security Council to preclude or prevent the exercise of jurisdiction by national courts with respect to such acts. Indeed national courts should be encouraged to exercise their jurisdiction in accordance with their relevant national laws and procedures.[47]

Due to the restrictions of time, funds and human resources, international courts will usually only choose to prosecute and try the leaders of the highest rank who bear the main responsibility for the crimes. Therefore, the limited ability to try specific cases in international tribunals means that many trials are processed in domestic courts. For instance, the ICTR

---

[44] Statute of the Special Court for Sierra Leone, 14 August 2000, Art. 1 (http://www.legal-tools.org/doc/aa0e20/).

[45] Agreement Between the United Nations and the Royal Government of Cambodia Concerning the Prosecution under Cambodian Law of Crimes Committed during the Period of Democratic Kampuchea, 6 June 2003, Art. 1 (https://www.legal-tools.org/doc/3a33d3/).

[46] Cambodia, Law on the Establishment of the Extraordinary Chambers in the Courts of Cambodia for the Prosecution of Crimes Committed during the Period of Democratic Kampuchea, with inclusion of amendments as promulgated on 27 October 2004, Art. 1 ((NS/RKM/1004/006) (http://www.legal-tools.org/doc/88d544/).

[47] United Nations Security Council, Report of the UN Secretary-General Pursuant to Paragraph 2 of Security Council Resolution 808 (1993), 3 May 1993, para. 64, UN doc. S/25704.

was granted primacy jurisdiction over war crimes when it was established. However, concurrent domestic jurisdiction replaced primacy jurisdiction because of the limited time and resources. During the completion strategy period supplemental jurisdiction emerged.[48]

Keenan, the head prosecutor of the IMTFE, made the following comment: "The persons who were crucial and occupied the highest place of domination were prosecuted in Tokyo Trial. From this perspective, it was a significant trial with symbolic meaning".[49] This observation is not obsolete even today. The virtue of an international court lies not in the number of cases and criminals it tries but in the powerful message it sends to international society: by establishing international tribunals, the persons who bear the greatest responsibility will be prosecuted and justice has long arms. In a similar way, the UN Secretary-General Ban Ki-moon addressed the same point during a speech at the Extraordinary Chambers in the Courts of Cambodia: "Putting the senior Khmer Rouge leaders on trial, even 30 years after, is itself a powerful message. A message that impunity will not be tolerant, neither by the people of Cambodia and their government, nor by the United Nations and the international community".[50]

5.2.4. The IMTFE as a Precedent for the Direct Enforcement of International Criminal Law

The IMTFE and IMT Charters have set examples for international tribunals in many aspects, such as the definition of core international crimes, the organisation of the court, jurisdiction, trial procedures, the qualification of prosecution, the specific penalties applied by the tribunal, evidence and the execution of judgment. Due to the successful operation of these two international tribunals, the General Assembly passed a resolution as early as 1948 requesting the ILC to pay attention to the possibility of es-

---

48 See LIN Yan, *The Theory and Practice of International Criminal Tribunal for Rwanda*, *World Knowledge Press*, Beijing, 2010, pp. 56–77.

49 See Awaya Kentarō, *The Secret History of the Tokyo Trial*, trans. LI Yin, World Knowledge Press, Beijing, 1987, p. 204.

50 United Nations News Centre, Secretary-General Ban Ki-moon: Remarks at Extraordinary Chambers in the Courts of Cambodia, 27 October 2010.

tablishing a criminal chamber of the International Court of Justice.[51] In 1950 the General Assembly decided to set up a criminal jurisdiction committee in order to frame a draft statute of an international criminal court.[52] After that, the issue of creating such a court was frequently discussed by the ILC, as well as other related organisations, all of which laid the foundations for the eventual official establishment of the ICC.

Direct enforcement of international criminal law creates an unprecedented way to solve criminal problems in armed conflicts through judicial resorts. Prosecuting wars of aggression and war crimes, instead of adopting traditional methods such as military retaliation, paying reparations and restrictions of sovereignty, necessitates an open trial. The accused is brought before an international court established by the international community, and an impartial trial would both punish the criminal and act as a warning, which demonstrates the progress of civilisation and rationality of human beings. Based on this successful experience, the international community reached a consensus to set up *ad hoc* international tribunals in order to punish crimes, after the large-scale armed conflicts on the territory of former Yugoslavia and the genocide in Rwanda. Since the formation of the ICC, it has become a common practice to submit a situation to the Court when international or domestic armed conflicts break out, or when there are large-scale violations of human rights as well as violations of international humanitarian law. In recent years, the conflicts in Sudan, Libya, Syria and Israel-Palestine have all sufficiently proved the point.

5.3. Implications of the IMTFE for the Development of International Criminal Law

It has been seven decades since the trial in Tokyo. Nevertheless, the problems and consequences triggered by the IMTFE still have a far-reaching influence in the present-day international criminal judiciary.

---

[51] United Nations General Assembly, Resolution 260 B (III), Study by the International Law Commission on the Question of an International Criminal Tribunal, 9 December 1948, UN doc. A/RES/3/260 B.

[52] United Nations General Assembly, Resolution 489 (V), International Criminal Jurisdiction, 12 December 1950, UN doc. A/RES/489 (V).

5.3.1. Who Should Be on the Bench?

After the First World War the plan of Allies to set up a special international tribunal to convict German war criminals failed. Hence, the highest court in Germany was designated to try criminals of its own country. It turned out that the Leipzig war crimes trials eventually became a symbol of a false trial and of harbouring criminals.[53] After the surrender of Japanese troops in 1945 Japan attempted to learn from the Leipzig trials and prosecute war criminals itself.[54] On the one hand, it could demonstrate the independent existence of Japanese sovereignty and judicial power; on the other hand, Japan would challenge the legitimacy of IMTFE under the principle of *ne bis in idem* (double jeopardy) because the defendants had already been convicted or acquitted by domestic courts.[55] Without the consent of the Allies, the Japanese Ministry of Defence had proceeded with unauthorised independent trials of a so-called "military law nature", and punished some heinous criminals with only symbolic slight penalties.[56] On 19 February 1946 the Allied headquarters issued a memorandum regarding the implementation of judicial criminal power, stating clearly that the Japanese had no right to try criminals who had committed war crimes with regard to the Allied countries. This order finally invalidated the trials in Japan.[57]

After the war the Allies apparently did not believe that the criminals' own countries would objectively try their own citizens. They decided to establish international tribunals to try class A war criminals, while the trials of class B and C war criminals were held in the victim states and states where the crimes were committed. Some argue that to prove the trials were not merely a form of revenge of the victors it was necessary to allow Japanese judges and prosecutors to participate in the trials. The

---

[53] In May 1920 the Allies submitted to the German government a list of 45 accused persons. In the event only 12 individuals were brought to trial; six of them were found not guilty and the others were sentenced to terms from six months to four years. See Claud Mullins, *The Leipzig Trials: An Account of the War Criminals' Trials and a Study of German Mentality*, H.F. & G. Witherby, London, 1921, pp. 9, 191.

[54] See SONG Zhiyong, "Tokyo Trial and Japan's Countermeasure", in *The Japanese Journal*, 2004, vol. 1, p. 122.

[55] *Ibid.*

[56] *Ibid.*, p. 123.

[57] *Ibid.*

suggestion was not carried out for two reasons. First, Japan put a major effort into hampering the international trial and replacing it with a domestic trial, and it forgot altogether to request to participate in the IMTFE. Second, there was much objection from the international prosecutors to Japan's participation.[58]

Although the IMTFE was established by the Allies, and the bench was composed of judges from the Allied states, the proceedings were not a mere "show trial" operated by the victors. It was not just a judgment compelled by victors, as Abe claimed. The Tokyo Trial adopted the strict evidential standards of the common law system, with the rights of the defendants fully protected and dissenting opinions fully expressed. The independence and due process of the tribunal entailed the fairness of the trial proceedings themselves.

The IMTFE was nonetheless condemned as a tool run by the occupying regime since the judges of the tribunal all came from the Allies.[59] The international tribunals established later learned lessons from the Tokyo Trial, and adopted the following rules: 1) judges were all elected by the United Nations; 2) the judges were assigned by state parties; and 3) international judges and domestic judges formed hybrid tribunals.

Judicial practice, however, has suggested that trials completely run by the states of the perpetrators could be acceptable to some extent. For example, after the IMT completed its work, the German government never stopped prosecuting criminals out of a feeling of national consciousness. The German prosecutor's agency set up Ludwigsburg-based Central Office of the State Justice Administrations for the Investigation of National Socialist Crimes in 1958 in order to pursue Nazi criminals.[60] Changes in the law and a revised statute of limitations – until 1979 when the statute of limitations was totally abolished – guaranteed that the perpetrators could be prosecuted at any time. Between 1945 and 1975 the Fed-

---

[58] See Kentarō, 1987, p. 59, see *supra* note 49.

[59] Cryer *et al.*, 2010, p. 118, see *supra* note 7; Ichirō, 1986, p. 195, see *supra* note 8; Futamura, 2014, p. 43, see *supra* note 9.

[60] Nomura Jiro, *Nachisu saiban* [The Nazi Trials], Kodansha, Tokyo, 1993, p. 95, quoted in SONG Zhiyong, "The Post-war Trials, Historical Understanding, National Reconciliation", in *The Study of Historical Theory*, 2011, vol. 1, p. 5.

eral Republic of Germany investigated 30,000 suspects, including 6,411 crime perpetrators who were eventually found guilty by domestic courts.[61]

The practice of the ICTY and ICTR indicate that international tribunals located far away from the crime location would inevitably involve a huge cost, which international society can hardly bear. Despite our reluctance, we have to admit that it is impractical idealism to try international war criminals based on moral standards. In recent years, hybrid tribunals have increasingly relied on the domestic resources provided by the states where international crimes were committed, including their legal systems and professionals, in order to reduce trial costs, provide opportunities for lawyers from the victim states to directly contribute to the retribution for war crimes, and even to improve the victim states' national confidence in their domestic judicial systems. Meanwhile, prosecuting international crimes under domestic law has become the primary method with which international criminal law is enforced. The Gacaca courts in Rwanda, the Iraqi High Tribunal, the War Crimes Section of the Court of Bosnia and Herzegovina, and other similar courts have all succeeded in employing the domestic resources of the victim states and played important role in improving reconciliation between different ethnic groups and rebuilding a normal life for their citizens.

5.3.2. Balance between Human Rights Protection and Judicial Economy

Compared to Nuremberg trial, the IMTFE took longer and cost much more. In the later stages of the trial, Britain expressed its disappointment in Tokyo Trial's inefficiency, and stated that it would not like to attend a similar international trial again. Should the need to prosecute crimes arise again, it should be held by domestic court.[62] On 31 March 1948 Keenan published a report on the achievements and future prospects of the Tokyo trial to the Far Eastern Commission in Washington. He reported that there was not enough time to try all the Japanese accused of committing crimes against peace. Keenan suggested that from then on there would be no new international trials and, if there were sufficient evidence to indict the re-

---

61 *Ibid.*
62 Kentarō, 1987, p. 204, see *supra* note 42.

maining perpetrators, it would be better to try them in small-scale tier B or C trial courts.[63]

Compared with the later international criminal tribunals, the relatively long time spent by Tokyo Trial should not be criticised so much. It took the ICC 10 years after its establishment to make its first judgment. The ICTR and ICTY only tried 93 and 161 cases respectively over a period of 20 years. For two and half years, the Tokyo Trial tried 28 defendants who committed countless atrocities in many countries, creating millions of victims. In these circumstances, it should not be condemned as "inefficient". It is well known that the Imperial Japanese Army avoided trial for many criminal acts committed in the Second World War, such as manslaughter, bacteriological attacks, poisonous gas attacks, sexual violence, indiscriminate bombardment, forced labour, sexual slavery against so-called "comfort women" and so on. Some crimes were not even mentioned in the trial, while some crimes were tried as crimes against the rules of war. The catastrophic crimes committed by the Japanese military were systematic and widespread in the pursuit of explicit and implicit national policies. Most of the crimes were not prosecuted during the Tokyo Trial. The workload of the court would have dramatically increased and become insurmountable had all the crimes been tried together.

The later international criminal tribunals bear some similarities with the IMTFE, as they have been subject to much criticism for inefficiency and extravagance.[64] The reasons for the low efficiency are the complexity of the indictment procedure, particularly because interpretation and translation between different languages are necessary in international trials. The latter is a common problem for international tribunals that cannot be easily resolved. Proper procedures are necessary for human rights protection in a modern criminal justice system. It is very hard to strike a proper balance between the requirement of due process and judicial economy.

---

[63] *Ibid.*

[64] The appropriation for 2010–2011 to the Special Account for the International Tribunal for the Former Yugoslavia was $327 million gross ($286 million net). See United Nations Security Council, Report of the Secretary-General: Second Performance Report on the Budget of the International Tribunal for the Former Yugoslavia for the Biennium 2010–2011, 15 November 2011, UN doc. A/66/555.

5.3.3. Political Considerations in International Justice

Political considerations at the IMTFE greatly reduced the quality of the trial, and it was a hidden danger for the present denial in Japan regarding its illegal invasion of China and other countries.

First, defendants at the IMTFE were named pursuant to political considerations rather than legal standards. This could be seen in the decision not to indict Emperor Hirohito of Japan. This decision was made because the United States needed to keep the emperor as a symbol of Japan's unconditional surrender and also because it would encourage the country's elites to co-operate politically.[65] It was a great deficiency of the IMTFE not to hold Emperor Hirohito responsible for the crime of aggression and the atrocities committed by the Japanese army. As the highest political leader and military commander, he was not prosecuted for any crime at all. He had enjoyed supreme power under the Japanese constitution. If his responsibility were not recognised, it would be impossible for Japan as a state to fully assume its liability for war crimes. International criminal tribunals have *ratione materiae* jurisdiction over the most serious crimes of concern to the international community as a whole, as well as *ratione personae* jurisdiction over leaders of a state, army leaders and senior government officials. Such cases, more often than not, have complex elements involved and complicated backgrounds. Political factors would be taken into consideration in terms of the suspect's arrest, extradition and transfer. The same could be said of the enforcement of the arrest warrants and judgments of the international tribunals. Apart from international tribunals empowered by the Allies (such as the IMTFE), even the treaty-based ICC has tried only African suspects in the past 12 years. The ICC still cannot get rid of the criticism that it employs only a selective application of law. This indeed undermines the cornerstone of international tribunals, that is, international judicial fairness and justice.

Second, the IMTFE's pursuit of justice was greatly hampered due to political considerations, as a result of which many crimes went unpunished. China suffered from invasion by Japan longer than any country. As defined by the IMTFE itself, Japan's invasion of China began in 1928 and lasted for 17 years. The war against Japan was the first real victory

---

65 M. Cherif Bassiouni, *Introduction to International Criminal Law*, trans. into Chinese by ZHAO Bingzhi *et al.*, Law Press, Beijing, 2006, p. 355.

achieved by China in nearly a century, since the First Opium War in 1839–1842. The Tokyo Trial allowed the Chinese people to believe that justice had finally been realised. The government consistently supported the trial from the establishment of the tribunal to the court hearing. China actively participated in the pre-trial proceedings, including drafting legal pleadings and composing a list of war criminals. China also sent judges and assistant prosecutors to participate in the trial, collected evidence, drafted complaints, and took part in witness examinations and cross-examinations. However, China's attention was being distracted by the pending civil war, for which it was heavily reliant on the United States, and it did not give the Tokyo Trial sufficient attention. Its evidence collection and production efforts were severely compromised, and its complaints were supported by weak arguments. As a result, the atrocities that Japan committed against China remained largely unpunished. Meanwhile, the United States started to reconsider Japan's strategic position in the context of the Cold War and intentionally adopted a benevolent policy in the trial of the Japanese war criminals.[66] The Tokyo Trial started with high expectations but ended with minimal effort, and was completed in a rush. Other than those sentenced to death, all the war criminals found guilty by the IMTFE were released by 1958.[67] Some of them even returned to work in prominent positions in Japan.

The political considerations of the IMTFE severely compromised its goal of enforcing justice and punishing war criminals. This heralded Japan's later attempt to deny the justification for the Tokyo Trial and to "rebuild the reputation" of the class A war criminals. Japan's recognition of the existence of its invasion of China, its willingness to reflect on its shameful criminals, and its promise to surrender its military power were the preconditions for it to gain forgiveness from international society. Many countries invaded by Japan consented to pardon Japanese war criminals and discharged Japan's pecuniary liabilities based on such an understanding.[68] The Truth and Reconciliation Commission in South Africa and Gacaca courts in Rwanda both adopted such principles – no admission, no

---

[66] See WANG Shizhou (ed.), *Contemporary Foundations of International Criminal Law*, People's Public Security University of China Press, Beijing, 2009, p. 38.

[67] *Ibid.*

[68] See "岂能无视人类共同价值观" [How Can We Ignore Common Human Values?], in *China Network*, 15 June 2005 (http://www.china.com.cn/chinese/zhuanti/rbzf/890180.htm).

forgiveness.[69] Japan's refusal to accept the Tokyo Trial's judgment not only impedes the co-existence between the different states in East Asia but also threatens the peace in this region.

The goal of criminal law is not only to punish criminals but also to prevent crimes. The value of criminal justice also lies in preventing potential crimes. The greatest value of Tokyo Trial is to prevent a revival of militarism, to keep the world peaceful and safe under the rule of international law.

---

[69] Republic of South Africa, Promotion of National Unity and Reconciliation Act 34 of 1995, Art. 20(1): "If the Committee, after considering an application for amnesty, is satisfied that – [...] the applicant has made a full disclosure of all relevant facts, it shall grant amnesty in respect of that act, omission or offence" (http://www.justice.gov.za/legislation/acts/1995-034.pdf). The Gacaca courts gave perpetrators the opportunity to confess their crimes, show remorse and ask for forgiveness in front of their community. Often, confessing prisoners returned home without further penalty or received community service orders. See outreach Programme on the Rwanda Genocide and the United Nations, "Background Information on the Justice and Reconciliation Process in Rwanda" (http://www.un.org/en/preventgenocide—/rwanda/about/bgjustice.shtml).

6

The Nanjing Trials – Victor's Justice? Revisiting the Case of Tani Hisao

LIU Daqun[*]

Immediately following the Second World War the Allies in Asia began to try Japanese war criminals. According to the special proclamation of the Supreme Commander for the Allied Powers on 19 January 1946, the International Military Tribunal for the Far East ('IMTFE') was established to prosecute Japanese war criminals.[1] The IMTFE convened on 29 April 1946 and delivered its judgment on 4 November 1948. The trial lasted two and a half years during which 28 defendants were charged as class A criminals for crimes against peace. Of these defendants, seven were sentenced to death by hanging and were executed at Sugamo Prison in Ikebukuro on 23 December 1948, 16 were sentenced to life imprisonment and two others were sentenced to lower prison terms.[2]

At the same time, China also established military tribunals in 10 different cities in order to prosecute Japanese war criminals (see Annex 1). The Nanjing War Crimes Tribunal ('Nanjing Tribunal'), organised under auspices the Ministry of Defence, was established on 15 February 1946 to deal with crimes committed mainly in Nanjing (Nanking) at the

---

[*] LIU Daqun is a Judge of the Appeals Chamber of the International Tribunals for the former Yugoslavia ('ICTY') and for Rwanda ('ICTR'), Professor at the Centre of Cooperative Innovation and Judicial Civilization of China University of Political Science and Law. The views expressed in this article are solely those of the author and do not reflect those of the ICTY, ICTR or the United Nations.

[1] Special Proclamation Establishing an International Military Tribunal for the Far East, 19 January 1946, Washington, DC, US Government Printing Office (https://www.legal-tools.org/doc/242328/).

[2] International Military Tribunal for the Far East ('IMTFE'), *United States of America et al. v. Araki Sadao et al.*, Judgment, 1 November 1948, the majority opinion of the Tribunal ('IMTFE Judgment') (http://www.legal-tools.org/doc/3a2b6b/). See also R. John Prichard (ed.), *The Tokyo Major War Crimes Trial: The Records of the International Military Tribunal for the Far East, with an Authoritative Commentary and Comprehensive Guide*, Edwin Mellen Press, New York, 2002, annex 4 of IMTFE Judgment.

end of 1937 and the beginning of 1938 ('Nanjing Massacre'). The Nanjing Tribunal concluded its proceedings on 26 January 1949 and acquitted General Okamura Yasuji, the commander-in-chief of the Japanese China Expeditionary Army in late 1944. Twenty-four suspects were tried: eight were sentenced to death, 14 were sentenced to imprisonment, one was acquitted and one died in custody.

Since the very beginning of their existence, both the IMTFE and Nanjing trials have been criticised as perpetuating victor's justice. Justice Radhabinod Pal, the Indian member of the IMTFE, said in his dissenting judgment:

> I might mention in this connection that even the published accounts of Nanking "rape" could not be accepted by the world without some suspicion of exaggeration. [...] Referring to the same incident, Sir Charles Addis on that occasion could say: "Between two countries at war there was always a danger that one or other of the combatants would seek to turn public opinion in his favour by resort to a propaganda in which incidents, inseparable alas from all hostilities, were magnified and distorted for the express purpose of inflaming prejudice and passion and obscuring the real issues of the conflict.[3]

Justice Pal's dissent was well received and welcomed by the Japanese who denied the occurrence of the Nanjing Massacre. Japanese war criminals executed as a result of the IMTFE and the Nanjing Tribunal were regarded as patriotic heroes, and since the 1970s their ashes have been placed at the Yasukuni Shrine in Tokyo. In recent years, the Japanese prime minister and cabinet ministers have paid regular visits to the shrine. The visits, sparking strong condemnation from Japan's neighbours such as China, Korea and Russia, have become a major diplomatic issue.

Nanjing Massacre deniers, such as Shūdō Higashinakano, argue that the Chinese Nationalists and Communists fabricated and spread claims about the Nanjing Massacre as wartime propaganda.[4] In his book, *"Nankin gyakusatsu" no kyokō* (The Fabrication of the "Nanjing Massacre"), Tanaka Masaaki also argues that the IMTFE and the Chinese government

---

3   IMTFE, *United States of America et al. v. Araki Sadao et al.*, Judgment of the Hon'ble Mr. Justice Pal Member from India, 1 November 1948 (http://www.legal-tools.org/doc/712ef9/).

4   Higashinakano Shūdō, *1937 Nanking Koryakusen no Shinjitsu* [The Truth of the Nanking Operation in 1937], Shogakukan, Tokyo, 2003, pp. 219–23.

fabricated the event as propaganda and that there was no indiscriminate killing in Nanjing. He further contends that the Tokyo trials represented "victor's justice" and were thus not fair.[5]

In light of this, the question arises: what is victor's justice? Does it mean that those who win the war have the right to take revenge on the vanquished? It is undeniable that, throughout human history, the defeated parties were always at mercy of the victors. International criminal tribunals are new creations of contemporary history and were established to try individuals who committed heinous crimes during war. As a matter of fact, only the winning party could be in a position to try war crimes. The only purpose of victor's justice is revenge. On the other hand, judicial proceedings seek to address crimes committed by the accused while providing him or her a chance to be heard. Justice should be rendered against the crimes committed, and should not depend on *who* committed the crimes.

Accordingly, this chapter submits four criteria to assess whether the Nanjing Tribunal amounted to victor's justice: 1) whether the Nanjing Tribunal was lawfully established; 2) whether the principle of *nullum crimen sine lege* was observed; 3) whether the trials were conducted according to due process and the fair trial rights of the accused were guaranteed; and 4) whether overwhelming evidence existed to justify the convictions.

6.1. Lawful Establishment

Even while fighting continued during the Second World War the Allies were already considering how to deal with war criminals after the war. Towards the end of the war in 1944 the British prime minister, Winston Churchill, preferred a policy of summary execution to avoid legal problems. The British government proposed to draw up a list of 50 to 150 Nazi leaders who should be summarily shot after their capture.[6] The proposal was met with strong opposition from the United States and the Soviet Union. They insisted on proper trials with carefully collected evidence, inde-

---

5 Tanaka Masaaki, *"Nankin gyakusatsu" no kyokō* [The Fabrication of the "Nanjing Massacre"], Nihon Kyobun Sha, Tokyo, 1984. p. 14.

6 In the British tradition, an act of attainder is an act of a legislature declaring a person or group of persons guilty of some crime and punishing them without a judicial trial.

pendent judges and the right of the accused to have defence lawyers.[7] The Allies decided to establish military tribunals to try those responsible for atrocities during the Second World War and determined that the tribunals should be set up upon sound legal basis.

The establishment of a war crimes tribunal to try Japanese military personnel responsible for the atrocities committed in China, especially during the Nanjing Massacre, took a long time, through careful contemplation and preparation. On 7 October 1942 the United Nations Commission for the Investigation of War Crimes was established in London. The Commission was to investigate war crimes committed against nationals of the United Nations, collect evidence on the atrocities, and name and identify persons responsible for the crimes.[8] On 17 December 1942 12 governments issued a declaration condemning German atrocities against the Jews and reaffirming their "solemn resolution to ensure that those responsible for these crimes shall not escape retribution and to press on with the necessary practical measures to this end".[9]

China began investigations against Japanese war criminals as early as 1943, while the fighting was still ongoing. According to instructions issued by the president of the Military Commission on 13 June, the Counsellor's Office of the Military Commission of China's national government was to appoint delegates to London for discussions and the establishment of a war crimes commission based on the British government's suggestions.[10] On 19 June 1943 the Counsellor's Office, acting upon suggestions of the British government, made a proposal to China's head of

---

[7] John Crossland, "Churchill: Execute Hitler without Trial", in *The Sunday Times*, 1 January 2006.

[8] UK Parliament, Parliamentary Debates, House of Lords, vol. 129, no. 86, col. 563, Printed for the Controller of HMSO by Harrison and Son, London, 1909–1947.

[9] Joint Declaration by Members of the United Nations against Extermination of the Jews, 17 December 1942, as reported by Anthony Eden, Secretary of State for Foreign Affairs to the House of Commons. See Hansard, HC Deb 17 December 1942, vol. 385, cols. 2082–7. The 12 governments were Belgium, Czechoslovakia, Greece, Luxembourg, the Netherlands, Norway, Poland, the United States, the United Kingdom, the Soviet Union, Yugoslavia and the French National Committee.

[10] China, National Archive No. 2, 761/208, 13 June, 1943, p. 8, The President of the Military Commission's Instruction to the Counsellor's Office on the Establishment of War Crimes Commission as Suggested by the Government of the United Kingdom. See HU Juron (ed.), *Nanking Trial: Collection of Historical Materials on the Nanking Massacre*, vol. 24, Jiangsu People's Press, Nanjing, 2006, p. 10.

---

state to establish a committee to investigate the crimes committed by the Japanese army. The proposal also set out the composition of the committee as well as the scope of investigations and the crimes.[11]

In October 1943 the foreign ministers of Britain, the United States and the Soviet Union issued the Moscow Declaration and declared their policy that German officers who were responsible for or took a consenting part in the atrocities "will be sent back to the countries in which their abominable deeds were done in order that they may be judged and punished according to the laws of these liberated countries and of the free governments which will be created therein".[12] This was to be done "without prejudice to the case of the major criminals, whose offenses have no particular geographical localisation and who will be punished by the joint decision of the Governments of the Allies".[13] This declaration was also applicable to Asia, covering the acts of alleged Japanese war criminals.[14]

In October 1943 the United Nations War Crimes Commission ('UNWCC') was set up in London to draft lists of criminals, record available supporting evidence, and make recommendations as to the tribunals

---

[11] National Archive No. 2, 2/5703. *Ibid.*

[12] Declaration of the Four Nations on General Security, Statement on Atrocities, Moscow, adopted 1 November 1943 (sometimes dated 30 October) ('Moscow Declaration') (http://www.legal-tools.org/doc/3c6e23/). There were actually four declarations, all arising out of the Conference of Foreign Ministers held in Moscow on 19–30 October 1943. China attended and joined in the general declaration, which included the commitment to set up an international organisation which eventually became the United Nations.

[13] *Ibid.*

[14] See The Inter-Allied Declaration on Punishment for War Crimes, St. James's Palace, London, 13 January 1942, Inter-Allied Information Committee, London ('St. James's Palace Declaration'), which referred not just to Germany but also to "associates of the Reich and in certain countries, by the accomplices of the occupying power" and the resolution of the states present "to see to it, in a spirit of international solidarity, that (a) those guilty or responsible, whatever their nationality, are sought out handed over to justice and judged, and (b) that the sentences pronounced are carried out". China attended this meeting, and later accepted the Declaration by way of a note. At the Cairo Conference (22–26 November 1943), the US president Franklin Roosevelt, British prime minister Winston Churchill and Generalissimo CHIANG Kai-shek of China agreed to a joint declaration that pledged, *inter alia*, the continuation of the war against Japan until she surrendered unconditionally, foreswore territorial ambitions, return of territories and eventual independence for Korea. It did not mention prosecutions. See M.E. Bathurst, "The United Nations War Crimes Commission", in *American Journal of International Law*, 1945, vol. 39, pp. 565–70.

trying alleged war criminals.[15] In May 1944 a Sub-Commission for the Far East was set up in Chongqing (Chungking), the temporary capital of China during the war, to gather information on crimes committed by the Japanese military in Asia.[16] The Sub-Commission was composed of representatives from 12 governments. The Chinese delegate, WANG Chung-hui, the secretary-general of the Supreme National Defence Council of China, was elected the first chairman of the Sub-Commission.[17]

In 1944 the Chinese National Office under the aegis of the UN-WCC was established to collect evidence on alleged war crimes committed by Japanese officials. Immediately following the war the Chinese government created a special investigation commission comprising various organisations, including the Nanjing municipal government, the police bureau, Nationalist Party department, the gendarmerie command, labour unions, farmers' unions, industrial unions, and the local courts and lawyers' association.[18] The Chinese government posted notices in the streets urging witnesses to come forward with evidence. From military troops to ordinary citizens, inquiry forms were handed out to victims of war to report atrocities they witnessed and losses they suffered.[19]

On 26 May 1945 the head of the Executive Yuan issued an order to investigate crimes committed by the Japanese army in China.[20] In early 1946 the special investigation commission received 1,036 letters of complaint, among them 320 were about the crimes committed by the Japanese

---

[15]   See United Nations War Crimes Commission, *History of the United Nations War Crimes Commission and the Development of the Laws of War*, His Majesty's Stationery Office, London, 1948.

[16]   R. John Pritchard, "War Crimes, International Criminal Law, and the Postwar Trials in Europe and Asia", in Loyd E. Lee (ed.), *World War II in Asia and the Pacific and the War's Aftermath, with General Themes: A Handbook of Literature and research*, Greenwood, Westport, CT, 1998, p. 459.

[17]   The 12 governments were Australia, Belgium, China, Czechoslovakia, France, India, Luxembourg, the Netherlands, Poland, the United Kingdom and the United States.

[18]   GUO Biqiang, "Investigation Statistics Conducted by Japanese War Crimes Investigation Commission", in ZHANG Xianwen (ed.), *Collection of Historical Materials on the Nanking Massacre*, vol. 20, Jiangsu People's Press, Nanjing, 2006, p. 1722.

[19]   See ZHANG Jing and L-V JING, "Crimes Investigation Forms filled out by Liao Tujin and Property Lost Form", in ZHANG Xianwen, *The Truth of the Nanking Massacre: Chinese Material*, Jiangsu People's Press, Nanjing, 2006, pp. 468, 495.

[20]   HU, 2006, p. 10, see *supra* note 10.

army and 67 were related to the Nanjing Massacre.[21] The Ministry of Justice also drafted a list of suspects responsible for the Nanjing Massacre. Among the 83 suspects listed, at the top was Prince Yasuhiko Asaka, the commander-in-chief of all Japanese forces during the Nanjing Massacre, as well as his subordinate, Lieutenant General Tani Hisao, commander of the 6th Division of the Imperial Japanese Army.[22]

On 15 February 1946 the Nanjing Tribunal was formally established under the Chinese Ministry of Defence.[23] The tribunal was composed of five judges, with Justice SHI Mei-yu as the president. Three of the judges were appointed by the Ministry of Defence and the other two by the Ministry of Justice.[24] The prosecution office comprised one to three chief prosecutors, with CHEN Guang-yu as the chief prosecutor. The Ministry of Justice was mandated to appoint one or two prosecutors from the high courts, and the Ministry of Defence was to appoint the other prosecutor. Every bench of the Nanjing Tribunal was stipulated to have one or two reserve judges or prosecutors so as to replace those who could not perform their duties.[25]

The discussions above demonstrate that the Nanjing Tribunal was established according to both international and Chinese domestic law and it went through a long period of preparation. Indeed, the Japanese government formally recognised its lawfulness and promised to implement and enforce the judgments and sentences rendered by the Nanjing Tribunal.[26] In the Instrument of Surrender the Japanese representative on behalf of the Japanese emperor and government declared:

---

21 *Central Daily News*, 6 January 1946.

22 The List of War Criminals of Nanking Massacre Prepared by Ministry of Justice, in HU, 2006, p. 54, see *supra* note 10.

23 See Detailed Rules for the Trial of War Criminals by Military Committee, *ibid.*, p. 38.

24 *Central Daily News*, 3 July 1946.

25 Law on Trial of War Criminals, Art. 21, in HU, 2006, p. 32, see *supra* note 10. This practice was very innovative at that time. After half a century, the Scottish court in the Lockerbie case began to utilise the practice of reserve judges. Later, in 2005, this rule was also incorporated into the International Criminal Tribunal for the former Yugoslavia ('ICTY'), Rules of Procedure and Evidence, as amended on 8 July 2015 ('http://www.legal-tools.org/doc/30df50/).

26 This was reflected in many international treaties, including: Instrument of Surrender by Japan, 2 September 1945 ('Instrument of Surrender') (https://www.legal-tools.org/doc/4059de/); Proclamation Defining Terms for Japanese Surrender, Potsdam, 26 July 1945 ('Potsdam Declaration') (http://www.legal-tools.org/doc/f8cae3/); and the Trea-

> We hereby undertake for the Emperor, the Japanese Government, and their successors to carry out the provisions of the Potsdam Declaration in good faith, and to issue whatever orders and take whatever action may be required by the Supreme Commander for the Allied Powers or by any other designated representative of the Allied Powers for the purpose of giving effect to that Declaration.[27]

In addition, the Potsdam Declaration, which defined the terms for the Japanese surrender, clearly stipulated: "We do not intend that the Japanese shall be enslaved as a race or destroyed as a nation, but stern justice shall be meted out to all war criminals, including those who have visited cruelties upon our prisoners".[28]

Officially, the Japanese government had accepted the judgments of the Nanjing Tribunal. Under Article 11 of the San Francisco Peace Treaty, signed on 8 September 1951, Japan formally recognised the jurisdiction and judgments of the IMTFE and the Nanjing Tribunal. Article 11 of reads:

> Japan accepts the judgments of the International Military Tribunal for the Far East and of other Allied War Crimes Courts both within and outside Japan, and will carry out the sentences imposed thereby upon Japanese nationals imprisoned in Japan. The power to grant clemency, reduce sentences and parole with respect to such prisoners may not be exercised except on the decision of the government or governments which imposed the sentence in each instance, and on the recommendation of Japan. In the case of persons sentenced by the International Military Tribunal for the Far East, such power may not be exercised except on the decision of a majority of the governments represented on the Tribunal, and on the recommendation of Japan.[29]

These Japanese declarations substantiate the legitimacy of the trials against Japanese war criminals in China and the Nanjing Tribunal's lawful establishment.

---

ty of Peace with Japan, San Francisco, 8 September 1951, United Nations Treaty Series 1952 (1832), vol .136, pp 45–164 ('San Francisco Peace treaty').

[27] Instrument of Surrender, para. 6, see *supra* note 26.

[28] Potsdam Declaration, para. 10 , see *supra* note 26.

[29] San Francisco Peace Treaty, see *supra* note 26.

6.2. Observation of the Principle of *Nullum Crimen Sine Lege*

Emulating the Charter of the International Military Tribunal at Nuremberg ('IMT Charter') and the Charter of the IMTFE ('IMTFE Charter'), and following extensive deliberations and consultations, the Ministry of Defence and the Military Commission of the Chinese government drafted a series of laws and regulations on issues relating to the arrest and trials of Japanese war criminals. On 4 July 1946 the Ministry of Defence submitted to China's State Council the outline for the trial of war criminals, which provided the subject-matter jurisdiction, temporal and personal jurisdiction, as well as the modes of liability.[30] In the same year the Military Commission also issued the Regulations on Procedure of Arresting Japanese War Criminals,[31] the Regulation on the Handling of War Criminals,[32] Rules for Implementation of the Regulation on the Trial of War Criminals,[33] the Amendment Draft of Rules Governing the Trial of War Criminals,[34] as well as the Document Comparing War Crimes between China's Criminal Code and International Law.[35]

The Nationalist government's Law Governing the Trial of War Criminals was promulgated on 23 October 1946.[36] Compared to the IMT Charter, the IMTFE Charter and Control Council Law No. 10,[37] the Law Governing the Trial of War Criminals is more detailed and specific. It is not an arbitrary exercise of power on the part of the victorious state. It is, rather, the expression of international law as it existed in 1946. According to its provisions, the tribunal shall apply the Law Governing the Trial of War Criminals and international law first. If there is no specific stipulation in the Law on the Trial of War Criminals, the tribunal shall apply China's Criminal Code. When doing so, the special law shall be applied first, which means, *inter alia*, the above-mentioned laws and regula-

---

[30] HU, 2006, p. 28, see *supra* note 10.

[31] *Ibid.*, p. 36.

[32] *Ibid.*, p. 37.

[33] *Ibid.*, p. 38

[34] *Ibid.*, p. 40.

[35] *Ibid.*, pp. 12, 24.

[36] *Ibid.*, p. 30.

[37] Control Council Law No. 10, Punishment of Persons Guilty of War Crimes, Crimes against Peace and against Humanity, Berlin, 20 December 1945 ('Control Council Law No. 10') (http://www.legal-tools.org/doc/ffda62/).

tions.[38] Various aspects of the Law Governing the Trial of War Criminals are examined and discussed below.

6.2.1. Personal Jurisdiction

The Law Governing the Trial of War Criminals was applicable to both military and civilians so long as the crimes committed were encompassed in its provisions and occurred during the period of time prescribed therein. The law only has personal jurisdiction over persons without Chinese nationality. Accordingly, the Nanjing Tribunal had no jurisdiction to prosecute Chinese nationals who collaborated with the Japanese during the war. They would be prosecuted and tried by Chinese domestic courts in accordance with domestic law. Article 6 provided that the Law Governing the Trial of War Criminals was also applicable to any suspect whose Chinese nationality was restored after 25 October 1945. This article mainly applied to Taiwanese, when Taiwan returned to China on that date after 50 years of Japanese occupation since the First Sino-Japanese War.[39]

6.2.2. Subject-matter Jurisdiction

The Law Governing the Trial of War Criminals also provided that the Nanjing Tribunal had jurisdiction over three major crimes: crimes against peace, war crimes and crimes against humanity. It thus recognised that crimes against humanity and crimes against peace were distinct under international law. According to the law, crimes against peace were defined as any foreign military or civilian planning, participating in a conspiracy, initiating or waging a war of aggression against China, before or during the war, in violation of international treaties, agreements or assurances, or engaging in other unlawful war. This definition was more or less identical to the definition in the IMT and IMTFE Charters.

---

[38] Article 1 of the Law Governing the Trial of War Criminals reads: "This law shall apply to the trials and punishment of the war criminals, besides the application of international law. If there is no specific stipulation in this law, the Criminal Code of the Republic of China should be applicable. When applying the Criminal Code of the Republic of China, special law shall be applied first".

[39] When the Japanese surrendered at the end of the Second World War, General Andō Rikichi, governor-general of Taiwan and commander-in-chief of all Japanese forces on the island, signed an instrument of surrender and handed it over to General CHEN Yi of the Kuomintang military to complete the official turnover in Taipei on 25 October 1945 at Taipei City Hall (now Zhongshan Hall).

As for war crimes, the Law Governing the Trial of War Criminals stipulated 38 sub-crimes, which were based on the 32 sub-crimes that the London war crimes investigation committee had suggested. According to the specific situation in China, more sub-crimes were added.[40] Those sub-crimes were:

1. Extermination, murder and other acts of terror in a planned way;
2. Killing hostages;
3. Intentional starvation of civilians to death;
4. Rape;
5. Abduction of children;
6. Collective punishment;
7. Intentional bombardment against undefended areas;
8. Attacking commercial and passages ships without warning and with disregard of the safety of the passengers and crew members;
9. Attacking fishing boats and relieving boats;
10. Intentional bombardment of hospitals;
11. Attacking or destroying hospital ships;
12. Employing poisonous gas and spreading gems;
13. Employing inhumane weapons;
14. Declaring no quarter will be given;
15. Poisoning drinking water or food;
16. Torture against civilians;
17. Abduction of women and forcing them to be prostitutes;
18. Deporting or transferring civilians;
19. Detention of civilians and inhumane treatment;
20. Compelling civilians to engaging in military activities for the adversary;

---

40 For instance: without warning and disregard of the safety of the passengers and crew members; declaring abolished, suspended or inadmissible in a court of law the rights and actions of the nationals of the hostile party during the period of occupation; collective arrest; and seizing historical or artistic subjects, and so forth.

21. Declaring abolished, suspended or inadmissible in a court of law the rights and actions of the nationals of the hostile party during the period of occupation;

22. Compelling the residents of the occupied area to serve in the forces of a hostile power;

23. Attempt at enslavement of the residents of the occupied area or depriving their inherited status and rights of a national;

24. Pillage;

25. Unlawful and excessively levelling tax and appropriation;

26. Devaluation of currencies and issuing forged money;

27. Extensive destruction of properties;

28. Violation of other rules laid down by the International Committee of the Red Cross;

29. Mistreatment of prisoners and the wounded;

30. Employing prisoners of war to engage in irregular work;

31. Making improper use of a flag of truce;

32. Collective arrest;

33. Appropriation of property;

34. Destruction of religious, charity, educational or historical buildings and monuments;

35. Intentionally committing outrages upon personal dignity;

36. Seizing or extortion of properties;

37. Seizing historical or artistic subjects;

38. Other acts in violation of war laws or customary of war, for instance, cruel acts beyond military necessity, or destruction, forcing civilians to anything beyond their obligations; or affecting the exercise of their legitimate rights.[41]

It is clear that the Chinese law emphasised the protection of basic human rights during wartime. And as noted, within the list of war crimes there was also an inclusive clause that identified "other acts in violation of war laws or customary of war".[42] Demonstrating the legality of the Law

---

[41] HU, 2006, p. 30, see *supra* note 10.

[42] *Ibid.*

Governing the Trial of War Criminals, it can be observed that the International Criminal Tribunal for the former Yugoslavia ('ICTY'), International Criminal Tribunal for Rwanda ('ICTR') and the International Criminal Court ('ICC') have adopted such a clause in their respective statutes. It gives the judges great discretion and, at the same time, it is not in violation of the principle of legality, since the acts in this clause should be as serious as other prohibited acts listed as war crimes. The Law Governing the Trial of War Criminals also stipulated that the statute of limitation, as described in Article 80 of China's Criminal Code, shall not be applicable to war crimes. As for crimes against humanity, the Law Governing the Trial of War Criminals criminalised the act of any foreign military or civilian, before or during armed conflict or hostility against China, that attempted to enslave, destroy or annihilate the Chinese nation. The following crimes were set out: 1) murder, starvation, extermination, slavery and deportation; 2) narcosis and control of ideology; 3) promotion, dissemination or forced use of narcotic drugs or planting of opium; and 4) forcible use or injection of narcotic drugs, or enforced sterilisation, or persecution on political, racial or religious grounds or other inhumane acts.

In accordance with the principle of *nullem crimen sine lege*, the Law Governing the Trial of War Criminals was largely based on existing international conventions. For crimes of breaches against peace, the Nanjing Tribunal referred to the text of the Pact of Paris of 27 August 1928, signed by 63 nations, including Japan, at the outbreak of war in 1931, thus making the waging of aggressive war illegal and those committing the act criminally liable. The Nanjing Tribunal also referred to the Nine-Power Treaty signed on 6 February 1922.[43] For war crimes, the national government published a document comparing war crimes with China's Criminal Code and with international law,[44] which traced the sources of the crimes in the Chinese law back to: the 1907 Hague Convention IV respecting the Laws and Customs of War on Land; the International Committee of the Red Cross conventions and international conventions on narcotic drugs; as well as customary international law. Accordingly, at the time crimes were committed during the Nanjing Massacre, pre-existing

---

[43] The Nine-Power Treaty, Washington, 6 February 1922, League of Nations Treaty Series 723. The nine powers were the United Kingdom, the United States, Belgium, China, France, Italy, Japan, the Netherlands and Portugal.

[44] HU, 2006, p. 30, see *supra* note 10.

international law bound and governed the acts of the defendants. It is clear that the Nanjing Tribunal did not apply *ex post facto* law, thus demonstrating that the principle of *nullem crimen sine lege* had been duly observed.

6.2.3. Temporal Jurisdiction

Article 4 of the Law Governing the Trial of War Criminals stipulated that the Nanjing Tribunal only had jurisdiction over crimes occurring between 18 September 1931, when the Japanese China Expeditionary Army invaded north-east China, and 2 September 1945, when the Japanese foreign minister signed the Instrument of Surrender on board USS *Missouri*. As for crimes against peace and crimes against humanity, the law did not apply to any crimes occurring before 18 September 1931.

6.2.4. Responsibility and Sentencing

The Law Governing the Trial of War Criminals also stipulated that a person who committed a crime within the jurisdiction of the Nanjing Tribunal shall not be relieved of his/her responsibilities on the following grounds: the implementation of superior orders, performing his/her job functions, promoting government policies and for political purposes.[45] A superior shall share the same criminal responsibility with his/her subordinates who committed war crimes, if he or she failed to prevent or stop the crimes.[46] According to the principle of *nullem crimen sine lege*, Chinese law stipulated the sentences of those convicted. Based on Articles 10 and 11 of the Law Governing the Trial of War Criminals, those convicted of crimes against peace and crimes against humanity, as well as grave violation of the laws of war, shall be sentenced to death or life imprisonment. Other offences mandate a sentence of seven or more years imprisonment.

6.3. Fairness of the Trials

The right to a fair trial is one of the cornerstones of a just society. Without fair trials, innocent people could be wrongfully convicted and the rule of law and public faith in the justice system would collapse. Irrespective of

---

[45] Article 8 of the Law Governing the Trial of War Criminals, in HU, p. 42, see *supra* note 10.

[46] *Ibid.*

---

the severity of the crimes alleged, the accused's legitimate right to fair proceedings should be guaranteed. With the development of human rights law, the standard and concept of a fair trial have greatly improved since the end of the Second World War. While alleged war criminals at the time could not benefit from present standards of trial fairness, the basic form of this right should still be guaranteed.

Article 26 of the Law Governing the Trial of War Criminals stipulated that the military prosecutor shall issue the indictment against the accused for war crime cases. In October 1946 an indictment against Doihara Kenji[47] and 30 other suspects was issued and it clearly and accurately listed the crimes charged with detailed descriptions of specific crime scenes.[48] On 31 December 1946 the chief prosecutor of the Nanjing Tribunal, CHEN Guang-yu, issued an indictment against Tani Hisao for his alleged crimes committed during the Nanjing Massacre. The attachment to the indictment listed 220 incidents of killing and massacres involving 924 victims. This was sufficient to provide the accused notice of crimes with which he was charged.[49] All of the Japanese accused tried by the Nanjing Tribunal received indictments before their trials. For instance, Okamuru Yasuji stated in his memoirs that he received the indictment against him on 2 August 1948.[50]

Taking Tani's case as an example, this chapter contends that all judicial activities were conducted according to the rules of procedure of the Nanjing War Crimes Tribunal. Tani was born on 22 December 1882. He was a lieutenant general in the Imperial Japanese Army during the Second World War. From 1935 to 1937 Tani was the commander of the 6th Division of the China Expeditionary Army, which was involved in battles in northern China and the attacks against Shanghai and Nanjing. After the war, the Allied powers arrested Tani on 2 February 1946 in Japan and interrogated him on 23 February at the Sugamo Prison in Tokyo. Tani said that his division had not committed any atrocities in Nanjing and added that he had not heard any stories of atrocities being committed.

---

47 A class A war criminal, indicted and tried by the IMTFE and sentenced to death.

48 HU, 2006, p. 15, see *supra* note 10.

49 *Ibid.*, p. 324, Indictment against Tani.

50 Inaba Masao (ed.), 冈村宁次回忆录 [Yasuji Okamura's Memoirs], trans. Tianjin Compilation and Translation Bureau of the Political Consultative Association, Zhonghua shuju, Beijing, 1981.

Nevertheless, the Chinese government demanded that Tani be extradited to China to stand trial for war crimes at the Nanjing Tribunal. He was extradited on 1 August 1946.[51] On 31 December 1946 CHEN Guang-yu filed a special indictment against him. The indictment charged Tani with crimes against peace, crimes against humanity and war crimes during the Nanjing Massacre for his participation in the atrocities. The indictment alleged that Tani was responsible for having killed several hundred thousand victims for the purpose of "crushing our nation's [China] will to resist".[52] The prosecution then claimed that Tani's military unit had committed massacres and rape in multiple locations in the vicinity of Zhonghua Gate, Nanjing and added that the incident was a "blot on the history of modern civilisation".[53] A document attached to the indictment listed specific evidence of killings, exterminations, lootings and rapes in Nanjing. These were 122 cases of shooting that resulted in the deaths of 334 people; 14 cases of stabbing causing the deaths of 195 people; 15 cases of group massacre that claimed the lives of 95 people; 15 cases of rape involving 43 women; three cases of property damage suffered by 17 people; and 69 instances of death for other reasons.[54]

In his opening statement on 8 February 1947 the prosecutor enumerated almost all alleged massacres in Nanjing within and outside of the operation area of Tani's 6th Division and declared the total number of victims as 400,000.[55] He also told the tribunal that the Nanjing Massacre was a "planned action" by the Japanese army, that it covered the whole city, and that while the accused only took part in a portion of the atrocities, "he should be held responsible for the whole massacre".[56]

Tani pleaded not guilty. In a statement submitted to the Nanjing Tribunal on 15 January 1947 he denied any knowledge of the alleged atrocities and added that the atrocities were made known to him when he returned to Japan. He also claimed that all the events happened in the op-

---

51 Telegraph sent by the Second Department of the Chinese Ministry of Defence to Nanking War Crimes Tribunal on the Arrival of Tani Hisao in Shanghai ('Telegraph'), on August 10, 1946, in HU, 2006, p. 61, see *supra* note 10.

52 *Ibid.*, Indictment, p. 325.

53 *Ibid.*

54 *Ibid.*, Attachment to the Indictment. p. 329.

55 *Ibid.*

56 *Ibid.*, p. 375, Opening statement by the chief prosecutor Chen Guang-yu.

eration theatre of the Nakajima Unit and that he played no part. He never gave his consent or issued any order for the killings. He never received any reports about the atrocities.[57] His trial started from 6 February 1947 and the judgment was delivered on 10 March 1947. The whole trial lasted approximately one month.

According to Article 27 of the Law Governing the Trial of War Criminals, the accused was entitled to choose defence counsel from the Nanjing Tribunal's list of accredited lawyers according to China's law. If the accused failed to appoint a defence counsel, the public defence counsel of the court shall be assigned to him. If the court had no public counsel available, it shall appoint a defence counsel. The Nanjing Tribunal appointed two Chinese lawyers, MEI Zufang and ZHANG Rende, to be Tani's defence lawyers.[58] Some defendants claimed that they were not allowed to be represented by Japanese lawyers. While this may be true, it is not a basis to claim that the trial was wholly unfair. The Nanjing Tribunal was not an international court, but a domestic one in China. According to the Detailed Rules for the Trial of War Criminals, promulgated by the Military Committee,[59] the accused could only choose Chinese lawyers according to China's Law on Lawyers, and only lawyers with Chinese nationality could appear before China's courts, which is the normal practice in most countries in the world. Of course, the Japanese defendants had the opportunity to seek advice from lawyers of their own and of other countries.

The accused was also entitled to have the free assistance of interpreters if he could not understand or speak the language used at the tribunal. The Nanjing Tribunal appointed three interpreters especially for Tani.[60] In order to allow audiences from other countries to follow court proceedings, the Nanjing Tribunal sent a request to the Ministry of Defence for English interpreters on 31 January 1947.[61]

Article 28 of the Law Governing the Trial of War Criminals stated that the trials at the Nanjing Tribunal as well as judgments shall be made public, thus guaranteeing transparency to the clearest extent. Throughout the investigation and trial stages, the trials were conducted in a way that

---

[57] Masao, 1981, see *supra* note 50.

[58] Letter of Acceptance of Mr. MEI Zugang, HU, 2006, p. 350, see *supra* note 10.

[59] Article 7 of the Detailed Rules, in *ibid.*, p. 39.

[60] *Central Daily News*, 6 February 1947.

[61] HU, 2006, p. 358, see *supra* note 10.

greatly encouraged public involvement. For the Chinese people, especially for the victims of the Nanjing Massacre, the public proceedings provided them with an opportunity to claim the damage they suffered, to be heard and to seek justice. Major Chinese newspapers such as the *Central Daily News*, the official news media of the Chinese government, the *Da Kong Pao*, and foreign media outlets all intensively and continuously covered important cases at the Nanjing Tribunal. Aside from newspapers, the Chinese government also used all possible ways to raise public awareness about the trials. For example, in July 1946 slide shows were made about the Nanjing Massacre and played before films in local cinemas.[62]

Tani, as a defendant, also had the right to examine the witnesses against him and to obtain the attendance and examination of witnesses on his behalf under the same conditions as witnesses against him. In this regard, Tani called Ogasawara Takeshi to testify during the proceedings. Ogasawara was a member of the research staff in the Japanese army. He claimed that, according to his research, no atrocities at all were committed in Nanjing because there was furious fighting around Zhonghua Gate and there were no residents in the area. The Nanjing Tribunal found that when Nanjing fell in 1937 Ogasawara was still a student at the Japanese Military Academy and was not a first-hand witness. Accordingly, his testimony was found to have no merit, to be insufficiently probative to raise reasonable doubt and to be incapable of demonstrating the Nanjing Tribunal erred in assessing the credibility of prosecution witnesses. Tani also requested the Tribunal to call other witnesses, including General Tanabe Moritake, chief of staff of the Yanagawa Division,[63] and General Shimadzu Ichi, deputy chief of staff of the 18th Division. The Tribunal found that these witnesses, generals of the Imperial Japanese Army, were co-perpetrators of the Nanjing Massacre, thus rendering the credibility of their testimonies in serious doubt. The accused did not provide their whereabouts, but only requested that they be extradited from Tokyo. The

---

[62] "Order of Nanking Society Bureau Ordering All Cinemas to Play the Slide Shows about Nanking Massacre Investigation Unit", in GUO Biqiang and JIANG Liangqin, *Collection of Historical Materials on the Nanking Massacre: Investigation Statics Conducted by Japanese War Crimes Investigation Commission*, Jiangsu People's Press, Nanjing, 2006, p. 1532.

[63] Tanabe Moritake was the commander-in-chief for the Japanese army in Indonesia in 1944. He was arrested after the war, sentenced to death by the Dutch Military Tribunal in Indonesia on 4 December 1948 and executed on 11 July 1949.

Nanjing Tribunal noted that Tani requested to call these witnesses several months after arrest. It determined that the purpose of his request was to delay the proceedings. Accordingly, the Nanjing Tribunal, acting within its discretion, rejected Tani's request.[64]

Some defendants alleged that they were deprived of the right to appeal against the sentence rendered by the Nanjing Tribunal in the first instance. At the time, appeal was not an absolute right. The IMTFE Charter did not grant defendants the right of appeals either, but they could seek administrative review of their sentences. The same was true for the Nanjing Tribunal. Article 32 provided that any judgment for conviction shall be approved by the Ministry of Defence, and those defendants who were sentenced to death and life sentence shall submit the verdict to the president of the Chinese government for approval via the Ministry of Defence. Tani, who was found guilty, could not accept the convictions rendered against him. In accordance with the Law Governing the Trial of War Criminals, he petitioned General CHEN Cheng, chief of staff of the Ministry of Defence, on 18 December 1946,[65] and SHI Mei-yu, president of the Nanjing Tribunal, on 15 January 1947.[66] Finally, he also pleaded to General BAI Chongxi, the minister of defence, on 18 March 1947. All these requests for review were submitted to the CHIANG Kai-shek and on 28 March 1947 the president decided to uphold the verdict rendered by the Nanjing Tribunal.[67] While his petitions and pleading were rejected, Tani nevertheless had the right to have his case reviewed. On 26 April 1947 Tani was executed.[68]

---

[64] National Archive No. 2, Newspaper Report, 25 February 1947, in HU, 2006, see *supra* note 10, p. 381.

[65] HU, 2006, p. 461, see *supra* note 10. Tani died a relatively honourable death as a military official by standing in front of an execution squad in comparison with the seven class A war criminals of the IMTFE who were hanged in the prison.

[66] *Ibid.*, p. 463.

[67] Cited from the confidential archive of the President's Office. Historical Materials of the Republic of China, the Period of Anti-Japanese Aggression, Second Section, Fighting, Committee of History of the Central Committee of the National Party, vol. 4, pp. 454–55.

[68] *Central Daily News*, 26 April 1947.

6.4. Overwhelming Evidence for Conviction beyond Reasonable Doubt

During trial and in the various requests to have his case reviewed, Tani and his defence lawyers raised several arguments, as summarised below:

- All evidence presented on the Nanjing Massacre was fabricated and lacked proof.

- Tani did not hear anything about the Nanjing incidents and did not see any dead bodies on the streets of Nanjing. He knew about the crimes only after the war while in prison in Japan.

- The army unit under Tani's command entered the city during the night of 12 December 1937 and pulled out of the city on 21 December 1937. The crimes had nothing to do with his army unit.

- The most serious crimes were committed in the middle of the city and along the Yangtze River. The responsibility for the alleged massacre rested with other units, such as those under the command of Generals Nakajima and Suematsu.

- The defendant's unit was well disciplined and orderly and did not kill anyone.[69]

The Nanjing Tribunal considered his arguments and evidence from both sides. More than 1,000 witnesses testified at his trial, recounting 460 cases of murder, rape, arson and looting.[70] Numerous eyewitness accounts of Westerners and Chinese citizens rebutted Tani's arguments as they demonstrated overwhelming evidence that Japanese troops engaged in rape, murder, theft, arson and other war crimes after the fall of Nanjing. The accounts included gruesome details of the Nanjing Massacre as thousands of innocent civilians were found to have been murdered, buried alive, used as targets for bayonet practice, shot in large groups and thrown into the Yangtze River. Evidence of rampant rape (and gang rape) of girls and women ranging from the age of seven to over 70 were presented. The international community estimated that within the six weeks of the Nanjing Massacre, 20,000 women were raped, many of them subsequently

---

[69]   HU, 2006, p. 463, see *supra* note 10.
[70]   Iris CHANG, *The Rape of Nanking: The Forgotten Holocaust of World War II*, Penguin, New York, 1998, p. 170.

murdered or mutilated, and over 300,000 civilians and prisoners of war were killed, often with the most inhumane brutality. The Japanese military looted the city and the surrounding area on a monumental scale, enslaved millions and exploited them as forced labourers.

LIANG Tingfang and BAI Zengrong, two survivors of the massacre, testified first. They told the Tribunal that at 18:00 on 16 December 1937 the military units under Tani rounded up approximately 5,000 refugees at the Overseas Chinese Hotel and drove them to a pier by the Yangtze River and shot them with machine guns. The bodies were then thrown into the river. The two survivors were seriously wounded and floated with other bodies in the river.[71] YAO Jialong also testified that on 14 December 1937 soldiers under Tani's command found his family at Zhanlong Bridge near Zhonghua Gate, where Tani's army was stationed. His wife was gang-raped and killed, and his two children were bayoneted to the fire and burned to death.[72] Another first-hand witness, FAN Shifu, testified that "subordinates under Tani Hisao committed murder, arson and rape without reason, and Tani's unit was identified as the most merciless, killing well over 100,000 people".[73] ZHANG Hongru told the Tribunal that the "Japanese army entered the city on 12 December 1937 and the army under Tani committed the most serious crimes of murder, arson and rape".[74] GUO Qi was a battalion leader of the Chinese army who hid in Nanjing for three months during the massacre and wrote a book entitled *Xiandu Xielei Ji* (A Record of Blood and Tears in the Fallen Capital), written in the first half of 1938. He also testified in Tani's case and pointed out that most of the atrocities described in his book happened around Zhonghua Gate, where Tani's troops were stationed.[75] The prosecution also presented in court the skulls of the dead, which were exhumed from the graveyard outside Zhonghua Gate.[76]

During the trial, the prosecution also called on foreigners who stayed in Nanjing during the Nanjing Massacre to testify. These foreigners included Miner Searle Bates, an American professor of history at Nan-

---

71 Judgment, HU, p. 388, see *supra* note 10.

72 *Ibid.*

73 *Ibid.*

74 *Ibid.*

75 *Ibid.*

76 *Ibid.*

jing University and one of the leaders of the International Committee for the Nanjing Safety Zone, who worked to secure the safety of the remaining population;[77] and Lewis S.C. Smythe, an American professor of sociology at Nanjing University, who testified about Japanese atrocities he saw when he served as the secretary of the International Committee for the Nanjing Safety Zone from 14 December 1937 to 10 February 1938.[78]

The Nanjing Tribunal also admitted into evidence written materials and books, including: *What War Means: The Japanese Terror in China* (the Chinese title translates as "Recorded Facts of the Japanese Army's Violence") by the Australian journalist H.J. Timperley; *War Damage in the Nanking Area December, 1937 to March, 1938* by Smythe; and *Xiandu Xielei Ji* (A Record of Blood and Tears in the Fallen Capital) by GUO Qi.[79] The diaries of John Rabe, a German national, and Minnie Vautrin, an American, as well as the field diaries and letters of both Chinese and Japanese military personnel and of staff members working in the Nanjing safety zone were also admitted as evidence. These materials, written during the Nanjing Massacre or shortly after, provide a candid description of the events. During court proceedings, a 16 mm film documentary, shot by the American missionary John Magee, was shown as well as photographs of the Nanjing Massacre, some of which were taken by the Japanese themselves.[80]

All this evidence, whether written or oral, was cumulatively corroborative of events during the Nanjing Massacre. According to the Tribunal, the only reasonable conclusion that could be inferred from the totality of the evidence on the record was that the Nanjing Massacre was a reality and that Tani contributed to this atrocity. Based on direct witness evidence, the Tribunal found that, despite Tani's duty to defend Zhonghua Gate, his troops committed a total of 459 separate incidents of arson, murder, rape and pillage in the vicinity.

---

[77] *Ibid.*

[78] *Ibid.*

[79] H.J. Timperley, *What War Means: The Japanese Terror in China: A Documentary Record*, Victor Gollancz, London, 1938; Lewis S.C. Smythe, *War Damage in the Nanking Area December, 1937 to March, 1938: Urban and Rural Surveys*, Mercury Press, Shangha, 1938.

[80] Timothy Brook (ed.), *Documents on the Rape of Nanking*, University of Michigan Press, Ann Arbor, 1999.

In pronouncing the judgment, the Tribunal enumerated almost all the large-scale massacres alleged to have taken place in Nanjing, and did so both in its verdict and the appendix before delving into the details of Tani's case. The major incidents attributable to Tani's unit included: an alleged massacre of 28,730 prisoners of war and civilians in Shangxinhe; the killing of 400 to 500 civilians in a refugee shelter in Sanyuhe; and the slaughter of approximately 5,000 refugees and 2,000 prisoners of war outside Zhonghua Gate. In addition, there were 487 cases of alleged individual murders, 25 cases of rape, nine cases of robbery and 90 cases of arson.[81] The Tribunal found "conspiracy" or "co-perpetratorship" among the Japanese military leaders in Nanjing and held Tani responsible as one of the contributors to the massacre.

The judgment discussed the findings as follows:

> Outline of the facts: The Japanese military clique saw our capital [Nanjing] as the centre of our resistance against them. The powerful, brutal and cruel 6th Division under Tani Hisao, the 16th Division under Nakajima, the 18th Division under Ushijima, the 114th Division under Suematsu and other units were joined under the command of General Matsui Iwane and attacked [Nanjing] in union. Our armies met them with unbending resistance, which enraged the enemy and in revenge, after the fall of the city, they carried out a planned massacre. The 6th Division under Tani Hisao acted as the spearhead and on the evening of December 12th, 1937, they took Zhonghua Gate by storm, the lead unit scaling the walls with rope ladders, entering the city and beginning the massacre. The following morning large armies led by Nakajima, Ushijima, Suematsu and others again advanced into the city and carried out large-scale massacres in different parts therein, accompanied by arson, rape and looting. The most violent massacres occurred that year from December 12th through December 21st, which is also the period when Tani division was stationed in Nanking. [...] The total number of victims was in excess of 300,000. It was the extreme of misery, and cannot be described in written or spoken words.[82]

---

[81] *Central Daily News*, 10 March 1947.

[82] Judgment, HU, 2006, p. 388, see *supra* note 10.

After examining and discussing the factual issues and evidence, the Nanjing Tribunal arrived at its verdict:

> Acts of cruelty by the accused during the war included violence encompassing such acts as killing prisoners of war and civilian non-combatants, accompanied by rape, looting, theft and destruction of property. This violates the Regulations Respecting the Laws and Customs of War on Land of the Hague Convention and Geneva Convention's rules for treating of war, and constitutes war crimes and crimes against humanity and should be punished with the death penalty.[83]

6.5. Related Legal Issues Regarding Tani's Case before the Nanjing Tribunal

Seventy years after the Nanjing Tribunal, the Nanjing Massacre remains a contentious political issue. Japanese historical revisionists and massacre deniers have disputed various aspects of the trials and have claimed that the massacre was either exaggerated or wholly fabricated for propaganda purposes. The most contentious issues include: 1) whether a policy, plan or common criminal design existed to kill civilians and prisoners of war; 2) whether the death toll in fact reached 300,000 during the Nanjing Massacre; 3) whether Chinese soldiers, who laid down their arms and changed into civilian clothes, were entitled to protection under international humanitarian law; 4) whether any evidence demonstrated that Tani had the knowledge of or intent to commit the crimes; and 5) the mode of his liability in the commission of the crimes. Each of these issues is discussed below.

6.5.1. Common Plan or Design

There is overwhelming evidence to show that the Nanjing Massacre was not a sporadic or isolated incident, but rather a systematic and widespread killing of civilians and prisoners of war. "Widespread" refers to the large-scale nature of the attack and the number of targeted persons,[84] to the cumulative effect of a series of inhumane acts or to the singular effect of an

---

[83] Ibid.

[84] ICTY, *Prosecutor v. Dario Kordić and Mario Čerkez*, Appeals Chamber, Judgment, 17 December 2004, IT-95-14/2-A, para. 94 (http://www.legal-tools.org/doc/738211/).

inhumane act of extraordinary magnitude.[85] "Systematic" refers to the organised nature of the acts of violence and the improbability of their random occurrence.[86] The massiveness of the crime automatically assumes a substantial degree of preparation and organisation which may serve as indicia for the existence of a murderous scheme or plan.[87] Judging from the magnitude of the atrocities that occurred in Nanjing, any reasonable person could arrive at the conclusion that "[t]he Rape of Nanking was not the kind of isolated incident common to all wars. It was deliberate. It was policy. It was known in Tokyo. Yet it was allowed to continue for over six weeks".[88]

The war diary of Lieutenant General Nakajima Kesago, commander of the 16th Division, was made public in 1984. He wrote on 13 December 1937:

1. Since our policy is, in principle, to take no prisoners, we attempted to dispose of all of them. However, they continued to surrender in droves, first 1,000, then 5,000, then 10,000. We could not begin to disarm such a large number of soldiers. They had completely lost the will to fight, and simply followed after us. They did not seem to present any threat, but if a riot had erupted, we would not have been able to control them. Therefore, I had additional units brought in by truck, and assigned them to guard and escort the Chinese.

2. On the evening of the 13th, we were required to make countless trips with the trucks. But since this event occurred immediately after a battle (which we had won), we were not able to act expeditiously. The Operations Section was unbelievably busy because we had to dispose of far more prisoners than we had anticipated.

3. Later, I learned that Sasaki's unit alone had processed approximately 15,000 individuals, that a company com-

---

[85] ICTY, *Prosecutor v. Vidoje Blagojević and Dragan Jokić*, Trial Chamber, Judgment, 17 January 2005, IT-02-60-T, para. 545 ('Blagojević and Jokić Trial Judgment') (http://www.legal-tools.org/doc/7483f2/).

[86] *Ibid.*, para. 94.

[87] ICTY, *Prosecutor v. Milomir Stakić*, Trial Chamber, Judgment, 3 July 2003, IT-97-24-T, para. 640 ('Stakić Trial Judgment') (http://www.legal-tools.org/doc/32ecfb/).

[88] Arnold C. Brackman, *The Other Nuremberg: The Untold Story of Tokyo War Crimes Trials*, William Morrow, New York, 1987, p. 28.

mander with the garrison at Taiping Gate had processed approximately 1,300, that there was a concentration of approximately 7,000 near Xianhe Gate, and that enemy soldiers were still surrendering.[89]

Given the "kill all captives" order allegedly issued by Prince Yasuhiko Asaka as well as the pattern of atrocities, the cumulative evidence suggests that the Nanjing Massacre had an organised and systematic nature. The common plan or common criminal design was to kill all the captives after the fall of the city. According to the jurisprudence of the two *ad hoc* international criminal tribunals, there is no necessity for such a plan, design or purpose to have been previously arranged or formulated. The common plan or purpose may materialise extemporaneously and be inferred from the fact that plurality of persons acts in union to put into effect a joint criminal enterprise.[90] Even if there was no specific written order, the participation of two or more persons in the commission of a particular crime may itself establish an unspoken understanding or arrangement amounting to an agreement formed between them to commit these particular criminal acts.

6.5.2. Form of Liability: Co-perpetration

Tani argued that his army unit entered the city during the night of 12 December 1937 and pulled out on 21 December 1937, thus staying in Nanjing for only nine days. He submitted that, since the most serious crimes were committed in the middle of the city and along the Yangtze River, the responsibility for the massacre rested with other military commanders and their units. According to Tani, his army unit had nothing to do with the atrocities.[91]

The indictment charged Tani as a co-perpetrator, through his action of inspiring, encouraging and authorising his subordinates to commit the crimes during the period from 13 December to 21 December 1937, when his army was stationed in the city. The indictment alleged that he "collab-

---

[89] Kimura Kuninori, *Kaisetsu: Nakajima Kesago chūjō to Nankin jiken* [An Explanation of Nakajima Kesago and the Nanjing Incident], Zoken rekishi to Jinbutsu, Tokyo, 1984, pp. 260–61.

[90] ICTY, *Prosecutor v. Duško Tadić*, Appeals Chamber, Judgment, 15 July 1999, IT-94-1-A, para. 227 (http://www.legal-tools.org/doc/8efc3a/).

[91] Masao, 1981, see *supra* note 50.

orated with other units, such as the unit under Nakajima Kesago", to commit the crimes.[92] The Tribunal convicted Tani as a co-perpetrator of the crimes during the Nanjing Massacre. The judgment stated:

> It is very obvious that Tani collaborated with other Japanese generals, based on the common agreement, jointly inspiring their subordinates and splitting up to take actions, to commit murder, arson, rape and looting in a pre-planned way. Although the army under the accused's command only perpetrates the crimes of murder in part of Nanjing in about 10 days time, he and other Japanese generals shared the same criminal intent, utilised each other to reach the purpose of revenge. According to the above analyses, Tani should share the criminal responsibility with Iwane Matsui, Nakajima Kesago, Suematsu and Yanagawa Hwisuke.[93]

Co-perpetration is a mode of liability in continental legal systems, while conspiracy or joint criminal enterprise, which evolved at the ICTY, are common law expressions that describe a situation in which the crime was carried out by a group of individuals acting in pursuance of a common criminal design and each accused contributed his/her part to this design. In joint criminal enterprise, while only some members of the group may physically perpetrate the criminal act (murder, extermination, wanton destruction of cities, towns or villages and so forth), the participation and contribution of the other members of the group are often vital in facilitating the commission of the offence in question.[94] The members of the group may participate in different ways at different times to accomplish criminal conduct on a massive scale.[95]

The *actus reus* of this mode of participation comprises three elements. The first is a plurality of persons, which need not be organised in a military, political or administrative structure. Second is the existence of a common plan, design or purpose which amounts to or involves the commission of a crime, without a necessity for this plan, design or purpose to have been previously arranged, formulated or even materialised. It is suf-

---

[92] *Ibid.*

[93] Judgment, HU, 2006, p. 388, see *supra* note 10.

[94] ICTY, *Prosecutor v. Miroslav Kvočka et al.*, Appeals Chamber, Judgment, 28 February 2005, IT-98-30/1-A, para. 80 (http://www.legal-tools.org/doc/006011/).

[95] Gideon Boas, James L. Bischoff and Natalie L. Reid, *Forms of Responsibility in International Criminal Law*, vol. 1, Cambridge University Press, Cambridge, 2007, p. 9.

fices that there was a mutual understanding, silent consent or meeting of minds. The common plan or purpose may materialise extemporaneously and be inferred from the fact that a plurality of persons acts in unison to put into effect a common criminal purpose. The third requirement is the participation of the accused in the common plan involving the perpetration of one of the crimes.[96]

The *mens rea* of the co-perpetration is that all the participants share the same intent to further the common design. The accused, even if not personally furthering the crime, intended the result. Indeed, co-perpetration is a form of commission. Thus, all the participants are equally guilty of the crime regardless of the part they each played in its commission. In other words, no matter what specific contribution each member makes, he or she is in the same position and everyone is regarded as principal perpetrators. Although Tani was only in the city for nine or ten days, he was held responsible for the whole period of the Nanjing Massacre, with other Japanese perpetrators. This form of participation is not novel in international criminal law or even in domestic law. Article 2 of the Law Governing the Trial of War Criminals stipulated: "In commission of above mentioned crimes, if a common plan or conspiracy is established, the masterminds, participants and aiders and abettors shall be held fully responsible for any act performed by any person in implementing the common plan or conspiracy".[97] The concept for this mode of liability could also be traced back to China's Criminal Code, where Article 28 stipulated: "each of two or more persons acting jointly in the commission of an offence is a principal of the offence".[98] Chinese law, especially the Criminal Code, was transplanted from Japan at the beginning twentieth century, and thus is in conformity with the principle of *nullum crimen sine lege*, as discussed earlier. It was groundless for Tani to claim that he had only stayed in the city for fewer than 10 days and should not have been responsible for the whole massacre.

---

[96] ICTY, *Prosecutor v. Milorad Krnojelac*, Appeals Chamber, Judgment, 17 September 2003, IT-97-25-A, para. 31 (http://www.legal-tools.org/doc/46d2e5/); and Blagojević and Jokić Trial Judgment, para. 698, see *supra* note 85.

[97] Control Council Law No. 10, see *supra* note 37.

[98] David C.C. Kang, *A Compilation of the Law of the Republic of China*, vol. 2, San Min Shu Jing Publishing House, Taipei, 1967.

As for Tani's personal contribution to the common criminal purpose to kill all the captives, the Tribunal found:

> [A]ccording to the investigation in all districts of the city, half of all the criminal activities in Nanjing, like murder, rape and looting took place from 12 December to 21 December and in the place where Tani's unit stationed as he himself told the court, that is, around the Zhonghua Gate area. The overwhelming evidence shows that there are 450 crimes of murder, arson, rape and looting occurred during this period of time and in this area.[99]

Based on the foregoing, it is suggested that the evidence against Tani was overwhelming, the legal reasoning was sound and the application of the law was correct. The judgment rendered by the Nanjing Tribunal could stand the test of time and the challenge of Nanjing Massacre deniers.

6.5.3. Tani's Knowledge

The Tribunal was not presented with direct evidence that Tani received any reports on the atrocities his subordinates allegedly committed or that Tani had the requisite *mens rea* for the commission of the crimes as a co-perpetrator. However, as a principle of international criminal law, convictions can be based on circumstantial evidence where it is established that the inference was the only reasonable one available on the evidence.[100] The Nanjing Massacre, as a pattern of purposeful action, shocked the conscience of humanity, even at that time. How could Tani, as the commander of the 6th Division and stationed in the city for 10 days, claim that he did not know about the crimes being committed?

According to his own statement from 18 December 1946, Tani was in Nanjing most of the time when his unit stationed there.

> In the afternoon of December 14 1937, I entered the city; December 15 and 16, I bid farewell to the units departing to Wuhu; December 17, I took part in the entry ceremony of General Matsui; December 18, I participated in the memorial ceremony for those lost their lives; December 19, I paid respect to the tomb of Sun Yat-sen; December 20, I did prepa-

---

[99] Judgment, see HU, 2006, p. 388, see *supra* note 10.

[100] ICTY, *Prosecutor v. Radislav Krstić*, Appeals Chamber, Judgment, 19 April 2004, IT-98-33-A, p. 41 (http://www.legal-tools.org/doc/86a108/)

ration for departure. In the morning of December 21 I left
Nanking for Wuhu.[101]

When General Matsui Iwane arrived in the city four days after the massacre had begun, he made a speech and issued strict orders to stop the killing and looting that resulted in the eventual end of the massacre.[102] Tani was present at the ceremony and heard Matsui's speech. From this fact alone there is evidence to show that both Matsui and Tani were aware of the grievous situation in Nanjing.

Prince Yasuhiko, who took over as commander of the entire Japanese army attacking Nanjing days prior to the fall of the city, allegedly issued an order to "kill all captives". Some authors recorded that Prince Yasuhiko signed the order himself; others claimed that Lieutenant Colonel Chō Isamu, the prince's aide-de-camp, sent this order under his sign without the prince's knowledge or assent.[103] Whether or not Yasuhiko personally issued this order, based on the behaviour of the Japanese army in Nanjing, including Tani's 6th Division, it appears that this order was received and followed. For instance, on 13 December the 66th Battalion received an order from Prince Yasuhiko: "All prisoners of war are to be executed. Method of execution: divide the prisoners in groups of a dozen, shoot to kill them separately".[104]

The Nanjing Massacre was so notorious that some of the Japanese military leaders, even those not in Nanjing, were aware of the event. For instance, General Okamura Yasuji, when questioned by Chinese investigators, testified to the Nanjing Massacre as follows:

> I surmised the following based on what I heard from Staff Officer Miyazaki, CCAA Special Service Department Chief Harada and Hangzhou Special Service Department Chief Hagiwara a day or two after I arrived in Shanghai. First, it is true that tens of thousands of acts of violence, such as looting and rape, took place against civilians during the assault on Nanking. Second, front-line troops indulged in the evil

---

[101] Statement by Tani on 18 December 1946, in HU, 2006, p. 462, see *supra* note 10.

[102] IMTFE Judgment, see *supra* note 2.

[103] CHANG, 1998, p. 40, see *supra* note 70.

[104] *Ibid.*, p. 41.

practice of executing POWs on the pretext of (lacking) rations.[105]

During the massacre, the International Committee for the Nanjing Safety Zone sent many letters of protest to the Japanese embassy. The judgment said:

> Foreigners in Nanking, on behalf of international organizations, from 14 December to 21 December, when the accused unit stationed in the city, 12 times respectively, lodged strong protest to Japanese army, authority and Japanese Embassy. The protest note also attached 113 cases of arson, killing, raping and looting committed by Japanese army and urged the Japanese army to exercise disciplines over the soldiers and to prevent the expansion of atrocities.[106]

Professor Bates provided evidence that the protests were forwarded to Tokyo and were discussed in great detail between Japanese officials and the American ambassador in Tokyo. Only a few days after the fall of Nanjing, Bates wrote his first letter to the Japanese embassy in Nanjing, protesting against atrocities that had been committed by members of the Japanese military against Chinese prisoners of war and civilians.[107]

It is not difficult for a reasonable person to know what had happened in Nanjing after the Japanese troops entered the city. Robert Wilson, a surgeon who was born and raised in Nanjing and educated at Princeton University and Harvard Medical School, testified that beginning with 13 December "the hospital filled up and was kept full to overflowing" during the next six weeks. He also stated that patients usually bore bayonet or bullet wounds, and that many of the women patients had been sexually molested.[108]

Based on the totality of the evidence and the discussion above, the only reasonable inference available on record demonstrated that Tani had the requisite *mens rea*. His submissions challenging the Tribunal's conclusions on his intent accordingly lacked merit.

---

[105] Telegraph, see *supra* note 51.

[106] Judgment, HU, 2006, see *supra* note 10.

[107] Letter of the International Committee of Nanking Safety Zone to the Japanese Embassy. December 18, 1937, cited from National Archive No. 2, Nanjing Municipal Archive, *Nanking Massacre of the Japanese Expeditionary Army*, Jiangsu Historical Book Publishing House, Nanjing, 1987, p. 128.

[108] See HU, 2006, see *supra* note 10.

6.5.4. The Number of Deaths

An accurate estimation of the death toll in the Nanjing Massacre was never established because most of the Japanese military records on the killings were deliberately destroyed or kept secret shortly after the surrender of Japan in 1945. In Tani's case, the prosecution claimed that there were 400,000 victims, the Tribunal determined the number to be over 300,000 and the IMTFE declared that "more than 200,000 civilians and prisoners of war were killed in and near Nanking".[109]

Estimates from Japanese historians vary widely, ranging from 20,000 to 200,000.[110] Some Japanese politicians bluntly deny the existence of the Nanjing Massacre. When interviewed by an American magazine, Ishihara Shintaro, a former governor of Tokyo and a former cabinet minister, maintained that the Nanjing Massacre was "a story made up by the Chinese".[111] Some Japanese scholars also deny that a widespread, systematic massacre occurred at all, claiming that any deaths were either justified militarily, accidental or isolated incidents of unauthorised atrocities. They claim that, while there were some killings, at most it could only be called the "Nanjing Incident" rather than the "Nanjing Massacre".[112]

According to a trial record, the Tribunal president SHI Mei-yu issued the conclusion of investigation on the Nanjing Massacre. The conclusion determined that the number of prisoners of war and civilians killed by the Japanese army totalled 350,000, of whom the Red Cross buried 43,071 of the dead and Chongshan Tong buried 112,666 others. The document further stated that more than 195,000 persons were collectively murdered by machine gun and their bodies burned, facts proven by eyewitness testimony. In addition, in the Temple of Huashen, outside Zhonghua Gate, over 7,000 refugees and prisoners of war were killed. Moreover, the mayor of Nanjing buried 3,000 unnamed bodies during the occupation and he erected a gravestone, which served as evidence of the deaths.[113]

---

[109] CHANG, 1998, p. 486, see *supra* note 70.

[110] Kitamuru Minoru, *The Politics of Nanjing: An Impartial Investigation,* trans. Hal Gold, University Press of America, New York, 2007, p. 7.

[111] *Playboy,* 1990, vol. 37, no. 10, p. 76.

[112] Minoru, 2007, p. 7, see *supra* note 111.

[113] National Archive No. 2, Conclusion by President SHI Mei-yu on the Investigation of the Nanking Massacre of the Military Tribunal, 593/870.

Formally, "massacre" is not a legal term and difficult to accurately define. In general terms, a massacre means the violent killing of many people, where the perpetrating party is in total control of the situation and victims are defenceless and innocent. No established criteria exist to determine when a mass killing becomes a massacre. Indeed, most crimes of similar nature are characterised as "extermination" within the framework of war crimes or crimes against humanity in international criminal law. Extermination is characterised as murder on a larger scale, where the killing must occur on a vast scale in a concentrated place over a short period of time.[114] While extermination generally involves a large number of victims, killings may be construed as exterminations even where the number of victims is limited. In the *Blagojević and Jokić* case before the ICTY, the Trial Chamber found that "the killings were part of one murder operation, which led to the death of 7000 Bosnian Muslim men and boys. The crime of extermination in the present case is clearly indicated by the massive scale".[115] In the *Stakić* case, the Trial Chamber concluded that killing more than 1,500 innocent people was extermination.[116] According to the most conservative estimation, the death toll during the Nanjing Massacre exceeded 20,000 victims. Based on the foregoing, it is not an exaggeration to claim that the killings of such a large scale amounted to a massacre.

6.5.5. Unlawful Combatants

Some authors allege that "prior to the capture of the city, Chinese troops stripped off their uniforms and mingled with the civilian population. By doing so, they became unlawful combatants not protected by the Regulations Concerning the Laws and Customs of War on Land annexed to the Hague Convention".[117] The concept of "unlawful combatant" has never been clearly established. No international treaty effectively provides a basis for its definition, and the term became better known only during recent conflicts in Afghanistan. Generally speaking, unlawful combatants refer to individuals who fail to follow the laws of war or to civilians who have organised themselves as self-styled paramilitary fighters and take

---

[114] Stakić Trial Judgment, para. 640, see *supra* note 87.

[115] Blagojević and Jokić Trial Judgment, para. 577, see *supra* note 85.

[116] Stakić Trial Judgment, paras. 651–55, see *supra* note 87.

[117] Higashinakano Shudo, *The Nanking Massacre: Fact Versus Fiction: A Historian's Quest for the Truth*, trans. Sekai Shuppan, Sekai Shuppan, Tokyo, 2005, p. 3.

part directly in hostilities.[118] Traditionally, unlawful combatants were spies and saboteurs who, wearing civilian clothing, infiltrated enemy territory to collect information or to destroy designated objects. Nowadays, it mostly refers to terrorist groups fighting on the battlefield.[119]

Chinese soldiers who lay down their arms and changed into civilian clothes did not meet these criteria when they were captured because they neither engaged in subversive activities nor took an active part in armed conflict. Even if these Chinese soldiers were regarded as unlawful combatants, and thus unable to obtain prisoner of war status when captured, they should still be entitled to some basic protection under international humanitarian law and provided with fair trials for acts which render their belligerency unlawful. In this regard, their summary execution at such a large scale without due process, as seen in the Nanjing Massacre, is not legally justified.

According to Article 4 of the Geneva Convention relative to the Protection of Civilian Persons in Time of War ('Fourth Geneva Convention'), which is the codification of customary international law, protected persons are those who "at the given moment and in any manner whatsoever, find themselves, in case of a conflict or occupation, in the hands of a Party to the conflict or Occupying Power of which they are not nationals".[120] A commentary on Article 45(3) of the Fourth Geneva Convention provides that "a person of enemy nationality who is not entitled to prisoner-of-war status is, in principle, a civilian protected by the Fourth Convention, so that there are no gaps in protection".[121] Thus, there should be no intermediate status between a prisoner of war and a civilian, and accordingly nobody in enemy hands shall be outside the law. The Protocol Additional to the Geneva Conventions of 12 August 1949, and relating to the Protection of Victims of International Armed Conflicts, "has adopted a so-called 'negative approach', which should ensure that each person in armed conflict belongs to one category or another; i.e., there are no uncer-

---

[118] Oscar Uhler and Henri Coursier, *Commentary on the Geneva Conventions of 12 August 1949*, vol. IV, International Committee of the Red Cross, Geneva, 1958, p. 243.

[119] Jason Callen, "Unlawful Combatants and the Geneva Conventions", in *Virginia Journal of International Law*, 2003/2004, vol. 1025, pp. 48–50.

[120] Convention (IV) relative to the Protection of Civilian Persons in Time of War, Geneva, 12 August 1949.

[121] J.S. Pictet (ed.), *Commentary: IV Geneva Convention relative to the Protection of Civilian Persons in Time of War*, International Committee of the Red Cross, Geneva, 1958, p. 51.

tainties, and no-one is left out". Thus, "the First Protocol explains that all persons who are not combatants are then inevitably civilians".[122] If there are doubts whether a person is a combatant or a civilian, that person must be considered to be a civilian.[123] The jurisprudence of the ICTY supports this view. The Trial Chamber in the *Mucić et al.* case emphasised the importance that there be no gap between the two statuses, as civilian or prisoner of war. If an individual is not entitled to the protections as a prisoner of war, he necessarily falls within the ambit of the Fourth Geneva Convention as a civilian.[124]

Since the Chinese soldiers laid down their arms, they should have been entitled to humane treatment and to be tried by a lawfully established military tribunal rather than be summarily executed, irrespective of their changing into civilian clothes.

6.6. Achievements and Shortcomings

For a long time, the Nanjing Tribunal faded in the memory of both the Chinese and Japanese people. Since the 1970s the Nanjing Tribunal has been the subject of heated exchange among Chinese and Japanese scholars and intellectuals over its legality, legitimacy and legacy. The various achievements and shortcomings of the Nanjing Tribunal are discussed below.

One shortcoming is that the Nanjing trials were conducted in great haste due to the domestic situation in China, and in particular the civil war between the Communists and Nationalists. As a result, many accounts listed in the indictment were not discussed or examined. The trials also did not delve into all the battles and atrocities in the rest of China, especially those occurring in the northern and north-eastern regions. For symbolic purposes, the Tribunal only chose to try a couple of events, such as the Nanjing Massacre, but the Japanese army killed far more people throughout China than in Nanjing alone. A lot of crimes committed dur-

---

[122] René Värk, "The Status and Protection of Unlawful Combatants", in *Jurica International*, 2005, vol. 10, p. 192.

[123] *Ibid.* See also Claude Pilloup and Jean de Preux, Commentary on the Additional Protocols of 8 June 1977 to the Geneva Conventions of 12 August 1949, ICRC, Martinus Nijhoff, Geneva, 1987, p. 152.

[124] ICTY, *Prosecutor v. Zdravko Mucić, Hazim Delić, Esad Landžo and Zejnil Delalić*, Trial Chamber, Judgment, 16 November 1998, IT-96-21-T, para. 271 (http://www.legal-tools.org/doc/6b4a33/).

ing the war were not even investigated and prosecuted, including the use of chemical weapons, bacteriological warfare and poison gas against Chinese soldiers and civilians; biological experiments on prisoners of war and Chinese civilians; the forced prostitution of so-called "comfort women"; and the subjugation of the Chinese as forced labourers in the Japanese domestic industry. Indeed, forced labour was not even mentioned in indictments the prosecution filed before the Nanjing Tribunal. This is partially because the trials concentrated only on the Nanjing Massacre and forced labour was briefly mentioned during the IMTFE and summarily rejected as unsupported.[125]

Another shortcoming was immunity. Immunity of a head of the state is a principle of international law, but it is not necessarily applicable to the alleged war criminals. Article 7 of the IMT Charter states: "The official position of defendants, whether as Heads of States or responsible officials in Government Departments, shall not be considered as freeing them from responsibility or mitigating punishment".[126] Unfortunately, the same article does not exist in the IMTFE Charter or the Law Governing the Trial of War Criminals. Immunity was not only granted to the Japanese emperor but also to his relatives. Prince Yasuhiko, an imperial kinsman and commander of the entire Japanese army that attacked Nanjing, was indicted as the principal perpetrator of the Nanjing Massacre due to his alleged order to "kill all captives". Whether or not he personally participated in the crimes, or whether his subordinates acted on their own volition, the prince, as the commanding officer in charge, gave no orders to stop the atrocities. The extradition request that the Chinese government filed against him was refused by General Douglas MacArthur because Prince Yasuhiko was a relative of the Japanese emperor and was thus granted immunity.[127]

---

[125] See CHANG, 1998, see *supra* note 70.

[126] International Military Tribunal, Nuremberg, Charter, 8 August 1945, in *Trial of the Major War Criminals Before the International Military Tribunal, Nuremberg, 14 November 1945–1 October 1946*, vol. 1. *Official Documents*, Nuremberg, IMT, 1947, pp. 10–16 (http://www.legal-tools.org/doc/64ffdd/).

[127] See Kyoko Inoue, *MacArthur's Japanese Constitution: A Linguistic and Cultural Study of its Making*, University of Chicago Press, Chicago, 1991, p. 162. After the war, Yasuhiko retired from the army and spent most of his time playing golf. He also took an active interest in golf course development. Asaka Yasuhiko died of natural causes on 13 April 1981 at his home at the age of 93.

Furthermore, convicted Japanese war criminals should have served their sentences in a special prison set up for this purpose. However, as the Nationalist government lost territory north of the Yangtze River to the Communist Party army in late 1948, it decided to send convicted individuals back to Japan to serve their sentences. Upon arrival in Japan, they were all released. Some even became important officials in Japanese government after the war, perpetuating the impunity of their criminal acts.[128]

Despite these problems, the Nanjing trials had great significance in China's history. The Nanjing Tribunal produced and preserved an important historic record through the indictments, judgments, testimonies of witnesses and victims, and records of the court proceedings. All of these records, tested through examination at trial, document the dark history of Japan's invasion against China. Accordingly, they render the commission of the atrocities very difficult to deny. Even now, these records serve as a historical reminder for the nation of China.

Furthermore, while the Nanjing Tribunal could not end the impunity of international crimes, its contribution is no less important to international justice. It was the first time that China, as a victorious nation, conducted public criminal trials instead of summarily executing war criminals. Historically, war criminals were summarily executed upon capture. Instead, a court was set up to address the question of responsibility after winning a war. This was a great step forward in China's long history. It was also a very important and inalienable component of the trials against fascism after the Second World War. The Nanjing trials, conducted in a fair way, fulfilled the requirement of justice and contributed to international and regional peace and stability. The trials raised moral and legal consciousness in the Chinese people and set a central milestone for the rule of law. While the Tribunal's procedures were not perfect, the precedents set by the judgments have undoubtedly constituted a landmark in international law.

6.7. Conclusion

The foregoing analysis demonstrates that Tani's trial did not amount to victor's justice. Indeed, his trial under the Nanjing Tribunal was lawfully

---

[128] For instance, Kishi Nobusuke was a class A war crimes suspect. He was released from prison in 1948 and elected as the prime minister of Japanese in 1957.

established. Since crimes he was convicted of were legally established at the time of his actions, the principle of *nullum crimen sine lege* was observed. Furthermore, the trials were conducted according to due process and Tani had the opportunity to defend himself and request the review of the Nanjing Tribunal's judgment at first instance. Finally, as extensively indicated above, there was overwhelming evidence to demonstrate the existence of the Nanjing Massacre, and of Tani's responsibility as co-perpetrator.

Sir Gerard Brennan, the former chief justice of Australia, has summarised the significance of war crimes trials such as the Nanjing Tribunal in the following terms:

> There are, no doubt, many lessons that can be drawn from war crimes trials. They do answer the deep-seated cry for retribution that moves victims of war crimes and their loved ones to demand condign punishment for the perpetrators of the crimes. They can affirm the continuing validity and operation of the international laws of war – laws that are not suspended by the outbreak of hostilities. Properly conducted, war crimes trials can be powerful examples of judicial impartiality and the rule of law.[129]

Understanding the past is crucial to addressing the challenges of today. We all must learn from the part to avoid repeating the same mistakes in the present and future. Since the achievement of an international order is based on reason and justice, we have the historical responsibility to provide definite and exhaustive answers about the value and place of the Nanjing Trials in China's history and its impact on the development of contemporary rule of law in China and in Asia.

---

[129] Sir Gerard Brennan, "Forward: Beyond Victor's Justice?", in Yuki Tanaka, Tim McCormack and Gerry Simpson (eds.), *The Tokyo War Crimes Trial Revisited*, Martinus Nijhoff, Leiden, 2011, p. xiv.

Annex I: Military Tribunals in China Trying Japanese War Criminals

Location	Duration	Accused on trial	Death penalty	Life sentence	Prison	Acquittal or natural death
Shanghai	April 1946–26 January 1949	116	14	22	25	5
Guangzhou	July 1946–10 March 1948	118	46	16	39	17
Nanjing	15 February 1946–26 January 1949	24	8*	2	12	2
Wuhan	June 1946–15 May 1948	80	7	20	26	27
Beijing	April 1946–17 December 1948	78	31	13	31	3
Jinan	August 1946–13 November 1947	19	9	1	7	2
Xuzhou	July 1946–12 July 1947	22	7	3	11	1
Taiyuan	December 1946–14 January 1948	7	3	0	4	0
Shenyang	July 1947–January 1948	38	23	4	9	2
Taipei	December 1946–22 December 1948	15	0	0	15	0
Total		**517**	**148**	**81**	**229**	**59**

* The eight accused who were sentenced to the death were:

Tani Hisao: commander of the 6th Division, Imperial Japanese Army ('IJA'), executed 26 April 1947.

Takashi Sakai: first Japanese governor of Hong Kong, executed 30 September 1946.

Mukai Toshiaki: second lieutenant, 16th Division, IJA, executed 28 January 1948.

Noda Tsuyoshi: second lieutenant, 16th Division, IJA, executed on 28 January 1948.

Gukichi Tanaka: captain, 45th Regiment, 6th Division, IJA, executed 28 January 1948.

Kiyoshi Matsumoto: captain of military police, Jiashan County, executed 11 June 1947.

Mitsukichi Tsurumaru: captain of military police, Wuxi, executed 22 April 1948.

Mitsuyoshi Tsurumaru: head of Military Police, executed 31 December 1946.

Takahashi Gako: lieutenant general, died in prison in Nanjing.

7

The Nanjing Trial and Its Impact on the Chinese and Japanese Peoples

WANG Xintong[*]

7.1. Introduction

From 15 February 1946 to early 1949 the Nanjing War Crimes Tribunal ('Nanjing Tribunal') of the Republic of China tried cases for class B and C Japanese war criminals, including leading Imperial Japanese Army officers who incited the Nanjing (Nanking) Massacre. Trials of high-level leaders for serious crimes have great significance which extends beyond events in the courtroom. Now, some seven decades after the tribunal concluded its work, it is time to assess its impact on both the victims' and defendants' countries. Consideration of the impact of the trial is constrained by the fact that no large-scale quantitative surveys or interviews have been conducted in China or Japan on this topic. Despite this limitation several noteworthy observations can be made.

On the Chinese side, in the late 1940s many people from affected communities were aware of the trial and actively participated in the trial process. For example, the Nationalist government of China had demonstrated a commitment to conducting outreach work with affected communities. Throughout the investigation, hearings and execution phases, the Nanjing Trial was conducted in a way that encouraged public involvement.[1] After the change of regime in China in 1949, however, there was

---

[*]   **WANG Xintong** is a licensed attorney working at the Beijing Yingke law firm. Her practice focuses on the representation of transborder crimes, international red notice cases, and white-collar criminal and complex civil litigation matters. Prior to her practice in China, she worked with three major international criminal courts in The Hague, the Netherlands, at the Office of the Prosecutor of the Special Tribunal for Lebanon, Trial Chamber I of the Special Court for Sierra Leone and Trial Chamber II of the International Criminal Tribunal for the former Yugoslavia. She obtained an advanced LL.M. in Public International Law with specialisation in international criminal law from Leiden University, the Netherlands.

[1]   A Nanjing Massacre crime investigation committee was set up in June 1946. By 11 November 1946 this committee had collected evidence and materials of 2,784 cases concern-

very little discussion of the Nanjing Tribunal in the Chinese media. The Nanjing Trial and other trials conducted by the Nationalists seem to have been forgotten or were shunned. It had only been since the 1980s that researchers began to revisit the war crimes trials conducted by the Nationalist government. Trial documents donated by individuals in Taiwan fostered new analysis and publications by legal professionals and historians.[2] Even so, this emerging research interest has largely remained in the academic discourse. Compared to the International Military Tribunal for the Far East ('IMTFE') in Tokyo or the Nanjing Massacre itself, which have been passionately debated among historians and intellectuals, discussion about the Nanjing Trial had been rather dispassionate. Furthermore, unlike the Nanjing Massacre, the Nanjing Tribunal is never mentioned in the curriculum of Chinese schools. Thus generations of post-war Chinese did not receive much historical education about the Nanjing Trial.

On the Japanese side, most people believed the Nanjing Trial was grossly unfair, and simply caused pain to the families of the accused. Holding to this belief, the public engaged in a campaign to release all imprisoned war criminals. This activity was successful, and as a result of their efforts all the imprisoned Japanese war criminals were released in 1958. This outcome itself limited the Nanjing Trial's impact in Japan. From 1970s onwards, with the rise of right-wing political forces in Japan, the Nanjing Trial was brought to the Japanese people's attention during a heated debate over the denial of the seriousness of the Nanjing Massacre. Encouraged by this trend, families of two convicted lieutenants filed a libel suit in 2003 against the *Tokyo Nichi Nichi Shimbun* and *Asahi Shimbun* newspapers and a publisher and writer who had published information regarding the occasion when the Japanese held a so-called "killing contest" during the invasion of Nanjing. The families that contested the media reports about the killing contest – reports that were used

---

ing Nanjing Massacre from local citizens. The trial proceedings for major cases adjudicated at the Nanjing Tribunal were fully covered by the media. See National Archive No. 2, Nanjing Municipal Archive, *Nanjing Massacre of the Japanese Invasion Archive*, Jiangsu Ancient Book Publishing House, Nanjing, 1981, p. 550; see also YAN Haijian, "Social Impact Assessment of Nanking Massacre Trial Conducted by Nationalist Government", in *Journal of Fujian Forum-Social Science*, 2011, vol. 4, pp. 109–11.

2   SHEN Zhengrong, "Relatives of the Nanking Tribunal Judge Donated 117 Japanese Criminals Trial Materials back to Nanking", in *Xinhua Daily News*, 14 December 2004.

as evidence by the Nanjing Tribunal – claimed they were fabricated.[3] The Tokyo District Court adjudicated the matter and rejected the case. The release of this judgment ended the killing contest debate, at least in the eyes of the Japanese legal field.[4] At the same time, intensive media coverage of this trial led the Japanese public to specifically differentiate the Nanjing Trial from the general national war crimes trials conducted by the Allied powers. The details of the Nanjing Trial are not widely known in Japan. In comparison to the Chinese, the Nanjing Trial has had even less impact on Japanese society.

7.2. Background to the Nanjing Tribunal

On 19 January 1946 the Supreme Commander of the Allied Powers, Douglas MacArthur, established the IMTFE. It was decided that the international tribunal would have prosecutorial authority over suspects charged with crimes against peace, who had became known as class A defendants, while national courts or commissions would have authority to try cases involving individuals recognised as class B and C criminals. Class B defendants were defined as those accused of committing war crimes and class C defendants were mostly senior officers who were accused of crimes against humanity. Besides the IMTFE, many military tribunals were set up either in occupied areas like Yokohama or within the national jurisdiction of the Allied powers. China was not part of the occupying force, so it could only establish military tribunals on Chinese soil. In order to establish the legal basis for national war crimes tribunals and regulate their work, the Nationalist government issued special rules, such as Regulations on the Handling of War Criminals, Regulations on the Trial of War Criminals, and Detailed Implementation Rules of the Regulations on the Trial of War Criminals, which were later replaced by the Amendment Draft of Rules Governing the Trial of War Criminals, promulgated by the committee dealing with war criminals in 1946.[5] According to these rules, China established 10 tribunals in Nanjing, Shanghai, Bei-

---

[3] Yumi Wijers-Hasegawa, "Wartime Killing Contest Trial Starts", in *The Japan Times*, 8 July 2003.

[4] Kasahara Tokushi, *Debate over the Nanking Issue: How Japanese Viewed History*, trans. LUO Cuicui and others, Social Science Press, 2011, p. 2.

[5] For the regulations and rules, see HU Juron (ed.), *Nanking Trial, Collection of Historical Materials on the Nanking Massacre*, vol. 24, Jiangsu People's Press, Nanjing, 2006, pp. 36–40.

---

jing, Hankou, Guangzhou, Shenyang, Jinan, Xuzhou, Taiyuan and Taipei. In total, 2,200 cases were tried, from which 145 people were sentenced to death, more than 400 sentenced to life imprisonment, while the rest were found to be not guilty and repatriated to Japan.[6] Based on territorial jurisdiction, many cases related to the Nanjing Massacre were adjudicated by the Nanjing Tribunal, which had the added effect of making the work of crime investigation, evidence collection and witness interview easier. Further, trying these cases in Nanjing, where the atrocities took place, had the potential of attracting attention and therefore enlarging the social impact of the work of the Nanjing Tribunal.

7.3. The Nanjing Tribunal and Its Work

The Nanjing War Crimes Tribunal was established on 15 February 1946 directly under the auspices of the Ministry of National Defence for the purpose of trying Japanese war criminals. The accused facing trial included both Japanese high commanders such as Okamura Yasuji, commander-in-chief of the Japanese China Expeditionary Army, and Japanese army contractors. The Nanjing Tribunal worked in co-operation with other jurisdictions to obtain evidence from Hong Kong,[7] Shanghai,[8] Guangzhou[9] and other places. The Tribunal also took judicial notice of findings from the Shanghai Supreme Court.[10] The judgments contained a verdict, sentence, facts and reasoning. The depth of reasoning varies between cases, and there were limited discussions concerning the criteria for the admissibility of evidence. The following sections examine five high-profile cases to provide an insight into the issues that came up during trial and to facilitate further discussion of the trial's impact.

---

[6]   ZHAO Lingyan, *Far East Committee and Japanese War Criminal Disposal Issues, 1994–2014*, China Academic Journal Electronic Publishing House, 2013, p. 55.

[7]   Nanjing War Crimes Tribunal ('Nanjing Tribunal'), *Prosecutor v. Sakai Takashi*, Judgment, 27 August 1946, pp. 2–4 ('Sakai Judgment') (http://www.legal-tools.org/doc/6ed3e2/).

[8]   Nanjing Tribunal, *Prosecutor v. Cui Bing Dou*, Judgment, 13 November 1946, p. 1 (http://www.legal-tools.org/doc/00b71d/); see also Nanjing Tribunal, *Prosecutor v. Matsumoto Kiyoshi*, Judgment, 28 May 1946, pp. 1–5 ('Matsumoto Judgment') (http://www.legal-tools.org/doc/0bf387/).

[9]   Sakai Judgment, pp. 2–3, see *supra* note 7.

[10] Matsumoto Judgment, p. 3, see *supra* note 8.

7.3.1. The Case of Lieutenant General Sakai Takashi

The first case tried by the Nanjing Tribunal was the case of the 26th Division company commander Lieutenant General Sakai Takashi. He served as a military commander in China during the war from 1939 to 1945.[11] The trial chamber was set up on 27 May 1946 and within three months Sakai became the first defendant to receive capital punishment. Sakai was a signature figure of the Japanese invasion. The charges laid against him included crimes against peace, war crimes and crimes against humanity for instigating terrorist activities in Beijing and Tianjin, setting up a puppet administration and "peace army" to overthrow the Chinese government, and encouraging his subordinates to commit atrocities in southern China and Hong Kong.[12] Sakai pleaded not guilty to these charges, arguing that he was just following orders and had no knowledge of wrongdoing committed by his subordinates.[13] These arguments were unsupported by international law and consequently rejected by the Nanjing Tribunal. He was convicted for inciting or permitting his subordinates to murder prisoners of war, wounding soldiers and non-combatants; to rape, plunder and deport civilians; to indulge in cruel punishment and torture; and to cause destruction to properties.[14] Thus, for his participation in a war of aggression Sakai was found guilty of crimes against peace. With regard to the atrocities he was found guilty of war crimes and crimes against humanity.[15]

The presiding judge for this trial, SHI Mei-yu, revealed a background story of this case during an interview conducted by a journalist.[16] Sakai led the 38th Division to invade Hong Kong, after which followed vast atrocities including a brutal massacre at St Stephen's Hospital. The British government wanted to extradite and try him in the Hong Kong war crimes tribunal. After the request was officially rejected by the Nanjing municipal government, a British judge was sent to the Nanjing Tribunal to

---

[11] LUO Junsheng, "Shi Mei-yu and Nanking Trial of Japanese War Criminals in the Aftermath of War", in *CPC History Review*, 2006, vol. 1, p. 22.

[12] United Nations War Crimes Commission ('UNWCC'), *Law Reports of Trials of War Criminals*, vol. 14, His Majesty's Stationery Office, London, 1949, pp. 1–7.

[13] *Ibid.*

[14] Judgment of War Criminal Sakai Takashi held by the National Archives Administration in Taiwan, cited in Suzannah Linton, "Rediscovering the War Crimes Trials in Hong Kong, 1946–48", in *Melbourne Journal of International Law*, 2012, vol. 13, no. 2, p. 340.

[15] UNWCC, 1949, p. 7, see *supra* note 14.

[16] LUO, 1995, p. 22, see *supra* note 11.

investigate the matter. The Tribunal responded with the following legal reasoning:

> Firstly, the suspect was arrested within Chinese territorial jurisdiction, Guangdong, and not in the British occupied area; secondly, although Hong Kong is a colony of the UK, it is still Chinese territory; thirdly, the number of Chinese victims is more than British victims, therefore, the Chinese military tribunal enjoys jurisdiction to entertain this case.[17]

Due to lack of legal support, and possibly fear of reciprocal requests for Chinese nationals involved in the British trials, the judge did not insist further. Instead, 12 British judges were sent to observe the trial proceedings. After attending the trial and reading the judgment in its English translation, the British observers expressed their satisfaction to Judge SHI and the entire judgment text was put in the UK National Archives as an important piece documenting the British–Japanese war.[18]

The trial of Sakai Takashi was the first case adjudicated by the Nanjing Tribunal. The newly established Tribunal gained practical experience from conducting its first war crimes trials. Positive responses from the British judges also evinced international recognition of the Tribunal's work, and also laid foundation for the following trials regarding the Nanjing Massacre.

7.3.2. Nanjing Massacre Cases

Much like the Holocaust in Europe, the Nanjing Massacre was one of the most brutal chapters in modern history. After Japanese forces captured Nanjing, a barbaric campaign of terror began against Chinese soldiers and non-combatant city residents. The Japanese military ordered the execution of Chinese prisoners of war.[19] Once these soldiers were killed, the Japanese forces proceeded to rape and kill civilians. Japanese soldiers murdered Chinese civilians through a variety of gruesome methods including burying people alive, extirpating body parts, using attack dogs and bayoneting babies. In total, more than 300,000 Chinese people were murdered.[20]

---

[17] *Ibid.*

[18] *Ibid.*

[19] Hisao Tani Judgment, in HU, 2006, pp. 388–95, see *supra* note 5.

[20] *Ibid.*

Four Imperial Japanese Army officers were tried before the Nanjing Tribunal for war crimes associated with the Nanjing Massacre. The first was Lieutenant General Tani Hisao, commanding officer of the 6th Division. His division was the first to invade Nanjing in December 1937.[21] The second case was brought against the company commander of the 45th Regiment, Captain Tanaka Gunkichi, and Second Lieutenants Mukai Toshiaki and Noda Tsuyoshi, who were made notorious for engaging in the so-called killing contest.

Tani was arrested by Allied forces in Japan in February 1946 and later extradited to Nanjing at the Tribunal's request.[22] The investigation and pre-trial stage lasted four months. The charges brought against him were crimes against peace and crimes against humanity for directing the invasion and ordering a massacre of non-combatant Nanjing citizens.[23] On 6–8 February 1947 the Tribunal conducted the public trial of Tani.[24] Approximately one thousand people attended the hearing.[25] During the trial session, the accused stated very clearly how his troops advanced into China, but completely denied their participation in the Nanjing Massacre. The prosecutor, however, introduced abundant evidence, including testimonies from survivors and witnesses of the Nanjing Massacre, news reports and photographs to show otherwise.[26] On February 1947 the Nanjing Tribunal announced its judgment and Tani was found guilty of instigating, inspiring and encouraging men under his command to stage general massacres of prisoners of war and non-combatants, and to perpetrate such crimes as rape, plunder and wanton destruction of property during the Battle of Shanghai, the earlier Battle of Nanjing and the Rape of Nanjing, and should be sentenced to death immediately.[27] Tani refused to accept this judgment and filed for a review by the president of the Nationalist gov-

---

[21] *Ibid.*

[22] LUO, 2006, p. 22, see *supra* note 11.

[23] Hisao Tani Judgment, in HU, 2006, pp. 388–95, see *supra* note 5.

[24] ZHANG Zhongxiu, "Witnessing the Trial of Nanking Massacre Criminal Hisao Tani", in *Journal of Essence of Literature and History*, 1994, vol. 3, p. 29.

[25] *Ibid.*

[26] LUO, 2006, p. 23, see *supra* note 11; See also Hisao Tani Judgment, in HU, 2006, pp. 388–395, see *supra* note 5.

[27] Hisao Tani Judgment, HU, 2006, pp. 388–95, see *supra* note 5.

ernment CHIANG Kai-shek and the chief of staff, who later approved the original sentence. Tani Hisao was executed on 26 April 1947.[28]

7.3.3. The Killing Contest

On their way to invading Nanjing, Japanese forces undertook a killing contest to boost morale and promote a more efficient way of murdering Chinese people. In order to raise awareness of what they considered to be a heroic competition, reporters and interview teams with the Japanese forces conducted interviews with contest winners, and such reports were published in prominent Japanese newspapers.[29] These news reports later became valuable evidence proving the existence and nature of this activity.

Tanaka, Mukai and Noda were jointly tried for participation in the killing contest. Tanaka was tried first, and charged with killing 300 people during the competition, after he initially denied any such involvement. However, when later shown evidence, including a photograph published in the Japanese book *Imperial Soldiers* documenting that Tanaka had killed "300 hateful Chinese enemies with his buddy sword Sukehiro", and a news report showing the accused beheading a Chinese using his sword, he rescinded his denial.[30]

After the Tanaka case, the Nanjing Tribunal opened a hearing for Mukai and Noda, infamous for their contest challenging soldiers to cut down a hundred people using their swords. The Tribunal admitted several news reports about this killing contest published in Japanese, Chinese and international newspapers, including *Tokyo Nichi Nichi Shimbun,* the Osaka newspaper *Mainichi Shimbun,* and the *Japan Advertiser* and *Shanghai Evening Post and Mercury.*[31] The facts covered in these reports were corroborative and together revealed the whole process of this contest. At the end of November 1937 Mukai and Noda had agreed to engage in a killing contest. Whoever could kill 100 people before the invasion and occupation of Nanjing were completed would win a prize. When the Japanese

---

28 LUO, 2006, p. 23, see *supra* note 11.

29 HU, 2006, pp. 487-488, see *supra* note 5.

30 LUO, 2006, p. 24, see *supra* note 11; see also "Justice Trial: Documenting the Chinese Trial of Japanese War Criminals", in *Xinhua News,* 12 August 2005.

31 HU, 2006, pp. 487–88, 495–99, see *supra* note 5; see also LUO, 2006, p. 24, see *supra* note 11.

forces arrived at Tang Mountain, Mukai had only killed 89 people, while Noda had killed 78. Having failed to reach their goal of 100 dead, the competition could not yet be brought to a close. Mukai and Noda continued their "competition" at the foot of the Purple Gold Mountain to the east of the city after Japanese forces had entered Nanjing. By then, Mukai had already killed 106 people and Noda had killed 105, but it was not clear who had reached the hundred mark first. Since there was no way to prove who had first reached the goal, they agreed to reset the target to 150 people. The vicious cycle continued without a definite ending mark in different reports.

The two accused claimed that all these reports were fabricated and that the Japanese news reporters did so in order to promote a heroic image of Japanese soldiers so it would become easier for them to get married after returning home.[32] Considering the Japanese military had extremely strict news censorship during the Second Sino–Japanese War, the Nanjing Tribunal also rejected this argument.[33] The presiding judge, SHI Mei-yu, announced at the end of the hearing that the two accused did indeed engage in killing prisoners of war and non-combatants, saw the killing contest as a game, and that these activities constituted a crime of war and against humanity in violation of the Hague Convention Respecting the Laws and Customs of War on Land and the Geneva Convention relating to the Treatment of Prisoners of War.[34]

7.3.4. General Okamura Yasuji

The trial of General Okamura Yasuji was a stain on the Nanjing Tribunal. Okamura was the commander-in-chief of the China Expeditionary Army from November 1944 until Japan's surrender. He was tried in July 1948 by the Nanjing Tribunal, but was immediately protected by the personal order of CHIANG Kai-shek,[35] who later retained Okamura as a military

---

[32] LUO, 2006, p. 25, see *supra* note 11.

[33] *Ibid.*

[34] *Ibid.*, p. 24.

[35] Herbert P. Bix, *Hirohito and the Making of Modern Japan*, HarperCollins, New York, 2000, p. 594.

adviser to the Nationalist government.[36] The unique features of his trial are discussed below in the concluding remarks.

7.4. The Nanjing Tribunal's Impact

As we have seen, Nanjing suffered grave atrocities during the war. Setting up the Tribunal provided the victims there with an opportunity to formally report the crimes they suffered and to make claims for their losses. Many people from the affected communities were aware of the trial and actively participated in the trial process. From its inception, the Nationalist government demonstrated a commitment to conduct outreach work with the affected communities. But after the change of regime in 1949 the trial was largely neglected and gradually forgotten except for some academic writings. Here we analyse the impacts of the Nanjing Tribunal on the Chinese and Japanese peoples.

7.4.1. Impact on the Chinese People

The Chinese public's awareness of and interest in the Nanjing Trial has fluctuated during different periods. Throughout the investigation, trial and execution stages, the Nanjing trials were conducted in a way that greatly encouraged public involvement. The Chinese people – and especially the survivors of the Nanjing Massacre – were able to use this opportunity to claim damages, have their voice heard and seek justice.

In 1944 the Chinese National Office under the auspices of the United Nations War Crimes Commission was established to collect evidence of Japanese war crimes. In Nanjing the Nationalist government created a special investigation commission that included various government organs and other organisations, including the Nanjing municipal government, police bureau, Nationalist Party department, gendarmerie command, labour unions, farmers' unions, industrial unions, local courts, lawyers' associations and so forth.[37] The Nationalist government posted notices in the streets urging witnesses to come forward with evidence. From military troops to ordinary citizens, inquiry forms were handed out to the

---

[36] ZHANG Xianwen, "Investigation Statistics Conducted by Japanese War Crimes Investigation Commission", *Collection of Historical Materials on the Nanking Massacre*, vol. 20, Jiangsu People's Press, Nanjing, 2006, p. 121.

[37] *Ibid.*, p. 121.

victims of war to report the atrocities they witnessed and the losses they suffered.[38] Major Chinese newspapers such as *Zhongyang Ribao* (*Central Daily News*, the official mouthpiece of the government), *Da Kong Pao* and foreign media outlets all intensively and continuously covered the important cases at the Nanjing Tribunal.[39] Aside from newspapers, the Nationalist government also used all possible means to raise public awareness about the issues at trial. For example, in July 1946 slide shows about the Nanjing Massacre were made and played before every film in local cinemas.[40]

The Nanjing Tribunal tried most of its cases publicly. The courtroom debate and reading of the judgment were open to the public so that more people could observe how the war crimes trials were conducted. In cases such as those of Sakai and Okamura, hearings were held in a local auditorium instead of the regular courtroom in order to host more observers.[41] Executions of criminals receiving the death sentence were also carried out publicly.[42] On 26 April 1947, the day of Sakai's execution, thousands of Nanjing citizens surrounded the execution site.[43] The crowd shouted out their relief after what they saw as Sakai finally taking responsibility for the Nanjing Massacre.[44]

The atrocities caused by Japanese troops, especially the Nanjing Massacre, had left great pain in the Nanjing community. Many witnessed their loved ones being violated or killed. After the war ended, many needed to see the war criminals brought to justice. The Nanjing Trial fulfilled this need to some degree.

---

[38] ZHANG Jing and L-V JING, "Crimes Investigation Forms filled out by LIAO Tujin and Property Lost Form", in ZHANG Xianwen, *The Truth of the Nanking Massacre: Chinese Material*, Jiangsu People's Press, 2006, pp. 468, 495.

[39] HU, 2006, pp. 63, 65, 68, 70–72, 318, 320–21, 349, 353, 358–60, 373–88, 494, 499, see *supra* note 5.

[40] GUO Biqiang and JIANG Liangqin, "Order of Nanking Society Bureau Ordering All Cinemas to Play the Slide Shows about Nanking Massacre Investigation Unit", in ZHANG, 2006, p. 1532, see *supra* note 36.

[41] LUO, 1995, p. 26, see *supra* note 11.

[42] Military Tribunal Announcement about Hisao Tani's Execution, HU, 2006, p. 456, see *supra* note 5.

[43] TAN Yugan, "Experiencing Nanking War Criminal's Trial and Execution", in *Journal of Guizhou World of Literature and History*, 1995, vol. 12, p. 16.

[44] *Ibid.*

The situation changed after the Nationalist Party lost power in China. In 1949 the Communists established the People's Republic of China, ousting the Nationalists from the mainland, who then retreated to Taiwan. Since then there has been very little discussion about the Nanjing Tribunal in the Chinese media. The Nanjing Trial and other trials conducted by the Nationalists seemed to have been forgotten or were actively shunned by many.

It was only from the 1980s that researchers began to revisit the war crimes trials conducted by the Nationalist government. In 1983 the Nanjing municipal government opened a full-scale research programme concerning the Nanjing Massacre and built the Nanjing Massacre Memorial Hall two years later. Great efforts have been made to collect documentary material and to conduct interviews with Nanjing Massacre survivors and witnesses. Based on these materials, researchers and experts have published many historical compilations and academic papers.[45] On the fiftieth anniversary of the victory of the Second Sino-Japanese War, the Communist Party's newspaper published an interview with the former presiding judge, SHI Mei-yu, who discussed his experience of conducting the trials.[46] Trial documents had been long kept by the Nationalists, and it was not until 2006 that the Memorial Hall had access to primary source trial materials, including indictments, judgments, meeting minutes and photographs. These documents, donated by individuals in Taiwan, fostered new analyses and publications by legal professionals and historians. Even so, this emerging research interest still only exists in the academic world.

Compared to the IMTFE or the Nanjing Massacre, which have been passionately debated among historians and intellectuals, discussions of the Nanjing Tribunal have been rather bland. Furthermore, unlike the Nanjing Massacre, the Nanjing Tribunal is not included in the Chinese school curriculum. Post-war Chinese generations have not received much historical education about the trial's significance.

In sum, during the trial itself, the proceedings and the decisions were generally conducted fairly, especially in light of the fact that the country had just suffered eight years of vicious war and the materials for trial were all gathered without the aid of modern technology and computer

---

[45] ZHU Chengshan and YUAN Zhixiu, "1982–2012: 30 Years Research about the Nanking Massacre", in *Journal of Japanese Invasion of China Research*, 2013, vol. 2, p. 1.

[46] LUO, 1995, p. 26, see *supra* note 11.

databases. The Nanjing Tribunal's efficacy, however, was affected by the changing regimes in Japan and China during the post-war period. All convicted Japanese prisoners were released based on a treaty concluded between Japan and the Nationalist Party in 1952.[47] The Communist government also upheld post-war clemency for Japanese war criminals. On 25 April 1956 the standing committee of the National People's Congress issued the Decision on the Handling of the Criminals in Custody from the Japanese War of Aggression against China. According to this decision, the Supreme People's Procuratorate announced the decision to exempt from prosecution and immediately release, in three batches in 1956, a total of 1,017 Japanese war criminals in custody who had committed relatively minor offences and had demonstrated good behaviour and shown repentance.[48] Thereafter, the Nanjing Tribunal was gradually forgotten until scholars developed a renewed interest several decades later. However, it still remains a purely academic interest. How much impact has it had on the Chinese people? It is difficult to provide a clear answer without conducting further research and social investigation. In light of the above discussion, the impact is probably very limited.

7.4.2. Impact on the Japanese People

In the post-war period, the work of Chinese military tribunals concerning accused war criminals did not attract much attention for most Japanese people. One reason was that they had very little knowledge about the atrocities committed by the Imperial Japanese Army in China. During the Second Sino-Japanese War, the Japanese government had very tight control over the news media. Reports about Japanese military actions in China were usually described as "heroic". For example, on 22 December 1937 *Tokyo Nichi Nichi Shimbun* published an article titled "Kindness towards Yesterday-Loving Scenario in Nanking City", accompanied by five photographs showing wounded Chinese soldiers receiving treatment

---

[47]   YAN, 2011, p. 112, see *supra* note 1.

[48]   "Decision of the Standing Committee of the National People's Congress on the Handling of the Criminals in Custody from the Japanese War of Aggression against China", in *People's Daily News*, 22 June 1956.

in a Japanese hospital after bombardment.[49] On 8 January 1938 *Xin Shen Bao*, a Japanese newspaper in Shanghai, reported:

> The streets in Nanking are still and quiet. Beautiful sunshine warms the refugee zone in the north-west corner of the city. Japanese royal military officers paid condolence to the Nanking refugees who escaped death. The refugees knelt down by the street showing their appreciation. Before the royal army came to town, they were suppressed by the anti-Japan Chinese army. The sick could not get medical care, and the hungry could not get any food. But now the royal army has come with mercy and kindness.[50]

Under such influence, when evidence about the Nanjing Massacre was presented at the IMTFE, the Japanese people were shocked, as it was the first time they had ever heard about it.[51] The Nanjing Tribunal adjudicated many cases concerning the Nanjing Massacre. However, these trials received very little publicity in Japan. *Mainichi Shimbun* only reported the execution of Japanese army officers in Nanjing three times, each given very little space on the page.[52] From the limited information available, most Japanese would not have known what really happened at the Nanjing Tribunal, and this likely caused the general impression that the class B and C trials conducted in Allied countries were unfair and unjust. The public also showed sympathy for the "misery and hardship of the families of war criminals".[53] Holding to this belief, the public engaged in a campaign to release all imprisoned war criminals, which succeeded in 1958.[54]

From 1970s onwards, with the rise of right-wing political forces in Japan, the Nanjing Trial was brought to the attention of the Japanese public in a heated debate over the denial of the Nanjing Massacre (the "Nanjing issue" as it was referred to by Japanese academics). A book titled *Nankin daigyakusatsu no maboroshi* [The Illusion of the Nanjing Massa-

---

[49] WANG Xingye, "Reasons for Nanking Massacre Denial Analysis", in *Journal of Nanking Massacre Historical Research*, 2012, vol. 9, p. 22.

[50] *Ibid.*

[51] YU Tianren, "Japanese View of the Nanking Massacre", in *Youth Reference*, 29 February 2012.

[52] Kasahara Tokushi, *Nanking Issue*, Boyan Press, 1997, pp. 7–8.

[53] Yuki Tanaka, "Crime and Responsibility: War, the State, and Japanese Society", in *Asia-Pacific Journal: Japan Focus*, 2006, vol. 4, no. 8.

[54] Wijers-Hasegawa, 2003, see *supra* note 3.

cre] published by a right-wing writer, Suzuki Akira, in 1973 denied the Nanjing Massacre and the existence of the killing contest, and went so far as to claim that the Japanese army officers were wrongfully convicted and executed.[55] Perhaps because this contention was more palatable to Japanese patriots, the book sold 200,000 copies and the author won the Soichi Oya Non-fiction Award in 1973.[56]

Encouraged by this trend, and as already noted, families of the two convicted lieutenants filed a libel suit for in 2003 against *Tokyo Nichi Nichi Shimbun* and two others who published information regarding the killing contest.[57] They contended that the 1937 *Tokyo Nichi Nichi Shimbun* report about the killing contest, which was used as evidence by the Nanjing Tribunal, was not based on the truth.[58] The Tokyo District Court rejected the case in August 2005. The presiding judge, Akio Doi, explained: "We cannot deny that the article included some false elements and exaggeration, but it is difficult to say the article was fiction not based on facts. Since a final historical assessment on whether the contest of killing 100 people has not yet been made, we cannot say [the article] was obviously false".[59] From a legal perspective, this case did not challenge the judgment made in other jurisdictional territory. According to Tokushi Kasahara, a leading Japanese historian, this judgment indeed ended the killing contest debate at least in the Japanese legal field.[60] At the same time, intensive media coverage of this trial caused the Japanese public to gain more knowledge about the Nanjing Tribunal and therefore to differentiate it from the general national war crimes trials conducted by the Allied powers.

Further details of Japanese perceptions of the Nanjing Trial are difficult to discern due to the author's limited language ability in researching Japanese-language materials. Based on the information available, howev-

---

[55] Suzuki Akira, *Nankin daigyakusatsu no maboroshi* [The Illusion of the Nanking Massacre], Bungei Shunjū, Tokyo, 1973; Kasahara Tokushi, "Memory of Nanking Massacre: The Lost Memory of Japanese People after Losing the War", in *Study of Japanese Aggression of China*, 2012, vol. 2, pp. 73–91.

[56] Hiroaki Gonoi, "Thorough Examination of the Reality at the Era of Non-Fiction", in *Journal of Truth of the Rumour*, 1987, vol. 4, p. 66.

[57] Wijers-Hasegawa, 2003, see *supra* note 3.

[58] *Ibid.*

[59] "Japanese Court Throws Out 'Killing Contest' Lawsuit", in *Taipei Times*, 24 August 2005.

[60] Tokushi, 2011, see *supra* note 4.

er, the evidence seems to suggest that the details of the Nanjing Trial are not widely known in Japan. In comparison to the Chinese, the Nanjing Tribunal has had even less impact on Japanese society.

7.5. Concluding Remarks

The Nanjing Tribunal was one of the most important domestic war crimes trials conducted by the Allied powers after the Second World War. It is astonishing to realise that the trial has had such limited impact on both the victims' and the defendants' countries, yet there are several clear reasons why this might be so.

Although the Nanjing Tribunal convicted several notorious Japanese war criminals, it has had a mixed reputation due to the lack of judicial independence. From the very beginning, CHIANG Kai-shek's regime adopted a magnanimous policy. He issued the famous radio speech "Letter to Soldiers and Civilians of the Whole Nation as well as the Peoples of the World after the Victory of the Anti-Japanese War" right after Japan's surrender.[61] He encouraged the Chinese to differentiate the oppressive Japanese war from the Japanese people as a whole by asking the public to not treat the Japanese as the enemy and to not seek retaliation.[62] In fact, this was a strategic political gesture aimed at helping the Nationalist Party to resume control over China. During the Second Sino-Japanese War, although the Communist forces and the Nationalist forces united to fight against the Japanese invasion, both parties controlled their respective areas of the country. The Nationalists controlled the south-west and north-west while the Communist forces were largely located in the north, closer to areas occupied by the Japanese. The Communists, therefore, had a geographical advantage to move in and take over locations under Japanese control.[63] In order to encourage Japanese troops to co-operate with the Nationalist Party instead of the Communists, CHIANG announced the policy of magnanimity, which served as the Nationalist Party's fundamen-

---

[61] QIN Xiaoyi (ed.), *The Thoughts and Speeches Collection of President Chiang Kai-shek*, vol. 32, Party History Committee of the Chinese Nationalist Party Committee Press, Taipei, 1984, pp. 121–23.

[62] *Ibid.*

[63] TANG Hongsen, "Communist Party and Nationalist Part's Strategy in Taking Over North-East China", in Chinese Modern and Contemporary Historical Material Academy (ed.), *Research on Anti-Japanese War and the Historical Material*, University Nankai Press, Tianjin, 1995, pp. 385–92.

tal principle in guiding the post-war treatment of the Japanese, including war crimes trials conducted in China.[64]

During the conference organised by the War Criminal Disposal Committee on 25 October 1946 the Nationalist government used this guiding principle to issue a decision "to punish the primary criminals of atrocities like Nanjing Massacre with severity, and to treat ordinary Japanese war criminals with lenience, not to press charges for those who did not commit major crimes or without substantive evidence".[65] This meant that CHIANG decided to narrow the scope of those eligible to be categorised as Japanese war criminals. The improper political interference seriously challenged the judicial independence of the Chinese war crimes tribunals. Instead of deciding cases based on the merits of law, the tribunals were subjected to the will of politicians. This was an injustice to the tens of thousands of men, women and children killed or injured during the war and their families.

This was most apparent in the Okamura case. As noted, Okamura was listed as a class A war criminal by the IMTFE for leading the aggressive war in China and, as such, he should have been sent back to Japan to face trial. However, in an effort to protect him, the Nationalist government went as far so setting up a Japanese liaison office in Nanjing and used Okamura's work in this office as an excuse to delay his repatriation.[66] He was later summoned by the IMTFE to testify in court as a witness and, again, CHIANG's government rejected the request.[67] Due to increasing public pressure, the Nanjing Tribunal finally tried him but granted probation pending trial and eventually issued a not guilty verdict.[68] The whole trial process was nothing more than a show to fool the public. As the former commander-in-chief of the China Expeditionary

---

[64] YUAN Chengyi, "Several Problems about Jiang Kai-Chang's Policy of Magnanimity towards Japan", in *Journal of Anti-Japanese War Research*, 2006, vol. 1, pp. 213–14.

[65] GUO Biqiang and JIANG Liangqin, "Japanese War Criminal Disposal Committee Meeting Minutes on Policy of Japanese War Criminals Disposal", in *Collection of Historical Materials on the Nanking Massacre: Investigation on Japanese War Crimes*, Jiangsu People's Press, Nanjing, 2006, pp. 28–29.

[66] Yedao Zhengfu and Yasuji Okamura, 冈村宁次回忆录 [Yasuji Okamura's Memoir], trans. Tianjin Compilation and Translation Bureau of Political Consultative Association, Zhonghua shuju, Beijing, 1981, p. 160.

[67] *Ibid.*

[68] *Ibid.*

Force and an arch-criminal, no court operating under the rule of law should have allowed a not guilty verdict for Okamura. And indeed, as soon as Judge SHI announced his verdict, people attending the hearing immediately shouted out in anger and questioned the ruling.[69] Angry journalists then went to SHI's office to protest against this unfair judgment.[70] People outside Nanjing sent many letters of protest to the Nanjing government.[71]

This verdict was unacceptable in the extreme to the Communist Party. The party had been prepared to try Japanese war criminals from early 1945. Okamura was listed as one the most important suspects to be tried due to his heavy involvement in the battles between the Japanese army and Communist troops in northern China. After the Nanjing Tribunal set Okamura free, the Communist Party formally condemned the trial as "betraying the interest of the people".[72] Therefore, the party denied the legality of the war crimes trials conducted by the Nationalist government and thus contributed to its limited impact among Chinese people after the war.

On the Japanese side, despite the large number of convicted verdicts issued by the Nanjing Tribunal and IMTFE, it was hard for the public to accept the harsh realities of the war and the Japanese soldiers' actions in perpetrating atrocities. According to a survey conducted in Japan, significant portions of the public saw themselves as victims of the war.[73] The typical historical image embedded in the minds of middle school students is one of victimhood: "I have always associated the war with Hiroshima and Nagasaki", said one student. "I could only think of Japan as the loser in the war".[74] This may be associated with a sentiment maintained

---

[69] WANG Junyan, "The Show of Yasuji Okamura's Trial under US and Mr. Jiang's Protection", in *Journal of Yanhuang Chunqiu*, 1995, vol. 11, p. 72.

[70] LUO, 1995, p. 26, see *supra* note 11.

[71] WANG, 1995, p. 73, see *supra* note 69.

[72] MAO Zedong, "On Ordering the Reactionary Nationalist Government to Re-Arrest Yasuji Okamura, Former Commander-in-Chief of the Japanese Forces of Aggression in China, and to Arrest the Nationalist Civil War Criminals-Statement by the Spokesman of the Communist Party on 28 January 1949", and "Peace Terms Must Include the Punishment of Japanese War Criminals and Nationalist War Criminals-Statement by the Spokesmen for the Communist Party of China issued on 5 February 1949", in *Selected Works of Mao Zedong*, vol. 4, People's Press, Beijing, 1993, p. 1394.

[73] HU, 2006, p. 4, see note *supra* 5.

[74] Ian Buruma, *The Wages of Guilt: Memories of War in Germany and Japan*, Farrar, Straus & Giroux, New York, 1994, pp.114–15.

by the annual Hiroshima Peace Memorial Ceremony. Every year at the precise time that the atomic bomb was dropped on Hiroshima, Japanese citizens, regardless of where they are situated, are asked to offer silent prayers for peace and to the souls of those victims attacked.[75] Furthermore, in stark contrast to Germany's actions following the war, there has never been any effort made by Japan to improve relationships by offering reconciliation to China. Instead, Japanese politicians regularly visit the Yasukuni Shrine, which commemorates not only those who died in the war but also 14 convicted class A war criminals. When they pay tribute at the Yasukuni Shrine, these politicians are also paying tribute, intentionally or otherwise, to an imperial order in which Japan violently subjugated its neighbours.[76] In addition, being constantly reminded of their victim status makes it very difficult for the Japanese people to develop a deeper understanding of the trials conducted in China. In their view, such war criminals were merely subordinates who followed imperial orders and should be honoured by their current leaders.

Although the Nanjing Tribunal has very limited impact on the Chinese and Japanese peoples, there are abundant trial records and public documentation from that time. But the tribunal still remains obscured in a lost legal and historical discourse. Despite its shortcomings, the Nanjing Tribunal formed an important part of the post-war justice system and contributed to increased expectations for the rule of law in the world. Alongside proceedings in Singapore, Malaya, North Borneo, Hong Kong, Taiwan and Burma, the Australian and Dutch trials, as well as the Nuremberg, Tokyo and Control Council Law tribunals, the Nanjing Tribunal presents great historical value for contemporary international criminal law. This is a part of history more people should be aware of. This is especially true after the establishment of the only independent and permanent International Criminal Court prosecuting war crimes. Not only can we learn lessons from the Nuremberg and Tokyo Tribunals, we should also reflect upon the impact of the class B and C trials in order to construct a fairer, truly impartial international justice system.

---

[75] "Hiroshima Marks 69th Anniversary of Atomic Bombing", in *The Japan Times*, 6 August 2014.

[76] Max Fisher, "Japan's No-Apology Diplomacy: Why a Small Tokyo Shrine Is Causing Big Trouble in Asia", in *Washington Post*, 23 April 2013.

8

On the Successor Commander's Responsibility: The Okamura Yasuji Case Revisited

YANG Lijun[*]

After the Second World War the Chinese Nationalist government set up 10 war crimes tribunals in 1945 in Nanjing (Nanking), Shanghai, Beijing, Hankou, Guangzhou, Shenyang, Jinan, Xuzhou, Taiyuan and Taipei to prosecute Japanese war criminals. Most of the trials were conducted in a fair way, with the legitimate rights of the accused guaranteed, the convictions based on profound evidence and the judgments convincing. However, some were not that satisfactory and contained obvious legal flaws, notably the Okamura Yasuji case. Listed as one of the most important Japanese war criminals, Okamura, the commander-in-chief of the Japanese China Expeditionary Army, was surprisingly acquitted and returned to Japan.[1] It is submitted here that, as a superior commander, he should have been held responsible for the atrocities committed by his subordinates, both during and before his tenure, due to his failure to punish those subordinates' crimes.

---

[*] **YANG Lijun** is an Associate Professor of International Law at the International Law Institute of the Chinese Academy of Social Sciences. She has focused her recent research on international criminal law and has published dozens of articles on issues relating to the International Criminal Court. She is also a Senior Research Fellow at the Erasmus China Law Centre, Rotterdam, the Netherlands, a board member of the Forum on International Criminal Law and Humanitarian Law, Brussels, Belgium, as well as a distinguished research fellow of the Collaborative Innovation Center for Judicial Civilization of the Chinese University of Political Science and Law.

[1] Okamura later wrote in his memoirs: "I was acquitted by the criminal tribunal, mainly due to the very strong proposition of military dignitaries led by HE Yingqin, especially the role of General TANG Enbo. I will never forget the consistent kindness towards me of the Chinese government, President CHIANG, and Generals in the Department of Defence, and in addition, devote myself to the Japan-China friendship so as to fulfil my long-cherished wish". See Inaba Masao (ed.) 冈村宁次回忆录 [Yasuji Okamura's Memoirs], trans. Tianjin Compilation and Translation Bureau of the Political Consultative Association, Zhonghua shuju, Beijing, 1981, pp. 159–60.

8.1. Introduction to the Case

Okamura Yasuji was alleged to have been involved in crimes of aggression against China as early as the 1920s. In 1928, as commanding officer of an infantry regiment, he took an active part in the war in which Japan attacked and seized Jinan where a massacre of civilians occurred. In 1932 he served as the deputy chief of staff of the Expeditionary Army that attacked and occupied Shanghai,[2] and he played a direct role in recruiting Korean-Japanese women from Nagasaki prefecture into military brothels in Shanghai, a fact noted in his memoirs.[3] Okamura was promoted to the rank of lieutenant general in 1936 with command over the Imperial Japanese Army's 2nd Division. In 1938, as the commander of the 11th Corps, he participated in a number of battles in China, including key battles at Wuhan, Nanchang and Changsha. In April 1940 he was promoted to the rank of a full general, followed by his appointment as the commander of the Northern China Front Army three months later. In December 1941 Okamura received and obeyed the scorched earth policies (also known as the "three alls policy") dictated by his superiors under Army Order number 575.[4] As a result of this order, his troops were responsible for the deaths of over two million Chinese, mostly civilians in Hebei and Shandong provinces. In 1944 Okamura was the commander-in-chief of the 6th Front Army. Later the same year he was appointed supreme commander of the China Expeditionary Army.[5]

---

[2] MAO Zedong, "On Ordering the Reactionary Nationalist Government to Re-Arrest Yasuji Okamura, Former Commander-in-Chief of the Japanese Forces of Aggression in China, and to Arrest the Nationalist Civil War Criminals-Statement by the Spokesman of the Communist Party on 28 January 1949", 28 January 1949, in *Selected Works of Mao Zedong*, vol. 4, People's Press, Beijing, 1960, p. 330, fn. 3.

[3] Masao, 1981, p. 351, see *supra* note 1.

[4] The three alls policy was a Japanese scorched earth policy adopted in China during the Second Sino-Japanese War. Generally considered a Japanese war atrocity, it was a policy that encouraged killing all the people, burning down all the villages and looting all the grain and other properties in guerrilla-active areas. This policy was also referred to as "the burn to ash strategy" in the Japanese literature. It was designed to uproot the guerrillas in northern China. After Okamura was appointed commander-in-chief of the Northern China Front Army he decided to implement the policy, which was the objective of more than a hundred military campaigns launched by Okamura. The three alls policy was responsible for the deaths of more than 2.7 million Chinese civilians. James Z. Gao, *Historical Dictionary of Modern China (1800–1949)*, Scarecrow Press, Lanham, MD, 2009, p. 359.

[5] Masao, 1981, pp. 4–5, see *supra* note 1.

Despite his use of chemical weapons during the war of resistance against Japanese aggression, which was specifically banned by the Geneva Convention, and his indiscriminate killing of Chinese civilians by enforcing the extremely brutal policy of "burn all, kill all, loot all", that is, the three alls policy,[6] Okamura was not charged with any such war crimes by the prosecutor at the Nanjing War Crimes Tribunal ('Nanjing Tribunal'). After the war Okamura, who was on the top list of war criminals issued by the International Military Tribunal for the Far East ('IMTFE'), and among the chief Japanese war criminals on the list published in Yan'an by the Chinese Communist Party in August 1945, was indicted by the Nanjing Tribunal under the auspices of the Ministry of Defence for his superior responsibility.[7] The public hearing of his case was not held until late August 1948. During the second hearing on 26 January 1949 Okamura was acquitted by the Nanjing Tribunal, to the surprise of the public. This result came even to his own surprise, for he himself had been convinced that he would be convicted as a war criminal and sentenced to death.[8]

According to Articles 2 and 3 of the Nationalist government's Law Governing the Trial of War Criminals promulgated on 23 October 1946, war crimes are atrocities such as killings, rape or robbery committed during war, or breaches of international conventions for a conspiracy of planning to launch or support a war of aggression. Article 9 of the law states that "a superior shall share the same criminal responsibility with his/her subordinates who committed war crimes, if he or she failed to prevent or stop the crimes".[9]

As noted, Okamura was appointed the commander-in-chief of the China Expeditionary Army on 26 November 1944. All the atrocities committed by the Japanese army in the battles of Changsha and Xuzhou, as well as massacres in Hong Kong and Guangdong led by Sakai Takashi, and the Nanjing Massacre led by Matsui Iwane and Tani Hisao, occurred before Okamura assumed his position as commander-in-chief. Therefore, the judgment found that the accused has nothing to do with these atroci-

---

6   MAO, 1960, see *supra* note 2.

7   Masao, 1981, pp. 142, 149, 152, see *supra* note 1.

8   *Ibid.*, p. 142.

9   HU Jurun (ed.), *Nanking Trial: Collection of the Historical Archive on the Nanking Massacre*, vol. 24, Jiangsu People's Press, Nanjing, 2006, p. 28.

ties.[10] (Sakai and Tani were found guilty and sentenced to death by the Nanjing Tribunal, and had already been executed.)

The reasoning outlined in the Nanjing Tribunal's judgment offered a number of contextual observations that allowed it to return a not guilty verdict in the Okamura case. The Tribunal recalled that during his tenure in office, the Allies had landed in Normandy in France and Saipan in the Pacific Ocean, while the Axis powers were collapsing and the Japanese army was largely isolated. Therefore, during the entire eight-month period from the date Okamura was appointed as commander-in-chief to that of Japan's surrender the Japanese army scattered all over China barely made any progress due to a low fighting spirit. And once the Japanese government formally surrendered, the accused immediately laid down arms, thereby leading millions of troops to obey the order to surrender.[11] After examining Okamura's actions during his command, the Nanjing Tribunal found that he was not involved in any of the above-mentioned massacres, nor rape, robbery, conspiracy or planning to launch or support a war of aggression. Therefore, it could not convict him based only on his *de jure* position as the commander of the China Expeditionary Army.[12] The Tribunal stated that although during Okamura's tenure there were sporadic atrocities committed by the Japanese army stationed at Lianhua in Jiangxi, Shaoyang in Hunan, Yongjia in Zhejiang and so on, it was the perpetrators and their direct superiors – Generals Ochiai Jinkuru and Hishida Motoshiro – who should be held responsible for these atrocities. Ochiai and the other accused had already been sentenced and convicted by the Nanjing Tribunal.[13] As for those sporadic atrocities that occurred during his tenure, the court found Okamura was in lack of the *mens rea* to be involved in the commission of the crimes. As a result, the Tribunal found that he should not be responsible for the crime of co-perpetration.[14] Based on this above reasoning and in accordance with Article 1(1) of the Law Governing the Trial of War Criminals and Article 293(1) of the Criminal Procedure Law, the Nanjing Tribunal found that the accused did not vio-

---

[10] The Military Tribunal of the Ministry of Defence of the Republic of China for the Trial of War Criminals, Case No. 28 of the War Criminal Trial, Judgment, in the 37th Year of the Republic of China ('Okamura Judgment'). Masao, 1981, p. 159, see *supra* note 1.

[11] *Ibid.*

[12] *Ibid.*

[13] *Ibid.*

[14] *Ibid.*

---

late any regulations of war nor international law, and he was acquitted of all charges in the indictment.[15]

It is submitted that the Nanjing Tribunal came to a totally incorrect conclusion in the Okamura case due to its purposely distorted interpretation of the principle of command responsibility in international humanitarian law. Okamura should at least have been convicted for failing to take reasonable and necessary measures to prevent or punish the acts of his subordinates when he knew or had reason to know that his subordinates were about to commit such acts or had done so before and during his tenure as commander of the China Expeditionary Army.

8.2. The Principle of Command Responsibility

The principle of individual criminal responsibility of superiors for failure to prevent or to punish crimes committed by subordinates is a well-established principle in conventional and customary international law.[16] It is now widely accepted that the purpose behind the concept of command responsibility is to ensure compliance with the laws and customs of war and international humanitarian law generally.[17] This protection is at the very heart of international humanitarian law. The principle is applicable both to international armed conflicts and domestic armed conflicts.[18] Based on state practice and the Second World War trial cases, it was formally codified into the 1977 Additional Protocol I to the Geneva Conven-

---

[15]   *Ibid.*

[16]   International Criminal Tribunal for the former Yugoslavia ('ICTY'), *Prosecutor v. Zejnil Delalić, Zdravko Mucić, Hazim Delić and Esad Landžo*, Appeals Chamber, Judgment, IT-96-21-A, 20 February 2001, para. 195 (http://www.legal-tools.org/doc/051554/).

[17]   ICTY, *Prosecutor v. Sefer Halilović*, Trial Chamber, Judgment, IT-01-48-T, 16 November 2005, para. 39 ('Halilović Judgment') (http://www.legal-tools.org/doc/abda04/); ICTY, *Prosecutor v. Dragan Obrenović*, Trial Chamber, Sentencing Judgment, IT-02-60/2-S, 10 December 2003, para. 100 ('Obrenović Judgment') (http://www.legal-tools.org/doc/3f6409/).

[18]   ICTY, *Prosecutor v. Enver Hadžihasanović, Mehmed Alagić and Amir Kubura*, Appeals Chamber, Decision on Interlocutory Appeal Challenging Jurisdiction in Relation to Command Responsibility, IT-01-47-AR72, 16 July 2003, para. 29 ('Hadžihasanović Appeal Decision'): "[C]ommand responsibility was part of customary international law relating to international armed conflicts before the adoption of Protocol I. Therefore [...] Articles 86 and 87 of Protocol I [the articles that address superior responsibility] were in this respect only declaring the existing position, and not constituting it". (http://www.legal-tools.org/doc/608f09/).

tions.[19] While Article 86(2) deals with the "failure to act", the same must be read in conjunction with the subsequent Article 87(1) and (3) that specifically addresses the issue of the responsibility or "duty of commanders".[20] Additional Protocol I attaches responsibility to superiors in those particular situations where they had knowledge, either actual or constructive, that would have given them reasons to believe that a prohibited act had either occurred or, in the alternative, was about to occur.[21] Liability would attach to the superior where information had been given and was then either disregarded or ignored by the superior.

While Article 86 addresses the issue of failure to act, it specifically uses the term "superior", suggesting that so long as the relationship between subordinate and superior is in existence, the obligation attaches. Article 87 is more specific in attaching liability to military commanders for actions of their military subordinates. It is further clear that this article also requires that a proactive posture be maintained on an ongoing basis

---

[19] Protocol Additional to the Geneva Conventions of 12 August 1949, and relating to the Protection of Victims of International Armed Conflicts ('Additional Protocol I'), 8 June 1977, Art. 86(2) (http://www.legal-tools.org/doc/d9328a/) stipulates:

> The fact the breach of the Conventions or of this Protocol was committed by a subordinate does not absolve his superiors from penal or disciplinary responsibility, as the case may be, if they knew, or had information which would have enabled them to conclude in the circumstances at the time, that he was committing or was about to commit such a breach and if they did not take all feasible measures within their power to prevent or repressed such a breach.

[20] Stuart E. Hendin, "Command Responsibility and Superior Orders in the Twentieth Century – A Century of Evolution", in *Murdoch University Electronic Journal of Law*, 2003, vol. 10, no. 1, para. 137.

[21] Additional Protocol I, Art. 87, see *supra* note 19:

> 1. The High Contracting Parties and the Parties to the conflict shall require military commanders, with respect to members of the armed forces under their command and other persons under their control, to prevent and, where necessary, to suppress and to report to competent authorities breaches of the Conventions and of this Protocol. [...]
>
> 2. The High Contracting Parties, and Parties to the conflict shall require any commander who was aware that his subordinates or other persons under it his control are going to commit or have committed a breach of the Conventions or of this Protocol, to initiate such steps as are necessary to prevent such violations of the Conventions or of this Protocol, and where appropriate, to initiate disciplinary or penal action against violators thereof.

by the superior to keep control of the activities of their subordinates.[22] In 1993 the International Criminal Tribunal for the former Yugoslavia ('ICTY') was established by United Nations Security Council resolutions 808 and 827 in response to the atrocities committed in the former Yugoslavia.[23] The ICTY Statute, in a sense, was the first international penal law incorporating the concept of command responsibility. Article 7(3) states:

> The fact that any of the acts referred to in Articles 2 to 5 of the present Statute was committed by a subordinate does not relieve this superior of criminal responsibility if he knew or had reason to know that the subordinate was about to commit such acts or had done so and the superior failed to take the necessary and reasonable measures to prevent such acts or to punish the perpetrators thereof.[24]

The statutes of other international judicial organs, like those of the International Criminal Tribunal for Rwanda ('ICTR'),[25] Special Court for Sierra Leone ('SCSL')[26] and Extraordinary Chambers in the Courts of Cambodia ('ECCC')[27] have similar provisions, while Article 28 of the Rome Statute of International Criminal Court ('ICC Statute') also adopt a similar approach, though with some differences.[28]

---

[22] Hendin, 2003, para. 139, see *supra* note 20.

[23] United Nations Security Council, Resolution 808 (1993), 22 February 1993, UN doc. S/RES/808 (http://www.legal-tools.org/doc/660ee3/); United Nations Security Council Resolution 827 (1993), 25 May 1993, UN doc. S/RES/827 (http://www.legal-tools.org/doc/0bff83/).

[24] United Nations, Updated Statute of the International Criminal Tribunal for the Former Yugoslavia, adopted 25 May 1993 by resolution 827 (1993), last amended 7 July 2009 by resolution 1877 (2009), Art. 7(3) ('ICTY Statute') (http://www.legal-tools.org/doc/b4f63b/).

[25] United Nations, Statute of the International Tribunal for Rwanda, adopted 8 November 1994 by resolution 955 ('ICTR Statute') (http://www.legal-tools.org/doc/8732d6/).

[26] United Nations, Statute of the Special Court for Sierra Leone by resolution 1315 (2000) of 14 August 2000 ('SCSL Statute') (http://www.legal-tools.org/doc/aa0e20/).

[27] Law on the Establishment of the Extraordinary Chambers in the Courts of Cambodia for the Prosecution of Crimes Committed during the Period of Democratic Kampuchea, with amendments as promulgated on 27 October 2004 (NS/RKM/1004/006).

[28] Rome Statute of the International Criminal Court, adopted 17 July 1998, entry into force 1 July 2002, Art. 28 ('ICC Statute') (http://www.legal-tools.org/doc/7b9af9/):

> (a) A military commander or person effectively acting as a military commander shall be criminally responsible for crimes within the jurisdiction of the Court committed by forces under his or her ef-

In practice, the most relevant precedent on command responsibility is the case of *United States of America v. Tomoyuki Yamashita* ('Yamashita case') which was heard in Manila, the Philippines by the United States Military Commission established under, and subject to, the provisions of the Pacific Regulations governing the trial of war criminals of 24 September 1945.[29] Yamashita was a lieutenant general of the Japanese army in Southeast Asia during the war. He was known as "Tiger of Malaya" since his army twice defeated the British army. On 9 October 1944 he was appointed as the commander of the Japanese army in the Philippines to defend the invasion of the US and British armies. Before his surrender on 3 September 1945 he was the commander of Japanese army and military governor in the Philippines. During his rule, hideous crimes

fective command and control, or effective authority and control as the case may be, as a result of his or her failure to exercise control properly over such forces, where:

(i) That military commander or person either knew or, owing to the circumstances at the time, should have known that the forces were committing or about to commit such crimes; and

(ii) That military commander or person failed to take all necessary and reasonable measures within his or her power to prevent or repress their commission or to submit the matter to the competent authorities for investigation and prosecution.

(b) With respect to superior and subordinate relationships not described in paragraph (a), a superior shall be criminally responsible for crimes within the jurisdiction of the Court committed by subordinates under his or her effective authority and control, as a result of his or her failure to exercise control properly over such subordinates, where:

(i) The superior either knew, or consciously disregarded information which clearly indicated, that the subordinates were committing or about to commit such crimes;

(ii) The crimes concerned activities that were within the effective responsibility and control of the superior; and

(iii) The superior failed to take all necessary and reasonable measures within his or her power to prevent or repress their commission or to submit the matter to the competent authorities for investigation and prosecution.

See also Paragraph 3 of Chapter VIII of the ECCC Statute.

[29] Trial of General Tomoyuki Yamashita, Case No. 21, vol. IV, *Law Reports of Trials of War Criminals 1, United States Military Commission, Manila, 8th October–7th December, 1945*, Published for the United Nations War Crimes Commission by His Majesty's Stationery Office, London, 1948, p. 2.

against the civilian population took place, especially during the last two weeks before Manila fell, when over 8,000 civilians were killed[30] and his subordinates raped 500 women.[31] In Batangas province, over 25,000 civilians were killed and in Laguna province almost 8,000 civilians were murdered.[32] He was charged for having "unlawfully disregarded and failed to discharge his duty as commander to control the operations of the members of his command, permitting them to commit brutal atrocities and other high crimes".[33] On 7 December 1945 the Military Commission convicted Yamashita and sentenced him to death. His defence team filed a motion for *habeas corpus* relief to the US Supreme Court. The Supreme Court denied the motion and upheld the findings of the Military Commission. On 23 February 1946 Yamashita was executed by hanging.

The Yamashita case opened a new chapter in the annals of the laws of war, by ascribing criminal liability to commanders on an individual basis.[34] The case was the only one concerning command responsibility reviewed by the US Supreme Court, which gives great precedential value to all the trials for the superior's responsibility cases after the Second World War, especially to the Okamura case heard by the Nanjing Tribunal.

In sum, the commander or superior carries two responsibilities during war. First, he should prevent or stop a criminal act that is about to be or being committed; second, he should punish the perpetrator who has committed the crimes. Failing to do so, he will take criminal responsibility. These responsibilities were detailed in the statutes of the *ad hoc* international criminal tribunals. For example, pursuant to Article 7(3) of the ICTY Statute, the principle of command responsibility consists of three elements: 1) the existence of a superior–subordinate relationship; 2) the

---

[30] William H. Parks, "Command Responsibility for War Crimes", in *Military Law Review*, 1973, vol. 62, p. 25; Weston D. Burnett, "Command Responsibility and a Case Study of the Criminal Responsibility of Israeli Military Commanders for the Pogram at Shatila and Sabra", in *Military Law Review*, 1985, vol. 107, p. 88.

[31] Richard L. Lael, *The Yamashita Precedent: War Crimes and Command Responsibility*, Rowman & Littlefield, Lanham, MD, 1982, p. 140.

[32] *Ibid.*, pp. 34–35, 140.

[33] US Supreme Court, *In re Yamashita*, 327 U.S. 1, 13–14, argued 7–8 January 1946, decided 4 February 1946); Department of Army, Pamphlet 27-161-2, International Law, vol. II, 241, 23 October 1962.

[34] JIA Bing Bing, "The Doctrine of Command Responsibility Revisited", in *Chinese Journal of International Law*, 2004, vol 3, no. 1, p. 12.

superior knew or had reason to know that the criminal act was about to be or had been committed; and 3) the superior failed to take necessary and reasonable measures to prevent the criminal act or punish the perpetrators thereof.[35]

The most crucial issue in the superior–subordinate relationship lies in whether the superior has effective control over his subordinates. In the Okamura case, with regard to the first element, a superior–subordinate relationship existed between Okamura and his subordinate troops in China. The fact that "once the Japanese government formally declared surrender, the accused immediately lay down arms, leading millions of troops to obey the order of surrender"[36] shows that Okamura had effective control and power over his subordinate troops.

As for the second element, Okamura knew or at least had reason to know the atrocities committed by the Japanese army – mentioned in the Nanjing Tribunal judgment – before and during his tenure as commander of the China Expeditionary Army. His knowledge of these atrocities is clearly shown in his memoirs[37] and in his testimony about the Nanjing Massacre in the trials of other Japanese accused. While he was questioned by the investigators, he testified about the Nanjing Massacre as follows:

> I surmised the following based on what I heard from Staff Officer Miyazaki, CCAA Special Service Department Chief Harada and Hangzhou Special Service Department Chief Hagiwara a day or two after I arrived in Shanghai. First, it is true that tens of thousands of acts of violence, such as looting and rape, took place against civilians during the assault on Nanking. Second, front-line troops indulged in the evil practice of executing POWs on the pretext of (lacking) rations.[38]

This second element is also supported by the Yamashita case which shows clearly that some degree of knowledge is required on the part of the

---

[35] ICTY Statute, Art. 7(3), see *supra* note 24. See also ICTY, *Prosecutor v. Zejnil Delalić, Zdravko Mucić, Hazim Delić and Esad Lan. žo*, Trial Chamber, Judgment, IT-96-21-T, 16 November 1998, para. 346 (http://www.legal-tools.org/doc/6b4a33/).

[36] Okamura Judgment, see *supra* note 10.

[37] Inaba Masao, 1981, p. 187, see *supra* note 2.

[38] Fujiwara Akira, "The Nanking Atrocity: An Interpretive Overview", in Bob Tadashi Wakabayashi (ed.), *The Nanking Atrocity, 1937–38: Complicating the Picture*, Berghahn Books, New York, 2008, p. 48.

superior of the crimes which are about to be committed or have already committed by his subordinates.

On the third element, Okamura failed to take necessary and reasonable measures to prevent the criminal acts or punish the perpetrators who had committed war crimes before and during his tenure. The judgment in the Okamura case does not mention any measures or steps taken by him to prevent or punish the criminal acts committed by his subordinates. Therefore, he should have been held responsible not for the crimes of his subordinates but for his failure to prevent the perpetration of the crimes of his subordinates or punish them for the crimes.[39] In other words, Okamura was guilty for "his failure to carry out his duty as a superior to exercise control".[40]

An important ground for the Nanjing Tribunal to acquit Okamura was that other Japanese commanders had already been tried and convicted for massacres in Hong Kong and Guangdong as well as in Nanjing. General Ochiai Jinkuru and the other accused had already been sentenced and convicted by the Tribunal for sporadic atrocities committed by Japanese army stationed at various locations in China. It is submitted that it does not make sense that the conviction of other commanders could be taken as an excuse to release Okamura from superior responsibility for his failure to prevent or punish the subordinates who committed crimes before his tenure and in office.

Furthermore, it should be pointed out that the Nanjing Tribunal failed to make the distinction between the responsibilities when a commander orders his subordinate to commit a crime and when he fails to prevent and punish crimes committed by his subordinates. For the former, it is one of the modes of participation of the crimes, namely planning, instigating, ordering, aiding and abetting or commission,[41] which generally

---

[39] ICTY, *Prosecutor v. Zlatko Aleksovski*, Trial Chamber, Judgment, IT-95-14/1-T, 25 June 1999, para. 67 (http://www.legal-tools.org/doc/52d982/).

[40] ICTY, *Prosecutor v. Milorad Krnojelac*, Appeal Chamber, Judgment, 17 September 2003, IT-97-25-A, para. 171 (http://www.legal-tools.org/doc/46d2e5/).

[41] Obrenović Judgment, para. 100, see *supra* note 17: "When a commander fails to ensure compliance with the principles of international humanitarian law such that he fails to prevent or punish his subordinates for the commission of crimes that he knew or had reason to know about, he will be liable pursuant to Article 7(3). When a commander orders his subordinates to commit a crime within the jurisprudence of the Tribunal, he will be held liable pursuant to Article 7(1) of the Statute".

requires the proactive action on the part of the accused. For the latter, it is the command responsibility for an omission, that is, the commander is responsible for the failure to perform an act required by international law. As an ICTY trial judgment notes:

> This omission is culpable because international law imposes an affirmative duty on superiors to prevent and punish crimes committed by their subordinates. Thus "for the acts of his subordinates" as generally referred to in the jurisprudence of the International Tribunals, it does not mean that the commander shares the same responsibility as the subordinates who committed the crimes, but rather that because of the crimes committed by his subordinates, the commander should bear responsibility for his failure to act.[42]

Therefore, although Okamura did not personally participate in all the atrocities, he should have been responsible for his failure to punish the subordinates who committed crimes under his effective control. It is a misinterpretation of the principle of superior responsibility to conclude that "he had nothing to do with all these atrocities", as the Nanjing Tribunal judgment claimed.

8.3. Superior Responsibility of a Successor Commander

In the Okamura case, the most controversial issue is whether a successor commander should be responsible for his failure in punishing his subordinates who had committed crimes before he was in office. In the judgment, the Nanjing Tribunal stated that Okamura was not guilty because "all atrocities committed by the Japanese army [...] occurred before the accused assumed his position as the supreme commander of the Japanese Expeditionary Forces in China. Therefore, the accused has nothing to do with all these atrocities".[43] Since then, the view that a successor commander is not responsible for a failure to punish his subordinates who committed crimes before his tenure has been subjected to a heated debate among judges in international tribunals.

In 2001 the Trial Chamber of the ICTY in the Kordić and Čerkez case pointed out:

---

[42] Halilović Judgment, para. 54, see *supra* note 17.

[43] Okamura Judgment, see *supra* note 10; Masao, 1981, p. 159, see *supra* note 1.

> The duty to punish naturally arises after a crime has been committed. Persons who assume command after the commission are under the same duty to punish. This duty includes at least an obligation to investigate the crimes to establish the facts and to report them to the competent authorities, if the superior does not have the power to sanction himself.[44]

However, this finding was overturned by the Appeals Chamber's majority verdict in the Hadžihasanović *et al.* case on 16 July 2003:

> Having examined the above authorities, the Appeals Chamber holds that an accused cannot be charged under Article 7(3) of the [ICTY] Statute for crimes committed by a subordinate before the said accused assumed command over that subordinate. The Appeals Chamber is aware that views on this issue may differ. However, the Appeals Chamber holds the view that this Tribunal can impose criminal responsibility only if the crime charged was clearly established under customary law at the time the events in issue occurred. In case of doubt, criminal responsibility cannot be found to exist, thereby preserving full respect for the principle of legality.[45]

In other words, the ICTY Appeals Chamber held that a superior could only incur criminal responsibility if the underlying crimes were committed at a time that the superior had effective control over the perpetrators.[46] Consequently, according to the Appeals Chamber's majority reasoning, a superior has no duty to punish subordinates for crimes that they committed before he assumed command, even if he has knowledge of them and has effective control over them when he took office. Two judges on that bench, Judge David Hunt and Judge Shahabuddeen, appended partially dissenting opinions. Judge Hunt considered that the situation at issue reasonably fell within the customary law principle of command responsibility, even though state practice was silent on this issue.[47] Judge Sha-

---

[44] ICTY, *Prosecutor v. Dario Kordić and Mario Čerkez*, Trial Chamber, Judgment, IT-95-14/2-T, 26 February 2001, para. 446 (http://www.legal-tools.org/doc/d4fedd/).

[45] Hadžihasanović Appeal Decision, para. 51, see *supra* note 18.

[46] *Ibid.*

[47] ICTY, *Prosecutor v. Enver Hadžihasanović, Mehmed Alagić and Amir Kubura*, Appeals Chamber, Separate and Partial Dissenting Opinion of Judge David Hunt, IT-01-47, 16 July

habuddeen held that: "A codification does not necessarily exhaust the principle of customary international law sought to be codified. The fullness of the principle, with its ordinary implications, can continue notwithstanding any narrower scope suggested by the codification".[48]

It is submitted that the plain and ordinary meaning of Article 7(3) of the ICTY Statute does not distinguish between crimes committed before and after the assumption of duties, so that a commander exercising effective control with the requisite knowledge can indeed be held liable solely for failing to punish his subordinates for crimes they committed before he assumed office.[49] The restrictive view of the Appeals Chamber to a certain extent defeats the objective of international humanitarian law and may have far-reaching consequences. It sends the signal that commanders are allowed to escape their responsibility to punish their subordinates for crimes committed before they assumed office. This does indeed create what Judge Hunt referred to as a "gaping hole".[50]

Further, in the Naser Orić case, in discussing whether Orić had a duty to punish crimes committed before he had effective control, the Trial Chamber followed the decision in Hadžihasanović et al. case, declaring in its judgment on 30 June 2006 that the defendant was not found responsible for the crimes perpetrated before he assumed his role as commander, because he was not found to have had effective control over the military police when the crimes were happening or had just occurred.[51]

Although the Trial Chambers, which, according to the jurisprudence of the ICTY, are bound to follow the decisions of the Appeals Chamber, have correctly respected the decision, they have nonetheless

---

2003, para. 8 ('Hadžihasanović Hunt Dissenting Opinion') (http://www.legal-tools.org/doc/876089/).

[48] ICTY, *Prosecutor v. Enver Hadžihasanović, Mehmed Alagić and Amir Kubura,* Appeal Chamber, Partial Dissenting Opinion of Judge Shahabuddeen, IT-01-47, 16 July 2003, para. 39 ('Hadžihasanović Shahabuddeen Dissenting Opinion') (http://www.legal-tools.org/doc/c348f4/).

[49] This approach is consistent with Article 31(1) of the Vienna Convention on the Law of Treaties which provides that, "a treaty shall be interpreted in good faith in accordance with the ordinary meaning to be given to the terms of the treaty in their context and in light of its object and purpose".

[50] Hadžihasanović Hunt Dissenting Opinion, para. 22, see *supra* note 47.

[51] ICTY, *Prosecution v. Naser Orić,* Trial Chamber, Judgment, 30 June 2006, IT-03-68-T, para. 708 ('Orić Trial Judgment') (http://www.legal-tools.org/doc/37564c/).

repeatedly expressed their dissatisfaction and frustration with this legal issue in the Hadžihasanović *et al.* case. For example, in the judgment of Hadžihasanović *et al.*, the Trial Chamber quite subtly considered that "the reasons given by the dissenting Judges merit further examination", supporting the pragmatic consideration set out by Judge Shahabuddeen in his dissenting opinion.[52] In the Orić case, the Trial Chamber explained in its judgment:

> A superior's duty to punish is not derived from a failure to prevent the crime, but rather is a subsidiary duty of its own. The cohesive interlinking of preventing and punishing would be disrupted if the latter were made dependent on the superior's control at the time of commission of the crimes. *Consequently, for a superior's duty to punish, it should be immaterial whether he or she had assumed control over the relevant subordinates prior to their committing the crime.* Since the Appeals Chamber, however, has taken a different view in the Hadžihasanović et al. Appeals Chamber Decision for reasons which will not be questioned here, the Trial Chamber finds itself bound to require that with regard to the duty to punish, the superior must have had control over the perpetrators of a relevant crime both at the time of its commission and at the time that measures to punish were to be taken.[53]

And again, the Appeals Chamber approved the view of the Trial Chamber in the Orić case, stating:

> The Appeals Chamber recalls that the *ratio decidendi* of its decisions is binding on Trial Chambers. Therefore, the Trial Chamber was correct in considering that it was bound to follow the precedent established by the Appeals Chamber in its decision of 2003 in the Hadžihasanović case.[54]

However, two more judges in the Appeals Chamber presented their dissenting opinions, disagreeing with the Hadžihasanović *et al.* Appeal decision on jurisdiction in this respect.

---

[52] ICTY, *Prosecutor v. Enver Hadžihasanović, Mehmed Alagić and Amir Kubura*, Trial Chamber, Judgment, IT-01-47-T, 15 March 2006, para. 199 (http://www.legal-tools.org/doc/8f515a/).

[53] Orić Trial Judgment, para. 335, see *supra* note 51. Emphasis added.

[54] ICTY, *Prosecution v. Naser Orić*, Appeals Chamber, Judgment Summary, IT-03-68, 3 July 2008, para.10 (http://www.legal-tools.org/doc/44a6f1/).

The author fully agrees with the views as well as the thorough and exhaustive analysis by at least four judges in the Appeals Chamber[55] that a commander should be held responsible for his/her failure to punish subordinates' commission of crimes committed prior to his/her assumption of command over the subordinates.

First, when a commander assumes his duties, he does not only take over the rights and privileges of his predecessor but also inherits his duties or obligations. A commander who possesses effective control over the actions of his subordinates, having the requisite knowledge, is duty bound to ensure that they act within the dictates of international humanitarian law and that the laws and customs of war are therefore respected. There is thus no justification for the distinction made before and after assumption of office by a commander. "What matters in this case is perhaps the point in time when the commander gained the knowledge of the subordinate crimes, not the one when he took up the post of command or established effective control".[56] There need not be a temporal concurrence between the commission of the crime forming the basis of the charge and the existence of the superior–subordinate relationship between the accused and physical perpetrator. Instead, such concurrence should be between the time at which the commander exercised effective control over the perpetrator and the time at which the commander is said to have failed to exercise his powers to punish.

Second, there are indications that support the existence of a customary rule establishing criminal responsibility of commanders for crimes committed by a subordinate prior to the commander's assumption of command over that subordinate.[57] Such indications stem, on the one hand, from a plain reading of the relevant provisions of the Chinese Nationalist government's Law Governing the Trial of War Criminals, Additional Protocol I, the ICTY and ICTR Statutes and, on the other hand, from an analysis of the objects and purpose of command responsibility. As worded, all these provisions concerned, including Article 6(3) of the ICTY Statute – which covers situations where the subordinate "was about to commit" any

---

[55] Judges Hunt, Shahabuddeen, LIU and Schomburg.

[56] JIA, 2004, p. 37, see *supra* note 34.

[57] ICTY, *Prosecutor v. Naser Orić*, Appeals Chamber, Judgment, Partially Dissenting Opinion and Declaration of Judge LIU, IT-03-68-A, 3 July 2008, paras. 29–32 ('Orić LIU Dissenting Opinion') (http://www.legal-tools.org/doc/e053a4/).

of the acts referred to in Articles 2 to 4 of the Statute or "had done so" – do not distinguish between crimes committed before and after the assumption of duties.[58] It is further noted that superior responsibility is meant to ensure that commanders comply with the laws and customs of war and international humanitarian law generally.[59] In this respect, the principle of superior responsibility may be seen to arise from one of the basic principles of international humanitarian law aiming to secure protected categories of persons and objects during armed conflicts.[60] By allowing commanders to escape their responsibility to punish their subordinates for crimes they committed before they assumed office, the Hadžihasanović *et al.* decisioncase creates a "gaping hole" in the protection provided by international humanitarian law.[61]

Third, the potential impact of the Hadžihasanović *et al.* decision's approach on the effective respect of international humanitarian law by military subordinates is more striking. In the event that the previous superior cannot himself be prosecuted, the criminal conduct of the subordinates would remain unpunished. Such absence of sanction would undoubtedly create a climate of impunity, which, in turn, would enable the unpunished subordinates to further their criminal conduct.

Fourth, provided that the basic requirements of command responsibility are established, more particularly the effective control and the knowledge requirements, it is submitted that a commander should be held responsible for his/her failure to punish subordinates' commission of crimes prior to his/her assumption of command over the subordinates. Therefore it is not necessary that a temporal concurrence existed between the commission of the crime forming the basis of the charge and the superior–subordinate relationship between the commander and the physical

---

[58] *Ibid.*, para. 29.

[59] ICTY, *Prosecutor v. Enver Hadžihasanović, Mehmed Alagić and Amir Kubura*, Appeals Chamber, Partially Dissenting Opinion and Declaration of Judge LIU, IT-01-47-T, 16 July 2003, para. 29; Hadžihasanović Shahabuddeen Dissenting Opinion, para. 39, see *supra* note 48; Hadžihasanović Hunt Dissenting Opinion, para. 40, see *supra* note 47.

[60] Halilović Judgment, para. 55, see *supra* note 17; Obrenović Judgment, para. 100, see *supra* note 17.

[61] Hadžihasanović Hunt Dissenting Opinion, para. 22, see *supra* note 47. As noted, the case against Okamura resulted in such a "gaping hole". See Philip R. Piccigallo, *The Japanese on Trial: Allied War Crimes Operations in the East, 1945–1951*, University of Texas Press, Austin, 1979, pp. 166–67.

perpetrator. In order for liability to arise, such concurrence must be between the time at which the immediate successor exercised effective control over the perpetrator and the time at which the successor is considered to have failed to exercise his/her powers to punish. By saying so, it does not mean that superior responsibility is a lasting liability; therefore President Barack Obama should not be held responsible for slavery two centuries ago. At least, the immediate superior or the commander assuming office before the end of a war should take effective measure to address the atrocities committed by his subordinates before he was in the office. Superiors cannot take advantage of a change of command to escape their duty to punish. As explained above, the restrictive approach adopted in the Hadžihasanović *et al.* Appeals Chamber may very well defeat the objective of command responsibility and may have far-reaching consequences on international humanitarian law.

Fifth, the function and nature of command responsibility does not support a distinction before and after a commander assumes effective control. The jurisprudence has recognised that causation is not a *conditio sine qua non* for the imposition of criminal liability on superiors for their failure to prevent or punish offences committed by their subordinates.[62] It has been held that requiring a causal link

> would change the basis of command responsibility for failure to prevent or punish to the extent that it would practically require the involvement on the part of the commander in the crime his subordinates committed, thus altering the very nature of the liability imposed under Article 7(3).[63]

Thus, if it is not necessary that the commander's failure to act caused the commission of the crime, and the essence of the commander's responsibility is his failure to punish under the second element of Article 7(3), there clearly is no basis for the distinction advocated by the Appeals Chamber in Hadžihasanović *et al.* Therefore, a plain reading of the ICTY Statute and an analysis of the objects and purpose of Article 7(3) responsibility shows that a commander can be held responsible for failing to punish crimes committed before he assumes effective control.[64]

---

[62] ICTY, *Prosecutor v. Tihomir Blaškić*, Appeals Chamber, Judgment, IT-95-14-A, 29 July 2004, para. 77.

[63] Halilović Judgment, para. 78, see *supra* note 17.

[64] Orić LIU Dissenting Opinion, para. 32, see *supra* note 57.

The conclusion to be drawn is that Okamura should have been held responsible for his failure to punish the crimes committed by his subordinates prior to his assumption of command. The failure to convict and the unsatisfactory judgment at the Nanjing Tribunal may constitute one of the reasons for disputes in contemporary Sino–Japanese relations.

The Fall of the Tigers of Hong Kong: Chinese War Crimes Trials of Three Japanese Governors of Hong Kong

ZHANG Tianshu[*]

9.1. Introduction

The day that the Imperial Japanese Navy launched a surprise military strike against the US naval base at Pearl Harbor, 8 December 1941, coincided with the day that Japanese units of the 23rd Army's 38th Division attacked Hong Kong.[1] Although under British administration, Hong Kong had been affected by Japanese aggression in China throughout the 1930s, particularly because it was a major supply channel for international goods destined for China.[2] It took a mere 18 days for Japan to defeat the British. On Christmas Day 1941 the British forces surrendered and Japan began its occupation of Hong Kong, which lasted for three years and eight months.[3] Winston Churchill described the collapse of the resistance in Hong Kong as one of "the worst things that happened".[4]

---

[*] **ZHANG Tianshu** is an LL.M. student at the University of Cambridge, UK. She graduated from China University of Political Science and Law (LL.M. specialising in International Law) and Wuhan University (LL.B.). She has interned at the Office of the Prosecutor at International Criminal Court with respect to the investigation of the situations of Darfur and Libya. She has published articles concerning international criminal law, international humanitarian law and international cyber law in Chinese and English.

[1] Ashley Jackson, *The British Empire and the Second World War*, Hambledon Continuum, London, 2006, p. 456.

[2] *Ibid.*, p. 453.

[3] Chi-Kwan Mark, *Hong Kong and the Cold War: Anglo-American Relations, 1949–1957*, Clarendon Press, Oxford, 2004, p. 14.

[4] Andrew Stewart, *Empire Lost: Britain, the Dominions and the Second World War*, Continuum, London, 2008, p. 90.

During the occupation, the governor general of Hong Kong served as the chief of the Japanese military administration in the occupied territory.[5] Lieutenant General Sakai Takashi,[6] who led the Japanese forces that invaded Hong Kong,[7] was the first governor general until 20 February 1942. After Sakai, Isogai Rensuke was appointed as the second governor general at the recommendation of the Japanese prime minister Tōjō Hideki.[8] Isogai retired from the post and returned to Japan in December 1944.[9] Subsequently, Tanaka Hisakazu served as the last Japanese governor general of Hong Kong from 16 December 1944 to the end of the war.[10]

When the war ended, a large number of war crimes prosecutions were conducted against Japanese perpetrators in Hong Kong, as part of war crimes trials promised by the Allied powers.[11] However, the three governors of Hong Kong were not among the 123 accused standing before British military courts in Hong Kong. Sakai, Isogai and Tanaka were sent to China after the war and convicted by Chinese military tribunals. Eventually, Sakai and Tanaka were condemned to death, while Isogai was sentenced to life imprisonment.

Although a more precise description of Hong Kong's history and the Chinese legal system seems necessary, it is not the purpose of this chapter to go through the details of all the Chinese trials. Rather, this chapter intends to critically review the trials of the three governors in order to observe how international law was involved before and during the court proceedings. The discussion is organised in three parts. First, it outlines how the Chinese war crimes tribunals were established and what

---

5   Yuma Totani, "The Prisoner of War Camp Trials", in Suzannah Linton (ed.), *Hong Kong's War Crimes Trials*, Oxford University Press, Oxford, 2013, p. 78.

6   For clarification, Japanese names, as well as Chinese names, of individuals mentioned in this chapter follow the format used by Hong Kong military courts and Chinese military tribunals, namely, surname first, personal name second. For example, Sakai Takashi refers to 酒井隆, in which 酒井 refers to Sakai as his family name, while 隆 refers to his personal name.

7   Philip Snow, *The Fall of Hong Kong: Britain, China and the Japanese Occupation*, Yale University Press, New Haven, 2003, p. 39.

8   *Ibid.*, p. 92.

9   *Ibid.*, p. 210.

10   *Ibid.*, pp. 210, 255, 305.

11   Suzannah Linton, "Introduction", in Suzannah Linton (ed.), *Hong Kong's War Crimes Trials*, Oxford University Press, Oxford, 2013, p. 1.

---

kind of legal sources were used in the trials. Second, it describes in detail the cases against Sakai, Isogai and Tanaka. Third, it discusses the distinct features of these trials from a contemporary international law perspective. In the conclusion, the chapter reiterates the need for a clearly articulated elaboration of the Chinese national trials against war criminals in the context of Second World War and international criminal adjudication.

9.2. An Overview of the Chinese War Crimes Trials

Before examining the cases, one question has to be answered: why did the British authorities agree to transfer the three governors of Hong Kong – who planned, ordered and committed atrocities – to the Chinese authorities to stand trial? As a British colony it would have been understandable if the British seized and tried them. The answer turns out to be relatively simple. Sakai retired after Japan established its occupation of Hong Kong and returned to Japan. The same situation applied to Isogai who had stepped down from his position as governor general on 24 December 1944. They were seized and transferred to China by the Supreme Commander for the Allied Powers ('SCAP'). The case of Tanaka is slightly different. Initially, a United States ('US') military commission in Shanghai tried him for his role in the extrajudicial execution of an American prisoner of war. However, the confirming authority disapproved his death sentence. The US authorities then turned Tanaka over to the Chinese military tribunal in Guangzhou for war crimes in connection with his command responsibility in China. Since both international law and domestic law are involved in these trials, it is necessary to take a closer look at the legal regime for the Chinese war crimes trials.

9.2.1. The Establishment of Chinese War Crimes Tribunals

9.2.1.1. Institutional Preparation

In June 1943 the Chinese authorities decided formally to set up a special commission for investigating all offences perpetrated on Chinese soil and the Rules of Establishment of an Investigation Commission on Crimes of the Enemy were drafted and enacted in late June 1943.[12] On 23 February

---

[12] HU Jurong, *Zhongwai Junshi Fating Shenpan Riben Zhanfan: Guanyu Nanjing Da Tusha* [Trials of Japanese War Criminals in Chinese and Foreign Military Tribunals: About the Nanjing Massacre], Nankai University Press, Tianjin, 1988, p. 110.

1944 a War Crimes Commission was officially established in Chongqing (Chungking) with a mandate to investigate all crimes perpetrated in China or against Chinese people in relation to the violation of the laws and customs of war, including:

1) Murder and massacres – systematic terrorism;

2) Rape or abduction of women for the purposes of enforced prostitution;

3) Forced labour of civilians in connection with the military operations of the enemy;

4) Pillage;

5) Imposition of collective penalties;

6) Deliberate bombardment of undefended places or other non-military objects;

7) Attacks of merchant ships without warning;

8) Deliberate bombardment of hospitals or other charitable, educational, and cultural buildings and monuments;

9) Breach of rules relating to the Red Cross;

10) Use of deleterious and asphyxiating gases;

11) Killing prisoners of war and wounded;

12) Producing, selling, transporting narcotic drugs, forced planting poppies, or opening opium dens providing narcotic drugs;

13) Illegal construction in occupied territory, and other acts of violations of the laws and customs of war.[13]

After Japan's surrender in August 1945 a special investigation commission for crimes committed in Nanjing was founded on 7 November 1945.[14] On 6 December 1945 the Chinese War Criminals Commission was established in Chongqing for handling issues of Japanese war criminals. It was not only municipal departments that participated in the preparation of war crimes trials. The Far Eastern Sub-Commission of the United Nations War Crimes Commission ('Sub-Commission'), an international body, was also engaged. Although the Sub-Commission was created to assist the function of the main Commission in London, it was not incorpo-

---

13   *Ibid.*, p. 111.

14   *Ibid.*, p. 112.

rated into the municipal law of China, but was a truly international body not subject to any specific municipal legal order.[15]

Various departments co-operated jointly in the preparation of trials and prosecution of Japanese war criminals: the Ministry of War issued warrants to arrest suspects and tackled general assignments; the Ministry of Justice embarked on investigating and drafting a war criminals list; the Department of Martial Law of the General Staff monitored war crimes trial proceedings and executions; the Ministry of Foreign Affairs handled the extradition of the accused from other countries, translated war criminals lists and submitted them to the Sub-Commission for final review.[16]

On 28 February 1946 the Military Affairs Commission reported to the Supreme National Defence Council the completion of the Japanese surrender in conflicts zones, and simultaneously handed in drafts of three legal documents with regard to war crimes prosecution.[17]

9.2.1.2. Legal Basis

On 12 August 1945 the Supreme National Defence Council of the Republic of China, as the highest military authority, declared its opinion that the basic principles for dealing with Japanese war criminals should be in accordance with the Potsdam Declaration and the principles jointly decided by the Allies powers.[18] The Potsdam Declaration laid a solid foundation for the legitimacy of the Chinese trials.[19] Article 10 of the declaration expressed that "stern justice shall be meted out to all war criminals, including those who have visited cruelties upon our prisoners".[20] As a living

---

15 United Nations War Crimes Commission ('UNWCC'), *History of the United Nations War Crimes Commission and the Development of the Laws of War*, His Majesty's Stationery Office, London, 1948, pp. 127–29.

16 *Ibid.*, p. 131; HU, 1988, pp. 112–13, see *supra* note 12.

17 QIN Xiaoyi, *Zhonghua Minguo Zhongyao Shiliao Chubian-Duiri Kangzhan Shiqi* [Important Documents Collection of the History of the Chinese Nationalist Party: Anti-Japanese War], vol. 2(4), Central Committee of Chinese Nationalist Party, Beijing, 1981, p. 397.

18 *Ibid.*, pp. 637–40.

19 LONG Xingang and SUN Jun, "1956 nian tebie junshi fating Shenyang Taiyuan shenpan yanjiu" [On the Special Military Tribunals Trials of Shenyang and Taiyuan in 1956], in *Literature on Party Building*, 2009, vol. 2, p. 10.

20 Proclamation Defining Terms for Japanese Surrender, Potsdam, 26 July 1945, Art. 10 (http://www.legal-tools.org/doc/f8cae3/).

demonstration of the declaration intent, the establishment of the International Military Tribunal for the Far East ('IMTFE') in Tokyo added more credence to the Chinese national war crimes trials.[21] Article 3 of the Special Proclamation for Establishment of an International Military Tribunal for the Far East pointed out: "Nothing in this Order shall prejudice the jurisdiction of any other international, national or occupation court, commission or other tribunal established or to be established in Japan or in any territory of a United Nation with which Japan has been at war, for the trial of war criminals". Correspondingly, every victim state that suffered from Japan's invasion and acts of violence was at least entitled to exercise jurisdiction over war criminals who had participated in the atrocities.

As noted, China built up the War Criminals Commission to formulate policies for war crimes trials, conduct investigations, arrests and extradition of war criminals, and monitor the proceedings of military tribunals in general.[22] In February 1946 the Supreme National Defence Council promulgated a War Criminal Process Regulation, Rules Governing the Trial of War Criminals[23] and Detailed Rules.[24] With more comprehensive and specific provisions, the Law Governing the Trial of War Criminals ('Law of War Crimes Trials') replaced Rules Governing the Trial of War Criminals on 24 October 1946.

While the IMTFE mainly focused on the prosecution of Japanese war criminals who perpetrated crimes against peace (class A) in the Asia-Pacific theatre of war,[25] the Chinese government was determined to target principally those who committed conventional war crimes (class B) and crimes against humanity (class C) on the territory of China. The accused detainees were placed in 10 separate war criminal detention facilities run

---

[21] WENG Youli, "Guomindang zhengfu, chuzhi Riben zhanfan shuping" [Comments on the National Government's Disposal of Japanese War Criminals], in *Journal of Southwest China Normal University (Philosophy & Social Sciences Edition)*, 1998, vol. 6, p. 112.

[22] HU, 1988, p. 112, see *supra* note 12.

[23] This chapter follows the translation of the related Chinese law provided by the UNWCC *Law Reports*. Thus, "Rules Governing the Trial of War Criminals" refers to "战争罪犯审判办法"; see UNWCC, *Law Reports of Trials of War Criminals*, vol. 14, His Majesty's Stationery Office, London, 1949, p. 3.

[24] REN Xiaoguang, *Zhonghua Minguo Shi* [History of the Republic of China], vol. 11, Zhonghua Book Company, Beijing, 2011, p. 232.

[25] International Military Tribunal for the Far East ('IMTFE'), *Araki et al.*, Indictment, 11 December 1948 (http://www.legal-tools.org/doc/58d995/).

by the Ministry of National Defence. According to the War Crimes Trials Procedure and its annexes, the military tribunals were independently located in Beijing, Nanjing, Shanghai, Hankou, Guangzhou, Taiyuan, Xuzhou, Jinan, Taipei and Shenyang.[26]

9.2.2. The Sources of Law

Given that neither precedent nor municipal law could be relied on to support the war crimes trials, the Supreme National Defence Council promulgated three pieces of war crimes legislation on 28 February of 1946: the War Criminal Process Regulation; the Rules Governing the Trial of War Criminals ('Rules of War Crimes Trials'); and the Detailed Rules of Rules Governing the Trial of War Criminals ('Detailed Rules').[27] These three legal instruments were the first batch of rules governing war crimes processes in China. Nevertheless, it must be pointed out that none of them crystallised laws and rules applicable to the court proceedings. Eventually, the Law Governing the Trial of War Criminals replaced these three laws.[28]

9.2.2.1. War Criminals Process Regulation

The War Criminals Process Regulation contains 15 articles with regard to the surrender, arrest, detention and execution of Japanese war criminals. According to Article 1, the Ministry of War handles the arrest of war criminals after the armies were disarmed. Articles 4 to 9 divide war criminals into three groups based on which authorities' control they were subjected to. For instance, Article 5 governs war criminals under the Japanese authorities' control. In this case, the War Crimes Commission should notify the Ministry of Foreign Affairs in writing; the Ministry of Foreign Affairs should then without delay present a note to the government of the United States, requesting the latter to transmit the note to the SCAP in Japan. After arresting the listed war criminals, the SCAP should extradite

---

[26] REN, 2011, p. 233, see *supra* note 24; HU, 1988, p. 129, see *supra* note 12.

[27] QIN, 1981, p. 397, see *supra* note 17.

[28] *Ibid.*, p. 408. United Nations War Crimes Commission ('UNWCC'), Chinese War Crimes Legislation: Law Governing the Trial of War Criminals, Misc. No. 120, 24 October 1946 ('Law of War Crimes Trials') (http://www.legal-tools.org/doc/74c87e/).

them to China.[29] This article played a vital role in extraditing Isogai who had been arrested in Tokyo by the SCAP and was sent back to China.[30]

9.2.2.2. Rules Governing the Trial of War Criminals and the Detailed Rules

The Rules Governing the War Crimes Trials embody 10 articles, structuring a framework for applying international law and municipal law together in war crimes trials. Article 1 defines the scope of the accused, which refers to the Japanese war criminals except for those who would be subjected to special military tribunals established by the Allied powers. It also sets the tone for applicable laws: "In addition to the present Rules, the Trials Procedure of the Army, Navy and Air Force and the Chinese Penal Code should apply". In the Rules, Article 8 provides that the tribunals should apply public international law, international customs, the Criminal Law of the Army, Navy and Air Force, other special criminal laws and the Chinese Penal Code. Although Article 8 does not explicitly reveal the hierarchy of the above laws, it can be plainly seen from the sequence that international law takes precedence over municipal law in these Rules. More than that, Article 8 also reflects the principle of *lex specialis derogat legi generali*.[31]

The later Detailed Rules are composed of 16 articles in furtherance of implementing the Rules. They set out procedures of recommendation and appointment of judges and prosecutors for each military tribunal; specify the composition of tribunals and their competence; empower the tribunal and its agencies with the right to search; and guarantee the rights of defendants and a public hearing.[32] However, the Detailed Rules again leave no interpretation of "public international law" or "international customs" referred to in Article 8 of the Rules. The vacuum in applicable laws in the three war crimes provisions awaited comprehensive and accurate clarification.

---

[29] QIN, 1981, p. 398, see *supra* note 17.

[30] Snow, 2003, p. 305, see *supra* note 7.

[31] QIN, 1981, p. 399, see *supra* note 17.

[32] *Ibid.*, pp. 400–1; SONG Zhiyong, "Chinese Foreign Policy Towards Japan and the Trial of Japanese War Criminals in the Years Immediately after the Second World War", in *Nankai Journal*, 2001, vol. 4, p. 44.

9.2.2.3. Law Governing the Trials of War Criminals

On 26 August 1946 a draft amendment to the Rules of War Crimes Trials with 40 Articles was submitted to the Supreme National Defence Council, addressing the concern about the absence of "appropriate standards for conviction and sentence measures".[33] With slight modification, the final text was named the Law Governing the Trial of War Criminals and announced on 23 October 1946.[34] The law encompasses 35 articles and is regarded in many aspects as guided by circumstances peculiar to China.

9.2.2.3.1. Jurisdiction and Applicable Laws

The Law of War Crimes Trials delineates the extent and scope of jurisdiction, which had not been regulated in the previous three war crimes provisions. Article 4 articulates temporal jurisdiction whereby the tribunals should only exercise jurisdiction over offences under Article 2, which took place after 18 September 1931 and before 2 September 1945. However, crimes under Article 2(1) and (3) constitute exceptions: these crimes, even if committed before 18 September 1931, still fall within the jurisdiction of the tribunals. The second sentence of Article 4 further points out that the statute of limitations provided by Article 80 of the Chinese Criminal Law does not apply to the cases of war criminals. As to personal jurisdiction, Article 5 elucidates the present law does not apply to offences committed after September 1945 by alien soldiers. Instead, these perpetrators should be subject to the Chinese Criminal Law by ordinary military tribunals.[35]

Article 1 identifies the extent and scope of the applicable laws:

> In addition to the Rules of International Law, the present Law is applicable to the trials and punishment of War Criminals. Cases not provided for under the Law of War Crimes Trials are governed by the Criminal Code of the Republic of China.
>
> In applying Criminal Law of the Republic of China, the present Law shall first be applied, irrespective of the status of the offender.[36]

---

[33] QIN, 1981, p. 408, see *supra* note 17.

[34] SONG, 2001, p. 45, see *supra* note 32.

[35] UNWCC, vol. 14, 1949, p. 156, see *supra* note 23.

[36] *Ibid.*, p. 152.

In particular, Article 1 not only reflects the principle of *lex specialis* but also rules out the application of the Criminal Law of Army, Navy and Air Force. Some commentators argue that this implicit exclusion of martial law can be interpreted as mirroring the lenient policy adopted by the Nationalist government.[37]

9.2.2.3.2. Definition of War Criminals

It is undisputable that the identification and clarification of war criminals are critical for war crimes trials. Article 2 gives a clear definition of war criminals and divides them into four groups:

1. Alien combatants or non-combatants who, prior to or during the war, violated an International Treaty, International Convention or International Guarantee by planning, conspiring for, perpetrating to start or supporting, an aggression against the Republic of China, or doing the same in an unlawful war.

2. Alien combatants or non-combatants who during the war or a period of hostilities against the Republic of China violate the Laws and Customs of War by having recourse to acts of cruelty directly or indirectly.

3. Alien combatants or non-combatants who during the war or a period of hostilities against the Republic of China or prior to the occurrence of such circumstances, nourish intentions of slaving, crippling, or annihilating the Chinese Nation and endeavour to carry out their intention by such methods as *(a)* killing, starving, massacring, enslaving, or mass deportation of its nationals, *(b)* stupefying the mind and controlling the thoughts of its nationals, *(c)* distributing, spreading, or forcing people to consume narcotic drugs or forcing them to cultivate plants for making such drugs, *(d)* forcing people to consume or being inoculated with poisons, or destroying their power of procreation, or oppressing and tyrannising them under racial or religious pretext, or treating them inhumanly.

4. Alien combatants or non-combatants who during the war with or a period of hostilities against the Republic of China, commits acts other than those mentioned in the

---

[37] QIN, 1981, p. 393, see *supra* note 17.

three previous sections but punishable according to Chinese Criminal Law.[38]

The definitions of the first three groups of war criminals echo three types of crimes under the Charter of the International Military Tribunal at Nuremberg ('IMT Charter'), the IMTFE Charter and Law No. 10 of the Allied Control Council for Germany ('Control Council Law No. 10'). Paragraph 1 of Article 2 covers the range of crimes against peace as manifested in Article 6(a) of the IMT Charter, Article 5(a) of the IMTFE Charter and Article II(1)(a) of Control Council Law No. 10; paragraph 2 covers the fields of war crimes as elaborated in Article 6(b) of the ITM Charter, Article 5(b) of the IMTFE Charter and Article II(1)(b) of Control Council Law No. 10; and paragraph 3 indicates crimes against humanity as incorporated in Article 6(c) of the IMT Charter, Article 5(c) of the IMTFE Charter and Article II(1)(c) of Control Council Law No. 10.

A significant feature of the Chinese definition of war criminals for crimes against humanity underlines the punishments on crimes in relation to narcotic drugs, opium and poison. Another emphasis is that the Law of War Crimes Trials criminalises "stupefying the mind and controlling the thought of the Chinese population".[39] This form of crime seems a departure from the recognised crimes against humanity, including psychological means of action.[40]

As Article 2 provides a practical scope of crimes for prosecution, it enhances the accuracy of establishing the accountability of the accused.

9.2.2.3.3. List of War Crimes

The amendment draft submitted on 26 August 1946 confuses the definition of war crimes with crimes against humanity. Article 3 of the draft affords the similar characterisation of war criminals as the later Law of War Crimes Trials. However, Article 4 of the draft articulates a list of offences that share almost identical descriptions of the third category of crimes, namely crimes against humanity.[41] In contrast to the draft, Article 3 of the final version of the Law of War Crimes Trials categorises the list

---

38 *Ibid.*, p. 409. The translation of the Law of War Crimes Trials is based on UNWCC, 1949, vol. 14, pp. 152–53, see *supra* note 23.

39 UNWCC, vol. 14, 1949, p. 153, see *supra* note 23.

40 *Ibid.*, p. 155.

41 QIN, 1981, p. 409, see *supra* note 17.

of crimes into the field of war crimes.[42] The description of war crimes under Article 3 is similar to that which was drawn up by the 1919 Commission on the Responsibility of the Authors of the War and on Enforcement of Penalties.[43] But it should be underscored that the list is in many respects wider than the 1919 list. The list given in Article 4 of the Law of War Crimes Trials is as follows:

1. Planned massacre, murder or other terrorist action;
2. Killing hostages;
3. Malicious killing of non-combatants;
4. Rape;[44]
5. Kidnapping children;
6. Imposition of collective penalties;
7. Deliberate bombardment of undefended places;
8. Destruction of merchant ships and passenger vessels without warning and without provision for the safety of passengers and crew;
9. Destruction of fishing boats and of relief ships;
10. Deliberate bombing of hospitals;
11. Attack or sinking of hospital ships;
12. Use of poison gas or bacteriological warfare;
13. Employment of inhuman weapons;
14. Directions to give no quarter;
15. Putting poison on food or drinking water;
16. Torture of non-combatants;
17. Kidnapping females and forcing them to become prostitutes;
18. Mass deportation of non-combatants;
19. Internment of non-combatants and inflicting on them inhuman treatment;

---

[42] Law of War Crimes Trials, see *supra* note 28.

[43] UNWCC, vol. 14, 1949, p. 153, see *supra* note 23.

[44] It is interesting to find that the crime of rape is missing in the draft but confirmed in the final version of Law of War Crimes Trials. QIN, 1981, p. 409, see *supra* note 17; Law of War Crimes Trials, see *supra* note 28.

---

20. Forcing non-combatants to engage in military activities with the enemy;

21. Usurpation of sovereignty of the occupied territory;

22. Conscription by force of inhabitants in the occupied territory;

23. Scheming to enslave the inhabitants of the occupied country or to deprive them of their status and rights as nationals of the occupied country;

24. Pillage;

25. Unlawful extortion or demanding of contributions or requisitions;

26. Depreciating the value of currency or issuing unlawful currency notes;

27. Indiscriminate destruction of property;

28. Violating other rules relating to the Red Cross;

29. Ill-treating prisoners of war or wounded persons;

30. Forcing prisoners of war to engage in work not allowed by International Conventions;

31. Indiscriminate use of the Armistice Flags;

32. Making indiscriminate mass arrest;

33. Confiscation of property;

34. Destroying religious, charity, educational, historical constructions or memorials;

35. Malicious insults;

36. Taking money or property by force or extortion;

37. Plundering of historical, artistic or other cultural treasures;

38. Other acts violating the laws and customs of war, or acts the cruelty or destructiveness of which exceed their military necessity, forcing people to do things beyond their obligation, or acts hampering the exercise of legal rights.

9.2.2.3.4. Sentence and Review Mechanism

Article 10 of the Law of War Crimes Trials prescribes punishments according to types of crimes under Article 2, specifying that the death penal-ity or life imprisonment will be imposed on "war criminals that are guilty of offences provided against under paragraph 1 and paragraph 3 of Article 2". The offences mentioned in this provision refer to crimes against peace and crimes against humanity contained in the first and third categories of the definitions of war criminals under Article 2 of the Law of War Crimes Trials. For these two categories of crimes, the punishment is limited to either death or life imprisonment.

As for war crimes offenders, punishments are more complicated. Article 11 prescribes penalties for war crimes in a narrower sense.[45] Penalties are set out on the basis of list of war crimes provided in Article 3:

(a) The penalties for offences provided against under items 1-15 of Art. III are death or life imprisonment;

(b) The penalties for offences provided against under items 16-24 of Art. III are, alternatively, death, life imprisonment, or imprisonment for a period of 10 years;

(c) Offences provided against under items 25-37 of Art. III are punishable for life imprisonment or imprisonment for not less than 7 years;

(d) Offences provided against under item 38 of Art. III are punishable by life imprisonment or imprisonment for not less than 7 years, with the proviso that offences of a more serious nature are punishable by death.[46]

Much as no appeal procedure is granted in the Law of War Crimes Trials, a review mechanism is set up to make sure that justice would be served properly. According to Article 31, if a trial reaches a verdict of not guilty, or if the prosecutor deems a prosecution unnecessary or unwarranted, the case shall be submitted to the Ministry of National Defence for confirmation. In case of doubt, the Ministry of National Defence may refer it back for retrial based on further investigation.

Article 32 regulates that a judgment for a guilty accused should also be submitted to the Ministry of National Defence for confirmation and approval to execution. Cases concerning life imprisonment or the death penalty should be further submitted to the president of the Chinese government for approval to execution. If the ministry or the president consid-

---

[45] UNWCC, vol. 14, 1949, p. 158, see *supra* note 23.
[46] *Ibid.*, 1949, pp. 158–59.

ers the judgment as contrary to the law or inappropriate, the judgment
should be referred to the original tribunal for retrial.[47]

9.3. The Trials of the Three Hong Kong Governors General

The British military authorities conducted the war crimes trials in Hong
Kong over a period of three years from 28 March 1946 to 20 December
1948.[48] Two military courts were constructed to try war crimes suspects
in a total of 48 cases involving 129 accused.[49] However, the three most
senior figures of the Japanese occupation regime were absent from the
Hong Kong proceedings. Sakai and Tanaka were captured by the Chinese
Nationalist forces on the mainland, while Isogai was arrested in Tokyo by
the SCAP and extradited to China.[50] They were put on trial before the
Chinese war crimes tribunals in Nanjing and Guangzhou.

9.3.1. Sakai Takashi

Of all the tribunals established on Chinese territory, the Nanjing War
Crimes Tribunal ('Nanjing Tribunal', officially the War Crimes Military
Tribunal of the Ministry of National Defence) was undoubtedly the one
with the highest profile.[51] The trial of Sakai was the first war crimes case
ever adjudicated by a Chinese military tribunal.[52] The proceedings lasted
nearly three months, from 30 May to 29 August 1946, when the judgment
was delivered. According to the judgment, Sakai was convicted of crimes
against peace, war crimes and crimes against humanity. He was found
guilty of participating in the war of aggression and of inciting or permitting his subordinates to murder prisoners of war, wounded soldiers or
non-combatants; to rape, plunder and forced deportation of civilians; to
indulge in cruel punishments and torture; and to cause the destruction of

---

[47] *Ibid.*, p. 160.

[48] Linton, 2013, p. 1, see *supra* note 11.

[49] Snow, 2003, p. 305, see *supra* note 7. Some say the number of the accused is 123. See
Suzannah Linton, "Table of Cases and Legal Materials", in Suzannah Linton (ed.), *Hong
Kong's War Crimes Trials*, Oxford University Press, Oxford, 2013, p. xi.

[50] Snow, 2003, p. 305, see *supra* note 7.

[51] REN, 2011, p. 233, see *supra* note 24; HU, 1988, p. 129, see *supra* note 12.

[52] LUO Junsheng, "Shi Mei-yu yu zhanhou nanjing dui Rijun zhanfan de shenpan" [Shi Mei-
yu and the Post-war Nanjing War Crimes Trials], in *The Scan of the CPC History*, 2006,
no. 1, pp. 20–26.

---

property. For the foregoing crimes he was sentenced to death on 27 August of 1946 and subsequently executed on 30 September the same year.[53]

9.3.1.1. Sakai's Role in the War of Aggression against China

Sakai was the first defendant handled by the Nanjing Tribunal. He served as a military commander in China from 1939 to 1945, and, prior to that, during the hostilities between China and Japan since the Mukden Incident of 1931.[54] Known as the Tiger of Hong Kong, Sakai commanded the 23rd Army which captured Hong Kong.[55] The fact-finding of the Nanjing Tribunal concerning Sakai's crimes in China is divided into two periods. First, between 1931 and 1939 Sakai was one of the Japanese leaders who were instrumental in the aggression against China. By creating disturbances in major Chinese cities, organising terrorist activities and assisting in setting up a puppet administration, Sakai instigated, planned and attempted to overthrow the Chinese government. Second, during the Second World War, as regimental commander of the 29th Infantry Brigade, Sakai incited or permitted his subordinates to indulge in acts of atrocity: the massacre of over a hundred civilians in Guangdong and Hainan; the torture of 22 civilians, rape and mutilation of women and feeding their bodies to dogs; setting fire to over 700 civilian houses and plunder.[56]

The crimes under Sakai's command and supervision committed in Hong Kong are separately described. The judgment notes that on 8 December 1948 Sakai personally directed the Japanese army to strike Hong Kong, assuming that the attack would easily succeed. Owing to the resistance of the defending troops, the Japanese army did not manage to land until 17 December 1941. In venting his frustration and anger, Sakai's troops massacred 30 prisoners of war at Lyumen and killed 24 more prisoners at West Point fortress. In addition to the prisoners of war, seven nurses were raped and three mutilated, 60 to 79 wounded prisoners of war were killed later. Moreover, the Nanjing Tribunal found that Sakai in-

---

[53] UNWCC, Chinese War Crimes Military Tribunal of Ministry of National Defence ('Nanjing Tribunal'): Trial of Takashi Sakai, Summary of the Proceedings (in English and Chinese), 27 August 1946, p.2 ('Sakai Proceedings') (http://www.legal-tools.org/doc/3789a0/).

[54] UNWCC, vol. 14, 1949, p. 1, see *supra* note 23.

[55] Snow, 2003, p. 63, see *supra* note 7.

[56] Nanjing Tribunal, *Prosecutor v. Sakai Takashi*, Judgment, 29 August 1946 ('Sakai Judgment') (http://www.legal-tools.org/doc/6ed3e2/).

dulged his soldiers looting and pillaging a large amount of valuable books and documents from libraries.[57]

9.3.1.2. Sakai's Defence

Sakai pleaded not guilty on three grounds: 1) the forced removal of the Chinese troops and the administrative chief in Hebei province was consistent with the Boxer Protocol that allowed foreign countries to base their troops in Beijing;[58] 2) the engagement in the war of aggression was based on the orders of the Japanese government; and 3) he had no knowledge of the war crimes and crimes against humanity perpetrated by his subordinates and hence he was not responsible for the acts of his subordinates.[59]

For the first plea, the Nanjing Tribunal examined every provision in the Boxer Protocol and confirmed that it bestowed no power upon Japan to either forcibly remove Chinese troops stationed in Hebei or to dismiss a Chinese administrative chief from his post.[60] Sakai's contention that their acts accorded with the Boxer Protocol was thus considered as a distortion of the provisions.

With regard to the second plea, the Nanjing Tribunal held that "the war of aggression is an act against world peace. Granted that the defendant participated in the war on the order of his Government, a superior order cannot be held to absolve the defendant from liability for the crime".[61] The rejection of the plea of superior orders was made on the basis of the generally recognised and already firmly established rule that to commit crimes upon superior orders, including those from a government, does not relieve the accused from criminal liability, but may be taken in mitigation of the punishment.[62]

---

[57] *Ibid.* UNWCC, vol. 14, 1949, p. 2, see *supra* note 23.

[58] Sakai Judgment, see *supra* note 56. The Boxer Protocol was signed on 7 September 1901 between the Qing Empire of China and the Eight-Nation Alliance (Austria-Hungary, France, Germany, Italy, Japan, Russia, the United Kingdom and the United States) plus Belgium, Spain and the Netherlands that had provided military forces after China's defeat in the intervention to put down the Boxer Rebellion at the hands of the Eight-Power Expeditionary Force.

[59] Sakai Judgment, see *supra* note 56; UNWCC, vol. 14, 1949, p. 2, see *supra* note 23; Sakai Proceedings, p. 4, see *supra* note 53.

[60] Sakai Judgment, p. 4, see *supra* note 56.

[61] Sakai Proceedings, p. 5, see *supra* note 53.

[62] UNWCC, vol. 14, 1949, p. 5, see *supra* note 23.

Regarding knowledge of Sakai's subordinates' actions, the Nanjing Tribunal held

> that a field Commander must hold himself responsible for the discipline of his subordinates, is an accepted principle. It is inconceivable that he should not have been aware of the acts of atrocities committed by his subordinates. All the evidence goes to show that the defendant knew of the atrocities committed by his subordinates and deliberately let loose savagery upon civilians and prisoners of war.[63]

In relation to offences that occurred in Hong Kong, the Tribunal found that "the defendant supervised the military operations in Guangdong and Hong Kong for almost two years; his troops committed acts of violence all over south-east China. It is unreasonable for the defendant to assert that he had no knowledge of the commission of those atrocities".[64] With the collaboration of testimonies from Sakai's subordinates and a witness statement from a Canadian military surgeon, the Tribunal observed that "the defendant knew the facts that his subordinates were committing massacres against civilian people and still indulged the occurrence of the horrific crimes".[65] Accordingly, the Nanjing Tribunal dismissed Sakai's defence of a lack of awareness of the commission of the crimes and did not consider this excuse as a mitigating factor either.

9.3.1.3. Findings and Sakai's Sentence

At the end of the proceedings Sakai was found guilty on all counts "of participating in the war of aggression" and "of inciting or permitting his subordinates to murder prisoners of war, wounded soldiers and non-combatants; to rape, plunder and deport civilians; to indulge in cruel punishment and torture; and to cause destruction of property".[66] With respect to charges of crimes against peace ("of participating in the war of aggression"), the Nanjing Tribunal examined evidence from various sources, including documents submitted by the administrative heads of northern China and written orders by Sakai himself to the Chinese authorities in northern China, which had been substantiated by evidence given by the

---

[63] Sakai Judgment, see *supra* note 56.
[64] *Ibid.*
[65] *Ibid.*
[66] Sakai Proceedings, p. 6, see *supra* note 53.

war crimes investigators before the Tribunal and corroborated by the deposition of Major General Tanaka Ryukich before the IMTFE. The Nanjing Tribunal found that Sakai had violated international law by undermining the territorial and administrative integrity of China. Accordingly, Sakai was held criminally responsible for violating the Nine-Power Treaty of 1922 and the Kellogg-Briand Pact,[67] thereby constituting crimes against peace. Moreover, it found that an offence against the internal security of China should be punished in accordance with Chinese criminal law.

With regard to the charges of war crimes and crimes against humanity, Sakai was found guilty as well. The Nanjing Tribunal confirmed that "a field commander must hold himself responsible for the discipline of his subordinates is an accepted principle" and

> in inciting or permitting his subordinates to murder prisoners of war, wounded soldiers, nurses and doctors of the Red Cross and other non-soldiers, and to commit acts of rape, plunder, deportation, torture and destruction of property, Sakai had violated the Hague Convention concerning the Law and Customs of War on Land and the Geneva Convention of 1929.[68]

In the last part of the judgment, the Nanjing Tribunal invoked the applicable law as follows:

> Article 1 and Article 8 of Rules Governing Trials of War Criminals; Article 291 of the ROC Criminal Procedure Law; Article 1 of the Nine-Power Treaty; Article 1 of the Paris Pact; Articled 4–7 Sub-sections 3 and 7 of Article 23; Articles 28, 46 and 47 of the Hague Convention;[69] Articles 1–6, 9 and 10 of the Geneva Convention;[70] Articles 3 and 4 of

---

67 Treaty between the United States and other Powers for the Renunciation of War as an Instrument of National Policy, Paris, 27 August 1928 ('Kellogg-Briand Pact') (http://www.legal-tools.org/doc/396040/). The government of China had adhered to Kellogg-Briand Pact after it became effective on 24 July 1929.

68 Sakai Judgment, see *supra* note 56.

69 Convention (IV) respecting the Laws and Customs of War on Land and Its Annex: Regulations concerning the Laws and Customs of War on Land, and, The Hague, 18 October 1907 ('Hague Regulations') (http://www.legal-tools.org/doc/fa0161/).

70 Convention relative to the Treatment of Prisoners of War, Geneva, 27 July 1929 ('1929 Geneva Convention') (http://www.legal-tools.org/doc/1d2cfc/).

Criminal Law of the Army, Navy and Air force; Paragraph 1
of Article 101 and Article 55 of the Criminal Code.[71]

In Sakai's case, the reason for applying the Rules of War Crimes Trials
instead of the Law of War Crimes Trials is that the trial started on 30 May
1946 and ended on 29 August 1946, whereas Law of War Crimes Trials,
as the amendment of the Rules, was only drafted. There was a wait of almost two months before it entered into force. But justice had no time. Sakai faced his destiny in Nanjing under the legal regime of both international law and municipal law and was sentenced to death.

9.3.2. Isogai Rensuke

On 20 February 1942 Isogai was appointed as governor general of Hong
Kong as successor to Sakai.[72] Long before this, he had volunteered to be-
come a military attaché in China in 1937, at the beginning of the war in
China.[73] He did not have this post for long, as he was soon assigned to
command the 10th Division of the Imperial Japanese Army.[74] In 1938
Isogai was transferred to Manchukuo (Manchuria) as chief of staff of the
Kwangtung Army shortly before the Battles of Khalkhin Gol (Nomonhan
Incident) which resulted in the defeat of the Japanese 6th Army. Isogai
retired on 24 December 1944 and returned to Japan.

At the end of the war Isogai was arrested and extradited to China.[75]
The Nanjing Tribunal was designated to process cases delivered by the
Chinese delegation in Japan assisting in extradition of Japanese war criminals to China.[76] There, he was confronted with a trial for war crimes, including those committed during the occupation of Hong Kong. Though
sentenced to life imprisonment, Isogai was released early in 1952.[77]

---

[71] Sakai Judgment, see *supra* note 56.

[72] Suzannah Linton, "War Crimes", in Suzannah Linton (ed.), *Hong Kong's War Crimes Trials*, Oxford University Press, Oxford, 2013, p. 114.

[73] Snow, 2003, p. 44, see *supra* note 7.

[74] ZHAI Xingfu, "Notes on 'Monument to the War Dead in the Thirteenth Army of the National Revolutionary Army in the Anti-Japanese War'", in *Journal of Nanyang Teachers' College*, 2005, no. 11, p. 96.

[75] XU Jiajun, "Nanjing Datusha Zhufan Gushoufu Guanya Tilanqiao Jianyu de Qianqian Houhou" [Principal War Criminal Tani Hisao and His Detention in Tilanqiao Prison], in *Zhong Shan Feng Yu*, 2005, no. 3, p. 13.

[76] HU, 1988, p. 118, see *supra* note 12.

[77] Linton, 2013, p. 115, see *supra* note 72.

9.3.2.1. Charges against Isogai

The prosecutor brought five charges against Isogai that ranged from crimes against peace to crimes against humanity. Isogai was charged with the following acts:

(1) Having served successively as military commander in the Japanese army and participated in military operations, the defendant shall be responsible for the initiation and support of a war of aggression;

(2) During the military presence in Shandong and Henan, the defendant shall be responsible for indulging his subordinates committed offences of murder, arson, rape and pillage;

(3) Serving as governor general of Hong Kong, the defendant shall be responsible for implementing the policy of poisoning by using drugs by selling narcotic drugs publicly;

(4) During the occupation of Hong Kong, the defendant shall be responsible as co-perpetrator for arbitrary detention and torture of Chinese and Alien citizens conducted by the Japanese military police;

(5) During the military occupation of Hong Kong, the defendant shall be responsible for the war crime of mass deportation of non-combatants.[78]

Of these charges, the Nanjing Tribunal only upheld the fifth, while the others were dismissed.

9.3.2.2. Findings

For the first charge, the Nanjing Tribunal, by referring to the crime of "the initiation and support of a war of aggression", found as follows: "It requires the accused, holding a principal position in a military organisation or a financial magnate, proposed the use of war as a method for the usurpation of sovereignty of the occupied territory or supported the war of aggression by finance and manpower".[79] In this instance, the Nanjing Tribunal held that "the defendant's positions were similar to a staff role, not

---

[78] Nanjing Tribunal, *Prosecutor v. Isogai Rensuke*, Judgment, 29 August 1946, pp. 2–3 ('Isogai Judgment') (http://www.legal-tools.org/en/doc/b9c3c1/).

[79] *Ibid.*, p. 3.

a principal in the organisations to which he belonged. Therefore, the defendant cannot be held responsible for the initiation and support of a war of aggression simply because he acted under orders to fight in battlefields".[80]

With regard to the second charge, the Tribunal noted the established facts that Isogai's subordinates committed assaults, rape, murder, arson, pillage and other offences in separate places as mere incidents at different times in different locations. Distinctions must be drawn between these incidents and the planned systematic offences of atrocities. Hence, the Tribunal concluded that "no sufficient evidence shows the defendant knew about the commission of the said crimes and indulged his subordinates to continue those actions, nor had he the capacity to foresee and prevent these incidents from happening".[81] Based on these reasons, the Tribunal believed that Isogai should not bear responsibility as a co-perpetrator for the crimes.

For the third charge, the Tribunal ascertained the facts that during the period Isogai served as Hong Kong's governor general he adopted a policy of gradually prohibiting opium, such as controlling the public sale of drugs, reducing consumption of narcotic products, hoping to eliminate narcotic drugs step by step. This fact was supported by evidence such as local news and reports of citizens' praise for this drug control policy. The Tribunal found these news and reports had credibility because they were released long before the surrender of Japan and could not possibly have been fabricated. "Even though the defendant only implemented a gradual control policy and did not definitively prohibit narcotic drugs in the market, this resulted in debatable administrative measures being adopted. However, it was not a case of poisoning and hampering the Chinese people with criminal intent. On the foregoing grounds, the defendant has no criminal responsibility on this count".[82]

For the fourth charge, the Tribunal confirmed the facts that the Japanese military police during the hostilities did arbitrarily detain and torture several Hong Kong citizens. However, the military police force constituted an independent system, differentiated from the ordinary military

---

[80]   *Ibid.*

[81]   *Ibid.*

[82]   *Ibid.*

organisation, and reported to their direct supervisor. "Acting as governor general of Hong Kong, Isogai assumed all overall duties of administration and hence was unable to prevent individual incidents committed by the Japanese military police". Since the prosecutor could not prove that Isogai had a common plan shared by the perpetrators, the Tribunal concluded that he should not be held responsible as a co-perpetrator.[83]

It was only in relation to the last charge that the Nanjing Tribunal acknowledged that Isogai confessed and admitted the deportation of non-combatants during the occupation of Hong Kong. Many witnesses, in collaboration with records of objections made by local civil groups against the deportations, demonstrated the facts of the occurrence of the crimes. Not surprisingly, Isogai retracted his confession, asserting that the deportations were to evict thieves and criminals and to evacuate Hong Kong citizens to their homes.[84] However, the Tribunal deemed this plea as pure fabrication, owing to the fact that in the previous proceedings of 21 April of that year Isogai had confessed: "The order to deport Chinese people was made in the name of the governor general of Hong Kong; the announcement of exiling Chinese to Mirs Bay was under my name. I cannot claim that I did not know their existence. But Mirs Bay is not entirely inhabitable".[85] The Tribunal found that Isogai knew and admitted that under his order people were forcibly deported to Mirs Bay. Consequently, the defence of "eviction of thieves and criminals and evacuation of Hong Kong citizens home" was proven untenable. "During the military occupation of Hong Kong, the defendant carried out massive deportations, disregarded the life and safety of civilians, and caused the old, weak, women and children to be homeless, resulting in death from cold and starvation".[86] Thus, the Tribunal opined that "it amounted to a grave breach of Article 46 of the 1907 Hague Regulations and constituted a war crime".[87]

---

[83]   *Ibid.*

[84]   *Ibid.*, p. 4.

[85]   *Ibid.*

[86]   *Ibid.*

[87]   *Ibid.* See also Linton, 2013, pp. 114–115, see *supra* note 72.

9.3.2.3. Isogai's Sentence

After discussion, the judges determined that both international law and municipal law were applicable to the case. At the time when Isogai's judgment was rendered, on 22 July 1947, the Law of War Crimes Trials was enacted and had entered into force. Therefore, the applicable laws were as follows: "Articles 291 and 293 of the Chinese Criminal Procedure Law, Article 46 of the Hague Regulations, Articles 1, 2(2), 3(18), and 11 of the Law Governing Trials of War Criminals; Articles 28, 56, and 57 of the Chinese Criminal Law".[88] Besides the applicable law, the Nanjing Tribunal further pondered over the means deployed in the crimes and the consequences generated from the deportation and found them quite severe. However, with regard to the deportations the Tribunal also observed that the primary reason for implementing the policy was because of the food deficit on Hong Kong island, which was supported by the records of the 135th Conference of Hong Kong Chinese Representatives.[89] Taking the purpose of the acts into account in mitigation, the Nanjing Tribunal decided that Isogai was responsible for the mass deportation of non-combatants and other crimes committed in China with a penalty of life imprisonment.[90]

9.3.3. Tanaka Hisakazu

Unlike the trials of Sakai and Isogai before the Nanjing Tribunal, Tanaka was tried by the military tribunal at Guangzhou Xing Yuan.[91] Taking a career path akin to that of Sakai, Tanaka was appointed as governor general

---

[88]   Isogai Judgment, p. 3, see *supra* note 78.

[89]   *Ibid.*, p. 4.

[90]   *Ibid.*, p. 5.

[91]   Xing Yuan (Chinese: 行辕) is usually translated as "mobile barracks of the high command". It is a Chinese term primarily referring to an Republic of China government regional special office opened on behalf of the military supreme commander in a particular region, where there is a high-ranking government or military official as the regional representative of the supreme commander-in-chief.

of Hong Kong on 16 December 1944,[92] and at that time held the post of commanding general of the 23rd Imperial Expeditionary Army in China.[93]

In the judgment of 18 October 1946 the Guangzhou Tribunal held that Tanaka was responsible for engaging in the war of aggression, violation of laws and customs of war, and the proliferation of narcotic drugs. Accordingly, it condemned him to death. Nevertheless, it should be highlighted that the Guangzhou Tribunal was not the only trial that Tanaka faced due to his crimes.

After acknowledging that Tanaka was arrested by the Chinese army, the US military commission in Shanghai requested the Chinese authorities to consign Tanaka to Shanghai for trial because he had directed offences against "a named United States Major" during his governorship of Hong Kong.[94] Although the US military commission sentenced Tanaka to death by hanging, the confirming authority disapproved the final result.[95] This disapproval may have allegedly been influenced by a request from the Chinese authorities, as the president of the Guangzhou Tribunal said: "The crimes Tanaka committed in southern China were much more severe than killing US pilots in Hong Kong. Whatever judgment the US military commission passed on Tanaka had no relevance to the Chinese trials".[96] Tanaka was condemned to hang for that offence, but it was never carried out. Instead, he was handed over to the Chinese authorities to answer for the depredations of the 23rd Army in mainland China. On 17 October 1946 Tanaka was sentenced to death after the final approval of China's president, CHIANG Kai-shek.[97]

---

[92] FENG Yingzi, "Biele, Xiang Gang Zongdu" [Farewell, Governors of Hong Kong], in *Century*, 1997, no. 4, p. 6.

[93] UNWCC, "Trial of General Tanaka Hisakasu and Five Others: United States Military Commission, Shanghai, 13th August–3rd September, 1946", in *Law Reports of Trials of War Criminals*, vol. 5, His Majesty's Stationery Office, London, 1948, p. 66.

[94] *Ibid.*, p. 70.

[95] *Ibid.*

[96] LIU Tong, "Guomin zhengfu shenpan Riben zhanfan gaishu" [General Introduction to the Chinese Nationalist Government's War Crimes Trials (1946–1949)], in *Republican Archive*, 2014, no. 1, p. 77.

[97] ZHANG Weizhen, "Research on the Acceptance of the Japanese Surrender in Guangdong after the Anti-Japanese War", in *History Teaching*, 2007, no. 9, p. 43.

9.3.3.1. Trial under the US Military Commission in Shanghai

The US military commission charged Tanaka with war crimes for the reason that he, as governor general of Hong Kong and commander of the 23rd Imperial Expeditionary Army, "did, at Canton [Guangdong], China and/or Hong Kong knowingly, willfully, unlawfully and wrongfully commit cruel, inhuman and brutal atrocities and other offences against" a named United States major, "by authorizing, permitting, participating in and approving of the illegal, unfair, false and null trial and the unlawful killing" of the major.[98] Unsurprisingly, Tanaka pleaded not guilty to all charges.

Evidence showed that the victim took part in an air raid on shipping and docks in Hong Kong harbour on 5 January 1945. He was shot down and captured by the Japanese. The major was charged with having bombed and sunk a Chinese civilian vessel on 15 January 1945, resulting in the death of eight Chinese civilians.[99] After a hasty hearing that lasted not more than two hours, all three judges decided that the major was guilty and unanimously voted for the death penalty.[100]

Despite pleading not guilty, Tanaka admitted that the court that the trial and execution of the major was under his jurisdiction and that all persons connected with the trial and execution were subordinates of his command as governor general and army commander in Guangdong. Tanaka admitted he knew the investigation of this case, as well as the hearing of the matter on 20 March 1945. Before returning to Guangdong on 21 March Tanaka endowed one of his subordinate staff with full powers to act on his behalf in all matters of the Hong Kong command.[101]

The US military commission found Tanaka liable for "willfully committed violations of the laws and customs of war against a certain United States prisoner by authorizing, permitting, participating in and approving of the illegal, unfair, false and null trial and the unlawful killing of the prisoner".[102] But the confirming authority disapproved the death penalty and observed that Tanaka was away from the scene at the time

---

[98] UNWCC, vol. 5, 1948, p. 66, see *supra* note 93.

[99] *Ibid.*, pp. 66–67.

[100] *Ibid.*, p. 68.

[101] *Ibid.*

[102] *Ibid.*, p. 70.

when the trial of the major was held, and did not return to his headquarters until the execution of the victim. In view of the confirming authority, given that Tanaka was the only person having power to legally approve the death sentence or order the execution by Japanese law, he was not proved to have known in advance that the trial would be unfair or to have known or had reasonable grounds to believe that, if the major were convicted, the execution of the sentence would be carried out without his consent and approval.[103] As a result, Tanaka was not executed but turned over to the Guangzhou Military Tribunal on the grounds of the crimes committed against Chinese people in the territory of China.

9.3.3.2. Trial under the Guangzhou Military Tribunal

Having been transferred to the Chinese authority, Tanaka was found guilty by the Guangzhou Tribunal for

> participating in the war of aggression, indulging subordinates to murder civilians, prisoners of war and non-combatants, to rape, to pillage, to deport civilians, to torture, to starve civilians to death, to force non-combatants to engage in military activities with the enemy, indiscriminately destroying properties, excessively confiscating or extorting properties, deliberately bombing historical constructions and spreading narcotic drugs.[104]

He was condemned to death and executed on 27 March 1947.[105]

9.3.3.2.1. Fact-Finding for the Prosecution

The Guangzhou Tribunal established the facts by virtue of the vast territorial scope in which Tanaka commanded his troops to perpetrate offences during wartime. These facts can be categorised into three groups according to the crimes charged.

First, subversion of the Republic of China and conspiracy to usurp the sovereignty of China. In October 1938 Tanaka landed his 21st Army at Bias Bay on the coast of Guangdong province, a short distance to the

---

[103] *Ibid.*, pp. 68, 79.

[104] Guangzhou Military Tribunal, *Prosecutor v. Tanaka Hisakazu*, 18 October 1946, p. 2 ('Tanaka Judgment') (http://www.legal-tools.org/doc/ca07a0/).

[105] ZHANG, 2014, p. 80, see *supra* note 97.

north-east of the New Territories. Tanaka's objective was not Hong Kong but Guangdong, which he duly captured after a nine-day campaign.[106] In 1940 and 1941 Tanaka was the regimental commander of the 21st Army and led the army to attack Jiangsu, Hebei, Henan and Shandong provinces. From 1943 to 1945 he was promoted as commander of the 23rd Imperial Expeditionary Army and conducted aggressive military operations in Jiangxi, Guangxi and Guangdong, where he ordered his forces to besiege cities and propped up a puppet government in order to subvert China.[107]

Second, the violation of the laws and customs of war. The Guangzhou Tribunal considered it evident that Tanaka indulged his subordinates to commit hideous offences against civilians, afflicting civilians with great suffering. In May and October 1943 two units under his command killed more than 10 children, destroyed civilian houses and forced over 500 civilians to construct fortifications. In 1944 his air force deliberately bombed hospitals, and his troops pillaged villages, committed arson, massacred hundreds of civilians, and destroyed historic and cultural sites. In 1945 the Japanese armed force under his command raped women, killed wounded and sick persons in hospitals, forced hostages to conduct military service, confiscated food supplies, extorted civilian properties and bombarded undefended cities. Under Tanaka's administration the military police and armed forces arrested large numbers of civilians in Guangdong and tortured them by affusion, beatings, being bitten by dogs, cutting off fingers, having the skin branded, beheading, starvation and other inhumane acts.[108] In addition, Tanaka's subordinates not only destroyed houses, dismantled water supply pipes, and damaged railways and tramways in Guangzhou City but also transported huge amounts of opium for distribution and sale in the market, aiming at implementing a policy of poisoning Chinese people.[109]

The authorities in each area concerned verified the above facts. The central government thus included Tanaka in the list of war criminals and arrested him for trial. The prosecutor filed charges according to the established facts.

---

[106] Snow, 2003, p. 27, see *supra* note 7.

[107] Tanaka Judgment, p. 2, see *supra* note 104.

[108] *Ibid.*

[109] *Ibid.*

9.3.3.2.2. Reasoning and Convictions

With regard to subversion of the Nationalist government, the Guangzhou Tribunal noted that Tanaka participated in the war of aggression by planning and directing the 21st Army to land and fight in southern China. Since October 1937 he had been promoted as commander of the South China Expeditionary Army and the 23rd Army, holding the highest command post in southern China.[110] He directed a series of major campaigns in relation to the overall war of aggression. Given that Tanaka had control over 100,000 soldiers in southern China, the Guangzhou Tribunal opined that it was ambiguous for him to assert that all the military operations were subject to the supreme command and that no communication existed between his operational decisions and those of the supreme command.[111]

The Guangzhou Tribunal maintained that Tanaka personally directed battles in the field, which established his participation, support and assistance in the war of aggression. What is more, the act of cultivating puppet governments to strengthen Japanese influence violated Article 1 of the Nine-Power Treaty that required the contracting powers to respect China's sovereignty and its territorial and administrative integrity. The Tribunal thereby deemed this act as undermining peace. By participating in the war of aggression and by analogy the Tribunal condemned Tanaka in light of Article 101 of the Chinese Criminal Law. Therefore, the defendant could not be exempted from responsibility by contending that he was just following orders from his supreme command.[112]

As to the 13 war crimes charges, the Guangzhou Tribunal examined each count separately. For the massacre and deportation of civilians in Guangdong and Hainan, the Tribunal noted that the commission of the offences took place prior to Tanaka's assumption of office as commander in March 1943. Rather, the perpetrators were members of the Japanese garrison in Hainan, which was not part of Tanaka's troops and hence fell

---

[110] *Ibid.*.

[111] *Ibid.*

[112] One question may be raised: why did the Guangzhou Tribunal not invoke the Law of War Crimes Trials whose Article 2(1) clearly criminalises the act of participating in and supporting the war of aggression against China? The reason is the same as the case of Sakai. Tanaka stood trial for crimes committed in the territory of China at a time when the Law of War Crimes Trials had not entered into force. As a result, the War Criminals Process Regulation, Rules of War Crimes Trials and the Detailed Rules were the applicable laws in Tanaka's trial.

outside his control. Therefore, the defendant should not bear responsibility for their commission of these crimes.[113]

However, in terms of the incidents of killing large numbers of children in May 1943 and destroying civilian houses in November of the same year, the Tribunal examined the witness statements and testimonies and concluded that the defendant could not argue that the offences occurred in a place belonging to the jurisdiction of Hong Kong, which was then outside of his authority, as he personally directed battle campaigns in that area and stationed his army there.[114] Further, with regard to the bombardment of St Joseph Hospital in Huizhou, Guangdong in January 1944, the Tribunal took the statements of the director of the hospital and a priest into consideration and dismissed Tanaka's defence that the air force was not subject to his command, since the air force was co-ordinated with the land troops in the field, and the bombardment formed part of the whole military operation.[115]

Therefore, the Guangzhou Tribunal found that Tanaka violated Articles 4(2), 23(7), 25, 28, 47, 46, 52 of the Hague Regulations by torturing and inhumanely treating prisoners of war, destroying property, bombarding undefended villages and cities, pillaging, confiscating private property, demanding requisitions and services from municipalities and inhabitants; and violated Articles 1 to 6 of the 1929 Geneva Convention by disrespecting prisoners of war. Remarkably, the Tribunal discovered that Tanaka's headquarters distributed opium and other narcotic drugs to businessmen in exchange for supplies in order to carry out the policy of poisoning Chinese people.[116] As a consequence, he was held liable for violation of Article 12(1) of the Interim Regulations on the Prohibition of Drugs.[117]

For the remaining charges, the Guangzhou Tribunal rejected all the pleas of Tanaka, even though he contended that he was not aware of the

---

[113] Tanaka Judgment, p. 2, see *supra* note 104.

[114] *Ibid.*

[115] *Ibid.*

[116] *Ibid.*, p. 5.

[117] *Shen Bao*, "Interim Regulations of Prohibition on Drugs, Promulgated on 2 August 1946", 16 December 1946 (http://contentdm.lib.nccu.edu.tw/cdm/ref/collection/38clip/id/74519).

crimes happening, or the army was not under his control, or the attacks were conducted by the United States.[118]

9.3.3.2.3. Command Responsibility and Sentence

The Guangzhou Tribunal noted that Tanaka either denied the charges or claimed he had no knowledge of the commission of the offences carried out by lower-ranked soldiers or puppet governments. However, the Tribunal also noted that the listed offences took place all over southern China and the case files related were piled up "like mountains", and were in no way accidental. Even those crimes perpetrated by *Hanjian*,[119] who acted either under Tanaka's supervision or in areas that Tanaka's army occupied and were stationed, were carried out under the orders from the puppet government subject to Tanaka's will. Having heard the testimony from the police commissioner of the puppet government in Guangzhou, the Tribunal considered that by no means could the defendant argue that he was not aware of the commission of the crimes in the areas concerned.[120] More importantly, the Guangzhou Tribunal opined that Tanaka as commander had failed to take precautionary measures in advance to repress the occurrence of the crimes and to punish the perpetrators afterwards; instead, the defendant indulged his subordinates in ravaging the Chinese people.[121] Therefore, he should bear criminal responsibility even though the crimes were not executed by him personally.

Apart from crimes against peace and war crimes, the Tribunal underlined that Tanaka connived in drug trafficking by his subordinates, resulting in the widespread distribution of narcotic products. Such acts constituted crimes analogous to Article 30 of the Criminal Law of Army, Navy and Air Force, and Article 12, paragraph 1 of the Interim Regulations on the Prohibition of Drugs.[122]

Turning to the sentence, the Guangzhou Tribunal held that the war crimes along with crimes in connection to narcotic drugs were implicated in Tanaka's participation in the war of aggression. Pursuant to Article 55,

---

[118] Tanaka Judgment, p. 2, see *supra* note 104.

[119] *Hanjian* (汉奸) is a specific term describing traitors to China.

[120] Tanaka Judgment, p. 5, see *supra* note 104.

[121] *Ibid.*

[122] *Ibid.*

paragraph 2 of the Chinese Criminal Law, if the method or consequence of committing a crime constitute another crime, punishment with the more serious crime should be imposed on the defendant. In this case, the Guangzhou Tribunal viewed that Tanaka directed aggressive operations and indulged his subordinates to commit the crimes all over southern China and thus deserved to be executed in order to demonstrate justice.

9.4. Contemporary Observations on the Three Trials

9.4.1. Mixed Regime of Applicable Laws

Together with other national war crimes trials after the Second World War, the Chinese war crimes trials adopted a mixed regime of applicable laws, where international law played a role as important as municipal law. In fact, international law took a lead in Chinese war crimes legislation and judicial decisions. In terms of legislation, the Nationalist government incorporated rules derived from international treaties or conventions that China had signed or acceded to at that time into national war crimes legislation. For instance, crimes listed in the Law of War Crimes Trials of 1946 echo provisions in the 1929 Geneva Convention and the 1907 Hague Regulations; it also presents more particular elaborations on how to apply international law. Furthermore, the law absorbs the latest developments of international criminal law at that time. To take examples from the three Hong Kong cases, four international treaties or conventions are highlighted in the judgments: the 1922 Nine-Power Treaty, the 1928 Kellogg-Briand Pact, the 1907 Hague Regulations and the 1929 Geneva Convention.

The judicial precedents also exemplify the successful incorporation of international law. In the Sakai and Tanaka cases, the Chinese tribunals invoked the Nine-Power Treaty and the Kellogg-Briand Pact to demonstrate the severity of the defendants' participation in the war of aggression, while realising that international treaties only impose obligations on states and not individuals. Hence, the judges looked into Chinese criminal law for a corresponding crime with only a distinction of subjects. Resorting to municipal law to accommodate the conviction also generates the question as to whether such an analogy violates the principle of legality. Fewer controversies exist in invoking the Hague Regulations and Geneva Convention, which cover most scenarios of violating the laws and customs of war and crimes against humanity.

9.4.2. Analogous Method: Violation of Principle of Legality?

As noted, in the Sakai and Tanaka cases, the tribunal used a method of analogy to connect the defendants' acts of subverting the Chinese government and fostering puppet governments to arrogate sovereignty with crimes under the Chinese criminal law, as the Nine-Power Treaty imposed obligations on state parties. In both cases, the Law of War Crimes Trials was not promulgated and thus no statute at the domestic level could be relied on to criminalise the acts. The question is: did the analogous method adopted by the Chinese military tribunals violate the principle of legality?

It is self-evident that the principle of legality had become fundamental to criminal law since the Enlightenment.[123] The Rome Statute of the International Criminal Court has codified this principle in Articles 22 and 23. Article 22 requires a strict interpretation of the definition of a crime and such interpretation shall not be extended by analogy, while Article 23 restricts the punishment rigorously to that stipulated in the Statute. The interdiction of analogy is directly linked to the prohibition against retroactivity, and hence a generally accepted component of *nullum crimen sine lege*, which means that a judge must not fill a gap in the criminal law by applying a statute beyond its wording or by extending a precedent through the creation of a new unwritten crime.[124]

As is well known, the first international trial for aggression, under the name of crimes against peace, was before the International Military Tribunal ('IMT') at Nuremberg that delivered its final judgment on 30 September–1 October 1946.[125] It must be pointed out that Sakai was tried before that date and Tanaka's judgment was rendered on 18 October 1946, when the results of the IMTFE were still two years away. So were the Chinese judges creating a totally new crime just to execute the ac-

---

[123] M. Cherif Bassiouni, *International Criminal Law: Sources, Subjects, and Contents*, vol. 1, 3rd ed., Martinus Nijhoff, Leiden, 2008, p. 73.

[124] Claus Kress, "*Nulla poena nullum crimen sine lege*", in Rüdiger Wolfrum (ed.), *Max Planck Encyclopedia of Public International Law*, Oxford University Press, Oxford, 2013, para. 28 (http://www.legal-tools.org/doc/f9b453/).

[125] Robert Cryer, Håkan Friman, Darryl Robinson and Elizabeth Wilmshurst, *An Introduction to International Criminal Law and Procedure*, 3rd ed., Cambridge University Press, Cambridge, 2010, p. 312.

cused in circumstances in which no precedent explicitly incorporated crimes against peace?

The answer can hardly be in the affirmative. Rather, the judgments seemed to proffer a clarification and prioritisation of existing laws instead of setting out completely new crimes. In both cases, Chinese war crimes tribunals did not mention the concept of "crimes against peace" as specified in the IMT Charter and the IMTFE Charter. By contrast, the tribunals criminalised the defendants in line with the crime of insurrection under the Chinese Criminal Law. One may argue that the aims of the crime of insurrection could be interpreted as similar to that of international law,[126] because the crime of insurrection under Article 101 of the Chinese Criminal Law punishes the acts that use violence to arrogate sovereignty and to subvert the legitimate government, while international law demands states respect other states' sovereignty, territory and administrative integrity. In addition, calling the Japanese war criminals to account for their perpetration of atrocities on Chinese territory was the primary responsibility of these war crimes tribunals, especially in the case of Sakai who was the first defendant before the Nanjing Tribunal.

9.4.3. Tanaka's Trials: Double Jeopardy?

Although the three governors general held different posts in the Japanese army, which meant that their offences occurred all over China, Tanaka was the only one tried before two judicial organs conducted by separate authorities. It is contended here that the principle of double jeopardy or *ne bis in idem* was not breached in this instance. Basically, the principle of double jeopardy states that a person should not be prosecuted for an offence which has already been prosecuted nor be convicted or acquitted of a different offence arising out of the same or substantially the same facts.[127]

---

[126] See also Anja Matwijkiw and Bronik Matwijkiw, "A Modern Perspective on International Criminal Law: Accountability as a Meta-Right", in Leila Nadya Sadat and Michael P. Scharf (eds.), *The Theory and Practice of International Criminal Law: Essays in Honor of M. Cherif Bassiouni*, Martinus Nijhoff, Leiden, 2008, p. 54; Douglas H. Fischer, "Human Shields, Homicides, and House Fires: How a Domestic Law Analogy Can Guide International Law Regarding Human Shield Tactics in Armed Conflict", in *American University Law Review*, 2007, vol. 47, p. 513.

[127] Olaoluwa Olusanya, *Double Jeopardy Without Parameters: Re-characterisation in International Criminal Law*, Intersentia, Oxford, 2004, p. 10.

In the Tanaka case, the Chinese authorities initially arrested him but the United States requested that he be transferred to Shanghai for trial. Tanaka was charged before the US military commission with war crimes of denying the right to fair trial against a US major.[128] Nevertheless, the US military commission found him not guilty on the grounds that he was not proven to have known in advance or have reasonable grounds to believe the commission of the crime.[129] In sum, the US military commission only exercised jurisdiction over Tanaka based on the victim's nationality and the crime prosecuted was limited to a war crime of denial of fair trial in Hong Kong during the Japanese occupation.

The case before the Guangzhou Tribunal was different. The prosecuted crimes varied from subversion of China and conspiracy to usurp sovereignty to diverse war crimes and crimes against humanity over a vast territory from 1938 to 1945.[130] Compared with the trial before the US military commission, the Chinese tribunal convicted Tanaka of different crimes committed in different geographical areas and temporal scope. Thus, the Guangzhou Tribunal did not violate the principle of double jeopardy.

9.4.4. Chinese State Practice on Superior Responsibility

A common feature is revealed in the trials of the three Japanese governors general: they were all indicted for superior responsibility. The Law of War Crimes Trials indicates superior responsibility as an independent criminal liability and addresses circumstances that could not relieve the accused of criminal responsibility.

It should be stressed that disparities emerge between the draft and the final text of the Law of War Crimes Trials. Article 10 of the draft reads: "The person who was in a position of authority or command and failed to prevent or repress the commission of the said crimes shall be criminally responsible for the crimes".[131] Article 9 of the final text states: "Persons who occupy a superior or commanding position in relation to war criminals and in this capacity have not fulfilled their duty to prevent

---

128 UNWCC, vol. 5, 1948, p. 66, see *supra* note 93.

129 *Ibid.*, pp. 68, 79.

130 Tanaka Judgment, pp. 1–2, see *supra* note 104.

131 QIN, 1981, p. 412, see *supra* note 17.

crimes from being committed by their subordinates shall be deemed as accomplices of the war criminals".[132] According to the final version, three elements must be fulfilled to establish a superior's criminal responsibility: 1) the accused has a superior or authoritative position; 2) this position needs to be related to war criminals who committed crimes punishable under the law; and 3) this person has not fulfilled his or her duty within his or her capacity to prevent crimes from being committed by the subordinates. In the third element, there is an implication of the actual perpetrator being a subordinate of the accused. However, the responsibility of the superior is not "principal"; on the contrary, Article 9 states that this superior's failure to prevent the commission of the crimes only constitutes an "accomplice" of the actual perpetrator. In this sense, and contrary to the current doctrine of superior responsibility established by cases of the International Criminal Tribunal for the former Yugoslavia and International Criminal Tribunal for Rwanda,[133] the Law of War Crimes Trials regards superior responsibility as an accomplice, not an independent form of responsibility.

Moreover, Article 8 of the Law of War Crimes Trials lays down grounds for not excluding the criminal responsibility:

(1) Crimes were committed by orders of his or her superiors;

(2) Crimes were committed as result of official duty;

(3) Crimes were committed in pursuance of the policy of his or her government;

(4) Crimes were committed out of political necessity.[134]

These exemptions for criminal responsibility are distinct from Article 6 of the IMTFE Charter, under which only two circumstances cannot be invoked to exonerate criminal liability: one is the official position and the other is acts under orders of his or her government or of a superior. Nevertheless, the IMTFE Charter allows these two circumstances to be con-

---

[132] Law of War Crimes Trials, Art. 9, see *supra* note 28.

[133] United Nations, Updated Statute of the International Criminal Tribunal for the Former Yugoslavia, adopted 25 May 1993 by resolution 827 (1993), last amended 7 July 2009 by resolution 1877 (2009), Art. 7(3) ('ICTY Statute') (http://www.legal-tools.org/doc/b4f63b/); International Criminal Tribunal of the former Yugoslavia, *Prosecutor v. Tihomir Blaškić*, Trial Chamber, Judgment, IT-95-14-T, 3 March 2000, para. 294 (http://www.legal-tools.org/doc/e1ae55/); Cryer *et al.*, 2010, p. 387, see *supra* note 125.

[134] Law of War Crimes Trials, Art. 8, see *supra* note 28; UNWCC, vol. 14, 1949, p. 157, see *supra* note 23.

sidered as mitigating factors, "if the Tribunal determines that justice so requires".[135]

Apparently, similar language is not incorporated in the Law of War Crimes Trials. That is to say, at least within the scope of these three cases, the Chinese war crimes tribunals did not accept the plea of superior orders as either a circumstance precluding criminal liability or a mitigating factor. It should be noted that the International Military Tribunal ('IMT') at Nuremberg took the same position: "There is nothing in mitigation. Superior orders, even to a soldier, cannot be considered in mitigation where crimes as shocking and extensive have been committed consciously, ruthlessly and without military excuse or justification".[136]

9.5. Conclusion

It is evident that the IMT at Nuremberg has compelled the most attention of commentators and scholars in the field of international law, in particular international criminal law.[137] The Western-centric point of view has more or less eclipsed the legacy of the IMTFE, not mention that of national war crimes trials. That is why presenting the Chinese war crimes trials on the accountability of war criminals helps raise awareness of the contribution of China to international law practice. Uncovering the forgotten judicial precedents not only helps to pull together the fragmented modern Chinese international law practice but also reveals China's efforts in punishing war criminals by the rule of law. Admittedly, Chinese war crimes tribunals were not only faced with issues of pure law but frequently with political needs and external pressures. Still, the trials mirror the concepts of crimes and modes of liabilities in international criminal law that were then emerging. The three trials of the governors general stand out among other Chinese war crimes trials for the unique role the defendants played in the Japanese war of aggression: they all served at the highest level in the occupation of Hong Kong while having committed crimes

---

[135] International Military Tribunal for the Far East, Charter, Tokyo, enacted 19 January 1946 and amended 25 April 1946, Art. 6 ('IMTFE Charter') (http://www.legal-tools.org/doc/a3c41c/)..

[136] International Military Tribunal ('IMT'), *Nuremberg Tribunal v. Goering et al.*, Judgment, 1 October, 1946, p. 110 ('IMT Judgment') (https://www.legal-tools.org/doc/ 45f18e/).

[137] See also Christian Tomuschat, "The Legacy of Nuremberg", in *Journal of International Criminal Justice*, 2006, vol. 4, no. 4, p. 830; Steven Fogelson, "The Nuremberg Legacy: An Unfulfilled Promise", in *Southern California Law Review*, 1990, vol. 63, p. 833.

in other parts of China. Their cases generated precious materials and precedents to disclose the Chinese mode of incorporating international law into municipal law and how superior responsibility was understood in the Chinese legal system. As a result, the cases reveal the great efforts China made in bringing substantial measures of accountability to the perpetrators of atrocities.

10

War Crimes Trials in China after the Second World War: Justice and Politics

ZHANG Binxin[*]

10.1. Introduction

When examining the war crimes trials after the Second World War, many have criticised the involvement of political elements in these trials.[1] Asia, in particular, seems to suffer most from the "illness" or "abnormality" of political involvement in the judicial process, from Tokyo to today's international criminal justice endeavours, such as in Cambodia, East Timor and so forth.[2] The Chinese trials of Japanese war criminals after the war have not received much attention because of the lack of first-hand records and many other reasons. But the political considerations in these trials are also obvious and have often been criticised by commentators.[3] By con-

---

[*] **ZHANG Binxin** is Assistant Professor at Xiamen University Law School, China and the first Peking University-Centre for International Law Research and Policy Research Fellow. She has previously worked as postdoctoral Research Fellow at Xiamen Law School, focusing on reparations for victims in international criminal proceedings; as a Legal Officer at the International Committee of the Red Cross Regional Delegation for East Asia; and as a trial monitor of the Asia International Justice Initiative Trial Monitoring group, monitoring the Duch case before the Extraordinary Chambers in the Courts of Cambodia. She holds a Ph.D. in international law from Renmin University, China. Her main research interest is international criminal law and procedure.

[1] See, for example, Richard H. Minear, *Victors' Justice: The Tokyo War Crimes Trial*, Princeton University Press, Princeton, NJ, 1971; M. Cherif Bassiouni, "Justice and Peace: The Importance of Choosing Accountability over Realpolitik", in *Case Western Reserve Journal of International Law*, 2003, vol. 35, no. 2, pp. 196–97; Matthew Lippman, "Prosecutions of Nazi War Criminals before Post-World War II Domestic Tribunals", in *University of Miami International and Comparative Law Review*, 1999/2000, vol. 8, p. 112.

[2] Simon Chesterman, "International Criminal Law with Asian Characteristics?", in *Columbia Journal of Asian Law*, 2014, vol. 27, no. 2, pp. 131, 143 ff.

[3] See, for example, ZHAO Lang, LIAO Xiaoqing and ZHANG Qiang, "沈阳审判与纽伦堡、东京、南京审判比较研究" [Comparative Study of the Shenyang Trials and the Nuremberg, Tokyo and Nanjing Trials], in 辽宁大学学报（哲学社会科学版）[Journal of

---

trast, others defend these trials by emphasising their adherence to judicial guarantees despite the political dimensions.[4] Both attitudes are based on the same presumption, that is, politics is an "evil" that should be separated from judicial processes. The latter should be "pure" and "just", and that means staying away from "dirty" politics.

This chapter considers it over-simplistic to make such a clear-cut separation between justice and politics, and to render it as a black-and-white dichotomy. By examining the trials of Japanese war criminals by both the Nationalist government in the immediate aftermath of the Second World War and by the People's Republic of China ('PRC') in the 1950s, the chapter seeks to demonstrate how politics plays out in the design and operation of judicial mechanisms. It argues that in a complex social background as existed at the end of a war, judicial proceedings are only one of the means available to meet the various needs of society. Justice might not be the sole, or the most important, goal of the judicial process, which might be designed and used by the decision makers to facilitate other priorities, such as the very existence of the nation or regime, or the maintenance of order and stability.

10.2. War Crimes Trials in China after the Second World War

As part of the Allied efforts in trying war criminals after the war, criminal trials of atrocities committed by the Japanese were carried out throughout China, as well as in Hong Kong, after the surrender of Japan. The Hong Kong trials were conducted by the British authorities and are thus not covered in this chapter.[5] The trials conducted throughout China are referred to in this chapter as the Nationalist trials, as they were conducted under the auspices of the Nationalist government. Less well know are the trials conducted by the PRC ('PRC trials') in 1956 of former Japanese soldiers or Kempeitai (Japanese military police) members transferred

---

Liaoning University (Philosophy and Social Sciences)], 2009, vol. 37, no. 6, pp. 65, 68–69.

[4] See, for example, YAN Haijian, "法理与罪责：国民政府对战犯谷寿夫审判的再认识" [Legal Principles and Responsibility for Crimes: Re-evaluate the Nationalist Government's Trial of the War Criminal Tani Hisao], in 江海学刊 [Jianghai Academic Journal], 2013, vol. 6, pp. 162–170.

[5] For a detailed account of the Hong Kong trials, see Suzannah Linton (ed.), *Hong Kong's War Crimes Trials*, Oxford University Press, Oxford, 2013.

from the Soviet Union. This section provides a brief account of both trials.

10.2.1. The Nationalist Trials

The Chinese national trials of class B and class C Japanese war criminals started in December 1945. Trials were conducted in 10 military tribunals established in Beijing, Shenyang, Nanjing, Guangzhou, Jinan, Hankou, Taiyuan, Shanghai, Xuzhou and Taipei. The preparation for the national trials actually commenced well before the end of the war. In October 1943 the Allied Powers set up the United Nations War Crimes Commission ('UNWCC') to investigate war crimes.[6] In 1944 a Sub-Commission of the UNWCC was established in Chongqing (Chungking) to examine evidence for atrocities committed in the Asia-Pacific region. The UNWCC and its Sub-Commission did not themselves carry out investigations. The investigations were conducted by national authorities which reported their findings to the UN commissions. In China, a National Office was established to investigate cases, reporting to the Chongqing Sub-Commission.

The Chinese National Office progressed rather slowly at the beginning due to various practical reasons as well as deficiencies concerning its structure and personnel.[7] It was reorganised in July 1945 and functioned more efficiently afterwards. It managed to take up some 170,000 cases and draw up a list of about 100 Japanese war criminals.[8] Further, the Executive Yuan promulgated the Investigation Guidelines on the Crimes of the Enemy in 1945, requiring local authorities across the country to conduct investigations of crimes committed by the Japanese during the war.[9] Through these nationwide investigations, considerable amounts of testimony were collected from victims and witnesses.

---

[6] For a more detailed account on the establishment of the UNWCC, see M.E. Bathurst, "The United Nations War Crimes Commission", in *American Journal of International Law*, 1945, vol. 39, no. 3, p. 565. The entire unrestricted part of the UNWCC archive is available in a designated collection in the ICC Legal Tools Database (http://www.casematrixnetwork.org/icc-legal-tools-database/).

[7] LAI Wen-Wei, "Forgiven and Forgotten: The Republic of China in the United Nations War Crimes Commission", in *Columbia Journal of Asian Law*, 2012, vol. 25, no. 2, p. 330.

[8] *Ibid.*, p. 331.

[9] LIU Tong, "国民政府审判日本战犯概述 (1945–1949)" [Overview of the Trials of Japanese War Criminals by the Kuomintang Government, 1945–1949], in 民国档案 [The Republic of China Archives], January 2014, p. 75.

Despite the efforts the Nationalist government, the investigations remained very difficult and the evidence collected was limited. On the one hand, the political situation at that time prevented the Nationalist government from moving into many of the rural areas controlled by the Chinese Communist Party ('CCP') where some of the worst atrocities were committed.[10] On the other hand, the displacement of civilians during the war made it difficult for local authorities to contact people under their jurisdiction. Further, very often the victims and witnesses were not able to identify the perpetrators when recounting the atrocities.[11] Thus, although a large amount of testimony was collected, much of it could not be used as evidence in a criminal trial.

From 1945 to 1947, 2,435 Japanese defendants were tried before the 10 tribunals. Of them 149 were sentenced to death.[12] The trials were based on several pieces of legislation promulgated by the Nationalist government concerning war crimes trials.[13] The basic legal instrument and foundation for these trials was the Law Governing the Trials of War Criminals, promulgated in October 1946. The law listed 38 war crimes, including murder, killing hostages, rape, using gas, torture, the mistreatment of prisoners of war, destroying religious or historical building or memorials and so on.

10.2.2. The PRC Trials

Because of the high profile of the Nanjing Massacre, the Nanjing trials were perhaps the best known of all the trials conducted by the Nationalist government. Less well known are the atrocities that occurred in other parts of the country, for example the north-east, a region which had been occupied by Japan since 1931, long before the general war started in

---

[10] *Ibid.*, p. 76.

[11] *Ibid.*

[12] *Ibid.*, p. 72.

[13] These included the National Government Law Governing the Trials of War Criminals (国民政府关于战犯审判条例), Military Commission Rules Governing the Trials of War Criminals (军事委员会关于战犯审判办法); Measures for the Implementation of the Military Commission Rules on Trials of War Criminals (军事委员会关于战犯审判办法试行细则), all promulgated in 1946, reprinted in HU Jurong (ed.), 南京大屠杀史料集 24：南京审判 [Collection of Historical Materials on the Nanking Massacre, vol. 24: The Nanjing Trials], Phoenix Publishing, Jiangsu Renmin Press, Nanjing, 2006, pp. 28–46.

1937. The north-east bore the full brunt of the unspeakable violence and brutality of the notorious Kempeitai throughout the occupation. However, although the Nationalist government sought to investigate the war crimes committed in the north-east and try those responsible it was unable to do so because the Japanese Guandongjun army (关东军) in the north-east numbered 664,000, surrendered to the Soviet Union, and around half a million of them were sent to Siberia for hard labour.[14] The Nationalist government's request to the Soviet Union for extradition of the suspects never received a response.[15]

It was only after the establishment of the PRC that the Soviet Union made the political decision to transfer the war crimes suspects among those captured back to China. Some of this group, sent to China in 1950, became the defendants at the PRC trials in 1956. The Soviet Union transferred 969 Japanese internees to the PRC.[16] They were then interned at the Fushun war criminals management centre. Another 140 Japanese fighting alongside the Kuomintang against the CCP were captured during the Chinese civil war and interned at the Taiyuan management centre. Altogether, there were 1,109 Japanese internees in China as of late 1950. The transfer of the internees from the Soviet Union was conducted with the understanding that the newly established PRC would try the suspects, as a symbolic event in exercising its sovereignty as an independent state. Investigations of the alleged war crimes started as early as January 1951,[17] but were soon interrupted, as the priority for the PRC at that time was clearly the Korean War. They only resumed in late 1953, after the end of the Korean War.

---

[14] The Soviet Union People's Defence Committee, Resolution No. 9898 on Accepting and Settling Down Japanese Prisoners of War for Labour, cited in CUI Jianping, "苏联政府战后对日战俘的政策评析" [Analysis on the Soviet Unions's Policy on Japanese Prisoners of War after the War], in 俄罗斯中亚东欧研究 [Study on Russia, Middle Asia and East Europe], 2009, vol. 2, p. 76.

[15] LIU, 2014, p. 82, see *supra* note 9.

[16] The word "internee" is used because their status is rather hard to determine at this point of time. Many might have qualified as prisoners of war as such; many others might not. Note also that in the official documents of the PRC at that time the term used to refer to these prisoners was "战犯", war criminals.

[17] See 关于侦查处理在押日本战争犯罪分子的通知 [Notice about Investigating Japanese War Criminals in Detention], announced by the Supreme People's Procuratorate and the Ministry of Public Security, 16 January 1951.

From the very beginning, the issue of how to deal with the Japanese internees was never seen as a purely juridical endeavour but also, and even more so, a political one. The process was thus always under the close monitoring of the very top of the CCP leadership. In 1955, when the Supreme People's Procuratorate working group in charge of the investigation concluded its work, it submitted its reports directly to the CCP Central Committee, the highest decision-making body within the CCP structure. Replying to the working group reports, Premier ZHOU Enlai instructed that a "policy of leniency" (宽大政策) was to be adopted. There would be no death sentence, no life imprisonment and only a small number of individuals would be put on trial.[18]

As China did not yet have a Criminal Code, the Standing Committee of the National People's Congress, the highest legislative body, adopted a special decision in April 1956 on the trials of the Japanese internees in Fushun and Taiyuan: the Decision on Dealing with the Detained War Criminals during the Japanese Aggressive War against China.[19] ZHOU's policy of leniency was officially stipulated in the preamble of this decision. The decision contained a rather brief six-provision text, including both the substantive and procedural rules to be followed at the trials.

Following the adoption of the National People's Congress decision, the trials took place in June to July 1956 in Shenyang and Taiyuan before two *ad hoc* military tribunals of the Supreme People's Court. Among the more than one thousand internees, only 45 were tried. The others were announced "exempt from prosecution", released and returned to Japan.[20] The 45 defendants who were selected to stand on trial because of the seriousness of their crimes were all convicted, with sentence terms ranging

---

[18] YUAN Qiubai and YANG Guizhen (eds.), 罪恶的自供状：新中国对日本战犯的历史审判 [The Confession of Guilt: New China's Historic Trials of Japanese War Criminals], Chinese People's Liberation Army Publishing House, Beijing, 2001, pp. 20–21.

[19] In Chinese, 关于处理在押日本侵略中国战争中战争犯罪分子的决定. See WANG Zhanping *et al.* (eds.), 正义的审判：最高人民法院特别军事法庭审判日本战犯纪实 [Just Trials: Documents of the Trials of Japanese War Criminals before the Ad Hoc Military Tribunals of the Supreme People's Court], People's Court Publishing, Beijing, 1991, p. 2.

[20] JIN Yuan, "再生之路—改造日本战犯的回忆" [The Journey to a New Life: Memories of Transforming the Japanese War Criminals], in 人民公安 [People's Public Security], 2000, vol. 8, p. 62.

from eight to 20 years.[21] The terms of their detention before trial were deducted from their prison terms.[22] Many of them received further deductions of their prison terms because of good behaviour. By 1964 all convicted war criminals – except for one who died of illness in prison – were released and returned to Japan.[23]

The 1956 PRC trials are in many ways fundamentally different from the Allied trials immediately after the Second World War. One very special feature worth mentioning here is the fact that all defendants at the trials pleaded guilty, showed great repentance, and some even pleaded for a severe penalty to be meted out.[24] Furthermore, after returning to Japan, the former internees in Fushun and Taiyuan devoted the rest of their lives to pacifist movements. They established the well-known pacifist organisation, Association of Returnees from China (中国归还者联络会, often abbreviated to Chukiren according to its Japanese pronunciation), carrying out anti-war and pacifist campaigns, and promote friendly relations between China and Japan.

The reason for this change was certainly not only the 1956 trials, but should be attributed mainly to the six-year "re-education and reform" process after their transfer from the Soviet Union. This was a process in which the internees received anti-militarism reading materials, participated in study and discussion sessions, and in the so-called "public confession" and "public accusation" sessions, where they revealed their own or others' criminal deeds.[25] While the Chukiren's pacifist efforts are widely respected, this "re-education" process and the methods adopted during it have been subjected to many controversies. At that time, in particular, the process was labelled as "brainwashing" both in the West and in Japan.[26] The legality and legitimacy of this process are beyond the scope of this

---

21   The two military tribunals issued four judgments. WANG, 1991, pp. 320–49, 495–504, 660–74, 729–32, see *supra* note 19.

22   See the judgments, *ibid*.

23   JIN, 2000, p. 62, see *supra* note 20.

24   See the transcripts of the trials, in WANG, 1991, *supra* note 19.

25   For a detailed account of the process of "re-education" and various means used, see XIONG Kan, 新中国处理日本战犯问题研究—过渡司法的视角 [New China's Dealing with Japanese War Criminals: From the Perspective of Transitional Justice], Ph.D. Dissertation, Renmin University of China, 2010, pp. 124–53.

26   Barak Kushner, *Men to Devils, Devils to Men: Japanese War Crimes and Chinese Justice*, Harvard University Press, Cambridge, MA, 2005, pp. 280, 294.

chapter, but in the next section the question of why and how this process was designed and carried out will be examined further, in order to help understand the politics involved in post-war dealings with war criminals.

10.3. Justice and Politics

The PRC trials were conducted under a clear policy of leniency, explicitly stipulated in the National People's Congress decisions. Interestingly, the Nationalist trials, though without an explicit legal pronouncement of a leniency principle, were also conducted under an overarching "magnanimous" policy announced by CHIANG Kai-shek immediately after the surrender of Japan. With their many differences, both endeavours amply demonstrate how political considerations and the quest for justice mingled in the post-war context.

10.3.1. The Nationalist Trials: "To repay hatred with kindness"

Almost immediately after the surrender of Japan, CHIANG delivered a speech in which he announced what was later to be called the "magnanimous" policy or the policy of "to repay hatred with kindness".[27] The speech emphasised that the "real victory" was not winning the war, but to make sure that "this war is the last war of civilised nations of the world".[28] For that purpose, CHIANG urged the Chinese people to uphold the Chinese tradition of "forgiving old wrongs" (不念旧恶) and to "be kind to others" (与人为善), and not to seek revenge or insult the "innocent people of the enemy".[29]

Though this was only a short speech delivered on radio, what CHIANG announced became the overarching guideline for the Nationalist government's foreign policy towards Japan after the war. The Japanese

---

[27] YUAN Chengyi, "战后蒋介石对日'以德报怨'政策的几个问题" [Several Issues Concerning Chiang Kai-shek's 'Magnanimous' Policy Towards Japan After the War], in 抗日战争研究 [Anti-Japan War Study], 2006, no. 1, p. 212.

[28] CHIANG Kai-shek, "抗戰勝利告全國軍民及全世界人士書" [Announcement to the Soldiers and People of the Whole Nation and People of the Whole World], in 總統蔣公思想言論總集（第三十二卷）[The Whole Collection of President Chiang's Thoughts and Speeches], vol. 32, Party History Committee of the Central Committee of China Nationalist Party, Taipei, 1984, p. 122.

[29] *Ibid.*, p. 123.

historian Iechika Ryoko even considered that this speech "determined [...] the basic structure of post-war China-Japan relations".[30] Unsurprisingly, the war crimes trials were also conducted under this overarching policy.

In October 1946, in preparing for the trials, the Commission on Dealing with War Criminals (战争罪犯处理委员会) held a meeting to discuss the policy on the forthcoming war crimes trials. The main agenda of the meeting was to discuss a proposal of the Second Bureau of the Ministry of Defence (国防部第二厅), in charge of dealing with war criminals. Before the specific proposal was put forward and discussed, the minister of defence, BAI Chongxi of the Nationalist government, spoke first. BAI mentioned CHIANG's speech and emphasised the "magnanimous" policy. He proposed that the policy on war crimes should follow the spirit of the speech, balance justice and the friendship between the two nations, and should be "lenient while not granting impunity" (宽而不纵).[31] In accordance with this guideline, the specific proposal concerning war crimes trials by the Second Bureau said that the "most important Japanese war criminals" should be tried and punished, but for other less important ones a policy of leniency was to be followed.[32] This proposal was largely endorsed at the meeting and the "lenient while not granting impunity" principle later became the guiding policy for the Nationalist trials.

According to the decision of the meeting, the principal war criminals of the Nanjing Massacre and other large-scale massacres were to be severely punished. For the trials of other war crimes, "leniency and promptness" should be the guiding principles.[33] All trials were expected to be concluded before the end of 1946. Suspects of less severe crimes were to be exempted from prosecution and repatriated. Suspects who per-

---

30 Iechika Ryoko, "蒋介石外交战略中的对日政策—作为其归结点的'以德报怨'讲话" [Japan Policy in Chiang Kai-Shek's Diplomatic Strategy: The "To Repay Hatred with Kindness Speech" as its Summary] in 近代中国与世界—第二届近代中国与世界学术讨论会论文集（第三卷）[Modern Times China and the World: Symposium of the Second Modern Times China and the World Academic Conference], vol. 3, Social Sciences Academic Press, Beijing, 2005, p. 273.

31 ZUO Shuangwen, "国民政府与惩处日本战犯几个问题的再考察" [Re-examining Several Issues concerning ROC and Punishing Japanese War Criminals], in 社会科学研 [Social Science Research], 2012, vol. 6, 2012, p. 151.

32 *Ibid.*

33 *Ibid.*

formed their duty well in the surrender process should also be treated differently, with the specifics to be decided after the end of the Tokyo trials.[34]

The Nationalist government's adoption of the magnanimous policy towards Japan was the result of the complicated political context of post-war China, and especially the looming civil war between the Kuomintang and the CCP. After the official surrender of Japan announced by Emperor Hirohito, there were still more than a million Japanese troops in China, practically controlling a large part of the country.[35] The smooth surrender of these troops required co-operation on the Japanese side. More importantly, CHIANG intended to encourage the Japanese to surrender only to the Nationalist government, and not to the CCP. Added to CHIANG's concerns was the fact that the bulk of the Nationalist forces were in the government-controlled areas, while the CCP presence in Japanese-controlled areas was significant.[36] Thus CHIANG had to make sure the Japanese troops would not surrender to the CCP forces which were geographically closer to them. CHIANG's speech successfully served this purpose. According to Okamura Yasuji, the commander-in-chief of the Japanese China Expeditionary Army, the Japanese troops under his command did hold their position against the CCP and surrendered only to Kuomintang forces.[37] The Kuomintang thus also felt a need to "reward" the Japanese commanders for this, for preserving order among the Japanese troops and facilitating the surrender process.

However, these political considerations and the decisions made accordingly were against the public sentiment of the time. The general public longed for justice. People expected trials and due punishment of those responsible. The investigation of war crimes and the subsequent trials at-

---

34 Research Association of Diplomatic Issues of the Republic of China (ed.), 中日外交史料丛编 (七): 日本投降与我国对日态度及对俄交涉 [Compilation of Historical Materials concerning China-Japan Diplomacy, vol. 7: The Surrender of Japan, Our Country's Attitude towards Japan and Negotiations with Russia], Kuomintang Central Committee, Taipei, 1995, pp. 458–59.

35 Imai Takeo, 今井武夫回忆录 [Memoirs of Imai Takeo], trans. Compilation and Translation Commission of the Tianjin Municipal People's Political Consultative Conference, China Culture and History Publishing, Beijing, 1987, p. 233.

36 YAN Haijian, "宽大抑或宽纵：战后国民政府对日本战犯处置论析" [Magnanimity or Impunity: Analysis on the Nationalist Government's Treatment of Japanese War Criminals after the War], in 南京社会科学 [Nanjing Social Sciences] 2014, vol. 7, p. 144.

37 Okamura's testimony at court, see *Takung Pao* [大公报], 24 August 1948.

tracted extensive public attention. In Nanjing, for example, an investigation commission was established and witnesses and victims could report cases and make claims to the commission. The commission received thousands of such reports.[38] The Nationalist government's magnanimous policy thus had to be carried out under pressure from the public.[39] Even within the Nationalist government, there existed different voices. This tension was perhaps most manifest in the Okamura case.

As noted, Okamura was the commander-in-chief of the China Expeditionary Army at the time of Japan's surrender. Before that, he had also been extensively involved in many other major battlefields across China since 1932. The Nationalist government's treatment of Okamura attracted tremendous public attention and controversy. He was listed as a major war criminal on the Communists' list, and also considered by the public as "the number one Japanese war criminal in China".[40] Even Okamura himself deemed a trial and his own death sentence "inevitable".[41] However, as the Nationalist government needed Okamura to maintain order among the one million Japanese troops after the surrender, they initially postponed his arrest and trial. Later, as Okamura did help to maintain order and, more importantly, held his troops against the CCP and only surrendered to the Nationalist government, within the government many felt that he should be "rewarded" for his co-operation.[42] Being an "expert" in fighting the CCP, Okamura also provided military advice to the Nationalist government, thus making himself an experienced and important military adviser for the government.[43]

---

[38] YAN Haijian, "国民政府对南京大屠杀案审判的社会影响论析" [Analysis on the Social Impact of the Nationalist Government's Trials of the Nanjing Massacre Case], in 福建论坛（人文社会科学版）, [Fujian Tribune (Humanities and Social Sciences)], 2011, vol. 4, pp. 109–10.

[39] *Ibid.*, p. 111.

[40] *China Press*, 3 and 14 August 1948 and 22 December 1945, cited in Philip R. Piccigallo, *The Japanese on Trial: Allied War Crimes Operations in the East, 1945–1951*, University of Texas Press, Austin, 1979, p. 155.

[41] Inaba Masao, 冈村宁次回忆录 [Memoirs of Okamura Yasuji], trans. Compilation and Translation Commission of the Tianjin Municipal People's Political Consultative Conference, Zhonghua Book Company, Tianjin, 1981, p. 142.

[42] ZUO, 2012, pp. 153–54, see *supra* note 31.

[43] *Ibid.*, p. 154.

For these reasons, the Nationalist government tried everything to shield Okamura from being prosecuted. Faced by the pressure from the Chinese general public, when they found it impossible to avoid a trial, the Nationalist government put Okamura on the defendant's stand, with a personal guarantee to Okamura that the death penalty was out of the question and that a prison sentence, if that verdict should arise, would not need to actually be served.[44] In the end, the verdict was beyond even Okamura's own expectation: not guilty. As Okamura himself recalled in his memoirs, upon the announcement of the verdict, the courtroom was in an uproar and he had to escape by the back door.[45] Okamura also stated that he "hoped" to receive a prison sentence, as that would "seem to be better".[46] This was not the result of an ordinarily functioning criminal justice process, but of personal interference from the very top of the Nationalist government leadership, and even CHIANG himself.[47]

The Okamura trial serves as a vivid example of how tensions between politics and justice play out. In particular, as war crimes trials often involve complex social and political contexts, it is certainly not rare that justice may not be deemed the priority. For the Nationalist government in the aftermath of the war, to guarantee a smooth surrender process of the one million Japanese troops and to win the imminent civil war with the CCP seemed to be more important than seeking justice. History is full of examples of this kind. The CCP fiercely criticised the Nationalist government for their "over-leniency" towards war criminals, and especially Okamura, demanding that he should be arrested again and tried by the CCP.[48] But in 1950s, faced with a new historical context, they decided to adopt an even more lenient policy, which was also against public sentiment.

---

44 Inaba, pp. 148, 150–54, see *supra* note 41.

45 *Ibid.*, p. 159.

46 *Ibid.*

47 *Ibid.*, pp. 150–51, 154.

48 This included statements by MAO Zedong, as well as editorials published in leading CCP newspapers. See ZHAO Shemin and MENG Guoxiang, "中共审判日本战犯工作述评" [Recounts and Comments on the CCP's Trials of Japanese War Criminals], 南京社会科学 [*Social Sciences in Nanjing*], 2009, vol. 8, p. 98. For the original text of MAO's statements, see 毛泽东选集（第四卷）[Selected Works of MAO Zedong], vol. 4, People's Publishing House, Beijing, 1991, pp. 1393–1403.

10.3.2. The PRC Trials: "Now that they are released, we should become friends"

The Nationalist government's magnanimous policy was announced by CHIANG through a broadcast speech and served as an overarching guiding principle for the trials. The PRC's policy of leniency, on the other hand, was officially adopted by a National People's Congress decision. The decision explicitly provided that "leniency in sentencing" was to be applied even to "war criminals who committed serious crimes", and that early release shall be possible in the case of good behaviour in prison.[49] It is worth remembering that the CCP strongly criticised the Nationalist government's leniency toward the Japanese war criminals; the Chinese general public still held a strong anti-Japanese sentiment and still considered that the Nationalist government failed to duly punish some of the main actors during the war, Okamura included. Why then, was such policy of "extraordinary leniency", which "ran counter to domestic anti-Japanese sentiment" adopted?[50]

When Premier ZHOU instructed that a policy of leniency was to be taken towards the Japanese internees transferred from the Soviet Union, many of the staff of the Fushun management centre, as well as members of the Supreme People's Procuratorate working group in charge of the investigations, found it difficult to appreciate the instruction,[51] let alone the general public. In his reply to the working group's report, ZHOU explained that he expected those Japanese internees, after being released and returned to Japan, could serve as "messengers".[52] He hoped that they could "tell the Japanese people what we the Chinese communists are really like [...] their words will carry more weight than what we Chinese communists say ourselves".[53] Thus, the 1956 PRC trials, conducted under the leniency policy, together with the "exemption from prosecution" and release of the majority of the Japanese internees, were meant to be a "friendly gesture", showing Japan the Chinese people's will to move on from the past and build new relations. The political and diplomatic aims

49 WANG, 1991, p. 2, see *supra* note 19.
50 Chesterman, 2014, p. 147, see *supra* note 2.
51 YUAN and YANG, 2001, p. 15, see *supra* note 18.
52 *Ibid.*, p. 21.
53 *Ibid.*

of restoring relations with Japan practically guided the design of the judicial process of release and trials.

Throughout the entire process, it was clear that the handling of the Japanese internees was deemed "not only a legal problem, but also a political problem".[54] In his speech at a meeting of the Standing Committee of the Chinese People's Political Consultative Conference, ZHOU explained in detail what he expected to be the "impact" of release: that the released internees would "say some good words" (说几句好话) about China.[55] Before the release, the PRC even organised tours for the former internees across the country, so that they could be left with "a good impression",[56] as ZHOU put it. "Now that they are released, we should become friends".[57]

At the same time, the PRC leadership was also keen to show the world that the new China was willing and able to handle the war criminals legally. The official records concerning the whole process show clearly that legal issues were always at the centre of the discussions.[58] Law was used as an instrument to achieve political goals, but it sometimes also became an obstacle to those goals. There was thus much struggling among the leadership to try to achieve their political goals without breaching legal principles.

One of the main legal issues discussed extensively was the applicable law. In 1956 China was still 23 years away from adopting its first Criminal Code. Neither were there any special laws or regulations on war crimes. Earlier drafts of the National People's Congress decision referred to "the principles of the Nuremberg and the Far East Military Tribunals",[59] or "well-established international law, especially laws and cus-

---

[54] Ministry of Foreign Affairs Archives ('MFA Archives'), 关于释放日本战犯问题的请示件、报告、命令等 [Requests, Reports and Instructions concerning the Issue of Releasing Japanese War Criminals], file no. 105-00220-06.

[55] ZHOU Enlai, "在二届政协常委会十九次会议（扩大）上的发言（一九五六年三月十四日）" [Speech at the 19th (Expanded) Meeting of the Standing Committee of the Second CPPCC (March 14, 1956)], in 党的文献 [Party Documents], 1995, no. 2, p. 20.

[56] *Ibid.*

[57] *Ibid.*

[58] The relevant official records and documents are available at the Chinese Ministry of Foreign Affairs Archives.

[59] MFA Archives, 关于处理在押日本战争罪犯的请示报告 [Report and Request of Instructions on How to Deal with the Japanese War Criminals in Detention], Annex, file no. 105-00501-02(2), 7 November 1955.

toms of war" as applicable law.[60] But these references were later deleted from the final draft. The ostensible reason was that this would not be in compliance with the newly promulgated 1954 Constitution, which required that international law could only be applied after being incorporated by domestic law.[61] However, the Supreme People's Procuratorate working group also mentioned that China "had not formally recognised international law",[62] and thus referring to international law might "give rise to some international controversies".[63] What exactly the expected "controversies" might be was not clearly stated. It seems that there was general distrust of international law and even the outside world. As it was deemed unpredictable what problems might arise if international law were to be applied, the safer choice would be to avoid referring to international law altogether. This distrust could be further observed in the discussions concerning a public trial. The PRC leadership struggled between a desire to send a message to the world, and deep concerns about foreign interference.

It was clear from very early on in the process that the PRC intended the trials of the Japanese war criminals to carry a message. They did not want the trials to be "just a formality".[64] They should be "serious", be "public propaganda and education to the Japanese people, and a public strike and fight against Japanese militarists".[65] The trials should thus obviously be held in public. However, the CCP leadership were also worried that if the news of the trials were announced, Japan would send people to attend them. While it would be difficult to refuse such a request, the leadership was worried that they would send people to deliberately carry out "sabotage activities" (破坏工作), such as encouraging the defendants to

---

60   MFA Archives, 关于审判日本战犯和伪满汉奸的请示报告 [Report and Request of Instructions on Trying the Japanese War Criminals and the Chinese Traitors of the Puppet Manchuria Regime], file no. 105-00501-06, 20 February–27 March 1956.

61   *Ibid.*

62   MFA Archives, 关于侦查日本战犯的主要情况和处理意见的报告等 [Reports about the Main Situation of Investigating Japanese War Criminals and about How to Proceed], Annex (1), file no. 105-00501-07, 16 March 1956.

63   *Ibid.*

64   MFA Archives, 关于处理在押日本战争罪犯的请示报告 [Report and Request of Instructions on How to Deal with the Japanese War Criminals in Detention], Annex, file no. 105-00501-02(2), 7 November 1955.

65   *Ibid.*

retract their confessions.[66] After many discussions, the final solution was to withhold the news about the trials until they actually started.[67] Thus the trials were theoretically still "public", but there would be no time for Japan or other countries to request attendance. Nevertheless, the PRC could still be able to claim that the trials were indeed held publicly.[68]

The tensions between political needs and legal requirements were obvious in the 1956 trials, as much as they were in the Nationalist government trials 10 years earlier. These two endeavours, though conducted by two opposing authorities of China at different stages of history, shared many similarities. Both were clearly designed and guided by political considerations. Both the Nationalist government and the PRC recognised the role of international law, and tried to comply with that body of law in seeking their respective political goals. But both followed a pragmatic approach towards the law. As Simon Chesterman puts it, they focused on "'output' legitimacy rather than input legitimacy".[69] They adapted international rules to their own political needs, and sought their own way out in their complex historical and political contexts. Today it might be more difficult to "adapt" international law in such ways, especially for international courts, but it is undeniable that law and politics still, and will always, mingle with each other, especially in situations involving international crimes.

10.4. Conclusion

From this account of the trials of Japanese war criminals in China, the interrelationship of law and politics is obvious, as was the case for the Nuremberg and Tokyo trials. However, it seems that today's international tribunals, as well as legal scholars, tend to view international trials as totally independent from politics, and international tribunals as apolitical institutions. Or at least, they seem to deem this the "ordinary" or "ideal" situation. International criminal proceedings should be "purely" judicial, since anything "political" becomes an "evil" that should be avoided.

---

[66] *Ibid.*

[67] *Ibid.*

[68] MFA Archives, "外宾对释放日本战犯可能提出的若干问题及回答提纲草稿", [Questions that Foreign Guests May Raise Concerning Releasing Japanese War Criminals and Draft Outline of Answers], file no. 105-00502-03, 29 April 1956.

[69] Chesterman, 2014, pp. 155–56, see *supra* note 2.

This attitude can be easily observed from some court documents or public statements of court officials. For example, the Office of the Prosecution of the International Criminal Court ('ICC') has made clear in a policy paper that the prosecutor is not concerned with considerations other than legal ones.[70] The then president of the ICC, Judge Philippe Kirsch, declared in 2006: "There's not a shred of evidence after three-and-a-half years that the court has done anything political. The court is operating purely judicially".[71] The Registry of the ICC also deemed the Court "*un organe judiciaire, lequel n'a pas vocation à être une tribune politique*".[72] These statements seem to presume that law and politics can be completely separated. The ICC, being a judicial organ, should operate "purely judicially", not with "a shred of" political influence. However, it is doubtful whether such an ideal apolitical process could actually exist, especially in terms of international tribunals and trials of international crimes. Obviously, the creation of international courts and tribunals is a political process. In the ICC's case, the drafting of its Statute was a political process and the final text reflects political compromise. In terms of its operation, political influence in the selection and initiation of a situation or case is obvious, no matter whether in the case of self-referral of a state or a UN Security Council referral. Even when the prosecutor initiates an investigation *proprio motu*, it is doubtful whether the decision could possibly be "purely" judicial.[73]

---

70 International Criminal Court ('ICC'), Office of the Prosecutor, "Policy Paper on the Interests of Justice", ICC-OTP-2007, September 2007, p. 9 (http://www.legal-tools.org/doc/bb02e5/).

71 "Japan's Expected to Support International Criminal Court", in *Voice of America*, 6 December 2006 (www.voanews.com/content/a-13-2006-12-06-voa14/311910.html).

72 ICC, Situation in Darfur, Sudan, The Registry, Conclusions du Greffier en vertu de la Norme 24bis du Règlement de la Cour en Réponse au Document Intitulé "Clarification for the Record of Annex 4 to the Application under Rule 103", ICC-02/05-222, 1 May 2009, para. 6 (http://www.legal-tools.org/doc/6bde54/).

73 For more discussion on the selection of cases at the ICC and the political elements involved, see, for example, William A. Schabas, "Victor's Justice: Selecting 'Situations' at the International Criminal Court", in *Journal of Marshall Law Review*, vol. 43, 2010, p. 549; Charles Chernor Jalloh, "Regionalizing International Criminal Law?", in *International Criminal Law Review*, vol. 9, no. 3, 2009, pp. 462–65; Yves Beigbeder, *International Criminal Tribunals: Justice and Politics*, Palgrave Macmillan, London, 2011, pp. 241–42; discussions by Antonio Cassese, Andrew Clapham and others at a conference, the proceedings of which can be found in *Journal of International Criminal Justice*, vol. 7, no. 1, 2009, pp. 97–119.

It is true that once the trial proceedings start, the judicial mechanism would operate by their own means and the political dimensions become less visible. In today's international criminal courts and tribunals, especially those with a "pure" international character, political interference with trial proceedings *per se* is rather rare, if not completely absent. However, even the most "political" trials would have a "judicial" cloak. And this is often found in the proceedings. The proceedings of the PRC trials were the closest to legality that could obtain at that time. Given the historical background, the efforts the PRC put into to making the trials meet legal standards were remarkable. But at the same time, there is no doubt that even those efforts were made out of political considerations, not legal ones. It is meaningless to single out the trial proceedings and pretend that they could be separated from the other aspects mentioned above: the establishment of an institution, definition of jurisdiction, the prosecutorial decision of investigation and bringing a charge, and so forth.

To recognise the political dimensions in the operation of international criminal justice is not to criticise them or deny their importance. As Sarah M.H. Nouwen and Wouter G. Werner put it, this is just "its real place": "not above the political world but in its very midst".[74] Some have criticised the current mainstream discourse of ignoring the broader political-economic context, and warned against the risk that such an approach would discourage efforts to address the issue of violence from a more systematic and broader perspective.[75] Indeed, depending on the specific historical and political context, a society may have multiple issues to be dealt with and the pursuit of criminal justice might not always be the priority. In the Chinese experience, political considerations were obviously deemed more important than legal principles in the decision-making process concerning war criminals.

Today many legal doctrines and principles are already well recognised internationally and cannot be simply set aside as in the mid-twentieth century. However, political dimensions are still clearly visible in judicial processes and will continue to be so. Judicial proceedings are

---

[74] Sarah M.H. Nouwen and Wouter G. Werner, "Doing Justice to the Political: the International Criminal Court in Uganda and Sudan", in *European Journal of International Law*, vol. 21, no. 4, 2010, p. 942.

[75] See generally Tor Krever, "International Criminal Law: An Ideology Critique", in *Leiden Journal of International Law*, 2013, vol. 26, no. 3, pp. 701–23.

never solely about the "pure" task of determining innocence or guilt. They always happen against a certain political and social background, and will always be influenced by such a background. In reality, international criminal trials are often expected to serve broader social and political purposes, such as promoting reconciliation and contributing to lasting peace.[76] These goals are sometimes difficult to reconcile, and many have rightly argued the need to manage expectations and recognise the limitations of criminal proceedings.[77] It is, however, still important to acknowledge the existence of different needs a society faces during and after conflicts, and to recognise that international criminal proceedings will always operate within such a context. International criminal justice cannot, and need not, be separated from this reality to be successful, but can only be successful when being consciously operated within this reality.

---

[76] See, for example, Extraordinary Chambers in the Courts of Cambodia, Internal Rules, Preamble, referring to "national reconciliation, stability, peace and security"; Security Council Resolution 827 establishing the ICTY, recognizing that the establishment of the ICTY "would contribute to the restoration and maintenance of peace", SC Res. 827, U.N. Doc. S/RES/827(1993), 25 May 1993.

[77] See, for example, Brianne McGonigle Leyh, *Procedural Justice? Victim Participation in International Criminal Proceedings*, Intersentia, 2011, p. 365; Philippe Flory, "International Criminal Justice and Truth Commissions: From Strangers to Partners?", in *Journal of International Criminal Justice,* vol. 13, no. 1, 2015, pp. 24–6.

11

The Progress of Historical Documents Acquisition and Compilation on Japanese War Crimes Trials after the Second World War in the National Library of China

GAO Hong* and LI Dan**

11.1. Introduction

The National Library of China ('NLC') serves as the repository of the nation's publications, a national bibliographic centre, as well as a national centre for the preservation and conservation of ancient books. The major mission of the NLC includes: the collection and preservation of domestic and foreign publications; the national co-ordination of document preservation and conservation work; the provision of information and reference services to the central government, other governmental organisations, social organisations and the general public; research in library sciences, development of library services and programmes, and guidance to other libraries in China with its expertise; the fulfilment of its role in international cultural exchanges through participation in the activities of the International Federation of Library Associations and Institutions and other related organisations worldwide, as well as the promotion of exchanges and co-operation with other libraries in China and abroad.

The NLC hosts vast and comprehensive holdings, including extensive collections in foreign languages and many historical books. At pre-

---

* **GAO Hong** is Research Librarian of the National Library of China (the 'NLC'). She began her research on documents on the Japanese war crimes trials after the Second World War in 2011, and was one of the first participants of the Minguo Documents Preservation and Conservation Programme. She currently serves as the Director of the Co-ordination and Operation Management Division, Office of Minguo Documents Preservation Project of the NLC.

** **LI Dan** is a Librarian of the NLC, and became a staff member of the Co-ordination and Operation Management Division, Office of Minguo Documents Preservation Project of the NLC in 2012.

sent, the NLC's collection totals about 33 million volumes and artefacts. It is renowned for its collection of ancient and rare materials. The NLC hosts a digital collection of 874.5 terabytes.

The NLC generally collects Chinese documents by legal deposit, purchase and donation, and foreign documents usually by purchase and exchange to build up a high-quality base to preserve national literature and create a system of information resources with abundant content, various forms, complete species and definite characteristics. The general principles of acquisition at the NLC are as follows: comprehensively collecting Chinese resources and selectively collecting foreign-language resources; and more titles and fewer copies. The NLC comprehensively collects all available documents in Chinese. The NLC also has special collections of manuscripts documents, classical collection and revolutionary history.

The Nationalist period of the Republic of China (Minguo), from 1911 to 1949, was an important and special era in Chinese history, when new and old ideas, Chinese or foreign, from ancient times as well as modern times, collided. The confluence of ideas developed a special cultural landscape during a time of social transition. In 2011 the NLC and related institutions in the field officially launched the Minguo Documents Preservation and Conservation Programme to conduct a full rescue and preservation of Minguo materials. The project started in 2012. The NLC launched projects in literature surveys, overseas documents collection, and compilation and publication, with the accent on basic research, methodological enquiry, exchange and co-operation, as well as project planning. In 2011 a special office was created in the NLC to take charge of the organisation and co-ordination of the Minguo Documents Preservation and Conservation Programme, to finalise the organisational structure and rules and regulations, as well as to prescribe the standards of related activities. A specialist committee was established, recruiting renowned specialists and experts in the field. It convened the first working conference in order to facilitate the role of experts in advising and directing, and providing academic support for the preservation project.

Compiling a collection on Japanese war crimes trials after the Second World War is an important part of the Minguo Documents Preservation and Conservation Programme. In this regard, the NLC conducts comprehensive acquisition and compilation of these materials by personal interviews and through agents, especially for American and Japanese collections on the International Military Tribunal for the Far East ('IMTFE') in Tokyo, in order to enrich the NLC's collection and acquire historical materials dispersed both at home and abroad.

11.2. Collection of Documents on Japanese War Crimes Trials

11.2.1. Archives

Because the means of collection and classification of government archives in the United States and Japan are different, the archives on Japanese war crimes after the Second World War are scattered in different organisations under a wide diversity of topics. Some of them have been split on purpose by intelligence agencies to keep them confidential. It is very difficult to collect these scattered archive documents. In recent years the NLC has collected 2,311 volumes of microforms on the Japanese war crimes trials from the United States, Japan, Taiwan and other locations. At present, the following documents have been organised.

- 50,000 pages of transcripts of the proceedings of the IMTFE (in English)
- 28,000 pages of evidence and testimony of the IMTFE (in Japanese)
- 372 volumes of microforms of the International Prosecution Section, Supreme Commander for the Applied Powers
- 32,000 pages of court documents on the Manila Tribunal
- 62,000 pages of court documents on the Yokohama war crimes trials
- 385 volumes of microforms (1941–1945) of documents from the Research and Analysis Branch of the US Office of Strategic Services
- 19 volumes of microforms on meetings of the US Department of State
- 6 volumes of intelligence and research reports of the US Office of Strategic Services and Department of State, concerning post-war Japan, Korea and Southeast Asia

- 24 volumes of special confidential archives of the US Department of State, concerning Northeast Asia (1943–1956)
- 21 volumes of core confidential archives of the US Department of State, concerning the Far East (1945–1949)
- 42 volumes of diplomatic post records of the Japanese political adviser (1945–1952)

Furthermore, the collection also includes 156 volumes of microforms of defence documents of 6,202 items under 176 categories for the Tokyo trial in the collections of the National Archives of Japan, covering court documents, archives of important events during the invasion of China by the Japanese army, testimonies, telegraph messages, diaries, reports and evidence archives of different types.

These archives are large in number and diverse in content. Yet there is repeated content, so it is urgent to organise them, compile a catalogue, and establish a platform for public access and research for the academic community.

11.2.2. Monographs, Newspapers and Periodicals

There are about 300,000 books, 400,000 periodical volumes of 15,000 different titles, and 5,000 kinds of newspapers of the Minguo period in the NLC. Some of these newspapers provided follow-up reports at great length on the Japanese war crimes trials at the IMTFE. The contents of these reports covered the trials of class A, class B and class C war criminals at Tokyo, the Manila Tribunal, the Yokohama war crimes trials, the Khabarovsk war crimes trials, the trials conducted by the Nationalist government in China and so on. From the perspective of the media, these daily updated news reports contain both introductions to the process of the trials and comments from different perspectives. These materials not only provide us with a window onto the reports from news media but also the historical condition presented from that window. Similar to the archives, they are also important historical documents for research on the Tokyo trial. In 2013 the NLC started to collect and organise related reports from more than a hundred different newspapers.

Moreover, relevant monographs are also important parts of the Tokyo trial collection. The monographs in the NLC's collections could be roughly divided into foreign monographs and domestic monographs, which cover fields like research on the history of the Second World War, international relations, international politics, international law and so on. The collections of foreign libraries are comparatively comprehensive and cover most of the representative research monographs in English, Japanese, French, Russian and so on. Examples include Yuki Tanaka, Tim McCormack and Gerry Simpson's *Beyond Victor's Justice? The Tokyo War Crimes Trial Revisited*; Timothy P. Maga's *Judgment at Tokyo: The Japanese War Crimes Trials*; the Nanjing International Relief Committee's *Documents of the Nanking Safety Zone*. As important documents for us to understand the research dynamics of the Tokyo trial in foreign countries, they are also effective methods for us to acquire relevant information.

11.2.3. Photographs and Videos

The NLC has collected over 1,800 historical photographs of the Asian war crimes trials, 615 photographs of the Tokyo trial, more than 3,000 photographs of the crimes of the Japanese invaders and the battlefield during the invasion of China, over 500 images of related historical documents like the maps seized by the US army and the Soviet army, statistical reports on the construction of the Japanese navy, 16,000 photographs taken in the China-Burma-India theatre of war, and more than 30 video clips showing the history of the Second Sino-Japanese War.

11.3. Publication of Documents on Japanese War Crimes Trials

Based on its collection and relevant materials, the NLC has actively carried out the publication of documents on the Tokyo trial. So far the following documents have been published: *Transcripts of the Proceedings of the International Military Tribunal for the Far East* (80 volumes and three volumes of indexes, co-published in September 2013 with Shanghai Jiaotong University Press). The volumes cover all the transcripts of the proceedings of the IMTFE from 3 May 1946 to 12 November 1948. Filling the gap because of the long-term absence of first-hand historical materials of the Tokyo trial in China, these transcripts provide not only precious original historical materials for the study of the crimes of the Japanese army during the Second World War, modern Sino-Japanese relations, international politics, international law and so on, but they also provide an historical basis for current struggles between China and Japan. Therefore, this publication is of great historical and practical significance.

After these volumes, the NLC published a series of books, including documents on Japanese war crimes trials after the Second World War and historical documents on the Second Sino-Japanese War, forming a complete document system. Each of the major publications is summarised here.

11.3.1. Evidence of the International Military Tribunal for the Far East (50 Volumes)[1]

The contents of these volumes are the evidence documents in Japanese adopted by the IMTFE. There is a total of 28,000 pages of evidence for the court organised in 50 volumes. As an important part of the documents on the IMTFE proceedings, the evidence documents reveal the war crimes of Japan in China and Southeast Asia during the Second World War. The books were published in the end of 2014. Meanwhile, three volumes of *Index for Proper Names in Evidence Documents* are being edited.

11.3.2. Collection of the Historical Documents on Special Events and War Criminal Suspects of the International Prosecution Section (Part I, 30 Volumes)[2]

As important first-hand historical documents on the trials of Japanese war criminals at the IMTFE, these documents were published in 2015 and are complementary to *Transcripts of the Proceedings* and *Documents of the International Military Tribunal for the Far East: Evidence and Testimony* to constitute core historical documents of the trials of Japanese war criminals. The NLC has also collected about 40,000 pages of International Prosecution Section documents on special events and suspected war criminals in 73 microform volumes.

---

[1] National Library of China (ed.), Evidence of the International Military Tribunal for the Far East, NLC Press, Beijing, 2014.

[2] The International Prosecution Section ('IPS') was a specialised agency for Japanese war crimes trials after the Second World War to investigate, prosecute war criminals in the Far East and the Pacific. From the end of 1945 to early 1948 the IPS finished the preparations for the IMTFE, drafting of the Charter, the suspected war criminals interrogation, evidence investigation and collection, and so on. Documents collected by the IPS include evidence of Japanese war criminals, indictments, transcripts of the court proceedings, document evidence and the judgment of the court. They all constitute important first-hand information.

11.3.3. Transcripts of the Court Proceedings of the Yokohama War Crimes Trials (105 Volumes)[3]

The English version of *Transcripts of the Court Proceedings of the Yokohama War Crimes Trials* of about 60,000 pages in 105 volumes has been organised on the basis of the original transcripts of the court proceedings at Yokohama collected by the NLC and was published in September 2014.

11.3.4. Transcripts of the Court Proceedings of the Manila Tribunal (53 Volumes)[4]

The NLC has collected 32,000 pages of microforms on the Manila Tribunal in 34 volumes from US National Archives and Records Administration. Based on these documents, the 53-volume *Transcripts of the Court Proceedings of the Manila Tribunal* has been organised and was published in December 2014.

11.3.5. Collection of News Reports on Japanese War Crimes Trials after the Second World War (8 Volumes)[5]

The collection of about 6,000 news reports has been organised and published in April 2014 after searching for related themes in over a hundred different newspapers collected by the NLC in its holdings, including: *Ta Kung Pao* (大公报), *Shen Bao* (申报), *North China Daily News*, *South China Morning Post, The Times* (London), the *New York Times*, *Yomiuri Shimbun* (読売新聞), *Sin Chew Daily* (星洲日報) and *Sin Pin Daily* (星檳日報). The contents include the preparations before the trials, the proceedings of the IMTFE, the China-led trials, and the trials with the United States, Britain and other countries taking leading roles. Among these news materials, the China-led trials account for the majority of the volumes. This is the first time that news reports relating to the Japanese war crimes trials have been compiled.

---

[3] Japanese War Crimes Trials Documents Editorial Board (ed.), *Transcripts of the Court Proceedings of the Yokohama War Crimes Trials*, NLC Press, Beijing, 2014.

[4] Japanese War Crimes Trials Documents Editorial Board (ed.), *Transcripts of the Court Proceedings of the Manila Tribunal*, NLC Press, Beijing, 2014.

[5] Japanese War Crimes Trials Documents Editorial Board (ed.), *Collection of News Reports on Japanese War Crimes Trials after the Second World War*, NLC Press, Beijing, 2014.

11.3.6. Historical Photographs Collection of the Tokyo Trial (1 Volume)[6]

The photographic collection selected over 400 fine examples from the tens of thousands of historic pictures in the US National Archives. With captions for each of the photographs, the book presents the background to the founding of the IMTFE, the tribunal, the prosecutors and judges participating in the trials, the class A Japanese war criminals, scenes of the trial, the sentence of the court and so on, in a vivid form. Showing the whole process of the Tokyo trial visually deepens the readers' understanding and recognition of the IMTFE. The book was published in November 2014.

11.3.7. Khabarovsk War Crimes Trial

The historical documents on the Khabarovsk war crimes trial include the indictment, testimony of the defendants and witnesses, transcripts of the court proceedings, document evidence and the judgment of the court. The NLC has collected the confessions of Japanese war criminals on the launching of germ warfare that were made at trial, in both the original English version and the Chinese translation. Supporting literature is currently being collected.

11.3.8. Documents of the South Manchuria Railway Company

This collection covers the South Manchuria Railway Company clippings and investigation documents. The thematic clippings of the South Manchuria Railway Company, whose Investigation Department was Japan's largest intelligence agency in China, comprise information collected via hundreds of agents for nearly 30 years (1918–1945). These are the clippings with the widest coverage, the most comprehensive classification, and the greatest amount of information on China and north-east Asia from the 1920s to 1940s anywhere in the world. It is planned that several years will be needed to compile and publish the classified documents of the South Manchuria Railway clippings in about five parts with 200 volumes, each based on the collections in the NLC and the Institute of Modern His-

---

[6] Japanese War Crimes Trials Documents Editorial Board (ed.), *Historical Photographs Collection of the Tokyo Trial*, NLC Press, Beijing, 2014.

tory, Chinese Academy of Social Sciences. The first batch of publications is on politics, diplomacy and the military.

11.3.9. Historical Documents on the Second Sino-Japanese War

Chosen mainly from the collections in the NLC, Chongqing Library and the Institute of Modern History, this publication covers thousands of important documents with regard to politics, economics and the military during the Second Sino-Japanese War in over 300 volumes. The first part covers 500 military documents in 100 volumes. The contents include China's strategy and tactics against the Japanese army; a summary and records of military meetings; combat reports, records, deeds, summaries and self-criticism materials; combat illustrations for the army, navy and air force; and confidential documents captured from the Japanese army and diary abstracts. Most of the original documents were compiled by the Military Committee, the Ministry of Defence, the war zones, troops participating in the war or their commanders and were published during the war itself. These documents are the basic materials for research on the history of the Second Sino-Japanese War.

11.3.10. Documents on the Home Front in the Second Sino-Japanese War

This set of books is divided into three parts: politics, economy and culture. The plan is to edit and publish thousands of important documents on the home front during the Second Sino-Japanese War together with major libraries and archives in south-west China, covering the moving of factories to inland area, economic surveys, social profiles, local autonomy and so on. The completed set will be over 100 volumes. In addition, the Nationalist government of China established military courts for trials of class B and class C Japanese war criminals at 10 locations: Nanjing, Shanghai, Beijing, Wuhan, Guangzhou, Xuzhou, Jinan, Taiyuan, Shenyang and Taipei. We are also actively collecting the related documents on these trials.

11.4. Future Plans for Collecting and Compiling Historical Documents

An information centre of these documents will be established. Based on the documents on trials collected by the NLC and relying on its rich collection, we plan to establish a data centre of Japanese war crimes trials to focus on the collection, acquisition and translation of related historical documents. With the help of the academic resources of research institutions, we will turn the information centre into a platform for academic institutions and knowledge generation, integrating reports on academic dynamics, publications of the collections of the library, the construction of digital resources, and exchange of academic information to promote research on the Tokyo trial and related fields.

A thematic directory will be formed after extensive literature surveys. We will conduct related literature surveys on a comparatively large scale to fully grasp the situation of collections in libraries and archives at all levels, in the hands of private individuals and those scattered overseas. Based on the existing achievements, we will accelerate the work on making a union catalogue for these documents to form a subject directory on Japanese war crimes trials. We will also establish a unified national literature retrieval platform for the documents on Japanese war crimes trials to facilitate the use of these documents in academic research.

The overseas collection of related documents will be accelerated. The NLC will perform in-depth research on the historical documents on the Tokyo trial and continue to search for overseas archives related to the Japanese war crimes trials and the related historical documents of the Allies during the Second World War and other countries that suffered during the war. We will introduce them to China, and collect archives on the war crimes of Japan, old photographs of the Nationalist period and related historical documents on Japanese war crimes trials. Meanwhile, we will strengthen the research on the trials of Japanese war criminals in China and explore co-operation with the archives to search for documents on the trials and publish them as soon as possible.

The scale of documents publication and compilation will be expanded. At present, the NLC has already made a three-year plan for publishing archival and historical documents from the Nationalist period: a series of materials will be published on a large scale, including the series of Japanese war crimes trials, the series of historical documents on the Second Sino-Japanese War, and the series of historical documents on the frontiers of China. The detailed content will cover the documents on Japanese war crimes trials, documents on the home front during the Second Sino-Japanese War, the investigation documents of the South Manchuria

Railway Company, and archives and documents on the south-west frontier of China.

A database will be established. The digitalisation of related documents on the Tokyo trial will put these documents into different formats to support academic research and facilitate their utilisation by the public. The content for digitalisation includes series of documents and books on the Tokyo trial that have been published and will be published, and books on the Japanese war crimes trials in the collection of the NLC.

Co-operation with academia and related organisations will be strengthened. The acquisition and collection of historical documents on the Tokyo trial is inseparable from the support and co-operation of academic and related organisations. Academic experts have been engaging in research on related topics for a long time. Their opinions and suggestions have helped us to grasp the overall policy and priorities of our work. Libraries, archives and research institutions in different places have rich collections of documents on the Nationalist period and on the trials of Japanese war criminals which are to be further protected and explored. The co-operation and exchange with all parties will hold us together to push the work on exploration on these documents to a greater depth.

Related promotion will be enhanced. Last year marked the seventieth anniversary of humanity's victory in the global war against fascism as well as China's victory in the Second Sino-Japanese War. The NLC made active preparations for it. On the anniversary the NLC, with its broad and extensive collection of historical archives and documents and the rich written materials and photographs collected in recent years, organised exhibitions on the Tokyo trial and history of the Second Sino-Japanese War together with the Museum of the War of Chinese People's Resistance Against Japanese Aggression and the Nanjing Massacre Memorial Hall. In addition, itinerant exhibitions on the latest achievements in publications have also been arranged in China and overseas to commemorate those important events.

12

Joint and Command Responsibility in Hong Kong's War Crimes Trials: Revisiting the Cases of Kishi Yasuo and Noma Kennosuke

Nina H.B. Jørgensen[*] and Crystal YEUNG[**]

12.1. Introduction

On 25 December 1941, shortly after the beginning of the war in the Pacific and on a day that would become known as Black Christmas, Hong Kong fell to Japan. Hong Kong's surrender was followed by over three and a half years of Japanese occupation during which civilians and prisoners of war suffered extensive and systematic maltreatment, especially at the hands of the Kempeitai (military police corps). The Emperor of Japan capitulated on 14 August 1945 after atomic bombs were dropped on Hiroshima and Nagasaki. This paved the way for the fulfilment of the Allied promise to hold trials of alleged war criminals in the Pacific as well as the European theatre of the Second World War.[1] Forty-six such trials were held by British war crimes courts in Hong Kong against 123 individual accused.[2] The courts were established pursuant to a Royal Warrant issued on 18 June 1945 which granted broad jurisdiction over violations of the

[*] **Nina H.B. Jørgensen** is a Professor in the Law Faculty at the Chinese University of Hong Kong and was a Visiting Fellow on the Human Rights Program at Harvard Law School in 2014/2015. She is a qualified barrister and has worked in different capacities for the Extraordinary Chambers in the Courts of Cambodia, the Special Court for Sierra Leone and the International Criminal Tribunals for the former Yugoslavia and Rwanda.

[**] **Crystal YEUNG** is a second-year student in the Juris Doctor programme at the Chinese University of Hong Kong. She has assisted with civil party representation at the Extraordinary Chambers in the Courts of Cambodia and worked with asylum seekers in the field of international human rights law. She also has advocacy and research experience in international criminal law and public international law.

[1] See, for example, Declaration of the Four Nations on General Security, Statement on Atrocities, 30 October 1943 ('Moscow Declaration') (http://www.legal-tools.org/en/doc/3c6e23/).

[2] See Hong Kong War Crimes Trials Collection (http://hkwctc.lib.hku.hk/—exhibits/show/hkwctc/home); Suzannah Linton (ed.), *Hong Kong's War Crimes Trials*, Oxford University Press, Oxford, 2013.

laws and usages of war during conflicts in which Britain had been engaged since 2 September 1939.[3] Regulations for the Trial of War Criminals were annexed to the Royal Warrant and provided the procedural framework for the trials,[4] supported by secondary legislation such as the Instructions issued by Allied Land Forces South-East Asia[5] and the provisions of the British Manual of Military Law 1929 (as amended).[6]

The governing rules and regulations did not specify modes of liability and all charges were brought under the umbrella concept of being "concerned" or "together concerned" in a crime. This formulation of the charges derived from English law and appeared designed to encompass various degrees of involvement in criminal conduct, ranging from aiding and abetting to direct, physical commission of the *actus reus*.[7] The phrase "being concerned in" therefore provided a catch-all charge and the precise degree of participation by an individual accused was expected to emerge at trial and to be reflected in the sentence upon a finding of guilt.

In the face of open-ended charges and few precedents, the British war crimes courts in Hong Kong had to develop their practice in addressing complex cases involving multiple accused or cases of commanders indicted in connection with crimes committed by their subordinates. The focus in this chapter will be on the biggest joint trial, that of Lieutenant Kishi Yasuo and 14 co-accused,[8] and arguably the most significant case of command responsibility, that of Colonel Noma Kennosuke.[9] All 15

---

[3] United Kingdom, Royal Warrant 0160/2498, 18 June 1945, promulgated by the War Office, Army Order 81 of 1945 ('Royal Warrant') (http://www.legal-tools.org/doc/65e2cb/).

[4] United Kingdom, Regulations for the Trial of War Criminals Attached to Royal Warrant 0160/2498, 18 June 1945, Promulgated by the War Office, Army Order 81 of 1945 ('Regulations for the Trial of War Criminals') (http://www.legal-tools.org/doc/386f77/).

[5] Allied Land Forces South-East Asia, War Crimes Instruction No. 1 (2nd ed.) (as amended) in File WO 32/12197, UK National Archives.

[6] Great Britain War Office, Manual of Military Law 1929 (7th ed., Great Britain War Office 1929) (Reprinted December 1939), His Majesty's Stationery Office, London, 1940, as amended in 1936 (the replacement of ch. XIV and in 1944 an amendment to para. 443 of ch. XIV) ('Manual of Military Law 1929').

[7] See further Nina H.B. Jørgensen, "On Being 'Concerned' in a Crime: Embryonic Joint Criminal Enterprise?", in Suzannah Linton (ed.), *Hong Kong's War Crimes Trials*, Oxford University Press, Oxford, 2013, pp. 137–67.

[8] Trial of Lt Kishi Yasuo and fourteen others, HKWCT Collection, file no. WO235/993 ('Trial of Kishi Yasuo').

[9] Trial of Col Noma Kennosuke, HKWCT Collection, file no. WO235/999 ('Trial of Noma Kennosuke').

---

accused in the *Kishi* case were charged with committing a war crime by "being together concerned in the beating, torture and maltreatment of the inhabitants of Silver Mine Bay district of Lantau and in the killing of nine of the said inhabitants".[10] The prosecution noted in final arguments that it was a "long and arduous case" in part due to the "all-embracing nature of the single indictment" and also "due to the multiplicity of the accused involved".[11] Kishi was convicted of the full charge and sentenced to death by hanging along with two of his co-accused. Nine of the other accused were convicted either in respect of the full or a reduced charge and sentenced to varying terms of imprisonment. Three accused were acquitted. Noma was charged alone with committing a war crime in that he was concerned in the ill treatment of civilian residents of Hong Kong "as a result of which numbers of them died or were unlawfully killed by members of the Japanese Forces, and many others underwent physical suffering".[12] The charge spanned the period from 25 December 1941 to 18 January 1945 while Noma was head of the Kempeitai, "and as such responsible for public order, the control of Kempei personnel, and for the management of places of detention".[13] He was found guilty and sentenced to death by hanging.

This chapter aims to assess the contribution of the *Kishi* and *Noma* cases to the development of principles relating to the use of evidence in joint trials and the doctrine of responsible command. It will be seen that a cautious approach to joint responsibility was taken in the *Kishi* case, avoiding direct reliance on a concept of common intent. In the *Noma* case, the challenge was to identify an appropriate standard for the mental element of command responsibility that would serve to reinforce the purpose of criminalising a commander's failure to prevent or punish international crimes.

There were no reasoned judgments in the Hong Kong proceedings and the analysis that follows is based on the presentation and treatment of the law and evidence by the parties, the verdict delivered and the review of the judge advocate. Comparisons with contemporaneous cases and

---

[10]   Trial of Kishi Yasuo, Judge Advocate's Report, slide 4, para. 1 of document.

[11]   Trial of Kishi Yasuo, Prosecution Closing Speech, slide 541, p. 515 of document.

[12]   Trial of Noma Kennosuke, Judge Advocate's Report, slide 4.

[13]   *Ibid.*

modern jurisprudence are drawn where appropriate but a full discussion of the current state of the law is beyond the scope of this chapter.

12.2. Joint Responsibility in the Case of Lieutenant Kishi Yasuo and 14 Others

The *Kishi* trial began on 28 March 1946 and was the first war crimes case to be heard before the British courts in Hong Kong. It concerned a massacre of local Chinese in the Silver Mine Bay district of Hong Kong's Lantau Island, which was under Kishi's command, just days after the Japanese emperor's capitulation but before Japan's formal surrender. In retaliation for an attack by Chinese guerrillas, Kishi's men, initially in his absence, raided several villages, burning and looting and carrying out arrests. The captives were beaten and several were then beheaded by Kishi and others in a punitive campaign lasting about a week.[14] At trial, Kishi admitted executing three villagers, claiming self-defence, while his subordinate, Matsumoto, admitted giving orders to kill two further villagers but also claimed self-defence or sought to justify his actions as preventative measures. Another accused, Uchida, admitted killing two villagers but asserted that he was acting on Matsumoto's orders. The remaining accused argued that they were not present at or in any way concerned in executions and/or maltreatment, or that the alleged maltreatment did not occur.

The trial presented the first opportunity to test the application of Regulation 8(ii) of the Regulations for the Trial of War Criminals. Regulation 8(ii), which reflected a recommendation of the United Nations War Crimes Commission for joint trials where crimes had been committed collectively by groups, formations or units, provided as follows:

> Where there is evidence that a war crime has been the result of concerted action upon the part of a unit or group of men, then evidence given upon any charge relating to that crime against any member of such unit or group may be received as prima facie evidence of the responsibility of each member of that unit or group for that crime.
>
> In any such case all or any members of such unit or group may be charged and tried jointly in respect of any such war crime and no application by any of them to be tried separately shall be allowed by the Court.

---

[14] Trial of Kishi Yasuo, Prosecution Opening Speech, slide 607, para. 22 of document.

In its opening speech, the prosecution argued that the actions forming the subject-matter of the charge were the "concerted actions of the members of the KISHI Unit".[15] The prosecution went on to say that the accused were "charged in this indictment with the result that having acted jointly and severally in the perpetration of these murders and cruel treatment of the villagers they must one and all accept the natural consequences of their actions by which nine of the inhabitants of Lantau Island met a sad, cruel and untimely death".[16] The prosecution returned to this theme in closing arguments, stating that "the execution of [...] all these villagers [...] was not a one man show"[17] and that each accused "was concerned in varying degrees of culpability, some playing a more active part than others, some acting with more enthusiasm" in the beating and maltreatment which resulted in the deaths of at least nine villagers.[18] Without being explicitly referenced, Regulation 8(ii) appeared to provide a centrepiece for the prosecution's case. It was argued that

> all the evidence before this court tends to prove that the cruelty, maltreatment, the torture and finally the murder of the unfortunate islanders was not the action of any one individual, however big a part he played in this crime, but was in actual fact the concerted action over a period of one week of a group of individuals belonging to one unit who acted jointly in the continued maltreatment of the civilian inhabitants in their custody and which group or unit having jointly and severally [*sic*] are thus jointly and severally responsible for the natural consequences of their actions which in this case was the cruel and untimely death of nine of the inhabitants of the said Lantau Island.[19]

Placing emphasis on the assistance and moral support provided within Kishi's unit, the prosecution elaborated that belonging to the same unit was "sufficient to support the Prosecution's contention that [the members] were together acting jointly and severally and must for this reason accept full responsibility for the actions of their group".[20]

---

[15] *Ibid.*, slide 607, para. 23 of document.

[16] *Ibid.*

[17] Trial of Kishi Yasuo, slide 548, p. 522 of document, see *supra* note 11.

[18] *Ibid.*, slide 549, p. 523 of document.

[19] *Ibid.*, slide 550, p. 524 of document.

[20] *Ibid.*, slide 551, p. 525 of document.

The arguments of the prosecution go further than treating Regulation 8(ii) simply as an evidential rule applicable to joint trials and hint at a theory of common purpose, though this was never openly brought forward. The 1929 Manual of Military Law contained a section on responsibility for crime based on "common intent" as follows:

> If several persons combine together for an unlawful purpose or for a lawful purpose to be effected by unlawful means, each is responsible for every offence committed by any one of them in furtherance of that purpose, but not for any offence committed by another member of the party which is unconnected with the common purpose, unless he personally instigates or assists in its commission. Thus, if a police officer goes with an assistant to arrest A in a house and all the occupants of this house combine to resist the arrest, and in the struggle the assistant is killed, the occupants are responsible. But if two persons go out to commit theft and one unknown to the other puts a pistol in his pocket and shoots a man the other is not responsible.[21]

While the prosecution appears to suggest that all of the accused in the *Kishi* case should be treated either as principals to the nine killings, or at least "concerned in" those killings on the basis of their participation in a common design, this implicit contention remained unexplored. It is furthermore not evident that the court accepted the possibility that all members of one unit acting in concert could be held fully liable for the actions of the group. Indeed, the charge was severed so as to individualise culpability, with certain accused being held responsible for the full extent of the crimes and others being exonerated from the accusation of involvement in the killings. The observations of the judge advocate make it clear that the degree of culpability was reflected in the sentences, with only Kishi, Matsumoto and Uchida being given the death penalty. The judge advocate also notes it was a long case in part due to the need to hear sufficient evidence to establish individual acts of torture and maltreatment against

---

21 Manual of Military Law 1929, para. 17: this paragraph featured in the *1914 Manual of Military Law* (89 para. 18) in identical terms save the first phrase which referred instead to "several persons" going out with "a common intent to execute some criminal purpose". The notion of "common intent" was known to United States military law as well, see United States War Department, *A Manual for Courts-Martial, Courts of Inquiry and of Other Procedure under Military Law*, Government Printing Office, Washington, DC, 1917, p. 34, para. 69.

those who were found guilty.[22] While it was logical to hold a joint trial of all those accused of involvement in a single series of events, the court did not appear to make significant advances in the use of evidence against multiple, jointly charged accused, or in the development of legal principles concerning joint participation. The concept of "common intent", which may be seen as a precursor to the modern notion of joint criminal enterprise, was available to the Hong Kong courts but remained dormant in the *Kishi* case.

12.3. Command Responsibility in the Case of Colonel Noma Kennosuke

The concept of a commander's responsibility for war crimes committed by troops under his direct command was recognised long before the Second World War;[23] however, the applicable legal principles were underdeveloped at the time of the Hong Kong war crimes trials. Most of these trials had been completed when the International Military Tribunal for the Far East ('IMTFE') delivered its judgment, expanding on the law in this area.[24] According to Article 7(3) of the Statute of the International Criminal Tribunal for the former Yugoslavia, which reflects the modern notion of command responsibility, criminal responsibility for a commander arises if he knew or had reason to know that the subordinate was about to commit such acts (as war crimes) or had done so *and* he failed to take the

---

22 Trial of Kishi Yasuo, slide 7, para. 5 of document, see *supra* note 10.

23 In 1625 Hugo Grotius wrote that "he who knows of a crime, and is able and bound to prevent it but fails to do so, himself commits a crime [...] unless he punishes or surrenders the guilty party". Hugo Grotius, *On the Law of War and Peace. De Jure Belli ac Pacis*, trans. A.C. Campbell, London, 1814, book II, ch. 21, sec. 2, para. 2.

24 See International Military Tribunal for the Far East ('IMTFE'), Indictment, Count 55, which charged high Japanese government and military officials with failing to take adequate steps to secure the observance and prevent breaches of conventions and laws of war in respect of prisoners of war and civilian internees (http://www.legal-tools.org/doc/59771d/); and IMTFE, *Prosecutor v. Araki et al.*, Judgment, 1 November 1948 (http://www.legal-tools.org/doc/3a2b6b/). See also B.V.A. Röling and C.F. Ruter (eds.), *The Tokyo Judgment: The International Military Tribunal for the Far East (I.M.T.F.E.), 29 April 1946–12 November 1948*, 2 vols., APA-University Press, Amsterdam, 1977, ch. IX, p. 1144

necessary and reasonable measures to prevent such acts or to punish the perpetrators.[25]

Re Yamashita was the first international trial in which a military commander was charged with disregarding and failing to discharge his duty to control the operations of his troops by "permitting them to commit" war crimes.[26] The legal charge and factual pattern in *Re Yamashita* were similar to that of *Noma* and shed light on two features of command responsibility which were reflected in both cases. First, the United States Military Commission sitting in the Philippines found that General Yamashita Tomoyuki, as the commanding general of the 14th Army Group of the Imperial Japanese Army in the Philippines during the war in the Pacific, was under a duty to take appropriate measures within his power to control troops under his command and prevent acts which violated the laws of war. The failure to fulfil this duty would potentially render him personally responsible when violations resulted. This echoes the charges of war crimes against Noma which were also primarily framed as crimes arising out of omissions.[27] Second, the US Military Commission asserted that in certain circumstances, a "failure to discover [criminal conduct]" could also lead to criminal liability. If "in certain circumstances" includes "receiving prior warnings", the language chosen by the Military Commission supports the prosecution's claim in the case of *Noma* in that the accused had "distained to follow up warnings he received [of crimes committed by his troops]".[28] Ultimately, the vague formulation of the knowledge re-

---

[25] United Nations, Updated Statute of the International Criminal Tribunal for the Former Yugoslavia, adopted 25 May 1993 by resolution 827 (1993), last amended 7 July 2009 by resolution 1877 (2009), Art. 7(3) (http://www.legal-tools.org/doc/b4f63b/). The International Criminal Court's definition of command responsibility under Article 28(a) of the Rome Statute differs in two respects. First, instead of "knew or would have reason to know" the *mens rea* standard is "knew or owing to the circumstances, should have known". Second, instead of "failing to prevent or punish", a commander is liable for "failing to prevent or submit the matter to the competent authorities for investigation and prosecution". Rome Statute of the International Criminal Court, adopted 17 July 1998, entry into force 1 July 2002 (http://www.legal-tools.org/doc/7b9af9/).

[26] *Re Yamashita*, 327 U.S. 1 (1946), reprinted in United Nations War Crimes Commission ('UNWCC'), *Law Reports of Trials of War Criminals*, vol. 14, His Majesty's Stationery Office, London, 1948, pp. 3–4.

[27] Trial of Noma Kennosuke, Charging Documents, slide 16, p. 8 of document. See also Prosecution's Opening Statement, slide 487, p. 479 of document.

[28] Trial of Noma Kennosuke, Prosecution's Closing Statement, slides 719–20, pp. 713–14 of document.

---

quirement in *Re Yamashita* brought about a long-standing debate on the standard of knowledge required for command responsibility as it is uncertain whether the Military Commission required commanders actively to find out about their subordinates' crimes.[29] The case at least underlined that actual knowledge would satisfy the *mens rea* requirement. These factors are pertinent in *Noma* as it was alleged by the prosecution that Noma was responsible because he failed to prevent war crimes or punish troops under his control despite possessing both actual and constructive knowledge of the repeated occurrence of such crimes.

Noma was both *de facto* and *de jure* commandant of the Kempeitai, responsible for maintaining civilian order in Hong Kong by carrying out military police functions while also assisting in war operations.[30] The prosecution maintained that from the time of the Japanese invasion of Hong Kong to the time Noma was relieved of command in February 1945, he inspired a policy of ill treatment of civilians amounting to violations of the laws and usages of war. These violations were classified into three categories:

1. The mismanagement of places of detention, inasmuch as prisoners were overcrowded, starved, tortured and refused medical attention with consequent suffering and deaths accruing as a result of all these contributing factors.

2. Illegal executions.

3. The mass deportation of civilians from Hong Kong [which] began in 1942 or 1943 and carried on throughout [the] Accused's term of office.[31]

Sixty witnesses were called to substantiate the allegation that Noma "with certainty and beyond the limit of contrary argument" was criminally liable "1) Where he orders criminal acts [committed by his subordinates] and 2) Where he knows of them, and either permits them, or fails to take adequate measures to prevent their continuance".[32] The prosecution added

---

[29] It has been argued that the Military Commission simply believed Yamashita either knew of the atrocities committed by his troops, or that he must have known in the circumstances. See William H. Parks, "Command Responsibility for War Crimes", in *Military Law Review*, vol. 62, 1973, p. 77, quoting the Military Commission's written opinion.

[30] Trial of Noma Kennosuke, Testimony of Col Noma Kennosuke, transcript 321, slide 338, p. 330 of document.

[31] Trial of Noma Kennosuke, slide 720, p. 714 of document, see *supra* note 28.

[32] *Ibid.*, slide 719, p. 713 of document.

that, as a projection of the second basis for liability, warning of wrongdoing and a failure to investigate also incurs criminal liability.[33]

It is worthwhile to note that questions of effective control and failure to prevent/punish were not contested for the most part. In regards to the former, it was undeniable that Noma, as its head, had command and control of the Kempeitai in Hong Kong.[34] On the topic of prevention/punishment, counsel for the defence recounted several incidents where Noma meted out severe punishment when he came to know of offences committed by his subordinates.[35] It was thereby argued that Noma would have prevented/punished crimes committed by his subordinates if only he had been made aware of them. The real argument, therefore, lay in the *mens rea* in relation to the alleged crimes, which was the heart of the legal dispute between the prosecution and defence.[36] In light of this, the question directed at the court was whether there were violations of the laws and usages of war and, if so, whether the accused knew of them or failed to discharge his responsibility to follow up on warnings. As the legal debate in Noma's case centred on his knowledge of the crimes committed by his subordinates, the focus here will be on the second basis for liability raised by the prosecution.

In explaining how Noma was "concerned in" the alleged violation relating to the mismanagement of places of detention by gendarmes under his control, the prosecution introduced several arguments based on witness testimony, to establish that Noma knew or at least "recklessly disregarded" proof of warning of the crimes.[37] First, the prosecution submitted that Noma retained actual knowledge of torture at places of detention. Colonel Kanazawa testified that Noma's superior, Governor General Isogai Rensuke, repeatedly admonished Noma following complaints re-

---

[33] *Ibid.*

[34] Noma agreed that he was "quite capable of taking charge of the Hong Kong Gendarmerie". Trial of Noma Kennosuke, transcript 356, slide 373, p. 365 of document, see *supra* note 30.

[35] Trial of Noma Kennosuke, transcript 329, slide 346, p. 338 of document, see *supra* note 30.

[36] Counsel for the defence submitted that because Noma had no knowledge of his troops' crimes, he cannot be said ever to have "committed such offences, be they of commission or omission, as those for which he is blamed in this trial". Trial of Noma Kennosuke, Defence's Closing Statement, slide 716, p. 710 of document.

[37] Trial of Noma Kennosuke, slide 720, p. 714 of document, see *supra* note 28.

ceived about the misconduct of gendarmes and torturing of prisoners.[38] Edward David Sykes testified that Noma stood by and watched for "about seven to ten minutes" as he [Sykes] was given the electric torture and that to do so, Noma had to have come through another room where people were being given the aeroplane torture.[39] The prosecution claimed that Sykes's account, if true, "would have put the Accused on enquiry as to the practices of his underlings".[40] Counsel for the defence flatly refuted the latter piece of evidence. Noma himself also denied ever having seen an instance of these inhuman practices and insisted that "if anyone [of the gendarmes] tortured suspects they would be severely punished".[41]

The prosecution claimed that in addition to actual knowledge of the gendarmes' conduct in torturing prisoners, Noma possessed what amounted to knowledge by inference. By presenting a procession of witnesses who described ceaseless persecution and suffering, the prosecution contended that there existed a calculated policy of sustained cruelty which "lasted throughout the Accused's term of office and the area under his jurisdiction [a part] of which were within a few miles of his own HQ".[42] In its submission, the prosecution presented and relied on circumstantial evidence. For instance, it suggested that the "screaming and wailing night and day" by prisoners being interrogated in the Supreme Court would have been heard by Noma in his nearby office which was in the same building. The prosecution further stated that an officer of normal intelligence upon hearing such sounds would have been moved to seek the cause.[43] In his defence, Noma replied that he "frequently had to leave his office during the day" and denied that any cries were audible to him.[44] His

---

[38] Trial of Noma Kennosuke, Prosecution Witness No. 8, slide 40, p. 34 of document. See also Prosecution's Closing Statement, slide 721, p. 715 of document on the first witness statement by Colonel Kanazawa.

[39] Trial of Noma Kennosuke, Prosecution Witness No. 29, slides 148, 164, pp. 140, 156 of document.

[40] Trial of Noma Kennosuke, slide 721, p. 715 of document, see *supra* note 28.

[41] Trial of Noma Kennosuke, transcript 336, 338, slides 353, 355, pp. 349, 347 of document, see *supra* note 30.

[42] Trial of Noma Kennosuke, slide 722, p. 716 of document, see *supra* note 28.

[43] *Ibid.*

[44] Trial of Noma Kennosuke, transcript 334, slide 351, p. 343 of document, see *supra* note 30.

counsel also claimed that there was considerable noise from outside traffic which obscured Noma's hearing range.[45]

The prosecution then turned to Noma's own testimony as further proof of his knowledge of the mismanagement of the places of detention. On the issue of torture, the prosecution emphasised that Noma himself said: "I was worried for it [torture] and I looked for it and I did not find such things. [...] I visited stations to look for instruments of torture but couldn't find any".[46] On the issue of overcrowding, the prosecution stated it was dubious Noma did not notice the cells were over capacity since he inspected them about once a week. Also, as Noma claimed he received reports of all arrests made, he would have known, through numerical calculation, that the cells were inadequate to hold all the prisoners. Regarding the final point which was on the issue of a lack of food and medical supplies, the prosecution alleged that Noma could not have reasonably failed to investigate whether his medical facilities were adequately available to detainees. To support this inference, it highlighted a request by the Chinese Peoples' Council ('CPC') for hospitalisation of the prisoners which Noma responded to by saying the hospitalisation matter "will be considered".[47] On the other hand, the arguments submitted by the defence were primarily based on the ground that the evidence of the witnesses called by the prosecution were neither credible nor accurate and did not bear up under close scrutiny.

In the end, it is uncertain how much weight the court placed on the prosecution's submission that Noma possessed actual knowledge of the

---

[45]   Trial of Noma Kennosuke, slide 723, p. 717 of document, see *supra* note 28.

[46]   Trial of Noma Kennosuke, slide 723, p. 717 of document on Noma's statements and evidence, see *supra* note 28. Transcript 376, slide 393, p. 385 of document on the first witness statement by Kanazawa, see *supra* note 30. Noma likely made the statement to show he was neither negligent nor reckless in failing to acquire knowledge of his subordinates' crimes.

[47]   Trial of Noma Kennosuke, slide 725, p. 719 of document, see *supra* note 28. In assessing how much weight the court placed on the CPC's request to establish Noma's knowledge of the first allegation, the *Boškoski and Tarčulovski* case is of value. There, the Trial Chamber held that information from outside of the commander's own organisation can constitute information that gives rise to knowledge. Although Boškoski was not a military commander, the ICTY Statute does not distinguish between the duties of military and civilian superiors. Therefore, it is applicable as a comparison to *Noma*. International Criminal Tribunal for the former Yugoslavia ('ICTY'), *Prosecutor v. Ljube Boškoski and Johan Tarčulovski*, Trial Chamber, Judgment, 10 July 2008, IT-04-82-T, para. 1 ('Boškoski and Tarčulovski Judgment') (http://www.legal-tools.org/doc/939486/).

---

mismanagement of places of detention considering the defence's claims that much of the evidence given by the prosecution witnesses was "full of false and exaggerated stories".[48] While it seems unlikely that Noma failed to "find any evil" despite the claims in his own testimony that he was alive to the possibility of torture of the prisoners,[49] the court's verdict in respect of this allegation may also have been grounded on knowledge derived from matters of inference. Indeed, the jurisprudence from *ad hoc* tribunals and the International Criminal Court today would support the notion that constructive knowledge is sufficient to give rise to criminal liability under command responsibility.[50] In the case of *Prosecutor v. Delalić et al.* ('*Čelebići*'), the Trial Chamber held that "depending on the position of authority held by a superior [...] the evidence required to demonstrate actual knowledge may be different".[51] However, in *Prosecutor v. Aleksovski*, the Trial Chamber held that while a superior position *per se* is a significant indicium for actual knowledge, there can be no presumption of such as it could automatically entail guilt which comes too close to making liability under command responsibility strict.[52] This indicates that the court would likely not have held that Noma had actual knowledge solely by virtue of his position as commandant. Separately, the Trial Chamber in *Čelebići* is of value in speculating as to the court's approach in assessing the circumstantial evidence in the case of *Noma*. In *Čelebići*, it was decided that indicia such as "the location of the commander at the time", "the number of illegal acts" and "the geographical location of the acts" can help determine whether or not a commander must have known about the acts of his subordinates.[53] Applied to the case

---

48   Trial of Noma Kennosuke, Defence's Closing Statement, slide 685, p. 679 of document. See also Prosecution Witness No. 18, slide 88, p. 80 of document.

49   Trial of Noma Kennosuke, slide 723, p. 717 of document, see *supra* note 28. See also transcript 376, slide 393, p. 385 of document, *supra* note 30; and slide 492, p. 484 of document, *supra* note 27.

50   For example, see ICTY, *Prosecutor v. Zdravko Mucić, Esad Landžo Hazim and Zejnil Delalić*, Trial Chamber, Judgment, 16 November 1998, IT-96-21-T, para. 393 ('Čelebići Trial Judgment') (http://www.legal-tools.org/doc/6b4a33/).

51   *Ibid.*, para. 428.

52   ICTY, *Prosecutor v. Zlatko Aleksovski*, Trial Chamber, Judgment, 25 June 1999, IT-95-14/1-T, para. 80 (http://www.legal-tools.org/doc/52d982/).

53   A list of 12 indicia of knowledge was provided in the Final Report of the Commission of Experts. The Commission of Experts was tasked to collect evidence of violations of humanitarian law within the former Yugoslavia. See Čelebići Trial Judgment, para. 386, *supra* note 50.

of *Noma,* this would suggest that Noma would have at least constructive knowledge regarding the torture taking place in the Supreme Court.

In alleging that Noma was concerned in illegal executions carried out by his subordinates, the prosecution raised three incidents which it claimed would point to the accused's knowledge. First, the prosecution addressed the testimony of Tsang Pei-Fu who claimed to have heard, while working in the prison of the Western Gendarmerie, that reports of illegal executions were sent to gendarmerie headquarters.[54] The prosecution contended that this hearsay evidence was corroborated by Noma's own affirmation that he received daily reports as to the progress of interrogations.[55] In the prosecution's view, this meant that Noma should have also received a report when action was taken "to eliminate an undesirable element" as that would remove the need for further interrogation. A more notable submission made by the prosecution revolved around the defence's cross-examination of Rampal Chilote. Chilote testified that following his arrest, a gendarme took him to a high official to request permission for Chilote's execution to which the high official responded "no, no, Indian can't be shot".[56] The prosecution held that Chilote's claim was again substantiated by Noma who referred to the episode in his testimony and said he "scolded" the gendarme for even asking for such a stringent measure.[57] While the witness was obviously not executed, the prosecution used the incident to illustrate that if executions without trials were as outlandish of an idea as Noma claimed them to be, the request would not have been raised in the first place. Surprisingly, the most unfavourable evidence to Noma in this allegation was volunteered by Noma himself. In his testimony, Noma asserted that after unsuccessfully protesting against an order by his superior to unlawfully execute some guerrillas, he "ordered [his] district commanding officer to execute these people on the spot".[58]

---

[54] Trial of Noma Kennosuke, Prosecution Witness No. 28, slide 144, p. 136 of document.

[55] Trial of Noma Kennosuke, transcript 328, slide 345, p. 337 of document referring to exhibit H, see *supra* note 30.

[56] Trial of Noma Kennosuke, Prosecution Witness No. 42, slide 253, p. 245 of document.

[57] Trial of Noma Kennosuke, slide 726, p. 720 of document, see *supra* note 28. See also transcript 338, slide 355, p. 347 of document, *supra* note 30.

[58] Trial of Noma Kennosuke, slide 727, p. 711 of document, see *supra* note 28. See also transcript 350, slide 367, p. 359 of document, *supra* note 30.

The court's affirmative verdict as to Noma's culpability clearly indicates that it was unconvinced there existed an absence of knowledge in the accused of the illegal executions. In *Prosecutor v. Orić*, the Trial Chamber concluded that actual knowledge of crimes committed, or about to be committed, was an indicium that the accused had reason to know about the crimes committed thereafter.[59] Transplanted to the case of *Noma*, this means that as long as Noma received a single report that showed his subordinates carried out illegal executions, he would possess information sufficient to give rise to constructive knowledge of subsequent illegal executions. By similar reasoning, a gendarme's request for Noma's permission to carry out an illegal execution would put him on notice of such parallel unlawful conduct thereafter. While it is unlikely that the court in the case of *Noma* was of the view that *any* lack of adherence to international humanitarian law would compel a commander to become extra prudent, it could have held that Noma was compelled to know under the circumstances since a close nexus in time and scope was present in the illegal executions. Nevertheless, what really incriminated Noma was his own confession that he ordered the illegal executions of guerrillas. This cemented actual knowledge of the violation and could not be defended via the superiors orders defence since the defence applies only if an order was not obviously unlawful.

The prosecution labelled mass deportation "a well authenticated war crime against humanity"[60] and, in alleging Noma's knowledge of the unlawful deportation scheme that existed under his command, the prosecution called upon several witnesses.[61] The testimonies of those witnesses were recounted in an attempt to demonstrate that the gendarmerie resorted to the law of the jungle in carrying out its duty of rounding up evacuees. The prosecution went on to say that while these testimonies alone could serve to impute knowledge in Noma, they were unnecessary to confirm the charge since proof of actual knowledge could be derived in statements made by Noma himself. First, the prosecution held that Noma openly admitted that "the persons deported were mostly beggars and vagrants" as

---

[59] ICTY, *Prosecutor v. Naser Orić*, Trial Chamber, Judgment, 30 June 2006, IT-03-68-T, para. 550 ('Orić Trial Judgment') (http://www.legal-tools.org/doc/37564c/).

[60] Trial of Noma Kennosuke, slide 727, p. 721 of document, see *supra* note 28.

[61] Trial of Noma Kennosuke, Prosecution Witness No. 50, slide 292, p. 284 of document.

opposed to persons facing deportation as a punishment after trial.[62] Second, the prosecution claimed that Noma's attention was specifically brought to the violation when the governor instructed him "to do some rectifications" following an incident whereby the CPC requested the gendarmerie to "be more careful in collecting evacuees and not arresting people who were not appointed to be evacuated".[63] In that incident, Noma acknowledged the governor's instructions and responded that he would "instruct his district commanders to be just as careful as before".[64]

The sheer number of testimonies regarding the gendarmes' impunity in respect of rounding up evacuees likely played a major role in the court's final decision as to Noma's culpability. At any rate, the court would have at least determined that the governor's admonishment and the CPC's request should have alerted Noma to his gendarmes' conduct. By way of comparison, it was held in the *Roechling* case[65] that "it is [a commander's] duty to know what occurs in his organization, and lack of knowledge, therefore, can only be the result of criminal negligence".[66] This inferred concept of a strict "duty to know" was later ruled out in *Čelebići* by the Appeals Chamber[67] which instead followed the practice dictated in military manuals such as the US Army Field Manual, stating a commander "should have had knowledge, through reports received by

---

[62]   Trial of Noma Kennosuke, slide 728, p. 722 of document, see *supra* note 28. See also transcript 379, slide 396, p. 388 of document, *supra* note 30.

[63]   Trial of Noma Kennosuke, slides 728–29, p. 722–23 of document, see *supra* note 28. See also transcript 343, slide 360, p. 352 of document, *supra* note 30.

[64]   *Ibid.*

[65]   *The Government Commissioner of the General Tribunal of the Military Government for the French Zone of Occupation in Germany v. Herman Roechling and Others*, Judgment on Appeal to the Superior Military Government Court of the French Occupation Zone in Germany, in *Trials of War Criminals before the Nuremberg Military Tribunals under Control Council Law No. 10*, vol. XIV, United States Government Printing Office, Washington, DC, 1949, appendix B.

[66]   *Ibid.*, appendix B, p. 1106.

[67]   The Appeals Chamber also held that the accused had actual knowledge in *Roechling* since "Roechling [...] had repeated opportunities during the inspection of his concerns to ascertain the fate meted out to his personnel, since he could not fail to notice the prisoner's uniform on those occasions". ICTY, *Prosecutor v. Zdravko Mucić, Esad Landžo Hazim and Zejnil Delalić*, Appeals Chamber, Judgment, 20 February 2001, IT-96-21-A, para. 239 (Čelebići Appeals Judgment) (http://www.legal-tools.org/doc/051554/).

him or through other means".[68] However, the Appeals Chamber in *Čelebići* interpreted "in possession of [reports]" and "[reports] available to" to mean that it was not necessary for a commander to have actually been acquainted with information in order to have constructive knowledge.[69] In other words, a commander need not have read or heard an oral report as long as he had the opportunity to do so. This means that the difference between what constitutes a "duty to know" in *Roechling* and *Čelebići* would not have affected Noma's *mens rea* in this case since Noma had warnings made available to him and would therefore be culpable regardless of the test.

12.4. Critique of *Noma* and Remarks on the Development of the Law

There is a conventional understanding in the military that a commander should be responsible for the actions of subordinates in the performance of their duties.[70] At the same time, while convention often informs the law, it does not always give rise to legal decrees. The cross-examination of Noma offers a glimpse into his personal perspective of responsible command. Noma was asked: "You thought it was fair to punish people for offences committed by their subordinates when they did not even know the things were being done?" He replied: "They should be punished because they had to supervise their subordinates". He was then asked: "And the man who does not supervise his subordinates correctly deserves punishment, is that right?" Noma answered: "That is correct".[71] Noma's responses illuminate that he believed a military commander should be conscientious in observing the conduct of his subordinates and diligent in exercising control over them with the failure to do so resulting in possible moral and legal responsibility.

---

68 United States, *Field Manual 27-10, The Law of Land Warfare*, Department of the Army, 18 July 1956, as modified by Change No. 1, 15 July 1976.

69 Čelebići Appeals Judgment, para. 239, see *supra* note 67.

70 The first time the notion of command responsibility was recognised internationally was in the trial of Peter von Hagenbach by an *ad hoc* tribunal in the Holy Roman Empire. The accused was convicted of crimes which he, as a knight, was deemed to have a duty to prevent. See Parks, 1973, p. 5, *supra* note 29. The first attempt to internationally codify the principle of command responsibility was in the Hague Convention (IV) respecting the Laws and Customs of War on Land, The Hague, 18 October 1907, Art. 1 (http://www.legal-tools.org/doc/fa0161/).

71 Trial of Noma Kennosuke, transcript 355, slide 372, p. 364 of document, see *supra* note 30.

It should be acknowledged that Noma's case was decided at a time when the doctrine of command responsibility was still emerging under international law. Yet, the accused was invariably charged through the elements of this incipient principle. As such, in evaluating the justness of the verdict, a pertinent question is whether criminal responsibility based on the principle of command responsibility was a fair burden to impose upon *Noma* in the momentous context of international crimes and with respect to the particular situation in Hong Kong at the relevant time. Judge Frank Murphy raised a forceful dissenting judgment in *Re Yamashita* in this regard, stating:

> There was no serious attempt to charge or to prove that he [Yamashita] committed a recognized violation of the laws of war. He was not charged with personally participating in the acts of atrocity, or with ordering or condoning their commission. Not even knowledge [actual knowledge] of these crimes was attributed to him. It was simply alleged that he unlawfully disregarded and failed to discharge his duty as commander to control the operations of the members of his command, permitting them to commit the acts of atrocity. [...] The established principles of international law afford not the slightest precedent for such a charge. This indictment, in effect, permitted the military commission to make the crime whatever it willed.[72]

This part of Judge Murphy's dissent has a certain resonance as a criticism of the verdict in the *Noma* case. For instance, the charge of being "concerned in" war crimes was framed atypically as it suggested complicity via an omission, namely the dereliction of duty, rather than positive acts. This legal construction was not well established in international law at the time of the trial. Further, in line with the above analysis of his alleged violations, with the exception of one case of illegal execution, it was unlikely that the prosecution succeeded in proving beyond a reasonable doubt that Noma had actual knowledge of the crimes committed by his subordinates. Yet, in both *Noma* and *Re Yamashita*, although the prosecution did not directly establish that the accused were aware of atrocities committed by their respective troops, the court found that they incurred liability by the mere fact that the atrocities committed by their troops were of a wide-

---

[72] *Re Yamashita*, pp. 26–41, see *supra* note 26.

spread and pervasive nature.[73] However, this is where the factual similarities between the two cases end. In assessing whether the principles of fairness, justice and due process were present in *Noma*, an important difference with *Re Yamashita* must be noted. Yamashita was the commander of an army "totally destroyed" by the superior power of the United States[74] and it was "while under heavy and destructive attack that his troops committed many brutal atrocities and other high crimes".[75] Since Yamashita assumed command in the midst of battle, he claimed he was never able to assert actual control over his subordinates. On the other hand, the atrocities committed by Noma's subordinates could not be said to have been carried out in the fury of combat and were, in almost all circumstances, acts which remained within Noma's effective control. On the face of the facts, it appears highly probable that if Noma had fully discharged his duties as a responsible commander, he would have been able to substantially reduce, if not eliminate, the ill treatment of civilians in Hong Kong. Therefore, Judge Murphy's dissent, regardless of its persuasiveness, cannot coherently be applied to the case of *Noma*.

According to *Čelebići*, it is not enough to ask if a commander had knowledge of a crime committed or about to be committed by his subordinate.[76] To allow criminal liability under command responsibility to attach to a commander, the commander must possess knowledge of "specific elements of the crime".[77] It is not an easy task to prove the existence of actual knowledge of the specific elements of a crime and, to do so in *Noma*, the prosecution would have to bring forward evidence to show that

---

[73] For *Re Yamashita,* per judgment delivered by the president of the Commission, see *ibid.*, p. 14. For *Noma,* see Trial of Noma Kennosuke, slide 491, p. 483 of document, *supra* note 27.

[74] *Re Yamashita*, p. 27, see *supra* note 26.

[75] *Ibid.*

[76] Čelebići Trial Judgment, para. 393, see *supra* note 50.

[77] After the First World War the Commission on the Responsibility of the Authors of the War and on the Enforcement of Penalties recommended establishing an international tribunal to try individuals for ordering, or, with knowledge thereof and with power to intervene, abstaining from preventing or taking measures to prevent, putting an end to or repressing, violations of the laws or customs of war. While the proposed tribunal was not established in the end, the Commission stipulated that under the rules of the tribunal, "specific knowledge" would have been required to hold military commanders liable for command responsibility. See International Law Commission, *Historical Survey of the Question of International Criminal Jurisdiction*, United Nations, New York, 1949, UN doc. A/CN.4/7/Rev.1, p. 7.

the accused had knowledge of both the *actus reus* and *mens rea* of his subordinates when they committed the crimes. While the *actus reus* could be logically inferred, the prosecution would likely have failed in establishing with certainty that Noma knew of his subordinates' culpable state of mind when engaging in the crimes. The Appeals Chamber in *Prosecutor v. Krnojelac* illustrated just how difficult it is to prove actual knowledge of a subordinate's *mens rea* in this regard.[78] The question in that case was whether Krnojelac, as a detention camp commander, knew of incidents of torture committed within his camp. Although it was established that Krnojelac witnessed and even knew of beatings, the prosecution was unable to prove that the commander knew they were being carried out "for one of the purposes provided for in the prohibition against torture" and as such could not be said to have actual knowledge of torture being committed by his subordinates.[79] Such an analysis supports the conclusion that Noma's actual knowledge of the allegations of mismanagement at places of detention and the unlawful deportation of Hong Kong civilians was likely repudiated by the court. However, the court could still have found him liable through constructive knowledge as it is recognised in international law today.

In *Prosecutor v. Boškoski*,[80] the Trial Chamber ruled that media reports and a report by Human Rights Watch regarding one single event was enough to give rise to constructive knowledge by declaring that in such circumstances, a commander "had reason to know" a matter required further investigation.[81] Under this view, Noma almost certainly had in his

---

[78] ICTY, *Prosecutor v. Milorad Krnojelac*, Appeals Chamber, Judgment, 17 September 2003, IT-97-25-A ('Krnojelac Appeals Judgment') (http://www.legal-tools.org/doc/46d2e5/).

[79] *Ibid.*, para. 155.

[80] Boškoski and Tarčulovski Judgment, see *supra* note 47.

[81] *Ibid.*, para. 527. This view is also supported in the *High Command* case where the US Military Tribunal stated a commander is charged with notice of occurrences which take place within [occupied] territory and that where he has received reports of crimes and he fails to require and obtain complete information, the dereliction of duty rests upon him and he is in no position to plead his own dereliction as a defence. The takeaway here is that if a commander has received 'reports' alluding to crimes committed by his subordinates, he cannot be protected from liability for command responsibility by pleading he had no 'actual knowledge' due to his dereliction of duty. See US Military Tribunal at Nuremberg, Military Government for Germany, *United States v. Wilhelm von Leeb et al.*, Judgment, 27–28 October 1948, reprinted in UNWCC, *Law Reports of Trials of War Criminals*, vol. 7, His Majes-

possession information of a nature which indicated a need to investigate. In ensuring that his subordinates were discharging their duties properly, Noma said he ordered his various district command officers to "cooperate with the Commandant as if they were one heart and one body [...] which meant reporting frequently as to their personal circumstances to their superior officers".[82] The witness, Captain Yatagoi Sukeo, verified that Noma had instructed the district command officers to know everything which took place within their districts and report the matters back to him.[83] Noma also claimed to have had actual "intimate knowledge of [my subordinates'] duties".[84] He maintained that the district command officers reported to him daily and on the occasions where any serious incidents had occurred, the matter had to be reported immediately to the commandant, regardless of the time of day. He further mentioned that another way to inquire into the methods of the district command officers was through seeking information from the lower staff of the gendarmerie and through rumours.[85] Finally, Noma said that since he had some doubts his subordinates reported the true facts to him, he stressed strongly that the reports made to him must be sincere. According to the 1929 Manual of Military Law, the duty of investigation requires deliberation and the exercise of temper and judgment.[86] Given Noma's military training, academic background in law and apparent good intentions, it is hardly likely that his investigations, if conducted attentively, failed to decipher information which could give rise to constructive knowledge of his troops' crimes.

Reference may also be made in this context to the International Law Commission's work on a draft Code of Crimes against the Peace and Security of Mankind which states that "the superior incurs criminal responsibility even if he has not examined the information sufficiently or, having examined it, has not drawn the obvious conclusions".[87] Since Noma testi-

---

ty's Stationery Office, London, 1949, p. 88 ('High Command Judgment') (http://www.legal-tools.org/doc/c340d7/).

82 Trial of Noma Kennosuke, transcript 326, slide 343, p. 335 of document, see *supra* note 30.

83 Trial of Noma Kennosuke, Defence Witness No. 2, slides 404–5, pp. 396–97 of document, see *supra* note 30.

84 Trial of Noma Kennosuke, transcript 327, slide 344, p. 336 of document, see *supra* note 30.

85 Trial of Noma Kennosuke, transcript 328, slide 345, p. 337 of document, see *supra* note 30.

86 Manual of Military Law 1929, ch. 4, para. 31, see *supra* note 6.

87 International Law Commission, Draft Code of Crimes against the Peace and Security of Mankind, Report of the International Law Commission on the work of its fortieth session,

fied to be a watchful and alert military commander, it would not be inappropriate to assume that the reason behind his alleged lack of knowledge was actually a wanton and immoral disregard of reported information and observed conduct amounting to acquiescence. Indeed, acquiescence was later held by the US Military Tribunal in the *High Command* case to meet the *mens rea* requirement of command responsibility in certain circumstances.[88]

The Appeals Chamber in *Prosecution v. Strugar* held that "sufficiently alarming information putting a [commander] on notice of the risk that crimes might subsequently be carried out by his subordinates and justifying further inquiry is sufficient to hold a superior liable".[89] The *Noma* case may be seen to set an early precedent for the notion of "alarming information" described in *Strugar*. In his testimony, Noma stated that one of the goals of the gendarmerie was to gain the trust of the public. Accordingly, he took two measures to achieve this goal. He installed letter boxes to follow the public opinion of the population so as "to know every complaint" and he took significant measures in monitoring the activities of his subordinates.[90] However, Noma claimed he did not receive any complaints about torture or very many letters at all in the letter boxes. He suspected that this was because the district command officers failed to report to him letters which were unfavourable to them. As a result of the initiative's lack of success, Noma discontinued the complaints system. The question that would have come to the court's mind at this point is whether the lack of complaints and Noma's suspicion of his subordinate's dishonesty constitute information which should have put him on inquiry of the risk that crimes may be committed. This in turn would have depended on whether the information should have enabled Noma to conclude that he needed to make further inquiries to affirm or discredit the information. The court's finding of Noma's guilt could very well have been founded, at least partially, on answering this question affirmatively. In fact, this deduction would be supported by the Appeals Chamber in *Čelebići* where

---

9 May–29 July 1988, *Yearbook of the International Law Commission*, vol. 1, 1988, UN doc. A/43/10, p. 71.

[88] High Command Judgment, p. 77, see *supra* note 81.

[89] ICTY, *Prosecution v. Pavle Stugar*, Appeals Judgment, 17 July 2008, IT-01-42, para. 304 (http://www.legal-tools.org/doc/981b62/).

[90] Trial of Noma Kennosuke, Testimony of Col Noma Kennosuke, transcript 372, slide 389, p. 381 of document.

---

reference was made to the International Committee of the Red Cross Commentary to the Additional Protocols to the Geneva Conventions to the effect that "alarming information" which gives rise to constructive knowledge does not have to encompass the *mens rea* and *actus reus* of a crime as required by actual knowledge.[91] Since, as mentioned above, the prosecution would likely have found it difficult to establish actual knowledge in Noma, the court may have relied on the existence of "alarming information" to assume the existence of constructive knowledge in the accused instead.

In the heat of battle, the possibility of deteriorating discipline is an ever-present risk. This was even articulated by Noma himself when appearing as a defence witness. War tends to breed atrocities and one of the vital roles of a commander is to ensure that his subordinates do not violate international humanitarian law. In this regard, an expansive *mens rea* standard for command responsibility is desirable as it may serve as a deterrent and promote vigilance on the part of leaders in preventing violations of international humanitarian law. A standard which only imposes a duty to investigate once the commander has been put on notice of criminal conduct permits, in effect, a plea of negligence as a defence. Such a standard would contradict the underlying purpose of command responsibility by allowing commanders to assert innocence on the basis of having negligently failed to carry out their duty to create a proper reporting system. In its closing statement in the *Noma* case, the prosecution stated that "[it is important] to point out to future potential men of Noma's calibre what would happen to men who behave in the fashion he has in a similar situation and it should be a very sobering deterrent".[92] Whether or not Noma's case has served as a deterrent, it is illustrative of the evolution of a coherent theory of command responsibility that is not so far removed from the modern doctrine.

---

[91] "For instance, a military commander who has received information that some of the soldiers under his command have a violent or unstable character, or have been drinking prior to being sent on a mission, may be considered as having the required knowledge". Čelebići Appeals Judgment, para. 238, see *supra* note 67.

[92] Trial of Noma Kennosuke, slide 734, p. 728 of document, see *supra* note 28.

12.5. Conclusion

Command responsibility is sometimes regarded as an interloper of international criminal law because it is a form of liability that applies solely to omissions. The Trial Chamber in *Prosecutor v. Orić* noted that "the superior bears responsibility for his own omission in failing to act" and is therefore not responsible in the same manner as the subordinate who physically commits the crime.[93] Nonetheless, command responsibility is not regarded as a form of strict liability.[94] The doctrine of command responsibility is in principle distinguishable from criminal liability for "complicity" by which commanders may be held responsible for providing assistance to the principal perpetrators.

It is not clear that command responsibility was regarded exclusively as a form of dereliction of duty in *Noma*. The prosecution in its closing address explained that the charge of "concern in" war crimes meant that the accused "was so senior in rank and appointment, and yet so closely tied to the Kempeitai personnel in the chain of command, that whatever operations they undertook, his planning and guidance were present and paramount".[95] Thus, "when those operations are tinged with illegality, the Accused can be said to be 'concerned in' the misdeeds and charged on that basis".[96] The manner in which the allegation was framed, in terms of a commander's concern in the crimes of his subordinates, suggests that the theoretical foundation of command responsibility came close to complicity.

The accused's knowledge of his subordinates' crimes formed the crux of the debate in Noma's trial. The arguments of both the prosecution and defence demonstrate that in determining whether the accused was "culpably concerned" (concerned to such an extent as to render him guilty of this charge and thereby deserving punishment), the court would place weight on the same characteristics of *mens rea* that have since been deliberated in other post-Second World War developments.

---

[93] Orić Trial Judgment, para. 293, see *supra* note 59.

[94] The International Criminal Tribunal for Rwanda ('ICTR') Trial Chamber in *Akayesu* noted that command responsibility is not a form of strict liability and that "it is certainly proper to [...] at least ensure that negligence was so serious as to be tantamount to acquiescence or even malicious intent". ICTR, *Prosecutor v. Jean-Paul Akayesu,* Trial Chamber, Judgment, 2 September 1998, ICTR-96-4-T, para. 489 (http://www.legal-tools.org/doc/b8d7bd/).

[95] Trial of Noma Kennosuke, slide 719, p. 713 of document, see *supra* note 28.

[96] *Ibid.*

If command responsibility is international criminal law's interloper, joint culpability based on common intent at the time of the Hong Kong trials appears as its trespassing cousin. There is nothing to suggest that Regulation 8(ii) was viewed by the courts as anything other than a directive to hold joint trials in factual scenarios such as the one presented in *Kishi* and an encouragement to take a holistic approach to the available evidence while individualising guilt.[97] As the *Kishi* case demonstrates, joint responsibility for participation in the same course of conduct was not to be permitted to give rise to guilt by association.

The Hong Kong trials, as illustrated by the *Kishi* and *Noma* cases, recognised emerging forms of participation in international crimes. While *Kishi* says little in direct support of joint criminal enterprise liability, *Noma* was not an anomaly in international law and aligns with the present-day doctrine of command responsibility. It is true that in the 70 years since *Noma* command responsibility has seen much progress and become customary international law. It is also notable that the *mens rea* standard of the doctrine remains ambiguous and contentious. How this question is navigated in the coming decade will in large part be shaped by further judgments of the *ad hoc* tribunals and new judgments handed down by the International Criminal Court.

---

[97] Regulation 8(ii) was interpreted more creatively by the prosecution in some contemporaneous cases. See further Jørgensen, pp. 160–62, *supra* note 7.

13

Overcoming Challenges in
Historical War Crimes Research:
The Hong Kong War Crimes Trials Project

Suzannah Linton[*]

13.1. Introduction

This chapter is a reflection on overcoming challenges to the historical academic research that I conducted in the course of my Hong Kong Research Grants Council-funded project into war crimes trials that were conducted in Hong Kong from 1946 to 1948. The project commenced when I was at the University of Hong Kong and concluded when I moved to Bangor University in the United Kingdom.[1] I hope that this reflection will provide encouragement to those who may be apprehensive about the challenges of such research, and I write with particular consideration of those who may one day tackle the monumental task of researching China's legal history. I believe that a fair-minded evaluation of what I write in the following pages will recognise many lessons about how, or perhaps how not, to conduct such challenging research. The Hong Kong War Crimes Trials project has been, in a personal sense, the most engrossing and satisfying academic project that I have engaged in. Reflecting on the years of work, I see the entire process as an archaeological excavation of

---

[*] **Suzannah Linton** began her research on the Hong Kong war crimes trials when she was Associate Professor of Law at the University of Hong Kong, and completed it as Chair of International Law at Bangor University, UK. Her contribution to this volume was facilitated through a fellowship at the Max Planck Institute for Comparative Public and International Law in Heidelberg, Germany. She teaches regularly in China, and in 2015 taught at the China University of Political Science and Law as well as at Zhejiang Gongshang University.

[1] I would like to acknowledge the wonderful support of my team at the University of Hong Kong: Ernest NG, Dixon TSE, Janet MAN, Yvonne NGAI, David Palmer and Dave LOW. I also acknowledge the superb contributions to the book Suzannah Linton (ed.), *Hong Kong's War Crimes Trials*, Oxford University Press, Oxford, 2013: Justice LIU Daqun, Justice Kevin Zervos, Alexander Zahar, Yuma Totani, Nina Jørgensen, JIA Bing Bing and Roger Clark.

---

a historic legal proceeding. Within that there was the "finding the needle in the haystack" challenge, and also that of "finding the pieces of the jig-saw" with a view to putting the picture together. In a way, this chapter is the telling of the story of the entire project, but it is a story told through identifying challenges and how I overcame them – or think I overcame them – or failed to overcome them.

In part 13.2. I address challenges relating to documents, or "files" as I call them. The files that I refer to are the compilations of materials gathered together under some kind of categorisation devised by the crea-tor of the collection. The word "file" is used in a general sense in this chapter to mean pre-existing compilations of documents on discreet top-ics, comprising correspondence, drafts, official documents, legal docu-ments, records, newspaper reports, case reports and so forth. Within this is a very specific category that I call "case files". These are to do with actu-al, concrete criminal proceedings, and are official documents that record the entire legal process from charge sheet onwards.

My first focus is on overcoming file-related challenges. This is bro-ken into identifying case files and locating them, and then on connecting the dots, connecting the files. My next focus addresses the difficult task of creating the database. My third focus considers the difficulties in finding direct participants in a process that took place from 1946 to 1948, and how that was eventually overcome. My fourth focus addresses specific academic challenges that arose and how I – and my colleagues who con-tributed to the book *Hong Kong's War Crimes Trials* – dealt with them. In part 13.3. I close with some general observations about what critical les-sons could be taken from these experiences.

13.2. Challenges and Overcoming Them

13.2.1. File-Related Issues

13.2.1.1. Identifying Case Files and Locating Them

I was inspired to conduct a full study of the trials, and create an online database, from my supervision at the University of Hong Kong ('HKU') of an excellent LL.M. dissertation that researched the trial of Colonel Noma Kennosuke, one of the commanders of the Japanese Kempeitai (military police) in occupied Hong Kong. The case file itself was located in the National Archives of the United Kingdom ('TNA'), and the HKU law librarian kindly purchased a digital copy to enable my supervisee, Paul Harris SC, to study the case in detail. I, of course, knew about the history of policy decisions about the prosecution of war crimes in international tribunals, military tribunals and domestic courts, and had a good understanding of Nuremberg, the European trials and also the Tokyo process. On a personal level, having been born and raised in a country once occupied by the Japanese, and having lived and worked in the region for years, I also was very aware of the realities of the occupation and how that lived on in public memory. However, at the initial stage of general interest in the topic of Hong Kong's war crimes trials, I could only say that there had been at least one war crimes trial in Hong Kong, and that some material was at TNA.

A reconnaissance visit to Kew to conduct preliminary examination revealed that there were more cases than *Noma*, and they were kept in original form at TNA. My list of questions kept growing, revealing how much more research needed to be done. Part of the problem was that while the processes against Germans – Nuremberg, occupation zone prosecutions and German prosecutions – were subject to extensive juridical analysis, there was a paucity of information about the Asian trials outside of a few well-known studies of the Tokyo trials.[2] I gained a helpful broad understanding about the national investigation and prosecutions programmes in Asia from *History of the United Nations War Crimes Commission*, but that did not explain to me what happened in Hong Kong.[3] John Pritchard has been a pioneer of the study of the war crimes trials in Asia, and while his work did not focus on Hong Kong it helped in the hunt for clues.[4] I discovered a work by Philip Picigallo about the Asian

---

[2]   See, for example, Arnold C. Brackman, *The Other Nuremberg: The Untold Story of the Tokyo War Crimes Trial*, William Morrow, New York, 1988; B.V.A. Röling and Antonio Cassese, *The Tokyo Trial and Beyond: Reflections of a Peacemonger*, Polity, Cambridge, 1994; Yuma Totani, *The Tokyo War Crimes Trial: The Pursuit of Justice in the Wake of World War II*, Harvard East Asian Monographs, Cambridge, MA, 2008.

[3]   United Nations War Crimes Commission ('UNWCC'), *History of the United Nations War Crimes Commission and the Development of the Laws of War*, His Majesty's Stationery Office, London, 1948.

[4]   R. John Pritchard, "Changes in Perception: British Civil and Military Perspectives on War Crimes Trials and Their Legal Context, 1942–1956", in Ian Gow, Yoichi Hirama and John Chapman (eds.), *The History of Anglo-Japanese Relations, 1600–2000: The Military Dimension*, vol. 3, Palgrave Macmillan, London, 2003, p. 243; R. John Pritchard, "The Gift

trials that was built on media reports; this had a section on Hong Kong that proved informative.[5] Lord John Russell's *Knights of Bushido*, drawing extensively from the judgment at Tokyo, provided me with a quick and easy reference, helped me to understand the Kempeitai, and also assisted me in my drawing links between what happened in Hong Kong and elsewhere.[6] An article by the military lawyer Tony Rogers was helpful for a legal perspective, but again not in relation to Hong Kong.[7] The materials at the Berkeley War Crimes Studies Research Center database did not provide insights into Hong Kong but contributed to broader contextualisation.[8] The eminent historians of wartime Hong Kong, Philip Snow and Tony Banham, relied in part on case files at TNA, confirming to me its critical role in the search for the case files.[9] No Hong Kong trials were reported in *Reports of Trials of War Criminals*, but a search through Hong Kong University Libraries ('HKUL') and Hong Kong Public Library archives in English and Cantonese unearthed that the local media had followed the trials closely, revealing not just details of the trials but also a high level of interest at the time. The Imperial War Museum in Duxford, UK, was another possibility; it held some interesting film footage and photographs, but in the final analysis did not yield critical materials for a legal study.

Rear Admiral C.H.J. Harcourt reclaimed Hong Kong on 30 August 1945.[10] In his proclamation, the rear admiral established an interim military administration, giving the commander-in-chief of the returning liber-

---

of Clemency Following British War Crimes Trials in the Far East, 1946–1948", in *Criminal Law Forum*, 1996, vol. 7, no. 1, p. 15.

[5] Philip R. Piccigallo, *The Japanese on Trial: Allied War Crimes Operations in the East, 1945–1951*, University of Texas Press, Austin, 1979.

[6] Lord John Russell of Liverpool, *The Knights of Bushido*, Cassell, London, 1958.

[7] Anthony P.V. Rogers, "War Crimes Trials under the Royal Warrant: British Practice 1945–1949", in *International and Comparative Law Quarterly*, 1990, vol. 39, no. 4, p. 78.

[8] Founded at the University of California–Berkeley in 2000, the War Crimes Studies Center is now housed at the WSD HANDA Center for Human Rights and International Justice at the University of Hawaii.

[9] Philip Snow, *The Fall of Hong Kong: Britain, China and the Japanese Occupation*, Yale University Press, New Haven, 2003, pp. 79–90; Tony Banham, *The Sinking of the* Lisbon Maru*: Britain's Forgotten Wartime Tragedy*, Hong Kong University Press, Hong Kong, 2006.

[10] "Proclamation", in Hong Kong, *Hong Kong Government Gazette*, nos. 1–2, 1 September 1945.

ating forces full judicial, legislative and executive powers.[11] Were the trials conducted under a civilian or military administration, I wondered. It took some time to unravel that. I learned from the 1946 *Hong Kong Annual Report* that in July 1946 some 10,000 Japanese prisoners of war were held in Hong Kong following the surrender, and that of these 239 were held on suspicion of having committed war crimes.[12] That year's report also revealed there was international collaboration in criminal proceedings – a difficulty that those pioneering investigators will have faced is that Japanese military personnel were deployed all over the Japanese Empire, and the location where they surrendered was not necessarily the place where the suspected war crimes had been committed. Some of the accused were also suspected of crimes in multiple locations. Towards the end of 1946, 58 Japanese and Taiwanese were sent to stand trial in Hong Kong in relation to prisoner of war camp atrocities on Taiwan, and 10 Japanese were sent from Japan to Hong Kong in relation to crimes committed in Shanghai against British nationals.[13] Fifty-five Japanese located in China were brought to Hong Kong in 1947, and 92 detained Japanese were repatriated that year.[14] One hundred and twenty-three persons were eventually to go on trial, and the rest were repatriated.[15] This fortified me in what I had to search for.

Further inquiries at TNA led to an initial list of Hong Kong case files within the WO 235 category, being the records of the Judge Advocate General's Office. However, there was no way of knowing if this was complete, nor did it indicate associated files for example about the establishment and administration of the military tribunals. I spent many hours looking at TNA's excellent database, and manually examining hundreds of files at Kew. Sometimes one file would directly link to another, sometimes reading a file sparked ideas that led to identification of a relevant file, more often than not the file was not helpful. I learned early on of the critical importance of having a good method of keeping track of files and recording what was and what was not relevant. Relevance in this context could mean directly to the matter at hand, being the Hong Kong trials

---

[11]   *Ibid.*

[12]   *Hong Kong Annual Report*, Hong Kong Government Printer, 1946, p. 72.

[13]   *Ibid.*

[14]   *Ibid.*, p. 94.

[15]   *Ibid.*, p. 72.

themselves, but also the broader picture. In the course of reviewing files, I was not just hunting for the trial materials (the case files), but anything that could help shed light on the entire process of the British process of accountability in Asia. I had to remain mentally alert throughout; I found that sometimes connections would suddenly become clear months afterwards.

I was initially confused to find that certain Australian trials were held in Hong Kong, the first of which began on 24 November 1947.[16] It was not clear if this was part of the British effort or an entirely separate one. I later established that this was entirely separate (see discussion below). Another matter that was initially confusing was microfiche material at the Hong Kong Public Records Office ('HKPRO') about the re-establishment of the judicial system and trials that appeared to be in connection with wartime activities being conducted in the civilian courts. Was this the war crimes process that I was hunting for? It turns out not, for this was about re-establishment of the colonial regime, including the courts, and trials of British nationals for collaboration, treason and other activities, with the Japanese (and Taiwanese) tried in the military courts established under the Royal Warrant.

Eventually, I settled on a final list of case files at TNA, and with the funding that I had, was able to purchase them in digital form for the purposes of uploading onto a public database. I kept an emergency fund in case other files would eventually be discovered. I will discuss the limitations placed by TNA later in this chapter, issues relating to the database created and challenges in academic analysis. The case files were rather daunting when received, because the process was still not entirely clear and to be able to understand them one had to have a thorough understanding of the broader context. There were links between the cases. So, it was essential that background research continued parallel to the process of the creation of the database and as a preliminary step to academic analysis. In truth, new materials would be identified throughout the project, and so that process of filling in gaps continued into the analysis phase. The process was rather like building up a filing system that one was in control of and eventually knowing when to use what.

---

[16] Among the Australian trials was that of Admiral Tahara Suzumi ("Puss in Boots") and 15 co-accused, including Matsukawa Chuzo ("Heavy Harry"), Tajuma Tanaki ("Friendly Fred" and later "Hateful Harry") and Shigetada Otsuki ("Gordon Coventry"), for war crimes at a prisoner of war camp on Hainan Island.

The affidavit of the Argentine diplomat and journalist Ramón Muniz Lavalle, relied on by the Tokyo Tribunal, captured the horrors of the fall of Hong Kong.[17] This recorded extensive sexual violence, which was not appearing in the cases – sexual violence was raised in the trial of Lieutenant General Itō Takeo in relation to the invasion of Hong Kong Island, but although serious this was not on the rampant scale of what Lavalle described in Kowloon. Even so, at the close of the proceedings against Itō, the prosecutor dropped the charges in relation to the rape of European and Chinese nurses at the Jockey Club emergency hospital and the rape of Chinese women at Blue Pool Road, along with several instances of mass killing including the St. Stephen's Hospital massacre: "the Prosecution feels that there is such a large element of doubt as to which Japanese troops were involved that it can in no way inculpate the accused".[18] Sexual violence was included in the charges against the former governor general, Lieutenant General Sakai Takashi in Nanjing (discussed below), but some of this was not pursued in Hong Kong. Thus, not just was there a limited effort to pursue sexual violence but there turned out to be no accountability because the evidence was insufficient to secure a conviction in the one Hong Kong case where it was charged. I feel that there must be a file on this somewhere in TNA, but I have not found it.

The work of Jean Gittins and Geoffrey Emerson revealed the extreme conditions endured in the civilian internment camp at Stanley.[19] However, I could find no prosecution in relation to the internment camp at Stanley among the files, and searches at TNA unearthed nothing of significance, and no explanation of why there was no prosecution. Here too, I feel that there must be a file out there, but I have not found it.

I found, from looking at a broader range of materials, that a number of cases had excited relatively recent interest: the violence against medi-

---

17 Dated 11 March 1943, reprinted as appendix 1 in Kenneth Cambon, *Guest of Hirohito*, PW Press, Vancouver, 1990.

18 Prosecution Closing Address, Trial of Lt Gen Ito Takeo, HKWCT Collection, file no. WO235/1107, slide 372, p. 3.

19 Jean Gittins, *Stanley: Behind Barbed Wire*, Hong Kong University Press, Hong Kong, 1982; Geoffrey Charles Emerson, *Hong Kong Internment, 1942–1945: Life in the Japanese Civilian Camp at Stanley*, Hong Kong University Press, Hong Kong, 2008.

cal personnel during the fall of Hong Kong,[20] torture in occupied Shang-hai[21] and the sinking of the MV *Behar*.[22] Digitalisation of news reports provided me with information that I would not otherwise have found – for example, the trial of the former Hong Kong governor, Lieutenant General Tanaka Kuichi, in Guangzhou (Canton).[23] However, I found it frustrating that materials would come online haphazardly, and am certain that there is now material in circulation from the post-war years that would have been helpful for my work.

13.2.1.2. Connecting the Dots, Connecting the Files

I continued to make trips to TNA when I could, searching for supporting files that would explain the Hong Kong process further. The hard slog, and an open and increasingly informed mind, facilitated successful re-search trips. Bit by bit, things fell into place, connections were made and the picture became more focused.

Quite early on, I came to realise that it was important to find mate-rials relating to China. There were several reasons: the status of Hong Kong as comprising both British and Chinese sovereign territory, the huge numbers of Chinese refugees in Hong Kong before and during the occu-pation, the invasion of Hong Kong from southern China and the rotation of troops in the region. In November 1944, just over a year after the Unit-ed Nations War Crimes Commission ('UNWCC') was set up in London to collect lists of criminals, record available supporting proof, and make recommendations as to the tribunals and the procedure for trying such criminals,[24] the UNWCC's Far East Sub-Commission was set up in Chongqing (Chungking), China and energetically collated evidence about

---

[20] Charles G. Roland, "Massacre and Rape in Hong Kong: Two Case Studies Involving Med-ical Personnel and Patients", in *Journal of Contemporary History*, 1997, vol. 32, no. 1, p. 43.

[21] Eric Niderost, "Hotel from Hell", in *World War II Quarterly*, 2011, Winter, p. 2

[22] National Ex-Services Association, *The Sinking of the SS BEHAR: Operation 'Sayo I'* (http://www.nesa.org.uk/features/page8.html); David Miller, "A Very Reluctant Mass Murderer", in *Royal United Services Institute Journal*, 1998, vol. 143, no. 3, p. 53.

[23] "Tanaka Executed", in *The Canberra Times*, 31 March 1947.

[24] UNWCC, 1948, pp. 2–3, see *supra* note 3.

---

suspected Japanese war crimes.[25] My inquiries revealed that there was no public access to the mainland's Chinese archives, and this continues to be the case – this is a major barrier to scholarship. However, through database and file searching, I found what I needed. In one file, WO 235/135, I picked up traces of the Chinese–British tensions over Hong Kong, and also international co-operation in criminal proceedings. Reading the file further, I came across more material relating to the trial of former Hong Kong governor general, Isogai Rensuke, in Nanjing, China. The file shows that after some lengthy internal deliberation and delicate communications with the Chinese, the British abandoned their earlier efforts to place either a British judge or prosecutor on the tribunal, which they were entitled to; the risk that they faced was that the Chinese would demand reciprocity in participating in trials in Hong Kong and that was intolerable for them.[26]

The Nanjing case against Isogai drew from evidence that had been prepared by a Hong Kong (British) war crimes investigation team; the charge against him included the allegation of "causing the wholesale arrest and deportation of Chinese civilians from Hong Kong".[27] There is, as I have noted, still no public access to the Chinese materials. However, in file WO 325/135 I found a trial observation report by Captain F.V. Collison of the No. 14 War Crimes Investigation Team, Hong Kong. In this, he reported to his commanding officer about the *Isogai* trial, and provided a "rough translation" of the judgment delivered on 22 July in the thirty-sixth year of the Chinese Republic (1947).[28] The charge that "he allowed his subordinates to arrest and deport non-army personnel" to Bias Bay continuously, and without taking care about the safety of those being banished, "causing the old, weak, females and children to be homeless, result-

---

[25] There are numerous files at TNA that deal with the UNWCC. Since the completion of this particular project on Hong Kong, the UNWCC material has been made available online at the United Nations War Crimes Commission Project (www.unwcc.org/).

[26] See The National Archives of the UK ('TNA'), File No. WO 235/135, Communication from Commander of Allied Land Forces South East Asia to the British representative in Nanjing: "further pressure believed undesirable because Chinese would be in a position to claim reciprocal rights in HONG KONG although would welcome Chinese Member on BRITISH Courts elsewhere […] in view above suggest BRIT observer only should attend ISOGAI rpt ISOGAI trial not member or prosecutor".

[27] *Annual Report on Hong Kong for the Year 1947*, His Majesty's Stationery Office, London, 1948, p. 95.

[28] See TNA, File No. WO 325/135.

ing in deaths from starvation and exposure" was proven to the satisfaction of the court, and he was convicted.[29] Isogai was, however, acquitted of the charges of responsibility for Kempeitai torture in Hong Kong and of pursuing a policy of public sale of opium in Hong Kong.

Another case of importance that related to Hong Kong but was tried in China was that of Lieutenant General Sakai Takashi. Sakai had, at the time of the invasion of Hong Kong, been regimental commander of the 29th Infantry Brigade; he was the "Conqueror of Hong Kong" and the commanding officer of the three Imperial Japanese Army officers who would stand trial in Hong Kong in relation to the invasion of Hong Kong Island. The trial, in Nanjing, raised war crimes in Hong Kong and was briefly reported in *Law Reports of Trials of War Criminals*.[30] It is studied as one of the earliest crime of aggression cases.[31] File WO 311/563 at TNA revealed that this report was actually based on a "summary translation" of the "Judgment of the Military Tribunal, Nanking, regarding Takashi Sakai, 27 August 1946". Thanks to Roger Clark, who was at the time also looking into Sakai, and also WANG Jingsi and Judge SHIH Muchin from Taiwan, I was able to access the judgment, in original language, from in the National Archives of Taiwan. Michael LIU, who heads the Chinese Initiative for International Criminal Justice, kindly provided an informal translation. This judgment is, of course, more valuable than the report of the case which appears in *Law Reports of Trials of War Criminals*. It contains an annex listing 22 atrocities in Hong Kong and Kowloon that the court found Sakai permitted his subordinates to carry out. These included some which were indeed tried in Hong Kong, such as the St. Stephen's Hospital massacre, and incidents of sexual violence (rape) and murder of civilians at No. 2 Blue Pool Road, Hong Kong, on 22 December 1941. Here, too, the evidence was compiled with the assistance of British investigators from Hong Kong. Sakai was sentenced to death.

---

[29] *Ibid.*, p. 2.

[30] United Nations War Crimes Commission ('UNWCC'), *Law Reports of Trials of War Criminals*, vol. 14, His Majesty's Stationery Office, London, 1948, pp. 1–7.

[31] See Roger S. Clark, "The Crime of Aggression: From the Trial of Takashi Sakai, August 1946, to the Kampala Review Conference on the ICC in 2010", in Kevin Jon Heller and Gerry Simpson (eds.), *The Hidden Histories of War Crimes Trials*, Oxford University Press, Oxford, 2013, pp. 387–90.

From one TNA file, I discovered that while the war was on, there was great British interest in the maltreatment of British and Commonwealth citizens in occupied Shanghai. The death of a British national, a chief inspector of the Shanghai police, William Hutton, was the first case which brought to light the maltreatment of British subjects in Shanghai. Documents in the file conclude that "William Hutton was murdered: dying as a result of torture by [the] Japanese".[32] How was it that the case was eventually heard in Hong Kong, I wondered. And why was it not the first case if official interest was so great? The Shanghai atrocities were, in fact, the last two cases to be tried in Hong Kong.[33] The Hutton matter turns out to have been a case transferred over from China, which had original jurisdiction.[34] One of the features to emerge from the files was Chinese–British tensions over Hong Kong. At the same time, my study of the Hong Kong files was showing that army officers from India, Australia and Canada were participating as judges and prosecutors. A file in the HKPRO helped clarify the situation. Crimes against an Allied national should first be available for trial by that nation, but "[i]f they do not desire to do so the accused may be tried by British court".[35] Where there were multiple Allied-nationality victims involved but without any British victims, "similar opportunity should be offered to each Ally in turn".[36] Where there were just British victims, a British court would try the case.[37] In the event of crimes against British and Allied nationals, they would be tried in a British court, but the respective Ally would be invited to be represented on the court.[38] Also, foreign nationality proceedings among the

---

[32] TNA, File No. WO 32/15509, List of Charges against Japanese in respect of Crimes Committed against British Subjects in Occupied China and Manchuria.

[33] See Trial of Lieutenant General Kinoshita Kiichi, HKWCT Collection, File No. WO235/1116; Trial of Sergeant Major Yokohata Toshiro, HKWCT Collection, File No. WO235/1117.

[34] TNA, File No. WO 32/15509, Communication from Major J.F. Crossley to the British Military Attaché, Nanking, 19 June 1945.

[35] Hong Kong Public Records Office ('HKPRO'), File No. HKRS-169-2-147 (War Criminals and Crimes), Communication from REAR SACSEA to Land Forces Melbourne, CHQ Wellington N.Z., C.N.Q. Ottowa, 26 M.M. Chunking, British Staff Section Tokio, C in C Hong Kong, Government of Burma, [date unclear, either October or November 1945] (Top Secret).

[36] Ibid.

[37] Ibid.

[38] Ibid.

Allies were allowed, for example, the Australian trials in Hong Kong and US trials in China. In this matter of the Shanghai atrocities, the British lobbied to have the case tried in Hong Kong. Major J.F. Crossley, commanding the No. 9 War Crimes Investigation Team in Shanghai asserted that

> [a]s this case is of such interest and importance to all British subjects who were in SHANGHAI at the time it is felt very strongly that it should be tried before a British Court at HONG KONG this is in accordance with instructions which I have received from HQ Allied Forces South East Asia and both the Consul General in SHANGHAI and the United Kingdom representative to the United Nations War Crimes Commission Mr Lambe agree on this point. We have consulted with the Chinese authorities here but they state they have not the power to give permission for this case to be tried in HONG KONG.[39]

This could have been a reason for the delay in prosecuting, but *The Argus*, an Australian newspaper, credits the case moving forward to the extraordinary efforts of Hutton's elderly father over three years.[40]

Many dots were joined up by looking at files in other locations, for example, at the Australian archives and the HKPRO. One of the initial peculiarities, as noted earlier, was the emergence of Australian trials that had been held in Hong Kong. I eventually learned from *History of the United Nations War Crimes Commission and the Development of the Laws of War* that the Australian War Crimes Section was established in Singapore in December 1945 to oversee investigations into war crimes against Australians in Malaya, on the Burma–Siam railway and in the Dutch East Indies.[41] I also learned more from presentations at a conference in Melbourne on the Hidden Histories of War Crimes Trials in 2010. This was not a British process, and was not part of the Hong Kong trials, although the process under the Australian War Crimes Act 1945 was very similar to the Royal Warrant procedure,[42] and the Australians worked closely with the Allied Land Forces in Southeast Asia ('ALFSEA') in

---

[39] *Ibid.*

[40] "Old Scots Pensioner Avenged Son's Death", in *The Argus*, 7 December 1948, p. 6.

[41] UNWCC, 1948, p. 388, see *supra* note 3.

[42] David Sissons, "Sources on Australian Investigations into Japanese War Crimes in the Pacific", in *Journal of the Australian War Memorial*, 1997, vol. 30, p. 1.

Singapore, the body that supervised the operation in Hong Kong through its War Crimes Legal Section. They held trials in locations such as Rabaul (Papua New Guinea), Singapore and Japan, and the last few cases from Japan were transferred to Hong Kong – *History of the United Nations War Crimes Commission and the Development of the Laws of War* revealed that the Australian War Crimes Section moved to Hong Kong following the end of the trials in Rabaul and the closing of 8th Military District headquarters, and pursuant to an agreement reached for the establishment of Australian courts in Hong Kong.[43] From the Australian archives, I learned that 13 Australian war crimes trials were held in Hong Kong.[44] From the HKPRO, I discovered that the court sat at Ma Tau Chung camp.[45] It closed down on 15 August 1948, with the Australian War Crimes Section leaving Hong Kong despite there being outstanding cases; this was apparently because of "accommodation problems" (the British administration in Hong Kong wanted the property back).[46] From my interviews with Major Murray I. Ormsby (see below), I learned that on the ground there was no contact between the British and Australian ventures or their personnel. History came together in a sufficient way for my purposes as a lawyer.

Research in the HKPRO files also helped clarify that there were two streams of British proceedings in relation to the war in Hong Kong itself. The first was the military proceeding against Japanese and Taiwanese. This was done under the Royal Warrant, and was the core of my project on Hong Kong's war crimes trials. The second stream concerned British and Commonwealth nationals accused of treason and other such acts. Files at the HKPRO revealed that British policy in relation to British subjects who had "assisted the enemy" emerged from an 18 May 1944 Home

---

43 UNWCC, 1948, p. 389, see *supra* note 3.

44 See National Archives of Australia, World War II War Crimes – Fact Sheet 61, 2012, (http://www.naa.gov.au/about-us/publications/fact-sheets/fs61.aspx); Australian War Memorial, Table B: Australian War Crimes Trials (Classified by Victim), *Journal of the Australian War Memorial* (http://www.awm.gov.au/journal/j30/trials.asp); Australian War Memorial, Table A: Statistics – Australian War Crimes Trials, *Journal of the Australian War Memorial* (https://www.awm.gov.au/journal/j30/wcrimes.asp).

45 HKPRO, File No. HKRS 156-1-1226, Australian War Crimes Court at Ma Tau Chung Camp No. 2.

46 HKPRO, File No. HKRS 163-1-210, Japanese War Criminals – 1. Question of Legal Position Re Hanging and Detention of [...] 2. Legislation to Provide for Detention of [...] after Conclusion of Peace Treaty, handwritten note dated 10 November 1949.

Office conference on how to deal with surrendering British "renegades" under the draft German armistice.[47] Unlike the military courts, the civilian authorities in Hong Kong relied on a Defence Regulation 27, also called the "Quisling Directive", on which prosecutions were based, in addition to the Treason Act 1351.[48] My researchers and I came across references, and sometimes discovered the direct case materials, relating to trials of local Hong Kong Chinese, Indians and Commonwealth nationals for collaboration with the enemy as treason.[49] The first treason proceedings appear to have been in February 1946 against the Red Cross employee Charles Alfred Gehring and five other local residents for allegedly "directing Japanese artillery fire across Hong Kong Bay in the first week of the war, and with having denounced nationals to the Japanese in 1942".[50] Some of the locals charged were the colleagues and collaborators of the Japanese who were standing trial in the military proceedings, held elsewhere in the territory, and some were called as witnesses. We discovered the microfiched case file of the notorious local policeman who collaborated with the Japanese, George WONG; he was sentenced to death.[51] Among the other cases examined were that of SO Leung[52] and LAU Kwing Wan,[53] both detectives working for the Kempeitai. Secondary files revealed that a number of Indians who had worked as guards for private corporations, with the Kempeitai and in the prisons, were tried in Hong Kong (one file showed that in April 1946 six Indians were detained in Hong Kong).[54] Others were brought back from India, with the assistance

---

[47] HKPRO, File No. HKRS 211-2-41, Secret correspondence containing annex I, Minutes of Conference on 18 May 1944; annex II, Report on Surrender of British Subjects in Enemy Territory Who Have Assisted the Enemy; annex III; annex IV, Draft Directive Concerning United Nations' Renegades and Quislings.

[48] *Ibid.*, Draft Directive Concerning United Nations' Renegades and Quislings. See also HKPRO, File No. HKRS 169-2-267.

[49] See for example, HKPRO, File No. HKRS 169-2-267, Arrest of Civilians Alleged by Service Departments to have been Guilty of Subversive Activities Collaboration with the Japanese Etc.; HKPRO, File No. HKRS 211-2-41, Questions as to the Treatment of Collaborators in the Far East; HKPRO, File No. HKRS No 169-2-266, Collaboration with Enemy.

[50] "Treason Charge in Hong Kong", in *The Courier-Mail* (Brisbane), 21 February 1946, p. 2.

[51] HKPRO, File No. HKRS No 41-1-1338, George Wong.

[52] HKPRO, File No. HKRS 41-1-1376, So Leung 1. Sentence of Death Passed on [...] for Guilty of High Treason 2. Petition from [...].

[53] *Ibid.*

[54] HKPRO, File No. HKRS 163-1-235, Renegades and Quislings: Papers Re Indians Whose Presence in Hong Kong is Required for [...] Trials; HKPRO, File no. HKRS 169-2-267,

of the British administration there, to testify as witnesses in such trials.[55] Files covering "collaboration with the enemy" indicated treason action against five released prisoners of war apparently repatriated to stand trial in Britain.[56] The files also revealed that in April 1946 there had, strangely, been public unease about the fact that only Chinese and Indians were being prosecuted for treason, and no "non-Asiatic British subjects".[57]

The labour-intensive task of trawling through the HKPRO files also solved a mystery concerning the case of Kanao Inouye, who was ethnically Japanese but born in Canada; he joined the Imperial Japanese Army as an interpreter. We already had the case file concerning his trial in a Hong Kong military court, where he was convicted of war crimes.[58] Kanao had all along protested that the court had no jurisdiction over him, claiming that he was a Commonwealth national. At the HKPRO, we discovered Kanao's case file of his trial for treason by the Supreme Court in Hong Kong.[59] The file revealed that the evidence from Canada finally arrived confirming Kanao's claim, and the war crimes conviction was overturned, to be followed by the treason proceedings (which also convicted him).

Visits to the HKPRO in Kwun Tong also illuminated the matter of sentencing in the Hong Kong trials. Post-war politics, above all Cold War politics, saw the rapid evolution of a policy of rapprochement with Germany and Japan. Pritchard has written extensively on this.[60] TNA case files themselves did not reveal anything beyond the sentence imposed with a confirmation that it was carried out, for example that the prisoner was taken into the custody of the prison warden at Stanley or executed. The HKPRO files, on the other hand, revealed how the wider global politics impacted on the men convicted in the Hong Kong War Crimes Trials. A file entitled "Japanese War Criminals – 1. Question of Legal Position

---

Arrest of Civilians Alleged by Service Departments to Have Been Guilty of Subversive Activities Collaboration with the Japanese etc.

55 HKPRO, File No. HKRS No 169-2-266, Collaboration with Enemy.

56 *Ibid.* See also TNA, File No. WO 203/5296B, Signal Form from Commander in Chief Hong Kong to War Office.

57 HKPRO, File No. HKRS 169-2-267, Arrest of Civilians Alleged by Service Departments to have been Guilty of Subversive Activities Collaboration with the Japanese etc. Communication from Commander in Chief, Hong Kong, to the Colonial Office, 2 April 1946.

58 Trial of Inouye Kanao, HKWCT Collection, File No. WO235/927.

59 HKPRO, File No. HKRS 163-1-216, War Criminals – Inouye Kanao.

60 Pritchard, 1996, p. 15, see *supra* note 4.

Re Hanging and Detention of [...] 2. Legislation to Provide for Detention of [...] after Conclusion of Peace Treaty" showed that there were 86 Japanese persons serving their sentences at Stanley Prison in Hong Kong on 10 December 1949: 55 were from military courts, 29 were from the Australian war crimes courts, and there was one from the Supreme Court of Hong Kong, which would have been Kanao referred to earlier.[61] Further to a petition from all of the prisoners in November 1949 seeking to be repatriated to Japan to serve their sentences,[62] the War Office Review Board considered their sentences, and did so again that year when the Japanese government sought remission. In the case of Colonel Tokunaga Isao, commandant of all the prisoner of war camps in Hong Kong, quantum of life sentence was set at 21 years' imprisonment, with no further reduction of sentence on the grounds that

> [t]his is one of the worst cases of a callous and vindictive senior officer in charge of prisoners-of-war who was not interested in their welfare. He ordered the executions, without trial, of some the said prisoners-of-war. He was very fortunate in having the death sentence commuted.[63]

Once in Japan, many repatriated war criminals benefited from a policy of amnesty: from 7 March 1950 General Douglas MacArthur's policy was "that within *his* command, those sentenced to less than ten years imprisonment would be released on parole".[64] A HKPRO file revealed that Major General Tanaka Ryosaburo, one of the senior officers, convicted of atrocities in relation to the invasion of Hong Kong, was refused sentence reduction on 3 February 1954.[65] Anthony Eden, as newly appointed British prime minister, could find no reason for reducing the sentence, recalling the earlier cabinet decision fixing quantum of 15 years for life sentences; however, he accepted that with allowance for good conduct, Tanaka would be entitled to release after 10 years in confinement, on 1

---

[61] HKPRO, File No. HKRS 163-1-210, see *supra* note 46.

[62] *Ibid.*

[63] HKPRO, File No. HKRS 163-1-1236, Japanese War Criminals – Remissions of Sentences, Note on Tokunaga Isao.

[64] Pritchard, 1996, p. 29, see *supra* note 4.

[65] HKPRO, File No. HKRS 163-1-1236, Japanese War Criminals – Remissions of Sentences, Note on Tanaka Ryosaburo from A.L. Mayall (Foreign Office) to Sir Esler Dening, Tokyo, 25 April 1956.

January 1957.[66] In 1956 the Japanese government again sought clemency, apparently repeating points that were rebutted at trial.[67] The request was rejected, the plea was said to have not put forward adequate grounds for setting aside the finding of the military court and the 20-year sentence.[68]

13.2.2. Challenges in Creating the Hong Kong War Crimes Trials Database

My vision for the project was that the war crimes cases from Hong Kong, a vital part of local history and an important link in the web of international criminal justice, should be digitised and made openly available to everyone, anywhere in the world, via a database housed at the HKUL. It was critically important, I felt, that something that had been forgotten about all these years should be made fully accessible.

This was, unfortunately, not to be, due to access restrictions that TNA imposed on my use of the case files. According to TNA, these case files are sensitive and liable to cause distress, and so they would only license the digital copies being made openly available through the institutions of higher learning in Hong Kong. In other words, only persons in Hong Kong, accessing through the libraries of the institutions of higher learning in Hong Kong, could view the entire files. I could, however, prepare my own casenotes as the next best thing. This was for me an illogical and unreasonable condition to impose from a freedom of information perspective. These materials date from well over half a century ago, were declassified over three decades ago, and relate to legal proceedings that were held in public and reported in the media at the time. The materials from today's international criminal tribunals are openly accessible on the internet unless subject to a judicial order, so why should TNA impose such a limitation on a historical process of accountability? There is no such limit placed on the materials from the Nuremberg, Tokyo or Control Council Law No. 10 cases. The imposition of such a draconian restriction on a scholarly project meant that people from outside of Hong Kong were denied access to the files. No amount of reasoning would shift TNA from this position, and I eventually decided to make the most out of the situation and accept their terms. It was better that people in Hong Kong had

---

66 *Ibid.*
67 *Ibid.*
68 *Ibid.*

access than no one at all. It is, after all, their history. To this day, people write to me to complain about this restriction on access. While I am very grateful for being able to provide some public access, I have directed complainants to TNA, but the restrictions remain in place.

As a Neanderthal on information technology ('IT') matters, I was very fortunate to have the full support of the HKUL in this project. The head of Digital Strategies and Technical Services, David Palmer, and Dave Low, an expert in IT and in databases, were indispensable members of the Hong Kong War Crimes Trials team. For the database and website (see http://hkwctc.lib.hku.hk/exhibits/show/hkwctc/home) we eventually settled on the Omeka system, a project of the Roy Rosenzweig Center for History and New Media, George Mason University. It is an open source web-publishing platform, designed with non-IT specialists in mind, allowing users to focus on content and interpretation rather than programming. For me, it was important to make it user friendly, and full of information that could go towards compensating for the lack of global access to the heart of the project, the case files themselves. Omeka allowed us to share the collections, display documents and oral histories, and create digital archives. We could also ensure that TNA's conditions on access were complied with. The layout was simple and logical. The technicians introduced plug-ins (Dublin Core Extended, Exhibit Builder, Geolocation, Simple Pages) and multiple functions enabling the searching of the database and facilitation of movement around the scanned files. Preparing the IT side of things and preparing the documents for uploading (inserting metadata an so on) was extremely time-consuming and meticulous – my research assistants were particularly helpful in this regard.

It would be wonderful if TNA would allow us to make the case files globally accessible. Had there been more time, and funding, I would have liked to have made the database available in Cantonese and Mandarin. Here, too, I have sought to do the next best thing, and am delighted that Hong Kong University Press are looking into publishing a Cantonese translation of *Hong Kong's War Crimes Trials* (the Chinese Initiative for International Criminal Justice has translated it), and Oxford University Press is investigating publishing a Mandarin translation.

13.2.3. Finding Eyewitnesses and Direct Participants

From the start of the project I tried to find persons who had been directly involved in the war crimes trials, whether in an official capacity, as an accused or as a witness, or had even observed the trials. It seemed vital to me to record that engagement, to memorialise those experiences. My project was not just about law but also the human beings involved, and an important historical period. One gem that eventually emerged was a paper in the *Hong Kong Branch of the Royal Asiatic Society* written by eminent local solicitor, Peter Vine, who had been the prosecutor of the *Lisbon Maru* case.[69] Peter Vine had eventually settled in Hong Kong. His account of his experiences of the Hong Kong trials was priceless for my project, and I contacted his son, Stephen, also a solicitor, to obtain permission to include the article on our website.[70] Stephen was later to speak at the March 2014 book launch of *Hong Kong's War Crimes Trials* at the Chinese University of Hong Kong, sharing what he could about his late father's life in that time. Colin Banfield, the son of a former defence lawyer, Lieutenant D.C.J. Banfield, also spoke at this event on behalf of his father who is still alive; Colin contacted me in 2013 as a result of reading an article about the project in the *South China Morning Post*.

I made inquiries through local historians and organisations. People were interested, but did not know anyone who had direct knowledge. I tried contacts abroad, including with the British army, but did not have any luck. I was perplexed when my request for assistance to the Taiwan POW Camps Memorial Society was met with suspicion, and there was unwillingness to circulate my request for information and assistance. There will have been prisoner of war survivors among its membership who could have contributed to our understanding of the Taiwanese camp trials, but without assistance I was not able to reach them.

---

[69] There were two trials that dealt with crimes committed in relation to the sinking of the *Lisbon Maru*. See Trial of Kyoda Shigeru, HKWCT Collection, File No. WO235/1114; Trial of Niimori Genichiro, HKWCT Collection, File No. WO235/892. Peter Vine was the prosecutor in the case brought against Kyoda Shigeru, who was the civilian captain of the vessel.

[70] Peter Vine, "Experiences as a War Crimes Prosecutor in Hong Kong", in *Hong Kong Branch of the Royal Asiatic Society*, 1995, vol. 35, pp. 205–9 (http://hkwctc.lib.hku.hk/—archive/files/petervine_f7cd6d7398.pdf).

It is not my style to engage much with the media, but in the interests of the search for survivors of that time who could assist with the project I knew I had to bite the metaphorical bullet. Discovering the case of LI Kam Moon provided me with a story that I knew the local media would jump at.[71] Late one dark evening in my office at HKU, my research assistant Dixon TSE and I were reviewing some files and casenotes. The prosecutor's opening statement in one case was unusually dramatic: "When the history of this Colony's part in the struggle against Japanese aggression comes to be written the name of LI KAM MOON will be inscribed upon its pages". Delving further, I found the defence also being similarly dramatic: "It is more important in this Honourable Court that the integrity of British Justice be maintained than that the blood of Li Kam Moon be avenged". My interest was piqued. I discovered the following. LI Kam Moon was a 20-year-old baker and confectioner from Kowloon, who worked at the Café Wiseman in Hong Kong. LI had a good friend from his school days, WONG Kai, who worked undercover for the British resistance organisation, the British Army Aid Group (BAAG). WONG Kai was a subject of interest for the Kempeitai, in particular one Sergeant Matsuda, known as 'Little Tiger' because he was aggressive. LI was arrested in Waichow by Matsuda and two Chinese detectives. He was first taken to the gendarmerie headquarters and then to Wai On Hospital. On 5 August 1945 his family were notified that he was dying, and his badly maimed body was buried by his two sisters on the grounds of Wai On Hospital. The torture and killing of LI was one of the first war crimes cases to be tried in post-war Hong Kong (10 May 1946–14 May 1946). The prosecution presented this as a tale of exceptional heroism, arguing that LI had preferred to die under torture rather than betray his friend to the Kempeitai. The trial came to turn on the conflicting accounts of LI's sister and Sergeant Matsuda about what happened to LI at the Wai On Hospital. The panel convicted the accused of "being concerned in" the war crime of maltreatment, but not of causing LI's death. Matsuda was sentenced to eight years' imprisonment.

With the assistance of the HKU assistant director of media, Trinni CHOY, I held a press conference and presented the work we had been doing on the Hong Kong war crimes trials, and specifically asked for help with my search for people who had had direct experience of the trials and

---

[71] Trial of Sergeant Matsuda Kenicihi, HKWCT Collection, File No. WO/235/846.

would be able to speak to me. Of course, I gave some illustrative cases and, as predicted, the LI Kam Moon story was indeed the one that the local media pounced on. There was extensive coverage in the English and Cantonese media, including making the front page of the *South China Morning Post*, and it also travelled to the Chinese mainland where it was picked up by the media there.[72] The emails and phone calls began with the very first of the publications, every one of them being positive and encouraging about the work that I was doing. To this day, I am contacted by strangers from around the world, asking for information about a family member or writing to provide some information.[73] Two particularly important people emerged from this round of publicity. One was a torture survivor, Stephen TSUI, who I interviewed at length about his experiences, which led to his testimony as a prosecution witness in the trial of Warrant Officer Omura Kiyoshi.[74] A second valuable account came from Luba Estes, of Russian background but living in Hong Kong as a child – her home in Kowloon was commandeered by the prisoner of war camp commandant Tokunaga Isao, while her father was incarcerated in one of the local prisoner of war camps under his control. She lived in the United States, but provided me with a valuable statement about her experiences.[75] People have continued to write to me and the media have continued to track the work on Hong Kong's war crimes trials over the years.[76] I was, of course, careful to obtain ethical clearance in advance of all interviews,

---

[72] See for example, Simpson Chueng, "Sad Tale of Unsung Hero's War Death Uncovered", in *South China Morning Post*, 13 September 2010; "Forgotten Hero of World War II Deeds Brought to Light" [in Chinese], in *South China Morning Post*, 13 September 2010; Wong Yat-hei, "Lessons from Our Darkest Era", in *Young Post, South China Morning Post*, 14 October 2010; "HKU Publish War Criminals Database", in *Mingpao News*, 13 September 2010; "rthk.hk 香港電台網站: Hong Kong Today Interview", on *Hong Kong Today*, Radio Television Hong Kong, 29 December 2010.

[73] For an informal account of my work with Stephen TSUI, see "China: Living the Law – How IHL Is Inspiring Lives", 22 December 2010 (https://www.icrc.org/eng/ resources/documents/feature/2010/china-moot-feature-2010-12-22.htm).

[74] HKWCT Collection, Interview Atendee Note, Mr. Stephen Sai-cheung, 17 September 2010 (http://hkwctc.lib.hku.hk/archive/files/img-y291702-0001_ac3a86c3ad.pdf). The case was the Trial of Warrant Officer Omura Kiyoshi, HKWCT Collection, File No. WO 235/893.

[75] HKWCT Collection, Statement of Mrs. Luba A. Estes (Nee Luba Alexandra Skvorzov) (http://hkwctc.lib.hku.hk/archive/files/luba-estes-statement_674d0cfb3d.pdf).

[76] See, for example, John Carney, "Book Sheds Light on Hong Kong's War Tribunals", in *South China Morning Post*, 28 April 2013.

and gain the consent of the interviewee/statement giver to the publication of the interview or statement.

Heartening as all of this was, I still did not have the testimony of any judge, prosecutor or defence lawyer. That changed one day in May 2011. I received an email from Donal Lowry, reader in imperial and commonwealth history and Irish history at Oxford Brookes University, UK. He had come across my work on the Hong Kong trials and told me that his former neighbour had been a war crimes prosecutor in Hong Kong. And, he said, the man was still alive. It was wonderful news and Lowry introduced me to Major Murray Incell Ormsby, formerly of the West Yorkshire Regiment. From 1946 to 1948 Ormsby had been a panel member (judge) and then a prosecutor of War Crimes Court No. 7 in Hong Kong. The whole situation was amazing. Ormsby was involved in more than half of the trials that were held in Hong Kong. Although he was 92 years old when I interviewed him, Ormsby's memory was extraordinarily clear. I was able to interview him at length at home in Gloucestershire and conducted a follow-up interview by telephone.[77]

In terms of research methodology, I obtained ethical clearance from my university, which by then had become Bangor University in the UK. The interviews, three in total, were recorded and then transcribed, and sent to Ormsby for verification. Ormsby had amazing recall of his days in Hong Kong. Sometimes he would repeat himself, and the event would be described in exactly the same way, virtually word for word. I would sometimes deliberately return to a topic and he would respond in exactly the same way. He did not embellish, and if he did not know the answer to a question he would say so. If his memory did not match exactly what I knew from the case files, for example over whether he had co-prosecuted with his friend, the Australian prosecutor McGregor, he would say that was the way he remembered things. He was able to rely on some documents that he kept from those times (since Ormsby died, I have become the proud and grateful custodian of them).

For me, the interviews with Ormsby were exquisite, not only because he was a wonderful person and the two of us shared some unforget-

---

[77] The interview is published as an annex to *Hong Kong's War Crimes Trials*, see *supra* note 1, and can be found online in original form at the Hong Kong's War Crimes Trials Project, Record of Interview, Major Murray I. Ormsby, 21 July 2011 (http://hkwctc.lib.hku.hk/archive/files/int-20110918_af84c07fa3.pdf).

table hours intensely talking about Hong Kong in the 1940s as if it were the present, but because he truly enlightened my understanding about the war crimes process and what it was like to be a participant in the proceedings. A year later I visited Ormsby with my researcher Ernest NG who was then at Cambridge. By then his memory had rapidly deteriorated. Ormsby passed away some months after that at the end of 2012. I am still awed by the incredible good fortune that led to our meeting, and that I was able to interview this 92-year-old man about his experiences at a moment in time when his memory about the 1940s was exceptionally sharp. My interview with Ormsby formed the basis of the obituaries written about him in *The Times* and the *Daily Telegraph*, and been recognised as one of the particularly important contributions to emerge from *Hong Kong's War Crimes Trials*.[78]

13.2.4. Academic Challenges

Overcoming the many hurdles described above facilitated the actual research that was carried out, leading to an article in the *Melbourne Journal of International Law* in 2012 that presented preliminary analysis, and the final work in *Hong Kong's War Crimes Trials* published by Oxford University Press in 2013, as well as numerous public lectures around the world. The contributors to the book have also taken their work further, for example Nina Jørgensen has expanded her work on joint criminal enterprise in the Hong Kong trials to a wider Asian study.

Perhaps perversely, I came to enjoy the constant challenges that emerged as I had a distinct sense that I was learning new skills at every turn, and also learning lessons in patience, methodology, control of a large amount of material and having to think laterally at all times. I was stretched in ways that I had not been stretched before, and I liked that. I am not sure if all the contributors to the book felt this way, but for me, I had to be on top of it all. It was, after all, my project and I was editing a collective effort, and I was undeniably driven to get the bottom of virtually every aspect.

---

[78] Justice LIU Daqun has written in his foreword to *Hong Kong's War Crimes Trials*: "Perhaps the most precious piece of history Professor Linton presents, though, is her interview with Major Murray Incell Ormsby, who was a panel member (that is, a Judge) and then a Prosecutor at War Crimes Court No 7 in Hong Kong". Linton, 2013, see *supra* note 1.

But, as a lawyer, how does one get to the bottom of a trial where there is no judgment? This was the first problem that we faced in analysing the case files. There were verdicts, but no judgments. I knew this from early on, and the need for special abilities lay behind my choice of contributors to the book. Although there were a few exceptions, the norm of the time was for the British military trials to be concluded by verdicts that were orally delivered, with no reasoned judgment.[79] In order to understand such cases, the entire contents of the case file need to be read. The entire file for the Hong Kong trials would include charge sheets, detailed and meticulously typed transcripts of every day of the proceedings, sworn affidavits, documentary evidence, opening and closing submissions of the lawyers, and closing orders. In order to understand the case one has to sieve through all of this. Sometimes our task was made easier by reviews of the proceedings by judge advocates who were based in Singapore and conducted file reviews in order to advise the commanding officer of land forces, Hong Kong whether or not to confirm the sentence. Not all of these reviews were of the detail one would have expected, but they were usually the first point from which one would enter the story told in the file. The quality of analyses contained in *Hong Kong's War Crimes Trials*, I humbly suggest, shows that in the right hands the "no written judgment" challenge is surmountable. This is not to suggest that we did not lament the absence of reasoning that could help us better to understand the decisions reached, but I believe that the product that emerged was rather different for that, and not the usual somewhat pedestrian black-and-white-letter reasoning exercise that one expects from legal analyses. One could say that we all had to think out of the box. Speaking for myself, I took the opportunity to illuminate the legal arguments being made by using the transcripts to tell the story of the war through the testimony that was provided in court. I particularly wanted the experiences of the forgotten victims of the Second World War to be heard in our day and age. In her chapter, Nina Jørgensen took the opportunity to go back to the basics of the joint enterprise doctrine in English common law, and in the process make an important doctrinal contribution. Alexander Zahar's laser-sharp scrutiny dissected the trials in a way that I have not seen elsewhere. Yuma Totani was able to draw from her formidable expertise as an historian to

---

[79] Several exceptions to the usual practice of non-reasoned decisions are pointed out in United Nations War Crimes Commission, *Law Reports of Trials of War Criminals*, vol. 15, His Majesty's Stationery Office, London, 1947, p. 20.

place the prisoner of war trials in their correct context. I could go on this way about every contribution to the book, but the point is sufficiently made.

The procedure used in the Hong Kong trials was that applicable in field general courts martial, regulated in the Army Act 1926 and the Rules of Procedure for Trials by Court Martial under the Army Act 1926.[80] This applied to the extent amended by the Regulations annexed to the Royal Warrant and other secondary legislation, such as the instructions issued by General Headquarters, ALFSEA. One challenge I had here was finding a consolidated version – none of the physical or online examples that I was able to examine of the *Manual of Military Law* that were supposedly relied on for the post-Second World War Royal Warrant prosecutions, including in Hong Kong, included the 1936 replacement of chapter XIV on the Laws and Usages of War on Land and the 1944 amendment on superior orders.[81] The consolidation took place after the war in the eighth edition.[82] To put it another way, it appears that the trials, including in Hong Kong, were conducted using physical copies of the *Manual of Military Law 1929*, which had been reprinted in 1939; this particular reprint did not include the 1936 amendment and obviously did not include the 1944 amendment which came after the reprint. Even so, the two amendments were part of British law and were in fact applied in the trials. The importance of being precise and not confusing anyone led me to employ the term *Manual of Military Law 1929 (as amended)* when referring to the *Manual of Military Law 1929* and the two amendments of 1936 and 1944 collectively, even though I never found a consolidated version. I used the terms *Manual of Military Law 1929 (Amendment No. 12 of 1936)* and *Manual of Military Law 1929 (Amendment No. 34 of 1944)* when referring to them separately.

I also discovered problems with finding a consolidated version of the ALFSEA Instruction, which was the primary document issued by

---

[80] Army Act 1881, 44 & 45 Vict, c 58, reprinted in Great Britain, War Office, *Manual of Military Law 1929*, His Majesty's Stationery Office, London, 1929, p. 418; Rules of Procedure 1926 (amended 31 December 1928), reproduced in *idem.*, p. 611.

[81] See the amendment to chapter XIV, Great Britain, War Office, *Manual of Military Law 1929*, ch. XIV (Amendment No. 12 of 1936); and the amendment to para. 443, Great Britain, War Office, *Manual of Military Law 1929*, ch. XIV (Amendment No. 34 of 1944).

[82] See Great Britain, War Office, *Manual of Military Law*, 8th ed, Her Majesty's Stationery Office, London, 1952.

ALFSEA headquarters to regulate trials under the Royal Warrant.[83] It transpired that the ALFSEA Instruction used was the second edition, and that it was amended eight times. Fortunately, during one of my TNA trips I was able to locate Amendment No. 1 of 12 June 1946, Amendment No. 2 of 27 June 1946, Amendment No. 3 of 16 July 1946, Amendment No. 4 of 21 November 1946, Amendment No. 5 of 4 December 1946, Amendment No. 6 of 22 January 1947, Amendment No. 7 of 14 March 1947 and Amendment No. 8 of 26 March 1947.[84] This meant that research using the ALFSEA instructions and the British military manual involved juggling additional documents.

The Regulations annexed to the Royal Warrant loftily declared: "The Court shall take judicial notice of the laws and usages of war".[85] That is good and well, but what were those laws and usages of war? That was actually a massive question that could be answered in many different ways, but had to be answered if one was to be able to conduct a legal analysis of the proceedings. How far one should go was a challenge that I personally faced in my own chapter on "War Crimes" in *Hong Kong's War Crimes Trial*. To start off, at a conceptual level, what were laws of war and what were usages of war in the period of the Second World War? There was, of course, the 1919 listing that emerged from the unsuccessful attempt to prosecute after the First World War. I also discovered that the *Manual of Military Law 1929 (as amended)* was actually incorporated by reference into the Regulations for the Trial of War Criminals, and this regarded the laws of war as the "rules respecting warfare with which, according to international law, belligerents and neutrals are bound to comply".[86] According to the *Manual of Military Law 1929 (as amended)*, the "laws and usages of war" were comprised

---

[83] TNA, File No. WO 32/12197, ALFSEA War Crimes Instruction No. 1 (2nd ed.).

[84] TNA, File No. WO 32/12197.

[85] Regulations for the Trial of War Criminals annexed to Royal Warrant 1945 (UK) AO 81/1945 Regulation 8(iii).

[86] *Ibid.*, para. 1. There was also, of course, the famous International Military Tribunal at Nuremberg declaration about where to find the law of war, which only reached Hong Kong during the *Lisbon Maru* trial. See International Military Tribunal, *Nuremberg Tribunal v. Goering et al.*, Judgment, 1 October 1946 (http://www.legal-tools.org/doc/45f18e/), reprinted in "Judicial Decisions", in *American Journal of International Law*, 1947, vol. 41, no. 1, p. 219.

partly of customary rules, which have grown up in practice, and partly of written rules, that is, rules which have been purposely agreed upon by the powers in international treaties. Side by side with these customary and written laws of war there are in existence, and are still growing, usages concerning warfare. While the laws of war are legally binding, usages are not, and the latter can therefore, for sufficient reasons, be disregarded by belligerents. Usages have, however, a tendency gradually to harden into legal rules of warfare, and the greater part of the present laws of war have grown up in that way.[87]

From the leading international law authority of the time, Hersch Lauterpacht, in the fifth edition of *Oppenheim's International Law*, I obtained confirmation of the 1937 position: "Custom is the older and the original source of International Law in particular as well as of law in general. [...] International jurists speak of a custom when a clear and continuous habit of doing certain actions has grown up under the aegis of the conviction that these actions are, according to International Law, obligatory or right".[88] He went on to explain the notion of usages in the following terms: "international jurists speak of a *usage* when a habit of doing certain actions has grown up without there being the conviction that these actions are, according to International Law, obligatory or right [...] a given course of conduct may be usual without being customary".[89]

That answered the abstract aspect, but what exactly was the content of those rules? One could answer this generally and then specifically in relation to Japan and the other states engaged in the Second World War in Asia. The issue of Japan and the laws of war, in particular her persistent objection to certain treaty provisions concerning the treatment of prisoners of war, fascinated me, not just from the international law aspects but also from the cultural perspective. This led to the wider issue of superior orders and Japanese law, and the extent to which it was right simply to override the categorical position in Japanese law on the grounds that "international law", as interpreted by the victorious Allies, had changed because two of them changed the rules during the war. The direction that

---

[87] Manual of Military Law 1929 (Amendment No. 12 of 1936), para. 2 (citations omitted).

[88] Hersch Lauterpacht (ed.), *Oppenheim's International Law*, 5th ed., vol. 1: *Peace*, 1937, Longmans, Green & Co., London, p. 25 para. 17.

[89] *Ibid.*

this discussion is going in illustrates the need to set parameters in research. This is something that I had difficulty with in researching and drafting my "War Crimes" chapter. I had already anticipated that the research would be inordinately slow as a single-person project, hence the role of my terrific contributors to *Hong Kong's War Crimes Trials*. They all pursued different aspects of the trials. But even with these certain critical issues distributed among my colleagues, there was so much to discuss on this massive topic of war crimes. I knew that if I made my study a comparison with contemporary processes, I would lose my desired focus on the Hong Kong trials, so rejected that option. I planned to contribute a chapter that would cover all the key war crimes issues. But the fantastical nature of that soon became clear as I endeavoured to get a grasp of the 46 case files. An overarching study in a situation of such complexity would be a very thin and insubstantial one, and I definitely did not want that. Even so, before I could focus on an appropriate topic within war crimes, I had to get a grasp of the entire picture. In other words, in order to map something one needs to know the terrain; I had to gain the big picture not just of the war crimes trials but also of the range of substantive legal issues that arose in relation to war crimes and then choose from among them what to focus on. I found this very difficult; there was so much material to get through and so many good possibilities. As it was, as explained in my chapter on "War Crimes", I settled for a focus on war crimes against civilians, which comprised the bulk of the cases, and raised some good substantive issues for closer consideration, namely involuntary displacement, torture and other ill treatment, and unlawful killing of civilians. Even within that, I must say that found the word limit constraining; there was so much more that I would have liked to discuss on those issues.

Apart from the widespread and systematic abuse of civilians by the Kempeitai, a particular feature of the Japanese maltreatment during the occupation concerned the removal of what the Japanese figures indicate was in excess of 973,000 persons, and that was over a period of under two years. [90] There were many different terms used to describe this – evacuation, compulsory evacuation, forced repatriation, deportation, banishment, forced displacement. In light of the particular circumstances, I

---

[90] Trial of Colonel Noma Kennosuke, HKWCT Collection, File No. WO235/999, translation of extracts from "Hong Kong under Military Administration" (Hong Kong Oriental Economics Co., 1944), exhibit ZZ, 2, slides 664–67.

thought it most appropriate, when myself referring to this, to use term "involuntary displacement"; for me, this included formally voluntary displacement under the coercive circumstances of the war and the occupation. The movement of people was massive and based on a policy response to the severe overcrowding of Hong Kong, and resulting famine. Japanese and local Hong Kong sources would confirm at trial that evacuation could be by persuasion which was free of charge, at own expense and compulsory, which was also free of charge.

The two Hong Kong cases dealing with the involuntary displacement were those of *Noma* and *Kanazawa,* the two Kempeitai commanders in Hong Kong.[91] Colonel Noma was convicted of a single war crimes charge that did not separate out the involuntary displacements from the industrial-scale torture and abuse by the Kempeitai in Hong Kong, but Kanazawa was acquitted of the specific charge dealing with deportation. These cases revealed the extent of the involvement of the governors general of Hong Kong. Fortunately, I had already discovered the cases in TNA, as discussed earlier in this chapter. Tried in Nanjing, Lieutenant General Sakai Takashi was convicted of "deportation of civilians". Sakai's successor, Lieutenant General Isogai Rensuke, who oversaw the scheme for most of its life, was also convicted of allowing "his subordinates to arrest and deport non-army personnel to Bias Bay continuously, and without taking care about the safety of those being banished, causing the old, weak, females and children to be homeless, resulting in deaths from starvation and exposure".[92] The Chinese cases at least had judgments, which was more than I had in *Noma* and *Kanazawa.* I extracted out what I could from those judgments, and then had to decide whether to enrich the discussion with consideration of the leading European deportation cases such as *Krupp*[93] and *High Command*[94] which actually came after the

---

[91] *Ibid.* See also Trial of Lt Col Kanazawa Asao, HKWCT Collection, File No. WO235/1093.

[92] TNA, File No. WO325/135, "rough translation" of the judgment of the Chinese Military Tribunal at Nanjing, 22 July in the 36th year of the Chinese Republic (1947).

[93] US Military Tribunal Nuremberg, *United States of America v. Alfried Felix Alwyn Krupp von Bohlen und Halbach et al.*, Judgment, 31 July 1948 (http://www.legal-tools.org/doc/ad5c2b/), in *Trials of War Criminals Before the Nuremberg Military Tribunal under Control Council Law No 10, October 1946–April 1949*, vol. IX, US Government Printing Office, Washington, DC, 1950, p. 1327 ('Krupp case').

[94] US Military Tribunal Nuremberg, *United States of America v. Wilhelm von Leeb et al.*, Judgment, 27 October 1948 (http://www.legal-tools.org/doc/c340d7/), in *Trials of War Criminals Before the Nuremberg Military Tribunal under Control Council Law No 10, Oc-*

Hong Kong trials were completed. In the course of reading Russell's *Knights of Bushido*, I came across a reference to deportation linked to food shortages in the Andaman Islands. I had the case pinpointed to TNA and reviewed the file in the summer of 2011. This was also an ALFSEA case, tried in Singapore, and it seemed to me to be a particularly suitable case to use for comparative purposes (it also had a far better judge advocate report than that in *Noma* and *Kanazawa*). I believe that the balance was right: the Hong Kong deportations took centre stage; the European cases were noted; and close consideration was given to a very similar situation on an Indian Ocean territory, and tried in Singapore using the same laws and procedures under ALFSEA supervision. I think, too, that this provides a good illustration of overcoming the "no judgments" barrier by drawing from a range of sources to form a coherent picture and novel analysis of the handling of war crimes cases involving involuntary displacement.

As a final point on the matter of academic analysis, I would like to raise the issue of how we assess a legal process that took place after the decimation of a world war, concerning crimes across swathes of Asian lands occupied by the Japanese, and using the standards and technology of that time. This was a challenge. I was very conscious of the need to be fair, but not to gloss over anything. It was inappropriate, to me, to use contemporary standards laid down in the International Covenant on Civil and Political Rights to evaluate the process. In his chapter in *Hong Kong's War Crimes Trials*, my colleague and friend Alexander Zahar rightly used the standards of the time, and was extremely critical of the process.[95] He demonstrated how the standards of fairness and due process were not just lower because this was a military process, but they were lower than what was usual in an equivalent British military proceeding. He expressed particular concern about the death penalties imposed, not just because of the flaws he found in the proceedings but in light of the eventual policy of appeasement and rapprochement with Japan. For myself, I have written about the weaknesses of the proceedings, but also balanced it against the achievements. For me, this was overall a surprisingly fair process, given

---

tober 1946–April 1949, vol. IX, US Government Printing Office, Washington, DC, 1950, p. 462 ('High Command case').

[95] Alexander Zahar, "Trial Procedure at the British Military Courts, Hong Kong, 1946–1948", in Suzannah Linton (ed.), *Hong Kong's War Crimes Trials*, Oxford University Press, Oxford, 2013, pp. 13–69.

the circumstances. It was certainly not a "kangaroo court", to borrow from my previous assessment in the *Melbourne Journal of International Law*.[96] Pritchard argues that "the evidence suggests that none of the trials which actually took place under British auspices in the Far East were prejudiced by direct intervention from political circles. [...] There was no effort to purge the Japanese leadership indiscriminately";[97] for him the British trial process upheld the "highest standards of British justice".[98] The point, in conclusion, is that this illustrates the importance of drawing in a range of expert contributions. In my view, one person's perspective is not enough. The study of Hong Kong's war crimes trials has been enriched by experts with different perspectives and reaching different conclusions.

13.3. General and Concluding Observations

There are of course other obstacles that I faced, but they are generic and arise at any time and place in collaborative academic projects. One is that contributors can let you down. There is a gap in *Hong Kong's War Crimes Trials* on command responsibility because at the very last minute, having promised for many months that the draft was in progress, the particular contributor dropped out. This left a gap in the book, but fortunately it was not fatal because command responsibility was an issue that was actually traced in all the chapters, and I had examined some of that in my *Melbourne Journal of International Law* article. Even so, it was a huge and unnecessary disappointment, especially in light of the enormous effort that went into the whole project. I am not sure how to advise future researchers in relation to this sort of thing. To be too heavy-handed with contributors can cause them to pull out, and making inquiries about reliability does not always yield what one needs to know. I guess one just has to manage situations as they arise.

Another more mundane issue relates to citations. Referencing the case materials for publications proved to be rather tricky, and I had some dramas with law journal editorial rigidity in relation to particular citation protocols. Referencing edits were unilaterally imposed, rendering the arti-

---

96   Suzannah Linton, "Rediscovering the War Crimes trials in Hong Kong, 1946–1948", in *Melbourne Journal of International Law*, 2012, vol. 13, no. 2, p. 359.

97   R. John Pritchard, "The Historical Experience of British War Crimes Courts in the Far East, 1946–1948", in *International Relations*, 1978, vol. 6, no. 1, p. 318.

98   *Ibid.*, p. 321.

cle inaccurate and unreliable. Major revisions then had to be made to enable publication to proceed. So, the lesson is that with publication of research into historical legal proceedings or any research using unusual sources, one has to be careful with the process of outside editing. Researchers will need to review and scrutinise edits to their work extremely carefully. The team at Oxford University Press was wonderful with *Hong Kong's War Crimes Trials*, and recognised that the project had its own internal discipline and so the publication needed to reflect the distinct referencing system. I sought to remain true to the documents, provide as much information as possible, to facilitate the work of others who may wish to retrace our steps.[99] I also made a particular effort to link citations not just to transcript pages, but to scan numbers so that those using the HKWCT Collection could find the source easily. The quest to remain true to documents sometimes meant that documents of the same class were called different things. This was because we adhered to the original name used by the author who created the document. Then, there were issues of nomenclature: Nanking/Nanjing, Formosa/Taiwan, Peking/Beijing. One has to be sensitive to sensitivities.

These then are some of the challenges that the Hong Kong War Crimes Trials project faced, and the ways that they were addressed. Projects like this are not for those who do pure black-letter lawyering, or philosophical abstractions, or those who like things to be all in one place and "just so". For those who can think out of the box, are flexible and creative yet can adhere to a strong and principled methodology, have an investigative or bloodhound streak in them, and can work with large amounts of material across multiple disciplines, I would warmly encourage them to consider embarking on legal time travel. It has been an incredible experience for me.

---

[99] This is described in the Introduction to *Hong Kong's War Crimes Trials*, see *supra* note 95.

14

Evidence Collection and Presentation in International Criminal Tribunals

Guido Acquaviva[*]

14.1. Introduction

This chapter mainly focuses on how the law of evidence – its collection and presentation in the courtroom – has evolved together with the evolution of international criminal courts and tribunals, from the experience of Nuremberg to the Special Tribunal for Lebanon, established in 2009, the latest court set up within the international community to deal with complex crimes.

As I have elaborated upon elsewhere, legal systems based on the common law tradition (adversarial systems) developed strict sets of exclusionary rules for the admission of evidence, for instance limiting the admission of written statements and hearsay in criminal proceedings.[1] These rules were premised, *inter alia*, on the assumption that in the courtroom juries should generally be exposed only to first-hand knowledge of the events in question. Thus, common law judges routinely exercise their duty of "screening" the evidence in order for jurors – the fact-finders – not to come in contact with evidence deemed unreliable or of unjust origin.[2]

---

[*]   **Guido Acquaviva** is Senior Legal Officer at the Special Tribunal for Lebanon (Chambers). Prior to that, he worked at the International Criminal Tribunal for the former Yugoslavia as a Legal Officer. He has lectured at the Geneva Academy of International Humanitarian Law and Human Rights, at the LL.M. in International Crime and Justice (University of Turin – UNICRI), at the University of Milan – Bicocca, and has published extensively on public international law and international criminal law. The views expressed in this chapter do not necessarily reflect those of the Special Tribunal for Lebanon or any other organisation with which Dr. Acquaviva is affiliated.

[1]   Guido Acquaviva, "Written and Oral Evidence", in Linda Carter and Fausto Pocar (eds.), *International Criminal Procedure: The Interface of Civil Law and Common Law Legal Systems*, Edward Elgar, Cheltenham, 2013, pp. 99–124.

[2]   When a jury trial is waived and a bench trial is conducted, the judge becomes the trier of fact and will also have the task of determining whether the evidence is both relevant and admissible. This is premised on the assumption that, unlike jurors, professional judges are

---

Although in most legal systems historically associated with English common law today the vast majority of criminal trials do not actually take place in front of a jury, but rather before professional judges, the evolution of the system – and of the evidentiary provisions within the system in particular – has undoubtedly been moulded by the necessities dictated by juries. The system therefore allows a sort of "duel" between the parties who, through strictly regulated examination and cross-examination procedures, are able to present evidence which will lead to a conviction only if guilt is demonstrated beyond reasonable doubt. In essence, according to the pure common law tradition, nothing really counts as "evidence" until and unless it is heard orally at trial.[3]

Civil law judges have instead historically been the adjudicators of both procedure and substance. This means that they will see all of the evidence, even that against which a party raises admissibility issues. In practical terms, of course, the standard of proof "beyond reasonable doubt" has come to be seen as essential in the civil law tradition too.[4] Nonetheless, in their quest for the truth, judges in these systems have traditionally been afforded greater latitude in admitting and assessing both oral and written evidence than in common law systems,[5] although this has been changing in recent times.[6]

---

conceptually able to distinguish the two tasks. The same assumption forms the basis of international criminal trials, where no juries exist.

[3] J.R. Spencer, "Introduction", in Mireille Delmas-Marty and J.R. Spencer (eds.), *European Criminal Procedures*, Cambridge University Press, Cambridge, 2002, p. 21.

[4] See, for example, France, Cour de cassation (crim.), 24 January 2007, Judgment n. 06-82.769; Italy, Cassazione Sezione Penale, 24 November 2003, n. 45276 (*Andreotti et al.*).

[5] See the German Code of Criminal Procedure (Strafprozeßordnung, StPO), section 244, which reads, in part: "In its search for the truth, the Court shall extend the taking of evidence to any fact or means of proof relevant to the decision" (http://www.legal-tools.org/doc/b96d81/). The Austrian Code of Criminal Procedure (Strafprozeßordnung 1975, StPO), section 258, provides in part: "The court shall examine the evidence carefully and conscientiously with regard to its trustworthiness and conclusiveness separately and as a whole. Judges shall not decide upon the question of whether or not a particular fact has been proven according to formal [or statutory] rules of evidence, but only according to their own conclusions drawn on the basis of their careful examination of all of the evidence on the record" (http://www.legal-tools.org/doc/b69e9e/). All translations of non-English case law and legislation in this chapter are by the author.

[6] J.R. Spencer, "Evidence", in Mireille Delmas-Marty and J.R. Spencer (eds.), *European Criminal Procedures*, Cambridge University Press, Cambridge, 2002, pp. 600–2. An extreme exception to the regime of free evidence is provided by the Netherlands Code of Criminal Procedure (Wetboek van Strafvordering), which requires that a conviction be based only on a list of enumerated "legal means of gathering evidence" (Articles 338 and

---

Contemporary international criminal tribunals have largely followed this model for the trial phase of the proceedings, and judges have – in relation to evidence – substantially relied on the material presented to them by the parties in the courtroom rather than investigating the crimes themselves. It is important in this context to appreciate what are the main factors in the use and assessment of the evidence during these extraordinarily complex criminal trials.

14.2. Evidence before International Criminal Tribunals

For the purpose of international criminal proceedings, evidence could be defined as all information admitted by a Chamber as tending to prove or disprove allegations contained in the document setting out the charges against the accused (usually referred to as indictment or document containing the charges).

International criminal tribunals are not endowed with juries, and thus it is judges who are called to assess the admissibility of evidence as well as its significance for the ultimate findings. It is therefore not so surprising that contemporary international criminal tribunals – essentially the ones from the International Criminal Tribunal for the former Yugoslavia ('ICTY') in 1993 onwards – have witnessed an evolution of at least part of the law applicable to the presentation, admission and evaluation of evidence. From their start, the *ad hoc* tribunals have relied on the traditional civil law approach of not burdening fact-finders with strict rules of evidence, doing without most of the complexities of the exclusionary rules so essential to common lawyers and, progressively, to most contemporary civil law systems. This is because it is often assumed that professional judges are more capable than lay jurors to assess themselves the reliability of evidentiary material tendered by the parties at trial.

The first substantive rule of evidence guiding judges of international criminal tribunals is, therefore, that a Chamber may admit *any relevant information* as evidence, taking into account its probative value.[7] This

---

339) (http://www.legal-tools.org/doc/612bb2/). A brief account of the evolution of the systems in the civil law tradition is John Henry Merryman and Rogelio Pérez-Perdomo, *The Civil Law Tradition: An Introduction to the Legal Systems of Europe and Latin America*, 3rd ed., Stanford University Press, Stanford, CA, 2007, pp. 125–33.

[7] International Military Tribunal, Nuremberg, Charter, Part of the London Agreement of 8 August 1945, Arts. 19 and 20 ('IMT Charter') (http://www.legal-tools.org/doc/64ffdd/). International Military Tribunal for the Far East, Tokyo, Charter, 19 January 1946, Art. 13(a)

essentially means that a Chamber, when ruling on the admission of evidence (oral or otherwise) will make a preliminary assessment of the likely probative value of the evidence in question vis-à-vis the charges contained in the indictment – while, of course, a final assessment of the probative value of each piece will only be made at the end of the trial, upon a full record. International criminal judges are generally – and subject to some exceptions – allowed great flexibility with respect to the admission of evidence, and their evaluation of what is relevant and what has probative value is largely left unchecked until the judgment is rendered.

As a corollary of this discretion, *international criminal tribunals are not bound by any national rules of evidence*, including the various exclusionary rules developed by most contemporary systems of criminal law and procedure.[8] The exclusion of domestic rules of evidence also means that documents or other exhibits that would formally have been inadmissible in certain (national) legal systems might nonetheless be legitimately considered by international judges in order to assess the guilt or innocence of an accused. For instance, telephone communications intercepted in contravention of the domestic legislation of various states of the former Yugoslavia have been admitted into the trial record of ICTY proceedings.[9] Similarly,

---

and (b) ('IMTFE Charter') (http://www.legal-tools.org/doc/a3c41c/); International Criminal Tribunal for the former Yugoslavia, Rules of Procedure and Evidence, as amended on 8 July 2015, Rule 89(C) ('ICTY RPE') ('http://www.legal-tools.org/doc/30df50/); International Criminal Tribunal for Rwanda, Rules of Procedure and Evidence, as amended on 13 May 2015, Rule 89(C) ('ICTR RPE') (http://www.legal-tools.org/doc/c6a7c6/); Rome Statute of the International Criminal Court, 17 July 1998, in force 1 July 2002, Art. 69(4), ('ICC Statute') (http://www.legal-tools.org/doc/7b9af9/); Special Tribunal for Lebanon, Statute, 30 May 2007, Art. 21(2) ('STL Statute') (http://www.legal-tools.org/doc/da0bbb/); Special Tribunal for Lebanon, Rules of Procedure and Evidence, 20 March 2009, Rule 149(C) ('STL RPE') (http://www.legal-tools.org/doc/3773bf/). These articles generally refer to "evidence" rather than information – while technically information becomes evidence only after being admitted into the record.

8   ICTY RPE, Rule 89(A), see *supra* note 7; ICTR RPE, Rule 89(A), see *supra* note 7; Special Court for Sierra Leone, Rules of Procedure and Evidence, amended 31 May 2012, Rule 89(A) ('SCSL RPE') (http://www.legal-tools.org/doc/4c2a6b/); Internatioanl Criminal Court, Rules of Procedure and Evidence, 9 September 2002, Rule 63(5) ('ICC RPE') (http://www.legal-tools.org/doc/8bcf6f/). The STL is an exception in this respect, since it provides that, in case of a lacuna, judges may apply provisions of the Lebanese Code of Criminal Procedure "consistent with the highest standards of international criminal procedure"; STL RPE, Rule 149(A), see *supra* note 7.

9   See, for example, ICTY, *Prosecutor v. Radoslav Brđanin*, Trial Chamber, Decision on the Defence Objection to Intercept Evidence, 3 October 2003, IT-99-36-T (http://www.legal-tools.org/doc/7efabf/); ICTY, *Prosecutor v. Astrit Haraqija and Bajrush Morina*, Trial

---

the International Criminal Court ('ICC') has held that search and seizure operations undertaken in violation of domestic procedures do not *per se* render the evidence gathered inadmissible.[10]

This in turns means that, in theory, each international criminal tribunal has its own self-contained system for the admission of evidence. In practice, however, the various courts and tribunals follow some shared rules and general principles, which form the kernel of what is developing as a body of international criminal procedure,[11] including the law dealing with evidence admission and evaluation. Some authors have suggested that the use of some exclusionary rules of evidence from the common law tradition would make international criminal trials more efficient[12] – but to date such critiques have not been heeded.[13]

14.3. Fundamental Principles on Admission of Evidence before International Criminal Tribunals

The post-Second World War international military tribunals – the International Military Tribunal at Nuremberg and International Military Tribunal for the Far East at Tokyo – had extremely lax rules of evidence, which allowed judges to exercise a very broad discretion in admitting evidence,

---

Chamber, Decision on Astrit Haraqija and Bajrush Morina's Joint Request for Reconsideration of the Trial Chamber's Decision of 4 September 2008, 24 September 2008, IT-04-84-R77.4 (http://www.legal-tools.org/doc/695b22/).

[10] ICC, Situation in the Democratic Republic of the Congo, *Prosecutor v. Thomas Lubanga Dyilo*, Pre-Trial Chamber, Decision on Confirmation of Charges, 29 January 2007, ICC-01/04-01/06, paras. 74–78 (http://www.legal-tools.org/doc/b7ac4f/).

[11] This international criminal procedural law appears to be developing a common set of basic due process guarantees that each international judicial body called to examine individual criminal responsibility is required to follow. In a similar vein, see Stefania Negri, "The Principle of 'Equality of Arms' and the Evolving Law of International Criminal Procedure", in *International Law Review*, 2005, vol. 5, no. 4, p. 513; Sergey Vasiliev, "General Rules and Principles of International Criminal Procedure: Definition, Legal Nature, and Identification", in Göran Sluiter and Sergey Vasiliev (eds.), *International Criminal Procedure: Towards a Coherent Body of Law*, Cameron May, London, 2009, p. 19.

[12] Peter Murphy, "No Free Lunch, No Free Proof: The Indiscriminate Admission of Evidence Is a Serious Flaw in International Criminal Trials", in *International Criminal Justice*, 2010, vol. 8, no. 2, p. 539.

[13] For a defence of the main features of the present system, see Christine Schuon, *International Criminal Procedure: A Clash of Legal Cultures*, T.M.C. Asser Press, The Hague, 2010, pp. 136 ff.

oral or written.[14] Despite witness evidence and various examples of masterful examination and cross-examination, at Nuremberg and Tokyo most of the most important evidence relied upon was *written* evidence, and specifically documents prepared by German and Japanese officials themselves to record their campaigns and operations. Indeed, the US prosecutor at Nuremberg even went so far as stating in court:

> There is no count in the Indictment that cannot be proved by books and records. The Germans were always meticulous record keepers, and these defendants had their share of the Teutonic passion for thoroughness in putting things on paper.[15]

Similarly, post-Nuremberg and Tokyo trials held in the zones of occupation by domestic military authorities against Germans, Japanese and collaborators under the aegis of the United Nations War Crimes Commission heavily relied on documents.[16] Such documents were easily retrieved by Allied military personnel during the occupation of Germany and of Japan or in liberated countries, with the help of some of the surviving victims, but without any real deep involvement of the victims themselves in presenting these documents in the courtrooms. It has been recently noted that in this respect the Nuremberg and Tokyo trials were not really akin to contemporary international criminal trials, in that only as of the *Eichmann* trial in Israel (1961–1962) was the voice of victims-witnesses seriously heard for the first time.[17] It is clearly against the backdrop of these precedents that one should understand contemporary international practice.

---

[14] IMT Charter, Art. 19 provided that "[t]he Tribunal shall not be bound by technical rules of evidence. It shall adopt and apply to the greatest possible extent expeditious and non-technical procedure, and shall admit any evidence which it deems to be of probative value", see *supra* note 7. IMTFE Charter, Art. 13 added that "[a]ll purported admissions or statements of the accused are admissible", see *supra* note 7.

[15] International Military Tribunal, *Trial of the Major War Criminals Before the International Military Tribunal*, Blue Series (42 vols.), vol. 2, IMT, Nuremberg, 1947, p. 102.

[16] On these efforts, see recently Carsten Stahn, "Complementarity and Cooperative Justice Ahead of Their Time? The United Nations War Crimes Commission, Fact-Finding and Evidence", in *Criminal Law Forum*, 2014, vol. 25, no. 1, pp. 223–60.

[17] Leora Bilsky, "The Eichmann Trial: Towards a Jurisprudence of Eyewitness Testimony of Atrocities", in *Journal of International Criminal Justice*, 2014, vol. 12, no. 1, p. 27.

It is essential to understand that contemporary international criminal tribunals are bound to respect international human rights standards.[18] This includes the presumption of innocence, and each one of the contemporary international criminal tribunals follows the strict rule according to which an accused may be convicted only if the evidence shows guilt *beyond reasonable doubt*. Most of this body of law, and specifically the areas related to the rights of the accused and the procedural guarantees afforded during criminal proceedings, has of course developed *after* the Nuremberg and Tokyo trials. This is certainly one of the most momentous differences between modern international criminal trials and the post-Second World War proceedings. Such human rights standards, and their interpretation by domestic, regional and international bodies, have a clear impact not only on the attitude of international judges but also – and more specifically – on the attention that international prosecutors and defence counsel have devoted to the issue of evidence, and of proof beyond reasonable doubt of all elements of each crime and the mode of liability charged, when arguing their cases before international judges.

International tribunals have undoubtedly heeded the prescription of the European Court of Human Rights ('ECtHR') that "all the evidence must normally be produced at a public hearing, in the presence of the Accused, with a view to adversarial argument",[19] a requirement aimed at ensuring that the defence is able to effectively challenge the case against the accused. This is in line with the requirement of Article 14(e) of the International Covenant of Civil and Political Rights ('ICCPR') and enshrined in all of the international courts' founding instruments, that an accused must be able to "examine, or have examined, the witnesses against him or her". Importantly, Article 14 has been interpreted as requiring not only equality between prosecution and defence in obtaining, leading and challenging evidence but also that each accused "must have the right to act

---

[18] United Nations Security Council, Report of the Secretary-General Pursuant to Paragraph 2 of Security Council Resolution 808, 3 May 1993, UN doc. S/25704 (1993), para. 106. See also ICC Statute, Art. 23(3), *supra* note 7. On the consequences for breach of human rights by international tribunals, see Guido Acquaviva, "Human Rights Violations before International Tribunals: Reflections on Responsibility of International Organizations", in *Leiden Journal of International Law*, 2007, vol. 20, no. 3, p. 613.

[19] See, for instance, European Court of Human Rights ('ECtHR'), *A.M. v. Italy*, no. 37019/97, ECHR 1999-IX, para. 25.

diligently and fearlessly in pursuing all available defences".[20] For these and other reasons – in proceedings before international criminal tribunals – preference is currently given to *oral* evidence presented through examination and cross-examination of witnesses before the fact-finders.[21] This is despite the fact that in recent years the scientific basis for preferring eyewitness testimony as the most reliable form of evidence in criminal proceedings has been strongly criticised, and largely proven wrong.[22]

It should be noted that, in interpreting human rights standards, international criminal tribunals have often made recourse to the decisions of the ECtHR, especially in the field of evidence. This is not, of course, because ECtHR rulings are *per se* binding on these jurisdictions, but rather because they deal with cases from a multitude of different jurisdictions applying a variety of different procedural rules through the prism of a provision (Article 6 of the Convention for the Protection of Human Rights and Fundamental Freedoms) which is very similar to the catalogue of fair trial rights enshrined in the ICCPR and in these tribunals' founding instruments.[23]

The ICTY, International Criminal Tribunal for Rwanda ('ICTR') and Special Tribunal for Lebanon ('STL') Rules of Procedure and Evi-

---

[20] United Nations, Human Rights Committee, CCPR General Comment No. 13: Article 14 (Administration of Justice), Equality before the Courts and the Right to a Fair and Public Hearing by an Independent Court Established by Law, 13 April 1984, para. 11.

[21] While the traditional English view enshrined in *Myers v. DPP* [1965] AC 1001 (HL), requiring oral evidence in all cases, has been gradually replaced by statutes allowing hearsay and records created in the course of business, it is still true that in common law countries the most important evidence is presented at an oral hearing. Thus, it is interesting that countries traditionally identified with the civil law tradition have been increasingly embracing the adversarial system of evidence presentation. See the Italian Constitution, Art. 111, amended in 1999, now stating: "In criminal law proceedings, the formation of evidence is based on the principle of adversary hearings. The guilt of the defendant cannot be established on the basis of statements by persons who, out of their own free choice, have always voluntarily avoided undergoing cross-examination by the defendant or the defence counsel".

[22] This point has been convincingly made in Nancy A. Combs, *Fact-finding Without Facts: The Uncertain Evidentiary Foundations of International Criminal Convictions*, Cambridge University Press, Cambridge, 2011, pp. 14–20 (but see also pp. 63–105 for problems specifically affecting international criminal tribunals).

[23] See, for instance, ICTY, *Prosecutor v. Jadranko Prlić et al.*, Appeals Chamber, Decision on Appeals Against Decision Admitting Transcript of Jadranko Prlić's Questioning into Evidence, 23 November 2007, IT-04-74AR73.6, para. 40 (http://www.legal-tools.org/doc/275012/).

---

dence provide that "[a] Chamber may admit any relevant evidence which it deems to have probative value"[24] (subject of course to a number of constraints and restrictions).[25] Similarly, the ICC Statute provides that the parties may submit evidence relevant to the case, and that the Court may rule on the relevance or admissibility of any evidence, taking into account its probative value.[26]

Contemporary international criminal tribunals therefore avoid complex technical rules of evidence. The only general exclusionary rule requires that judges in all contemporary courts and tribunals exclude evidence obtained by methods which cast substantial doubt on its reliability or if its admission is contrary to, and would seriously damage, the integrity of the proceedings, for example, by being contrary to the basic legal instruments of these courts and/or in violation of established human rights.[27] To this general principle, one should add that international criminal tribunals have excluded evidence gathered in *serious* violation of their own procedures, such as those rules requiring counsel to be present during suspect interviews.[28] Moreover, the fact that international judges are required to issue reasoned written judgments which may be appealed for lack of reasoning, abuse of discretion, and other legal or factual errors, provides an important safeguard against them using inappropriate evidence to reach a conviction.

Unlike the simple finding by common law juries that an accused is "guilty" or "not guilty", with no written reasons and justifications for such a finding, international criminal judgments therefore tend to be rather lengthy, because trial judges must duly explain their assessment of the relevance and probative value of the (main) evidence, as well as their own

---

24 ICTY RPE, Rule 89(C), see *supra* note 7; ICTR RPE, Rule 89(C), see *supra* note 7; STL RPE, Rule 149(C), see *supra* note 7.

25 ICTY RPE, Rules 89–98, see *supra* note 7; ICTR RPE, Rules 89–98, see *supra* note 7.

26 ICC Statute, Art. 69(3) and (4), see *supra* note 7. See also ICC RPE, Rule 63(2), *supra* note 8.

27 ICTY RPE, Rules 89(D) and 95, see *supra* note 7; ICTR RPE, Rule 95, see *supra* note 7; ICC Statute, Art. 69(4) and (7), see *supra* note 7. See also STL RPE, Rule 149(D), *supra* note 7.

28 See, for instance, ICTR, *Prosecutor v. Théoneste Bagosora et al.*, Trial Chamber, Decision on Prosecutor's Motion for the Admission of Certain Materials under Rule 89(C), 14 October 2004, ICTR-98-41-T, para. 21 (http://www.legal-tools.org/doc/d6aea0/).

reasoning in reaching the verdict.[29] Even though judges are not required to articulate each and every step of their reasoning for each specific finding,[30] what triers of fact are encouraged to do is, for instance, to discuss *why* they rely on certain parts of a witness's testimony, while they reject other parts as not credible.[31] The same applies to documents, in particular those bearing directly on the guilt or innocence of the accused. This is not dissimilar to what civil law systems provide, and actually human rights bodies tend to require, when mandating judges to give reasons for their decisions.[32]

14.4. The Interaction between Law and Technological Advances in Evidence Gathering

However, the practices of gathering and presenting evidence before international criminal tribunals are not just a consequence of the applicable rules of evidence and the fundamental rights of the accused. There is another aspect of the problem that has been largely overlooked by scholars and commentators in the international field (far more, at least, than in domestic systems): the impact of new discoveries and technologies. As technology advances, new methods of identifying and gathering evidence are discovered or invented (DNA sampling techniques, ability to intercept telephone communications, analyses of call data records and electronic communications and so forth), and new modalities of presenting this evidence in court – while fully respecting the rights of each accused – must

---

[29] The requirements may actually have unintended consequences: the Trial Chamber in the *Sainović et al.* judgment (a 1,700-page ruling) stated: "The Prosecution chose to present a case founded upon a multitude of alleged events in [13] separate municipalities [...]. The Prosecution led evidence from a small number of people in relation to each of the municipalities, but invited the Chamber to make wide-ranging findings about the perpetration of crimes and the movement of hundreds of thousands of people and the murders of many hundreds of people. [...] The net effect is that the Chamber had the very onerous task of carefully considering whether the witnesses presented were sufficiently reliable to enable such wide-ranging conclusions to be based on their evidence". ICTY, *Prosecutor v. Sainović et al.*, Trial Chamber, Judgment, vol. 1 of 4, 26 February 2009, IT-05-87-T, para. 45 (http://www.legal-tools.org/doc/9eb7c3/).

[30] See ICTR, *Prosecutor v. Alfred Musema*, Appeals Chamber, Judgment, 16 November 2001, ICTR-96-13-A, para. 18 (http://www.legal-tools.org/doc/6a3fce/).

[31] See, for instance, ICTY, *Prosecutor v. Momcilo Krajišnik*, Appeals Chamber, Judgment, 17 March 2009, IT-00-39-A, para. 150 (http://www.legal-tools.org/doc/770028/).

[32] ECtHR, *Garcia Ruiz v. Spain* [GC], no. 30544/96, ECHR 1999-I, 21 January 1999, para. 26 (http://www.legal-tools.org/doc/e4bae4/).

---

be developed. The modalities of presentation of evidence before international tribunals (and any court, in reality) can therefore be said to be a function of the applicable procedural rules as well as of the level of technological development relevant for the specific trial in question. These could be said to be two of the main forces driving the development of international criminal procedure, one (technology and new discoveries) potentially expanding the sources of evidence, the other (the rights of the accused, but also the interests of other stakeholders within the international criminal process, such as victims) aimed at ensuring that no unfair verdict ensues.

Once again, the caveat is that this dichotomy – between technological advances, on the one side, and the protection of human rights, on the other – is a crude and simplistic one: of course technology and technical expertise may benefit the defence as much as prosecuting authorities, so long as actual equality of arms is procedurally and substantively ensured and safeguarded. But such simplification may assist in discussing the tensions building up within the international criminal justice system – and any justice system, really – which should be kept under close scrutiny by all involved actors.

14.5. Gathering and Presenting in Court Different Types of Evidence

14.5.1. The Practice of International Courts and Tribunals

14.5.1.1. Evidence from Previous Investigations

More generally, during contemporary international criminal trials, evidence comes from a variety of sources.

The first scenario is common to some of the international criminal justice systems, at least in their preliminary stages: investigative commissions are at times set up even before the creation (or the concept) of an international tribunal.[33] In these cases, which include the ICTY and the

---

[33] See examples and a brief discussion in Karel de Meester, Kelly Pitcher, Rod Rastan and Göran Sluiter, "Investigation, Coercive Measures, Arrest, and Surrender", in Göran Sluiter, Håkan Friman, Suzannah Linton, Salvatore Zappala and Sergey Vasiliev (eds.), *International Criminal Procedure: Rules and Procedure*, Oxford University Press, Oxford, 2013, p. 181. See also, importantly, works such as Stephen Wilkinson, *Standards of Proof in International Humanitarian and Human Rights Fact-Finding and Inquiry Missions*, Ge-

STL, which based themselves heavily on the work of previous UN-mandated investigating commissions, evidence is collected when the procedural and evidentiary system of the future court is not yet in place, which of course poses great challenges.

14.5.1.2. Courts' Investigators

The second scenario is evidence gathered by investigators from the courts themselves, who however do not of course have enforcement powers in the various jurisdictions, and in practice have to rely on the co-operation of states or, in case they are on the ground, peacekeeping forces or other authorities. This evidence may consist of statements taken from witnesses, but also of physical objects and archived documents.

Investigating commissions and even non-governmental organisations further often assist international criminal courts and tribunals in providing material, open-source documents but also contacts and statements by witnesses – they often act as intermediaries "on the ground", which at times has created problems in assessing the reliability of witnesses, but is necessarily of pivotal importance when an international institutions wishes to get into a new – and potentially unknown – environment to investigate.[34]

While witness statements and transcripts of previous proceedings are generally gathered and prepared in view of future litigation, a variety of other documents may thus be relevant in criminal trials, such as minutes of meetings, military orders, newspaper articles, forensic and medical reports, personal diaries, photographs and so on.[35] Such material often amounts to tens of thousands of pages tendered into evidence, especially at the ICTY. Indeed, the trend has been that of an exponential increase in the submission of documents before the judges, such that the

---

neva Academy of International Humanitarian Law and Human Rights, Geneva, 2011 (http://www.geneva-academy.ch/docs/Standards%20of%20proo%20report.pdf).

[34] Amal Alamuddin, "Collection of Evidence", in Karim A.A. Khan, Caroline Buisman and Christopher Gosnell (eds.), *Principles of Evidence in International Criminal Justice*, Oxford University Press, 2010, pp. 231 ff.

[35] On this topic generally, see Marc Nerenberg and Wibke Timmermann, "Documentary Evidence", in Karim A.A. Khan, Caroline Buisman and Christopher Gosnell (eds.), *Principles of Evidence in International Criminal Justice*, Oxford University Press, 2010, p. 443.

ICTY is now inundated with this type of evidence.[36] Parties have made somewhat less use of exhibits at the ICTR and ICC, probably owing to the smaller number of documents generated during the conflicts in question and the more limited temporal scope of each case there. In any event, lengthy documents, such as books or other compilations of material, are not usually admitted in full, but rather a selection is usually made of the passages relevant for the given trial.[37]

14.5.1.3. Witnesses and Other Material

Third, various international tribunals have seen journalists and other professionals who spent time on or around the various "crime scenes" giving evidence and providing their own material and/or expertise. During the siege of Sarajevo, to mention only one example, various journalists covered the difficult life conditions of the civilian population and were later called to testify at the ICTY about their impressions and the information that they had gathered.

Moreover, states and intergovernmental organisations themselves at times provide evidence, whether *proprio motu* or upon request. It is interesting in this respect to note that, apart from the ICC, the founding legal instruments of international criminal courts and tribunals do not generally explicitly allow them to request co-operation (and evidence) from intergovernmental organisations, but only from states: nonetheless, judges and parties have generally assumed an implicit power to request – and even, in some cases, to *order* – the production of relevant evidentiary material from non-state actors, thus possibly giving rise to a rule of international law in this respect.[38]

---

[36] While in the first ICTY case, *Tadić*, a total of 386 exhibits were admitted, the number had already risen to 1,268 in the 2001–2003 trial of *Galić* and then to more than 3,800 in the *Krajišnik* case (2004–2006). See the table in Chris Gosnell, "The Changing Context of Evidentiary Rules", in Karim A.A. Khan, Caroline Buisman and Christopher Gosnell (eds.), *Principles of Evidence in International Criminal Justice*, Oxford University Press, 2010, p. 221.

[37] ICTY, *Prosecutor v. Momcilo Krajišnik*, Trial Chamber, Decision on Admission of Material Sought by the Chamber and Other Exhibits, 14 July 2006, IT-00-39-T, para. 13 (http://www.legal-tools.org/doc/276602/); ICTY, *Prosecutor v. Sainović et al.*, Order on Procedure and Evidence, 11 July 2006, IT-05-87-T, para. 6 (http://www.legal-tools.org/doc/54ecb0/).

[38] For examples of co-operation by international intergovernmental organisations with international tribunals in the evidence-gathering process, and its theoretical underpinnings, see,

In general, these would be items such as archival material and maps, but could also consist of expertise provided by national experts as well as other forms of evidentiary material, such as intercepted telephone communications or other sensitive material. The gathering, preservation (through reliable chain of custody) and presentation in the courtroom of each of these types of evidentiary material of course poses various questions, not just technological ones but also issues related to the rights of the accused, in particular the right to have adequate time and facilities to prepare their case, and therefore to be provided of the resources necessary to effectively challenge the prosecuting authorities' strategy and evidence.

Despite the various sources of evidence outlined above – to which others may of course be added – it is easy to understand how important it is for international criminal tribunals to receive strong co-operation from states and other international actors; since these courts have no police or other law enforcement agencies of their own with enforcement authority, they will almost invariably have to rely on those who possess such powers. As the former ICTY president, Antonio Cassese, stated: "the ICTY remains very much like a giant without arms and legs – it needs artificial limbs to walk and work. And these artificial limbs are state authorities. If the cooperation of states is not forthcoming, the ICTY cannot fulfil its functions".[39] Similar co-operation will have to be in turn ensured also to defendants, if they elect to defend themselves by running investigative inquiries opposed to those of the prosecution.

14.5.1.4. Presentation of the Evidence in Court

Regardless of the model chosen by international courts and tribunals to allow the presentation of evidence to the judges,[40] all of these evidentiary sources are then used in particular to present to the court (expert or fact)

---

for instance, Guido Acquaviva, "Non-state Actors from the Perspective of International Criminal Tribunals", in Jean d'Aspremont (ed.), *Participants in the International Legal System*, Routledge, London, 2011, p. 185.

[39] Antonio Cassese, "On the Current Trends Towards Criminal Prosecution and Punishment of Breaches of International Humanitarian Law", in *European Journal of International Law*, 1998, vol. 9, no. 1, p. 13.

[40] For an analysis of the various models of presentation and examination of evidence, see Sergey Vasiliev, "Fairness and Its Metric in International Criminal Procedure", in Sergey Vasiliev (ed.), *International Criminal Trials: A Normative Theory*, Oxford University Press, Oxford, 2016, pp. 648–799.

witness testimony, written statements of witnesses who are unavailable to come to court or whom the parties and the judges considered unnecessary to summon,[41] various documents produced as exhibits (expert reports, forensic and medical reports, dossiers of contextual documents, transcripts of intercepted communications, minutes of meetings, military orders, newspaper articles and so on), or physical objects (body parts, but also personal diaries, photographs, supports for video or audio recordings and so on). While, as mentioned above, preference is generally given to oral presentation of evidence in the courtroom – especially for evidence that is deemed pivotal to the prosecution case against the accused – material can be presented "from the bar table" and admitted without actual in-court challenge.[42] In all such instances, of course, the development of new technologies may impact on how these different types of evidence are gathered, but also – crucially – on how the evidentiary material in question is later actually presented in court to the other parties and to the judges, while ensuring no unfairness ensues.

14.5.2. The Special Tribunal for Lebanon: Challenges from Technical Evidence

The Special Tribunal for Lebanon – in particular – has been at the forefront of the impact of new technological advances in the use of eviden-

---

41 While oral evidence is very important before international criminal tribunals, as time has progressed the disadvantages of unnecessarily time-consuming live testimony have become apparent, in particular in interrelated international criminal cases, which deal with extremely similar factual bases. The ICTY and ICTR – followed by other courts and tribunals – have therefore introduced over the years a series of provisions to facilitate the admission of written statements of witnesses, while at the same time striving to maintain the adversarial nature of the system. On this trend, see Acquaviva, 2013, see *supra* note 1.

42 In theory, the ICTY, ICTR, SCSL and STL generally allow written statements in lieu of oral testimony when the statement does not go to "the acts and conduct of the accused". This language – though by now established as a fundamental feature of the procedures at the *ad hoc* courts and tribunals – is unsatisfactory. What the provision in question is meant to ensure is that no conviction be based on untested evidence. Thus, what appears critical is that, under the circumstances of each case, judges are prevented from considering statements containing information essential to the prosecution case – *whether or not these relate to the acts and conduct of the accused*. Statements regarding the accused's conduct might, for instance, be favourable to the accused and against the prosecution case theory – there is no reason why these should not be admitted without cross-examination, at least in cases when this material comes from prosecution repositories of material. Moreover, facts that are strictly speaking unrelated to the acts and conduct of the accused can be pivotal to the prosecution case in other ways.

tiary material. So far, this has had an impact mostly on investigations, but since its first trial started in early 2014 this will soon need to translate into new legal and practical solutions, as the parties begin presenting and contesting this evidence in the courtroom. Specifically, Lebanese investigating authorities, the UN International Independent Investigative Commission, as later the Special Tribunal for Lebanon's prosecution have made extensive use of so-called call data records from mobile phones. This is an investigative technique developed by several domestic law enforcement agencies and already used in national investigations and criminal proceedings, and based on the analysis of metadata that that may reveal details as to an individual's relationships with associates, communication and behaviour patterns, and even location data that can establish the whereabouts of an individual during the entirety of the call.[43] This is because call data records contain information such as incoming and outgoing phone numbers, the date and time of a call, its duration, call type (whether voice or text message), and the approximate location of mobile phones by reference to the cell towers that carried a specific call.

Under certain circumstances, therefore, call data records enable investigators to locate the user of a particular phone at a specific time and location. This would not, of course, be enough to identify the identity of the callers (except in the rare cases when the text message carries identifying information), a process that is usually defined as "attribution". In order to proceed to this attribution, various techniques can be used to identify the user of a SIM card or phone during a particular period of time. Mobile phone SIM cards may provide the subscriber details, for instance, because when individuals buy a new card they are often required to identify themselves. Nonetheless, of course, subscriber details may be false or absent, in an effort to mislead phone companies or even law enforcement agencies. In these more complex cases, witness statements and third party documents (bank or insurance contracts, for instance), but also telephone contacts and/or geographical lifestyle of the phone user, can theoretically be used to "attribute" a phone to a specific individual.

STL prosecutors have argued that they have used this methodology to identify five individuals, who are now standing trial before an STL Trial Chamber for the killing of the former Lebanese prime minister Rafiq

---

[43]   See, for instance, Gregory Kipper, *Wireless Crime and Forensic Investigation*, Auerbach Publications, New York, 2007.

Hariri and 21 other persons on 14 February 2005 in downtown Beirut.[44] Only time will tell if this circumstantial evidence – coupled with the rest of the evidentiary material which the parties will bring to the STL's attention – will convince the judges *beyond reasonable doubt* of the guilt of the five accused, as required by the fundamental legal principles involved in any criminal trial worthy of its name.

14.6. Conclusions

This brief chapter, after providing a tentative definition of evidence relevant to international criminal proceedings from Nuremberg to the Special Tribunal for Lebanon, has discussed the sources of evidentiary material more commonly used by international criminal courts and tribunals, as well as the legal principles underpinning their presentation in court for the purpose of international trials. In doing so, it has identified two of the main factors that shape the type of evidence presented during these trials: the fundamental rights of the accused, including the right to be put in a position effectively to challenge the evidence against them, on the one side; and technological advances, which make available to all courts new techniques to gather and present evidence, on the other.

I have then tried to highlight some of the interactions between these factors by presenting various kinds of evidentiary material used during these trials, from documentary evidence, to witness testimonies and telephone intercepts, and even to judicial use of so-called call data records, something used for the first time at the international level during the investigations of Rafiq Hariri's murder. More domestic and international practice on the use of this type of evidence, and its testing through in-court examination and cross-examination of experts called to discuss it, will certainly open new areas for legal debate.

---

44 STL, *Prosecutor v. Salim Jamil Ayyash, Mustafa Amine Badreddine, Hassan Habib Merhi, Hussein Hassan Oneissi, and Assad Hassan Sabra*, Redacted Version of the Prosecution Submission of Consolidated Indictment, Witness and Exhibit Lists, 10 March 2014, STL-11-01/T/TC.

INDEX

A

Abe Shinzō, 95
accomplice liability, 91
acquiescence, 284
actual knowledge
    evidence, 281
    ICTY, 275
    superior orders, 277
actus reus, 139, 282
Acquaviva, Guido, 321–37
admission of evidence
    exclusionary rule, 321
    flexibility, 324
    human rights, 329
    ICTY, 323
    international criminal tribunal, 325
    probative value, 324
aggressive war
    IMTFE Charter, 98
    international crime, 9
    Kellogg-Briand Pact, 99
Akio Doi, 167
Al-Bashir, Omar, 46
Annan, Kofi, xiv
anti-Western imperialism, 70
Asaka Yasuhiko, iv
Association of Returnees from China, 237
atomic bombs, 64–65
attribution of responsibility, 84
Australian War Crimes Act, 300
Australian War Crimes Section, 300

B

BAI Chongxi, 239
BAI Zengrong, 133
Ban Ki-moon, 103
Bandō Junkichi, 70
Banfield, Colin, 307
Banfield, D.C.J., 307
Banham, Tony, 292
Bataan Death March, 75
Bates, Miner Searle, 133

Bernard, Henri, 61, 78
    class A war criminals, 88
    collection and analysis of the evidence, 87
    conventional war crimes, 83
    crimes against prisoners of war, 83
    duty as a judge, 91
    and Emperor Hirohito, 80, 87, 90
    evidence, 90
    French civil law, 87
    imputation of knowledge, 84
    legal positivism, 81, 86
    legitimacy of the tribunal, 79
    majority judgment, 88
    modes of liability, 80
    natural and universal law, 86, 89
    natural law, 81, 86
    omissions, 84
    planning and preparation of aggressive war, 80
    standard of liability, 85
    substantive law, 86
    violations of fair trial rights, 88
    war criminality, 86
biological experiments, 49
Bischoff, James L., 24
Boas, Gideon, 24
Boxer Protocol, 209
brainwashing, 237
Brennan, Gerard, 150
British war crimes courts
    command respnsibility, 269
    in Hong Kong, 263, 293
    Kishi case, 266
    Manual of Military Law, 264
    Royal Warrant, 264, 294
    sentence, 303
Buergenthal, Thomas, viii

C

Cairo Declaration, 10, 33, 93
capital punishment, 157
Cassese, Antonio, xxviii, 334

TOAEP TEAM

OTHER VOLUMES IN THE
FICHL PUBLICATION SERIES

Morten Bergsmo, Mads Harlem and Nobuo Hayashi (editors):
Importing Core International Crimes into National Law
Torkel Opsahl Academic EPublisher
Oslo, 2010
FICHL Publication Series No. 1 (Second Edition, 2010)
ISBN 978-82-93081-00-5

Nobuo Hayashi (editor):
National Military Manuals on the Law of Armed Conflict
Torkel Opsahl Academic EPublisher
Oslo, 2010
FICHL Publication Series No. 2 (Second Edition, 2010)
ISBN 978-82-93081-02-9

Morten Bergsmo, Kjetil Helvig, Ilia Utmelidze and Gorana Žagovec:
The Backlog of Core International Crimes Case Files in Bosnia and Herzegovina
Torkel Opsahl Academic EPublisher
Oslo, 2010
FICHL Publication Series No. 3 (Second Edition, 2010)
ISBN 978-82-93081-04-3

Morten Bergsmo (editor):
Criteria for Prioritizing and Selecting Core International Crimes Cases
Torkel Opsahl Academic EPublisher
Oslo, 2010
FICHL Publication Series No. 4 (Second Edition, 2010)
ISBN 978-82-93081-06-7

Morten Bergsmo and Pablo Kalmanovitz (editors):
Law in Peace Negotiations
Torkel Opsahl Academic EPublisher
Oslo, 2010
FICHL Publication Series No. 5 (Second Edition, 2010)
ISBN 978-82-93081-08-1

Morten Bergsmo, César Rodríguez Garavito, Pablo Kalmanovitz and Maria Paula Saffon (editors):
Distributive Justice in Transitions
Torkel Opsahl Academic EPublisher
Oslo, 2010
FICHL Publication Series No. 6 (2010)
ISBN 978-82-93081-12-8

Morten Bergsmo, César Rodriguez-Garavito, Pablo Kalmanovitz y Maria Paula Saffon (editors):
Justicia Distributiva en Sociedades en Transición
Torkel Opsahl Academic EPublisher
Oslo, 2012
FICHL Publication Series No. 6 (2012)
ISBN 978-82-93081-10-4

Morten Bergsmo (editor):
Complementarity and the Exercise of Universal Jurisdiction for Core International Crimes
Torkel Opsahl Academic EPublisher
Oslo, 2010
FICHL Publication Series No. 7 (2010)
ISBN 978-82-93081-14-2

Morten Bergsmo (editor):
Active Complementarity: Legal Information Transfer
Torkel Opsahl Academic EPublisher
Oslo, 2011
FICHL Publication Series No. 8 (2011)
ISBN 978-82-93081-55-5 (PDF)
ISBN 978-82-93081-56-2 (print)

Sam Muller, Stavros Zouridis, Morly Frishman and Laura Kistemaker (editors):
The Law of the Future and the Future of Law
Torkel Opsahl Academic EPublisher
Oslo, 2010
FICHL Publication Series No. 11 (2011)
ISBN 978-82-93081-27-2

Morten Bergsmo, Alf Butenschøn Skre and Elisabeth J. Wood (editors):
Understanding and Proving International Sex Crimes
Torkel Opsahl Academic EPublisher
Beijing, 2012
FICHL Publication Series No. 12 (2012)
ISBN 978-82-93081-29-6

Morten Bergsmo (editor):
Thematic Prosecution of International Sex Crimes
Torkel Opsahl Academic EPublisher
Beijing, 2012
FICHL Publication Series No. 13 (2012)
ISBN 978-82-93081-31-9

Terje Einarsen:
The Concept of Universal Crimes in International Law
Torkel Opsahl Academic EPublisher
Oslo, 2012
FICHL Publication Series No. 14 (2012)
ISBN 978-82-93081-33-3

莫滕·伯格斯默 凌岩 （主编）：
国家主权与国际刑法
Torkel Opsahl Academic EPublisher
Beijing, 2012
FICHL Publication Series No. 15 (2012)
ISBN 978-82-93081-58-6

Morten Bergsmo and LING Yan (editors):
State Sovereignty and International Criminal Law
Torkel Opsahl Academic EPublisher
Beijing, 2012
FICHL Publication Series No. 15 (2012)
ISBN 978-82-93081-35-7

Morten Bergsmo and CHEAH Wui Ling (editors):
Old Evidence and Core International Crimes
Torkel Opsahl Academic EPublisher
Beijing, 2012
FICHL Publication Series No. 16 (2012)
ISBN 978-82-93081-60-9

YI Ping:
戦争と平和の間——発足期日本国際法学における「正しい戦争」
の観念とその帰結
Torkel Opsahl Academic EPublisher
Beijing, 2013
FICHL Publication Series No. 17 (2013)
ISBN 978-82-93081-66-1

Morten Bergsmo and SONG Tianying (editors):
On the Proposed Crimes Against Humanity Convention
Torkel Opsahl Academic EPublisher
Brussels, 2014
FICHL Publication Series No. 18 (2014)
ISBN 978-82-93081-96-8

Morten Bergsmo (editor):
Quality Control in Fact-Finding
Torkel Opsahl Academic EPublisher
Florence, 2013
FICHL Publication Series No. 19 (2013)
ISBN 978-82-93081-78-4

Morten Bergsmo, CHEAH Wui Ling and YI Ping (editors):
Historical Origins of International Criminal Law: Volume 1
Torkel Opsahl Academic EPublisher
Brussels, 2014
FICHL Publication Series No. 21 (2014)
ISBN 978-82-93081-11-1

Morten Bergsmo, CHEAH Wui Ling and YI Ping (editors):
Historical Origins of International Criminal Law: Volume 2
Torkel Opsahl Academic EPublisher
Brussels, 2014
FICHL Publication Series No. 22 (2014)
ISBN 978-82-93081-13-5

Morten Bergsmo, CHEAH Wui Ling, SONG Tianying and YI Ping (editors):
Historical Origins of International Criminal Law: Volume 3
Torkel Opsahl Academic EPublisher
Brussels, 2015
FICHL Publication Series No. 23 (2015)
ISBN 978-82-93081-15-3 (print) and ISBN 978-82-93081-14-6 (e-book)

Morten Bergsmo, CHEAH Wui Ling, SONG Tianying and YI Ping (editors):
Historical Origins of International Criminal Law: Volume 4
Torkel Opsahl Academic EPublisher
Brussels, 2015
FICHL Publication Series No. 24 (2015)
ISBN 978-82-93081-17-7 (print) and ISBN 978-82-93081-16-0 (e-book)

Morten Bergsmo and SONG Tianying (editors):
Military Self-Interest in Accountability for Core International Crimes
Torkel Opsahl Academic EPublisher
Brussels, 2015
FICHL Publication Series No. 25 (2015)
ISBN 978-82-93081-61-6 (print) and ISBN 978-82-93081-81-4 (e-book)

Wolfgang Kaleck:
Double Standards: International Criminal Law and the West
Torkel Opsahl Academic EPublisher
Brussels, 2015
FICHL Publication Series No. 26 (2015)
ISBN 978-82-93081-67-8 (print) and 978-82-93081-83-8 (e-book)

All volumes are freely available online at http://www.fichl.org/publication-series/. Printed copies may be ordered from distributors indicated at http://www.fichl.org/torkel-opsahl-academic-epublisher/distribution/, including from http://www.amazon.co.uk/. For reviews of earlier books in this Series in academic journals, please see http://www.fichl.org/torkel-opsahl-academic-epublisher/reviews-of-toaep-books/.

CPSIA information can be obtained
at www.ICGtesting.com
Printed in the USA
LVOW01*0103100916

504020LV00018B/119/P